American Public Opinion

Its Origins, Content, and Impact

Fifth Edition

Robert S. Erikson
University of Houston

Kent L. Tedin
University of Houston

ALLYN AND BACON

Boston   London   Toronto   Sydney   Tokyo   Singapore

Library of Congress Cataloging-in-Publication Data

Erikson, Robert S.
  American public opinion : its origins, content, and impact /
Robert S. Erikson, Kent L. Tedin. — 5th ed.
    p. cm.
  Includes bibliographical references and index.
  ISBN 0-02-334042-8
  1. Public opinion—United States.   I. Tedin, Kent L.   II. Title.
HN90.P8E74   1994
303.3'8—dc20   94-21993
                                                           CIP

Series Editor: Steve Hull
Editorial Assistant: Brenda Conaway
Cover Administrator: Suzanne Harbison
Manufacturing Buyer: Louise Richardson
Editorial-Production Service: Electronic Publishing Services Inc.

Copyright © 1995 by Allyn and Bacon
A Division of Simon & Schuster, Inc.
160 Gould Street
Needham Heights, Massachusetts 02194

Printed in the United States of America

10 9 8 7 6 5 4 3   99 98 97

0-02-334042-8

Contents

Preface

In this fifth edition of *American Public Opinion*, we present an accounting of the role of public opinion in the democratic politics of the United States. As in previous editions, we base our analysis on the most recent data available. Our discussion of public opinion and election results, for instance, draws on survey data from the 1992 election. Our examples of public opinion poll findings include data from as recent as 1994. We also review and analyze the most recent research in the scholarly literature on public opinion.

As this book has evolved through five editions over twenty years, so too has the list of authors. The first edition (1973) was authored by Robert S. Erikson and Norman R. Luttbeg. With the second edition (1980), Kent L. Tedin joined the team as the third author. That triumvirate held through three editions. When the time came to produce a fifth edition, Luttbeg decided that it was time to pursue new scholarly challenges. *American Public Opinion* again has but two authors, this time Erikson and Tedin. Luttbeg's intellectual contribution to the book remains, most notably in the five linkage models of public opinion, which he originated.

Because the data and literature are always changing, most of the chapters have been extensively rewritten for this edition. But readers familiar with our previous editions will find few changes in the basic structure of the book. Two exceptions are the reorganization of Chapters 3 and 4. Previously, these chapters were organized in terms of "Opinion Polls and Public Opinion" (Chapter 3) and "Ideology, Partisanship, and Political Opinions" (Chapter 4). The material formerly in these chapters is now updated and reorganized into two chapters on "microlevel opinion" (Chapter 3) and "macrolevel opinion"

(Chapter 4). Another minor change is the switching in the order of Chapter 5 and 6.

The preparation of this volume relies heavily on the survey data of the National Election Studies, conducted by the Center for Political Studies at the University of Michigan, supported by grants from the National Science Foundation, and made available by the Inter-University Consortium for Political and Social Research. We have also relied extensively on the General Social Surveys conducted by the National Opinion Research Center, also funded by NSF. The organizations bear no responsibility for the analysis and interpretations presented here. We are greatly indebted to them for making their data available to us, and to other scholars upon whose research we depend.

We thank the supportive staffs of the Social Science Data Laboratory and the Department of Political Science at the University of Houston. We owe special thanks for the research assistance of Darren W. Davis, Callie Hernandez, Sondra Richards, and Toshi Yuasa and for the secretarial assistance of Tiffany Quaranta. The manuscript has benefited from the careful reading by our colleague Christopher Wlezien. Finally, we thank Robert Miller of Macmillan Publishing and Stephen Hull of Allyn and Bacon Publishers for skillfully guiding this project to completion.

R.S.E
K.L.T

Credits

Table 3.9: From Paul R. Hagner and John C. Pierce, "Correlative Characteristics of Levels of Conceptualization in the American Public: 1956–1976," *Journals of Politics* 44 (August 1982), pp. 779–809; updates compiled by Paul Hagner and Kathleen Knight.

Table 5.1: From Roberta S. Siegel and Marilyn B. Hoskin, *The Political Involvement of Adolescents* (Table 3.1: Affect for Political Objects). Copyright 1981 by Rutgers, The State University. Reprinted with permission of Rutgers University Press.

Tables 5.2 and 5.3: From M. Kent Jennings and Richard G. Neimi. *The Political Character of Adolescence.* Copyright 1974 by Princeton University Press. Tables 2.2 and 3.4 reprinted with permission of Princeton University Press.

Table 6.1: From John L. Sullivan, James Pierson, and George E. Markus, *Political Tolerance and American Democracy* (Chicago: University of Chicago Press, 1982), p. 67.

Table 8.1: From William Schneider and I. A. Lewis, "Views on the News," *Public Opinion* 8 (Aug./Sept. 1985), p. 7. Reprinted with permission of the American Enterprise Institute.

Table 8.2: From Norman R. Luttbeg, "News Consensus: Do U.S. Newspapers Mirror Society's Happenings?" *Journalism Quarterly* 60 (Autumn 1983), p. 486.

Table 8.3: From John P. Robinson and Mark R. Levy, *The Main Source: Learning from Television News*, Chapter 4: "Comprehension of Week's News" (Beverly Hills, Calif.: Sage Publications, 1986), p. 91. Copyright © 1986 by Sage Publications, Inc. Reprinted by permission of Sage Publications, Inc.

Table 10.3: From Eric M. Uslaner and Ronald E. Weber, "Policy Congruence and American State Elites: Descriptive Representation versus Electoral Accountability," *Journal of Politics* 45 (February 1983), p. 188.

Figure 10-2: From James H. Kuklinski, "Representation and Elections: A Policy Analysis," *American Political Science Review* 72 (March 1978), p. 174.

Figure 10-3: From Martin Thomas, "Election Proximity and Senatorial Roll Call Voting," *American Journal of Political Science* 29 (February 1985), p. 103.

Table 11.4: From Robert S. Erikson and Gerald C. Wright, "Voters, Issues, and Candidates in Congressional Elections," in Lawrence C. Dodd and Bruce I. Oppenheimer (eds.), *Congress Reconsidered*, 3rd ed. (Washington, D.C.: Congressional Quarterly Press, 1985), p. 94.

CHAPTER 1

Public Opinion in Democratic Societies

Few Americans in the 1990s can remember a time when public opinion polls—like television, shopping malls, and eight-lane freeways—were not part of the popular landscape. Polls tell us which television shows are the most popular, how frequently people attend church, what person Americans most admire, plus a myriad of opinions on political topics currently in the news. We shall see, however, that the study of public opinion is much broader than simply gauging popular reaction to recent events. It is, for example, also concerned with how people learn about government, their trust in existing political institutions, their support for the political "rules of the game," the interrelationships among their opinions, or their beliefs about the effectiveness of political participation. The list could go on. But more than anything else, the study of public opinion is justified by the simple notion that democratic institutions should result in government decisions that reflect the views of everyday people. It is this presumption, and its implications, that guides the systematic analysis of mass opinion.

1-1 Public Opinion and Government

Rousseau, in 1744, was among the first to use the term "public opinion" (*l'opinion publique*), meaning the customs and manners of all members of society (as opposed to some elite). By 1780 French writers were using the term interchangeably with "common will," "public spirit," and "public conscience" to refer to the political aspects of mass opinion (V. Price 1992, 8). "Public opinion" soon came into common usage among those writing about government.

However, long before scientific methods were developed to measure attitudes or the term "public opinion" gained currency, political theorists speculated about the "group mind" or "the general will" and how it might influence the political order. Writers beginning with Plato and Aristotle, through Locke and Hobbes as well as Rousseau, did not see "public opinion" as an aggregation of individual opinions, as is common today. Rather they saw the whole as greater than the sum of its parts, much in the way a mob with a united purpose behaves in a fashion that would be foreign to any individual member. To these predemocratic theorists, public opinion was a mass entity, which if brought to bear on public affairs had potential for enormous influence. It was like a force in nature, constrained perhaps by certain regularities, but a unified whole that changed continually, like the currents in the ocean (Palmer 1936; Spitz 1984).

It was not until the rise of popular sovereignty that thinking about public opinion began to consider individual or group characteristics. By the eighteenth century, no Western political regime could afford simply to ignore the views of the masses. This change was brought about by the construction of electoral institutions and parliamentary bodies for regular consultation with the public, and the gradual extension of the franchise to the lower classes. Henceforth, governments would find it necessary to take account of public opinion and its distribution throughout the polity. This "accounting" was not simply a question of government responsiveness to mass policy desires. Government also had to take account of popular support for the ongoing political order. A strong argument can be made that only when the political status quo was threatened did political elites, in an act of self-preservation, grudgingly extend the franchise to portions of the mass public (Ginsberg 1982). But in granting the franchise, there soon developed an ethical imperative that governments are morally obligated to heed public opinion in formulating policies.

In the early years of the American republic, to speak of "public opinion" was mostly to speak about a thin layer of the educated, affluent public in a position to communicate their views to government. While the Founding Fathers agreed on the principle of popular government, they greatly distrusted the wisdom and good judgment of the masses on matters political. To Alexander Hamilton:

> The voice of the people has been said to be the voice of God; and however generally this maxim has been quoted and believed, it is not true in fact. The people are turbulent and changing; they seldom judge or determine right (Farrand 1961, 299–300).

While not all took such an uncharitable position, it was generally thought that public opinion was easily swayed and subject to fits of passion. Thus institutions were developed, such as the electoral college and the indirect election of senators, to distance political leaders from the opinions of everyday citizens.

Nevertheless, by the mid-nineteenth century, many who followed the American political scene voiced concern about an excess of influence on political decision-making by public opinion. One reason was the integration of the working class into the electorate via the universal franchise. By the 1850s it became impossible to argue that the public's opinion could be ignored. Writing in 1848, Alexis de Tocqueville, perhaps the most astute observer of nineteenth-century America, thought "there was no country in which . . . there is less independence of mind and true freedom of discussion than in America" (Tocqueville 1969, 254). He felt the numerical majority intimidated the minority, so that only a narrow range of opinion could be expressed. In the end he feared that the views of the majority could result in either social or governmental tyranny (Spitz 1984, 70). History was, of course, to prove him wrong. But those writing later agreed with his assessment of the importance of public opinion. In 1888, the perceptive British journalist and author James Bryce would claim that "[i]n no country is public opinion so powerful as in the United States" (Bryce 1900). He also noted, "[t]he obvious weakness of government by opinion is the difficulty of ascertaining it."

Of those writing before the development of the modern opinion poll, perhaps the most influential critic of public opinion was Walter Lippmann. Like many of the Founding Fathers, he believed mass opinion was subject to passions that could be induced by elite propaganda. He was convinced that the manipulation of public opinion by those opposed to the League of Nations was responsible for the tragedy of America's failure to join. He perceptively observed that the images of politics received by the public are not direct pictures of events, immediate experiences of action, or provable economic and social theories. Rather, they are "pictures in people's heads" generated by political interests to benefit their cause. In a prescient analysis of major findings by modern survey research, Lippmann challenged traditional democratic theory and its notion of an informed and rational public basing opinions on a considered judgment of the facts. He argued that the average person had little time for affairs of state, and would rather read the comics than consider the pros and cons of weighty political issues. It should not be expected, therefore, that the mass public would be competent in matters of state. Lippmann's prescription for democracy was for the public to choose leaders, but for public policy to be developed and implemented by scientifically oriented experts (Lippmann 1922; Lippmann 1925).

The debate over the role of public opinion in democracy was given a new focus by the appearance of scientific polling in 1936. Among the most outspoken proponents of polls as a guide to government decision-making was George Gallup, a pioneer of the new technology (Gallup and Rae 1940). Gallup was a "prairie populist" with a Ph.D. in psychology who believed in the collective wisdom of everyday citizens. He distrusted intellectuals and experts, and thought elite rule and democratic government were incompatible. The challenge for democracy, as he saw it, was "shall the common people be free to express their basic needs and purposes, or shall they be dominated by a small ruling clique?" In other words, how does one make those holding high public office responsive to the needs and wishes of the public?

Poll results, Gallup argued, could be considered a "mandate from the people," a concrete expression of the policies the public desires the government to enact. No longer would elected officials have to rely on the ambiguities of elections, self-serving claims by interest groups, or other nonrepresentative channels of public sentiment. Rather, they could turn to the latest opinion poll. In the past, claims that elected officials should heed popular preferences directly when formulating policy could always be countered with arguments like those of Montaigne (1957) that "[p]ublic opinion is a powerful, bold, and unmeasurable party."

Gallup saw the modern opinion poll as the high-tech equivalent of the New England town meeting—an opportunity for all citizens (or at least a representative sample) to voice their opinions. The scientific poll gave crispness, clarity, and reliability to mass opinion. Gallup and his supporters argued that through polls the will of the people could accurately be determined. No longer could failure to take seriously popular preferences when enacting public policy be justified by claims that public opinion is unknowable. With the aid of the modern opinion poll, it was the moral responsibility of elected officials to convert the public will into public policy.

Not all were enthusiastic about the new technology and George Gallup's prescriptions for it. Sociologist Herbert Blumer and political scientist Lindsay Rogers soon launched frontal assaults on the opinion poll and its implications. Blumer (1948) asserted the "one person, one vote" definition of public opinion inherent in polls was precisely what public opinion *was not*. Public opinion could not be reduced to a nose count among citizens. Rather, it was the interactions and communications among functional groups that percolated through society and came to the attention of government. These interactions and communications were not aggregations of individual opinions, but "an organic whole of interacting, interrelated parts." To Blumer, not all opinions counted equally. They merited the label "public opinion" only to the extent opinions surfaced in a public forum and were taken seriously by those in government with power and influence.[1] This view, of course, clashed directly with the populist inclinations of Gallup and other early pollsters.[2]

Lindsay Rogers, on the other hand, was convinced that the public was not intellectually or emotionally fit to play the role Gallup's opinion-poll democracy required of it. But, in any case, polls were not technically able to ascertain the public's message. Rogers (1949) reformulated the position of the English philosopher Edmund Burke that it is the duty of elected representatives to follow their conscience and best judgment, and not be slaves to moments of popular passion.[3] Only in this fashion, argued Rogers, could the true public interest be served. Rogers was also one of the first to raise serious methodological questions about polls—that is, to challenge pollsters on their own turf. He addressed questions of measurement, opinion aggregation, intensity, and framing effects that occupy a great deal of attention among contemporary students of public opinion. In essence, he claimed that polls of public opinion did not really measure "public opinion." Rogers argued that "Dr. Gallup does not make the public more articulate. He only estimates how in replying to certain questions it would say 'yes,' 'no,' or 'don't know.' Instead of feeling the pulse of democracy, Dr. Gallup listens to its baby talk." (Rogers 1949, 17).

A somewhat related argument holds that public opinion changes in a capricious fashion—that over short periods of time policy preferences shift rapidly, frequently, and arbitrarily. This belief was used by the author of the Federalist Paper No. 63 for an indirectly elected senate, which would serve as "an anchor against popular fluctuations" and protect the people against their own "temporary errors and delusions" (Federalist No. 63). In 1950, this same sentiment was reflected by political scientist Gabriel Almond (1950, 53), when he noted that on matters of foreign policy the public reacts with "formless and plastic moods which undergo frequent alteration in response to changes in events."[4] This view of public opinion was used to buttress arguments about limiting the role of mass opinion in policy decisions, and is still a touchstone of the "realist" school of foreign policy (Russett and Graham 1989).[5]

On the other hand, the liberal democracy school of thought (Dahl 1989) holds that an essential element of democracy is the creation of institutions and practices that allow for meaningful public input into the governing process. Democratic government works best when elected office-holders and appointed officials respond to the popular will. Citizens are more likely to comply with government decisions when they are backed by the moral force of popular approval. In addition, advocates of liberal democracy argue that decisions based on popular will are most likely to be the correct decisions. This idea traces its heritage to Aristotle's view that the pooled judgments of the many are likely to contain more wisdom than the judgments of the few.[6] The liberal democratic model does not hold that public policy must be driven only by the engine of public opinion. Rather, public opinion must count for something of consequence in government decision-making.

The arguments we have just outlined are still occasionally elaborated upon today. However, most current research on public opinion does not address normative issues about the proper role of opinion in the governmental process. Rather, empirical questions dominate the field—that is, questions about "what really is" as opposed to "what ought to be." But empirical questions often have important normative implications. Clearly of consequence is, "How much does the public know about public affairs and how is that knowledge organized?" Or, "How is public opinion articulated?" "Whose voices are heard?" Are some segments of society (presumably the more affluent) better able to communicate their opinions to political decision-makers than those with fewer economic resources? The answers to these questions are important for theories of how the just polity should be structured.

1-2 Public Opinion Defined _____

Public opinion is notoriously difficult to define.[7] There are scores if not hundreds of variations on a definition (see Childs 1965 for a sampling). A standard definition of "public" is a group that has something in common. Some argue that there is no such thing as a single public; rather, there are many publics (MacDougall 1966). Thus one can refer to the tennis-playing public, the snowmobiling public, or the television-watching public. Others, however, take a broader view. For political scientists, what members of the "public" in public opinion have in common with each other is a connection to government. At a minimum, all citizens 18 and older have the right to vote. That binds them together with a common interest, even if they choose not to exercise the right.[8] And, of course, everyone is impacted in some way by government. That creates a common interest as well. Students of government also regularly speak of several specialized publics. They talk of the "attentive public," those persons who generally pay close attention to politics; or "issue publics," those persons who focus on specific issues while paying less attention to others. It is perhaps helpful to think of these as "subpublics" of the overall public (i.e., the adult population).

We may first describe an opinion as a verbal expression of an attitude.[9] There are, of course, other ways in which attitudes can be expressed, such as marches, demonstrations, or riots. But we reserve the term "opinion" as the manifestation of attitudes in words or writing.[10] Attitudes are "latent"; they cannot be directly observed. Social psychologists typically define an attitude as an enduring predisposition to respond. Normally, attitudes do not change on a weekly or monthly basis. Although change is clearly possible, attitudes are mostly stable over extended periods of time. Opinions are imperfect indicators of the underlying, unobserved attitude. Because opinions are imperfect measures, we sometimes find they are inconsistent or display contradictions. We shall deal with this problem at length in Chapter 3.

Second, opinions are disagreements about matters of preference, which cannot be resolved using the rules of science. Thus, when it comes to music, I may prefer opera. You may prefer hard rock. But there is no systematic way of demonstrating the virtue or goodness of one over the other. The same is true for opinions about welfare policy, foreign aid, or gays in the military. Disagreements about questions of fact are not opinions, but beliefs.[11] There was once disagreement as to whether the earth circled the sun. Some believed the reverse, that the sun revolved around the earth. That disagreement has been resolved by scientific methods. There is still disagreement over whether massive doses of vitamin C will prevent colds and other illness. Some believe this notion is nothing more than a hoax; others take large doses of the vitamin on a daily basis. But one's position on this issue is a belief, not an opinion, because in principle the question may someday be resolved with finality. Disagreements over classical vs. rock music will not be resolved.

No one has yet advanced a definition of public opinion that satisfies a substantial number of students in the field. We prefer to keep our definition short and simple. We define public opinion as *the preferences of the adult population on matters of relevance to government*. The first implication is that not all opinions are "public opinion." Thus one's preference for computer operating systems—DOS, UNIX, OS/2—is excluded from our definition because it has nothing to do with government. The second caveat is that while in the broadest sense we are talking about all adults, that does not exclude the possibility of referencing subgroups, such as the attentive public. A third point is that by the term "preferences" we mean more than simply the *affective* component of an opinion. "Affect" refers to feelings—like or dislike, approve or disapprove. But, we must also be concerned with the cognitive component of an opinion. "Cognition" refers to the process of knowing, to the intellectual sophistication one brings to the ordering of political opinions. Obviously, the amount of political information one has affects the ability to link one political concept with another, and is important for our understanding of public opinion. Finally, while we have defined "opinions" as verbal manifestations of attitudes, events such as riots, demonstrations, and marches are also indicators of "public opinion" for certain attentive publics.

In the recent era, the meaning of public opinion sometimes seems to have evolved into whatever opinion polls show public opinion to be. In many ways, the findings of public opinion polls (or survey research in general) should inspire trust. Counterintuitive though it may seem, mathematical statistics and decades of experience reveal that one can generalize from a random sample of one or two thousand individuals to the nation as a whole. And one rarely has reason to believe that survey respondents systematically lie to pollsters.

We must be careful, however, not to reify. Public opinion and the results of public opinion polls are not necessarily the same thing. As shown in later chapters, the results of opinion polls must be interpreted with great care. Findings can vary considerably with different question wordings or different shadings of how the issues are presented. Also, survey respondents sometimes tend to give socially desirable responses. For this reason, surveys often underreport attitudes and behaviors such as nonvoting, racist feelings, or tolerance for pornography because of a tendency for respondents to give socially desirably answers.

1-3 The Evolution of the Public Opinion Poll _____

Before the appearance of the modern public opinion poll in 1936, popular sentiment was assessed by newspapers and magazines through a variety of informal and haphazard soundings called "straw polls."[12] The *Harrisburg Pennsylvanian* is credited with conducting the first of these polls, in the summer of 1824. It showed Andrew Jackson, with 63 percent of the vote, an easy winner over John Quincy Adams and Henry Clay.[13]

But it was not until 1896 that straw polling became a serious business. In that year the *Chicago Record* conducted an elaborate and very expensive straw poll to tap voter preferences in the bitterly fought presidential contest between William McKinley and William Jennings Bryan. It sent out postcard ballots to every eighth voter in twelve midwestern states, as well as ballots to every registered voter in Chicago.[14] The owner of the *Chicago Record* had clear Republican sympathies, and the Democratic party feared the poll was nothing more than a Republican trick. The party urged Democrats not to return the ballots. Nevertheless, with the aid of a team of eminent mathematicians, the *Record* predicted in October that McKinley would win Chicago with 57.95 percent of the vote. Amazingly, he received 57.91 percent on election day. Outside of Chicago, however, the *Record*'s predictive record was a failure (Jensen 1968).

With the dawn of the twentieth century, straw polls were becoming a regular feature in many magazines and newspapers. Like today, the poll results were "newsworthy." Approximately 84 straw polls were conducted during the 1928 presidential election, of which six were national. The straw polls occupied thousands of column inches in the print media. If anything, they were featured even more prominently than is currently the case.[15] The polls were of major importance to their sponsors as a promotional gimmick. They created interest in the publication. Also, those publishers using mail-out ballots usually included a special subscription offer along with the ballot. By all indications, the scheme worked remarkably well to boost circulation (Robinson 1932).

And like current opinion polls, the straw polls did not limit themselves simply to electoral contests. They polled on the issues as well, most notably the burning issue of the 1920s: Prohibition. The wet-dry controversy was as emotion-laden as any issue to surface in American politics. If popular sentiment on the issue was to be measured by a cutout ballot from a newspaper, one side would sometimes attempt to secure a monopoly on that issue and send in all the ballots. Or one side would urge its people not to participate in a straw poll when the sponsor's sentiments on the issue were known. Thus a poll in Delaware sponsored by Pierre du Pont, a well-known wet, was boycotted by drys. It wound up showing 97 percent of its respondents in favor of repeal. Mr. du Pont wisely decided against publishing the poll results as an indicator of public opinion. Rather, he submitted the returned ballots as a petition to the Delaware legislature urging the repeal of Prohibition (Robinson 1932).

The straw polls were a public relations disaster waiting to happen. By the 1930s, considerable advances had been made by market researchers in the field of applied sampling. However, the magazines and newspapers sponsoring the straw polls were oblivious. Their major concern with straw polls was how they contributed to profitability, not the technical quality of the poll itself. Methodologically, straw polls stayed in the rear guard, learning nothing from the advances in sampling methods, using the same outdated methods year after year.

Straw polls were, in fact, known to be notoriously unreliable. In 1932 Claude Robinson published an analysis of the state-by-state error margins of the major straw polls of the day.[16] The average error of the polls conducted by the Hearst newspapers was 12 percent in 1924. The poll by *The Pathfinder*, a weekly magazine, was off by an average of 14 percent in 1928. The *Farm-Journal* poll of 36 states in 1928 had an average error of 17 percent. Even the best-known and most professionally operated of the straw polls—the *Literary Digest* poll—was off the mark by an average of 12 percent in both 1924 and 1928.

It was the 1936 election and the notorious misprediction of its outcome by the *Literary Digest* that brought an end to the era of straw polls. The *Literary Digest* was the largest-circulation general magazine of its time, with over two million subscribers. Much of this success could be traced directly to its straw poll, a regular feature since 1916. While the *Digest* poll experienced more than its share of mispredictions, it had managed each time to get the winner of the presidential election right. And it was not modest. The *Digest* claimed "uncanny accuracy" for its poll, congratulating itself frequently on its amazing record. But in the 1936 presidential election, the *Digest* poll wildly mispredicted the outcome, giving Alf Landon 57 percent of the vote and Franklin Roosevelt 43 percent. Roosevelt won with 62.5 percent of the vote. The *Digest* was off the mark by almost 20 percentage points. Its credibility shattered, the *Literary Digest* went bankrupt a year later.

In that same year, three young pollsters with backgrounds in market research, using "scientific" methods of sampling, did correctly predict the win by Roosevelt. The three were Archibald Crossley, Elmo Roper, and George Gallup, each of whom went on to found his own poll. The best-known of these was, of course, George Gallup, founder of the Gallup Poll.

Gallup was a talented self-promoter. In the 1936 election, he taunted the *Literary Digest*, offering clients a money-back guarantee that his poll would be closer to the actual vote on election day than the *Digest*'s.[17] He urged newspapers and magazines to run the two polls side-by-side (J. Converse 1987, 116–20).

Gallup used in-person interviews as opposed to mail questionnaires, and employed "quotas" to insure that his samples looked demographically like the overall population. His poll forecast Roosevelt with 55.7 percent of the vote—6.8 percent off the mark. But he got the winner right, and he used that fact along with the *Digest*'s disaster to quickly become the nation's preeminent pollster.

But all was not right with the Gallup Poll. While Gallup continued to forecast the correct winner in the 1940 and 1944 presidential contests, his surveys consistently overestimated the Republican vote (Moore 1992, 66–68). Then in 1948 the Gallup Poll incorrectly forecast that Republican Thomas Dewey would defeat Democrat Harry Truman by a margin of 49.5 to 44.5 percent. It is important to note that the Crossley Poll and the Roper Poll also predicted a win by Dewey. Roper had the margin at 52.2 percent Dewey and 37.1 percent Truman. Something was clearly wrong with the sampling methodology used by all three of these polls. That something was quota sampling. In a comprehensive study of the failure of the polls in 1948, the Social Science Research Council recommended the abandonment of quota samples and their replacement with probability samples (Bradburn and Sudman 1988). Probability sampling is the method used in today's public opinion polls (see Chapter 2).

Gallup, Crossley, and Roper were commercial pollsters. They did polls for clients, and by necessity were concerned with costs and profitability. They had little incentive for pure research, or for the lengthy surveys necessary to answer complex academic questions.[18] Those topics would be addressed by the major academic survey organizations, most notably the National Opinion Research Center (NORC) at the University of Chicago and the Survey Research Center (SRC)[19] at the University of

Michigan. NORC was founded in 1941, and its associates produced several classics in the field of public opinion, including *The American Soldier* (Stouffer 1949) and *Communism, Conformity and Civil Liberties* (Stouffer 1955). The SRC, founded in 1946, has focused on studies of the American electorate. Perhaps the most influential book to date on public opinion and voting, *The American Voter* (A. Campbell et al. 1960), was published by a group associated with the SRC.

Both the NORC and the SRC devote considerable resources to technical issues involving sampling and question wording. The NORC pioneered the "split ballot technique," in which different forms of a question are asked of random halves of a sample to investigate the effects of question wording. Researchers associated with the SRC have also devoted extensive time and energy to problems of question wording (Schuman and Presser 1981). But most important are the periodic surveys conducted by each of these institutions. Since 1948, the SRC and the Center for Political Studies have been conducting, on a biennial basis, the National Election Studies (NES).[20] These are large, in-person national surveys of issues relevant to elections. Respondents are interviewed in Autumn before an election, then reinterviewed after the election is over. The total interview time is often three to five hours, and hundreds of questions are asked. Since 1971, NORC has sponsored the General Social Survey (GSS), usually conducted on an annual basis. The GSS has a general set of questions, often repeated from year to year, and a topical module that addresses a specific substantive concern at considerable length. Both the NES and GSS are publicly available, formatted and ready for analysis with common computer statistical packages. A great deal of the data presented in this book comes from these two sources.

Both the NES and GSS surveys interview people in their homes, a very expensive undertaking. By the early 1970s, techniques were being developed to scientifically sample telephone numbers using a random-digit-dialing methodology. This greatly reduced the cost of surveys, and encouraged the media to conduct their own public opinion polls, much as they did in the days of the straw polls. In 1976, CBS News and the *New York Times* went into partnership to conduct their own polls. They were soon followed by the NBC/*Wall Street Journal* and the ABC/*Washington Post* polls. Others, such as CNN, also poll on a regular basis.[21] The principal advantage to the media of in-house polls is that they can decide on the topics and timing of the surveys, rather than being confined to the topics and timing of independent pollsters like Gallup. In-house polls also free the media from having to rely on leaks from political campaigns about how candidates are faring with the voters. They can find out for themselves on an impartial, firsthand basis. Media polls are occasionally of interest to academic students of public opinion. But their value is limited by their interest in topical issues, and the abbreviated number of questions they ask.

The most recent polling innovation is the election day exit poll, developed by CBS News in the late 1960s (Moore 1992, 255). It did not, however, gain prominence until the 1980 election, when it was first used to forecast the outcome of a presidential election. With an exit poll, one chooses a representative sample of precincts in a state and interviews voters as they leave the polling place. The networks usually know by 3:00 P.M. who has won the election, although they do not reveal this information for any one state until the polls have closed in that state. Beyond forecasting, exit polls have proven extremely valuable for understanding why people voted for specific candidates. Until recently, each network conducted its own exit polls. But in 1990, the major networks along with CNN and the Associated Press, formed a consortium, Voter News Service (VNS), to conduct common exit polls and share the information.

A final innovation in polling worth mentioning is the development of a code of standards for those in the field of public opinion. Unlike physicians, lawyers, or morticians, pollsters are not subject to government regulation. On occasion there have been calls by some in Congress for regulation. The first of these came in 1948, with many Democrats charging that the polls were biased in favor of Republicans. Another came in response to using exit polls to call the winner of the presidential election in 1980 before the voting booths had closed on the West Coast. It was argued that many Democrats failed to vote once they learned that President Carter had been defeated. However, most attempts by the government to regulate opinion polls would probably run afoul of the First Amendment's guarantee of the right of free speech.

In 1986 the American Association for Public Opinion Research (AAPOR) adopted a code of ethics and practices for the profession.[22] Among the major features of this code are full disclosure, confidentiality, and responsibility to those being interviewed. Pollsters must make available full information about who sponsored the survey and give details of relevant methodology, such as how the sample was selected. They must hold as confidential the responses to questions by specific individuals. They must avoid any practice that would harm or mislead a respondent. While the AAPOR has a standards committee, its only power of sanction is the glare of adverse publicity.

1-4 The Modern Opinion Poll and Its Consequences _____

Change is not neutral. New innovations benefit some at the expense of others. Benjamin Ginsberg (1986) makes the counterintuitive argument that replacement by the modern opinion poll of traditional methods for expressing public opinion has served to "domesticate" public opinion. In other words, public opinion is a less potent force in American politics now than it was prior to scientific polling.

By traditional methods of expressing public opinion, we are referring to letters to newspapers and public officials, personal contact, elections, advocacy group activity, marches, demonstrations, and riots—to list the more obvious. Such methods are still available, but when these indicators of public opinion differ from those reported in polls, it is universally assumed that polls are more representative. If one conceives of public opinion as an aggregation of equally weighted preferences, that assumption is almost certainly correct. However, polling by simply totaling individual opinions has, according to Ginsberg, changed some very important aspects of "public opinion" as expressed by methods commonly employed before the advent of the scientific survey.

For example, public opinion was once largely a group phenomenon. At election time, elected officials would consult closely with the leaders of various advocacy groups, such as farmers or organized labor, to be informed of membership opinion. Opinion polls have undermined the ability of group leaders to speak for their membership, as the members can now be polled directly. Any difference between the polls and the characterization of group opinion by leaders is usually resolved in favor of the polls. During the Nixon administration, wage and price controls were strongly opposed by organized labor. However, polls showed Nixon was popular with the rank and file, thus undercutting the ability of union leaders to threaten reprisals at the voting booth.

Where it had once been a behavior (letter writing, marches, etc.), public opinion is now mostly a summation of attitudes. In fact, the citizen is relieved of all initiative whatsoever. Pollsters contact respondents, determine worthwhile questions, analyze the results, and publicize them. If a citizen feels strongly about an issue, one mode of expression not available is to call a survey house and demand to be included in the next opinion poll.

Polls weaken the connection between opinion and intensity. It requires little effort to "strongly agree" with a statement proffered by an interviewer. Converse et al. (1965) have demonstrated that public opinion as measured in surveys is much less intense than that offered in voluntary modes of popular expression. Polls, in practice, submerge intense opinions with those held by the much larger, more apathetic population. This characteristic of opinion surveys can be employed by elected officials to promote their policy choices. Both Lyndon Johnson and Richard Nixon used evidence from polls to justify their policies in Vietnam as being in step with majority preferences, despite widespread public protests. Ginsberg claims a good argument could be made that if decision-makers had accepted the more intense behavioral indicators of sentiment about the Vietnam War, as opposed to the evidence from polls, the Vietnam War would have ended much sooner.

Finally, modern opinion polls have changed the character of public opinion from an assertion to a response. Before polling, citizens themselves chose the topics on which to express their opinions. Now, according to Ginsberg, these subjects are chosen mostly by polling technocrats. Most publicly expressed opinion is based less on the concerns of citizens than on the concerns of whomever is paying for the poll. Thus in 1970, a year of both racial strife and antiwar protest, the Gallup Poll devoted 5 percent of its questions to American policy in Vietnam, less than one percent to race relations, and had no questions on student protests. On the other hand, 26 percent of its questions (in a nonpresidential year) concerned the electoral horserace.

Whatever the merit of Ginsberg's arguments, they suffer from the same problem as those of Lippmann, Blumer, and Rogers—a rejection of the normative view that all opinions ought to count equally. In the last years of the twentieth century, there are few who endorse less democratic input into the political system as opposed to more democratic input, whatever might be the imperfections of the latter. Polls may have shortcomings, but as measures of public opinion they are clearly more representative of all opinion than are the traditional measures. In fact, the traditional measures may be even more nonrepresentative today than they were in the past. In recent years, paid political consultants have become very sophisticated at marshaling local interest groups on issues of importance to their clients, raining letters, faxes, and phone calls on Congress and the White House, as well as newspapers and talk shows (Engelberg 1993). It is often difficult to distinguish between these mobilized outbursts of public sentiment and those that are genuinely spontaneous.

Implicit in Ginsberg's analysis is an assumption that modern opinion polling has discouraged the communication of public opinion by other methods. But all the means available to express public opinion prior to 1936 are still available, and are often used effectively. One need only witness the controversy over the confirming of Zoe Baird as attorney general, or lifting the ban on homosexuals in the military during the early months of the Clinton administration, to appreciate the efficacy of the old ways.

Explicit in the analysis is a claim that the appearance of public opinion polls has domesticated public opinion—that it is not as powerful a force in political decision-making as it was once. There is, however, no systematic, hard evidence to support this assertion. The simple truth is that poll results are brought forcefully to the attention of government authorities at all levels (P. Converse 1987, 14). The relationship of public opinion to public policy in the modern era is an empirical question, about which we will have much to say in this book.

1-5 Sources of Information on Public Opinion _____

Since the 1930s, tens of thousands of surveys have been conducted, hundreds of thousands of questions have been asked, and millions of respondents have been interviewed (T. Smith 1990). Much of this data has been housed in several "data libraries" or archives. The most comprehensive and up-to-date method for finding particular public opinion items is a computerized data base called POLL (the Public Opinion Location Library), located at the Roper Center in Storrs, Connecticut. For members, the Roper Center archives can be accessed by computer over the phone or through most university computer networks. One simply enters one or more key words, such as "gun control," and the question wording, item frequencies, and basic documentation will appear for questions housed at the archive. The surveys themselves are available from the Roper Center, but at a cost. The Harris Center at the University of North Carolina houses the surveys conducted by Lou Harris and Associates plus several others. The holdings of the Harris Center can be accessed via computer through CDNet.

For academic students of public opinion, including undergraduate and graduate students, the most valuable data archive is the Inter-University Consortium for Political and Social Research (ICPSR) at the University of Michigan. Many colleges and universities are members of "the Consortium," while membership in the Roper Center, and particularly the Harris Center, are less frequent. Like Roper and Harris, the Consortium's holdings can be accessed by computer through a data base called "VARIABLES." The Consortium also publishes annually a complete catalog of its holdings and distributes a newsletter informing members of new acquisitions. Most important, the Consortium disseminates the National Election Studies and the General Social Survey. Each of these studies comes with a completely documented codebook. These codebooks and the data sets are routinely received by universities who are Consortium members.[23]

In addition, there are a number of journals that publish opinion data on a regular basis. Each issue of the *Public Opinion Quarterly* has a section called "The Polls," in which survey data on a specific topic is reviewed. General compilations of public opinion data are also published in *Public Opinion*,[24] the *Public Perspective*, and *American Enterprise* magazine. The best source for academic studies of public opinion is the

Public Opinion Quarterly. One might also consult the major journals in political science and sociology.[25]

1-6 Linkage Models Between Public Opinion and Public Policies

In a democracy, public opinion is supposed to influence the decisions by the elected leaders. The mechanisms linking public opinion to government policies are more complicated than we might think. In this final section we outline five models, originally proposed by Luttbeg (1968), by which public opinion can be reflected in public policy.

The Rational-Activist Model

This model is the basis for the widely accepted concept of the ideal citizen's role in a democracy. Voting on the basis of issues is at the heart of the Rational-Activist Model. By the standards of this model, individual citizens are expected to be informed politically, involved, rational, and, above all, active. On the basis of an informed and carefully reasoned set of personal preferences, and an accurate perception of the various candidates' positions, the voter is expected to cast a ballot for those candidates who best reflect the voter's issue preferences. The model suggests that elected officials who are not held accountable by an informed electorate will not responsibly enact public preferences into policy. Instead, such representatives may vote their own preferences or the preferences of limited segments of society, such as wealthy professional groups.

This model places great burdens on both elected officials and citizens, expecting both to be informed and to communicate with each other. In a complex and increasingly technical society, the task of the voter who seeks to be informed is indeed formidable. As we have noted, politics does not play a salient role in the lives of most Americans. Many people rarely or never vote. Those who do are often ill-informed, particularly when they participate in nonpresidential elections.

Certainly issue voting allows for some modest influence of public opinion on government policy. But in our search for methods by which political leaders can be held accountable, we must look beyond the Rational-Activist Model.

The Political Parties Model

The Political Parties Model greatly reduces the political demands placed on the citizen. The model depends on the desire of political parties to win elections as a mechanism for achieving popular control. According to the model, a party states its positions on the various issues of the day in its platform. Because of their interest in winning elections, parties can be counted on to take stands that appeal to large segments of the electorate. The voter then selects among platforms, giving support to the candidate of the party whose platform most conforms to his or her personal preference. Instead of facing multiple decisions for the numerous offices up for election, the voter need only make a single decision among the available choice of parties.

A number of questions are raised by a consideration of this model. For example, do people simply adopt the party identification of their parents and loyally support that party throughout their lives? Such loyalty violates the model's expectations that voters rationally chose the party most closely standing for issue positions they prefer. Does a party's electoral fortunes reflect the degree of public support for its policies, or is a party's vote largely independent of the policies it advocates?

The Interest Groups Model

In the preceding models we have emphasized the central importance of communication between elected officials and their constituents. For representatives to respond to public demands, they need to know what these demands are. For the public to achieve accountability from representatives, they need to know what the representatives have done, and what alternatives were available. Interest groups can perform this function. They can serve as a link between the people and their representatives.

Numerous organized groups in society claim to speak for various segments of the electorate—the Sierra Club, the National Organization for Women, and the National Rifle Association, to mention a few. At one extreme, these groups could be so inclusive of individuals in our society and could so accurately represent their members' opinions that representatives could achieve accountability merely by recording the choice of each group, weighing them by the number of voters they represent, and voting with the most sizable group. This would be in accord with what might be called the Interest Group Model of popular control.

Under ideal circumstances interest groups might succeed in communicating public opinion to officials between elections and with greater clarity than can be communicated through election outcomes. Interest groups, like political parties, could simplify the choices for the individual voter, making it possible for an electorate that is largely disinterested in politics to nevertheless achieve accountability.

Several questions arise out of the Interest Groups Model. Are the opinions of those citizens within an interest group similar, and do they differ from members of other groups? Does "group opinion," the somehow combined opinions of all those persons in all the relevant interest groups, coincide with public opinion? Or, do the opinions carried to government by interest groups reflect only the opinions of the wealthy or the business sector of our society? Who among everyday citizens belongs to interest groups? Are some segments of society overrepresented, while others are mostly uninvolved in any type of group activity?

The Role Playing Model

The Role Playing Model builds on the sociological concept of "role," or widely shared beliefs about how people in various social positions should act. The judge is supposed to be fair-minded, the doctor both expert and comforting, and the political representative willing to work to enact the preferences of his or her supporters. If elected officials believe they should learn constituency opinion and enact it into public policy, public policy may well reflect public opinion. Even if the public votes for candidates and parties with no concern for their positions on issues, public policy would still reflect public opinion because of the role orientation of the representative. He or she would attempt to learn public opinion and translate it into public policy regardless of the electorate's motives in casting the ballot. Of course elected leaders will be more likely to heed public opinion if they perceive that the people are paying attention to what they do. Thus, representation of public opinion can be enhanced simply because elected leaders believe that they will be thrown out of office if they do not attend to voter opinion—whether or not the voters would actually do so.

Questions raised by the Role Playing Model are: Can elected officials accurately learn public opinion, or do they receive a distorted view? To what extent do elected officials actually heed public opinion as they perceive it? What do elected leaders view as the consequences of ignoring public opinion? Finally, how often do elected officials see their role as representing consistituency preferences, as opposed to their (possibly conflicting) personal views of the constituency's best interests?

The Sharing Model

Because as a society we do not designate leaders early in life and hold them as a class apart throughout their early lives, it is unlikely that the personal opinions held by elected officials on the issues of the day differ diametrically from those held by the rest of the electorate. This possibility is the final model of political linkage: the Sharing Model. This model simply states that since many attitudes are broadly held throughout the public, elected leaders cannot help but satisfy public opinion to some degree, even if the public is totally apathetic. Unilateral disarmament, total government takeover of the economy, a termination of public education, a complete disregard for the preservation of the environment—all are examples of actions so contrary to broadly held American attitudes that they would be rejected by any set of government leaders. Even on issues that provoke substantial disagreement, the distribution of opinion among political leaders may be similar to that among the public. If so, even when leaders act according to personal preference and are ignored by disinterested citizens, their actions would often correspond to citizen preferences. For this model, we need to consider how broadly opinions on national issues are shared, and how similar are views of elected officials to the public at large.

1-7 Plan of the Book _____

Necessarily, we have ordered facts into various chapters that strike us as convenient. Chapter 2 discusses the science of assessing public opinion. Chapter 3 is concerned with the psychology of opinion-holding, and focuses on the role of political ideology and party identification. Chapter 4 chronicles trends in public opinion over time. Chapter 5 discusses the formation of political attitudes. Chapter 6 evaluates data on broad public acceptance of certain attitudes that may be necessary for a stable democratic government, and Chapter 7 delves into the group basis of public opinion. Chapter 8 analyzes the effect of the media on those attitudes. Chapter 9 is an analysis of public opinion and elections, and Chapter 10 views the reverse aspect of political linkage—how elected officials respond to the views of their constituents. Chapter 11 considers the importance of political parties and interest groups in achieving correspondence between public opinion and public policy. In the final chapter, we assess the linkage models and draw conclusions about public opinion in the United States based on the data presented throughout this book.

Notes _____

1. The Blummer view of public opinion is one still held by many in the field. For a recent statement, see Zukin (1992).
2. The term "pollster" was coined by political scientist and pollster Lindsay Rogers to evoke in the minds of readers the word "huckster" (Hitchens 1992, 46).

3. Or as Winston Churchill put it, "Nothing is more dangerous than to live in the temperamental atmosphere of a Gallup Poll, always feelings one's pulse and taking one's temperature.... There is only one duty, only one safe course, and that is to try to be right and not to fear to do or waver in what you believe to be right." (Quoted in Bogart 1972, 47.)

4. Almond moderated his opinion on this point in the reissue of his book in 1960.

5. For a detailed argument that the change in public opinion is not capricious but ordered and rational, see Page and Shapiro (1992).

6. The eighteenth-century French mathematician Marquis de Condorcet, using jury decisions as an example, was able to demonstrate mathematically a greater probability that the majority would come to the right decision than the probability the minority would come to the right decision.

7. For an analysis of the dimensions possible, see Herbst (1993).

8. Choosing not to vote may well be as much of a political statement as casting one's ballot. A nonvote can mean alienation from government, or may indicate acceptance of the status quo.

9. It also includes the functional equivalent of verbal expressions, such as filling out a written questionnaire.

10. One ambiguity with this conceptualization is that some people may never express orally or in writing some of their opinions. We could possibly conceptualize such opinions as internal, but that has the unhappy consequence of muddying the distinction between attitudes and opinions. Our simple solution for unexpressed opinions is to assert that if expressed they would have the same characteristics and qualities of expressed opinion.

11. It should be noted that our distinction between opinions and beliefs is not universal across all fields. In a court of law, for example, an expert witness is frequently asked to give an "expert opinion" on a matter of fact. In everyday conversation, it is quite frequently that someone asserts, "It is my opinion that ..." followed by some assertion of factual truth.

12. The name apparently comes from a practice in rural areas of throwing straw into the air to see which way the wind is blowing. Presumably, a "straw poll" is a method for determining the direction of the political winds. Pioneer pollster Claude Robinson (1932, 6) defined a straw poll as "an unofficial canvass of an electorate to determine the division of popular sentiment on public issues or on candidates for public office." Today the term generally refers to any assessment of public opinion based on nonscientific sampling methods.

13. The sample consisted of 532 respondents from Wilmington, Delaware, selected "without Discrimination of Parties" (Gallup and Rae 1940, 35). Other straw polls were conducted in 1824 as well (see Smith 1990).

14. Straw polls used three methods to gather data. One was the "ballot-in-the-paper" method, in which the reader filled out the ballot, cut it out of the paper, and mailed it to the sponsoring organization. The second was the personal canvass, in which solicitors would take ballots to crowded locations, such as theaters, hotels, and trolleys, and get willing citizens to complete them. Sometimes ballots would simply be left in a crowded area in the morning, and those completed would be retrieved in the evening. The third

method was to send out ballots by mail to a specified list of people, and ask that they send them back by return mail.

15. In publications such as the *Chicago Record*, there was a daily front-page feature from September 1896 through election day. The same was true of the *Literary Digest*.

16. The sample sizes for the straw polls were so large that they typically made projections on a state-by-state basis.

17. Gallup marketed a column to newspapers based on his polls, called "America Speaks."

18. Although early on, Gallup did do split-ballot question-wording experiments. These were not, however, publicly released.

19. Now a division of the Institute for Social Research.

20. Over the years, these University of Michigan–based surveys have undergone a number of name changes. In the early years, they were dubbed the "SRC" surveys, after the Survey Research Center. Then they became the "CPS" surveys, named after the Center for Political Studies, a division of the Institute for Social Research. Currently they are referred to as the "National Election Studies" (NES).

21. However, only the CBS News/*New York Times* has its own in-house polling operation. ABC, NBC, and CNN contract with outside commercial polling houses for their opinion surveys.

22. For a copy of the code of the ethics and a discussion, see Cantril (1991, Ch. 4).

23. For more information on data archives, see Smith (1990) or Kiecolt and Nathan (1985).

24. Public Opinion ceased publication in 1991, but is still a good source of opinion data from 1978 to 1991.

25. One might consult the *American Political Science Review*, the *Journal of Politics*, the *American Journal of Political Science*, *Political Research Quarterly*, *Political Behavior*, the *American Sociology Review*, the *American Journal of Sociology*, *Social Forces*, *Sociological Quarterly*, and the *Social Science Quarterly*.

CHAPTER 2

Polling: The Scientific Assessment of Public Opinion

Analysis of public opinion and elections using modern survey methods has now been part of the public landscape for over fifty years. Yet few among the mass public have even a rudimentary understanding of how a public opinion poll works. In a recent study, the Roper Poll asked a national sample whether interviews with 1,500 or 2,000 people (typical sample sizes for national polls) "can accurately reflect the views of the nation's population," or whether "it's not possible with so few people." Only 28 percent said a sample of that size could yield accurate results; 56 percent said it was not possible, with the remaining 15 percent having no opinion (Sussman 1985, 37). While the public may not understand the technicalities of polling, a sizable majority, nevertheless, believes polls are always accurate or almost always accurate, and 75 percent believe they work "for the best interest of the general public" (Sussman 1986, 37).

In the popular press, however, polls have frequently been the subject of severe criticism. Following the 1980 presidential election, the *Detroit Free Press* ran a story headlined "Pollsters Kissed Off by Electorate: Have 1,001 Excuses" (Ladd and Ferree 1981, 13). Similar complaints were heard in other years. In 1986, an ABC polling analyst was quoted in the *New York Times* as saying, "I don't think it was a great year for pollsters" (Tolchin 1986, 17). In 1988, according to *Newsweek*, "polls are more accurate than in the past, but they are still wrong more often than their sponsors admit" (21 Nov. 1988, 26). The author then went on to criticize the Gallup misprediction of a win by Republican senator Robert Dole in the New Hampshire primary and the underestimate of Senator Albert Gore's showing in the Super Tuesday Primary. In 1989, much critical analysis was directed at polls in New York and Virginia, where the percentage of the vote received by black candidates David Dinkins and Douglas Wilder were greatly overstated in preelection surveys (Rosenthal 1989). In November 1992, the polls mostly performed well in estimating the division of the presidential vote. Only the Gallup Poll suffered a major embarrassment, overstating Clinton's share of the vote by 6 percent. But there were numerous missteps on the way to November. The polls were inconsistent in defining the election day voting population, leading to artificial surges in support for President Bush late in the contest. And in the first primary of the year, the VRS[1] exit poll in New Hampshire caused a feeding frenzy among the media when it predicted a close contest between challenger Patrick Buchanan and President Bush. Mr. Bush ultimately won an easy victory, with 16 percentage points separating him from Buchanan (Traugott 1992). Finally, in 1993 the polls suffered a major embarrassment in New Jersey, where every public poll save one gave incumbent Democratic governor Jim Florio a substantial lead. On election day his Republican opponent, Christine Whitman, won with 52 percent of the vote (Kolbert 1993). This "misprediction" along with others gave the popular press yet another opportunity for a journalistic coup on "What went wrong with the polls."

Polling certainly deserves a critical look. Many surveys are badly conceived, poorly executed, and incorrectly interpreted. Nevertheless, much popular criticism of public opinion polls seems ill-informed. Few outside the professional survey community have an appreciation for why candidates who lead in the final preelection poll do not always win; why two surveys taken at the same time report different results; or even why Truman beat Dewey when the Gallup Poll predicted otherwise.

The news media are now saturated with polling reports. In 1992, *Hotline*, the daily campaign newsletter, reported 198 different presidential polls between September 1 and election day.[2] Countless others were undoubtedly conducted as well. Furthermore, polls are no longer confined predominantly to the analysis of elections. In the last several years, abortion has been a major issue on the public agenda. Hardly a month goes by without a survey report on how Americans currently feel on the abortion issue.

An understanding of what can and cannot be inferred from political polls has a practical importance that lies beyond the academic world. It is now agreed that a candidate's poor showing in preelection polls makes fund raising difficult and dampens volunteer enthusiasm. To quote from Richard Nixon in 1968, "When the polls go good for me, the cash register really rings."[3] When the polls go good, it also results in more media attention (Traugott 1992b, 126). In addition, a strong showing in the polls can legitimize a candidate, insuring that he or she is taken seriously. A good example is the third-party candidacy of John Anderson in 1980. In June of that year, an ABC poll showed that 31 percent of the electorate would vote for Anderson, a clear asset for an unconventional candidate in attracting volunteers and raising money (Broh 1983, 32–33). The same could be said for Ross Perot in 1992, who at one point in June led both major party candidates in the polls. He did not, of course, need a strong showing in the polls to finance his campaign.

Polls also create expectations about who is the likely election winner. Larry Bartels has demonstrated that in presidential primaries with a number of more or less unknown candidates—such as 1988 for the Democrats—expectations about who will win are a major factor in determining candidate choice on election day (Bartels 1988, Ch. 6). Thomas Patterson makes a compelling argument that the standing in the polls of a presidential candidate determines the way the candidate's personal qualities are described by the media. Candidates who are ahead in the polls are described in very flattering terms, while those behind are depicted as bumblers. In an analysis of reporting in *Newsweek*, Patterson shows that in 1988 when Michael Dukakis was doing well in the polls, he was described as "relentless in his attack" and "a credible candidate." As he later dropped in the polls, *Newsweek* described him as "reluctant to attack" and "trying to present himself as a credible candidate." Interestingly, the change in descriptors coincided quite closely with the point he fell behind George Bush in the polls (Patterson 1989, 104–06). Finally, standing in the polls can determine whether or not a candidate is invited to participate in the presidential debates. For example, when John Anderson's poll numbers fell below 10 percent in 1980, he was excluded from the final debate (Polsby and Wildavsky 1984).

Presidential popularity is now gauged at least every two weeks, and is watched with considerable interest by members of Congress as well as others in the political community. It is argued that one very important aspect of presidential power is the chief executive's personal standing with the public. A president may also use polls to gauge the popularity of his policies among certain segments of the population, or to try to identify those segments that are not supportive. Specific programs may then be targeted for the nonsupportive group. For example, in the spring of 1982, Ronald Reagan's advisors found his popularity was slumping badly with Roman Catholics. In an attempt to remedy the problem, President Reagan flew to Chicago, home of the largest Catholic school system in the nation, and announced a proposal to give tuition credits to allow families to send their children to private (e.g., Catholic) schools (Bradburn and Sudman 1988, 47–48). Survey results also directly affect who gets what from government. Formulas for allocations of federal grant money are based on surveys such as the monthly Current Population Surveys (CPS) done by the Bureau of the Census. Finally, democratic governments (as well as others) justify their existence by claiming to respond to "the will of the people." Public opinion polls have become the commonly accepted tool for uncovering the hopes, fears, wishes, preferences, and values of those whom government serves. In this chapter we shall outline the major procedures used in conducting surveys of public opinion and how they can go awry.

2-1 Sampling

Most public opinion polls are based on samples. When the Gallup Poll reports that 50 percent of adult Americans approve of the way that the President is handling his job, it is obvious that the Gallup organization has not gone out and interviewed 190 million American adults. Instead it has taken a sample. The reasons for sampling are fairly straightforward. First, to interview everyone would be prohibitively expensive. The 1990 census cost over 2.5 billion dollars. Second, to interview the entire population would take a very long time. Months might pass between the first and last interviews. Public opinion might, in that period, undergo real change.

Sampling provides a practical alternative to interviewing the whole population—be it national, state, or local. Furthermore, when done correctly, sampling can provide very accurate estimates of the political opinions of a larger population. The theory of sampling is a branch of the mathematics of probability, and the error involved in going from the sample to the population can be known with precision. However, many surveys of public opinion do not meet the demanding requirements of sampling theory. The attendant result, of course, is a loss in accuracy.

Sampling Theory

The *population* is that unit about which we want information. In most political surveys three different populations are frequently polled: (1) those 18 and older, (2) those who are registered voters, and (3) those who will (or do) vote in the next election. These are three quite different groups. It is very important that the population be clearly specified. When one sees a poll addressing abortion, presidential popularity, or voter intent in an upcoming election, those reporting the poll should provide a clear description of the population about which they speak. It has been shown, for example, that Senator Edward Kennedy is more highly rated among all adults than among registered voters (Roper 1980, 48). Evaluations of Kennedy are, in part, determined by how one defines the population.

The *sample* is that part of the population selected for analysis. Usually, the sample is considerably smaller than the population. National political surveys conducted by reputable firms employ samples of 1,000 to 1,500 respondents, although smaller samples are sometimes used in state and local contests. But as samples get smaller, the probability of error increases. Sample size should always be reported along with the results of a survey. If that information is missing, the alleged findings should be treated with a great deal of caution.

When samples accurately mirror the population, they are said to be *representative*. The term "randomness" refers to the only method by which a representative sample can be scientifically drawn. In a simple random sample, each unit of the population has exactly the same chance of being drawn as any other unit. If the population is American attorneys, each attorney is required to have exactly the same probability of being selected in order for the sample to be random. Attorneys in big cities could not have a greater likelihood of getting into the sample than those from rural areas. This situation obviously requires a detailed knowledge of the population. In the case of attorneys, one could get a list from the American Bar Association and then sample from that list. But suppose the population was unemployed adults. To specify the population in a fashion to be able to draw a random sample would be very difficult. As a consequence, obtaining a representative sample of the unemployed is not easy.

A probability sample is a variant on the principle of random sampling. Instead of each unit having exactly the same probability of being drawn, some units would be more likely to be drawn than would others. But this would be a *known* probability. For example, if one were sampling voter precincts in a state, it is of consequence that some precincts contain more people than do others. To make the sample of people in those precincts representative, the larger precincts must have a greater likelihood of being selected than smaller ones.

We will use *simple random sampling* (SRS) to illustrate how the principle of probability works in selecting a representative sample. Let us assume our population is a large barrel containing 100,000 marbles, some of which are red and some of which are green. We do not know the percentage of each. Instead of counting them all (a long and tedious job), we will draw a random sample. The question is: How? We could just dip in our hand and take some out, but that would mean that those within our reach would be picked and those close to the bottom would have no chance of being selected. Or we could spin the barrel and take one out after every spin. That would probably work reasonably well, but it still would not be "scientific." Even with a spin, those marbles at the bottom might never get close enough to the surface to get picked. If we are insisting on a pure random sample, we would have to employ a table of random numbers, and give each marble a numeral between 1 and 100,000. Random number tables are computer-generated digits that are completely unrelated to one another (i.e., random). They can be found in the appendix of virtually any statistics book. Let us assume we sample 600 marbles. Our first random number might be 33,382. We would then find the marble with that number and note if it is red or green. Our next random number might be 12,343. We would again note its color. The process would continue until we drew 600 marbles and recorded the color of each.

Having completed that task, let us say our sample shows 65 percent red marbles. Given the sampling method, we now know some things about the population. Sampling theory (the central limit theorem) tells us that the most likely percentage of red marbles is 65 percent. Of course, it is very unlikely that the real percentage of red marbles is precisely 65 percent. It might be 65.5 or 64.3, for example. The sample will not get the population value exactly correct for the same reason that flipping a coin 100 times will not likely yield exactly 50 heads and 50 tails—although it should be close if the coin is honestly flipped.

We need at this point to introduce the concepts of *confidence level* and *sampling error*. A sample will rarely hit the true population value right on the nose. The confidence level tells us the probability that the population value will fall within a specified range. The sampling error specifies that range. A commonly used confidence level is 95 percent (it is sometimes higher, but almost never lower). For a sample of 600, the sampling error is 4 percent. What all this means is that if we took 100 samples from our population, and each of these samples consisted of 600 marbles randomly drawn, then 95 out of 100 times we would be plus or minus 4 percent of the true population value. Our sample came up 65 percent red. While this figure may not be exactly correct, we at least know that 95 out of 100 times (our 95 percent confidence level) we are going to be within four points—one way or the other—of the true proportion of red marbles in the barrel. This much can be proved mathematically.

Let us turn to a political example. The *New York Times* reported that President Clinton's popularity his first week in office was 58 percent approval. By May 27, his popularity had dropped to 36 percent, the lowest of any president at the same point in his term (*New York Times*, 29 May 93, Section A). Since the sample size in the May survey was 750 adults, we know that if the poll were repeated 100 times, 95 of the 100 repetitions (the 95 percent confidence level) would produce results that are plus or minus 3.5 percent (the sampling error) of what we'd find if we interviewed all adult Americans.[4] Thus Clinton's popularity on or about May 27, 1993, could have been as high as 39.5 percent or as low as 32.5 percent. The "best estimate" (according to the central limit theorem) is 36 percent. Sampling error decreases as we move away from a 50/50 split, and it increases as the population has more heterogeneous political attitudes. But by far the most important factor is the size of the sample.

The importance of sample size for sampling accuracy can be easily demonstrated by flipping a coin. In theory we know if a coin is flipped honestly a large number of times it should come up about equal proportions of heads and tails. Suppose we flipped a coin ten times. Given a large number of repetitions of ten flips we might frequently get seven heads, eight tails, etc. But if instead of flipping the coin ten times we flipped it 100 times, then our large number of repetitions would only occasionally yield 70 heads or 80 tails, and if we flipped it 1000 times, our repetitions could tend to cluster around 500 heads and 500 tails, with 700 heads or 800 tails being rare events indeed. The larger the size of the sample (i.e., the number of times the coin is flipped), the closer we will come to the theoretical expectation of one-half heads and one-half tails.

Unlike the size of the *sample*, the size of the population is of little consequence for the accuracy of the survey. That is, it does not make much difference if we are surveying the city of Houston or the entire United States. With a sample size of 600, the sampling error would be identical for both the city and the nation—all other things being equal.[5] Presented in Table 2.1 are the sampling errors associated with specific sample sizes.

Note that when the sample size drops to around 150, the sampling error gets very large. While one rarely sees a public opinion survey of 150 people, one often sees survey subgroups (men, college-educated, blacks, Republicans, etc.) analyzed where the number of respondents falls below 150. For example, a poll done following the 1992 election showed George Bush leading Bill Clinton among partisan

TABLE 2.1 Sampling Error and Sample Size Employing Simple Random Sampling*

Sample Size	Sampling Error (plus or minus)*
2,430	2.0
1,536	2.5
1,067	3.0
784	3.5
600	4.0
474	4.5
384	5.0
267	6.0
196	7.0
150	8.0
119	9.0
96	10.0
42	15.0

*This computation is based on the assumptions of a simple random sample (SRS) with a dichotomous opinion that splits 50/50.

Independents by a margin of 39 to 31 percent.[6] However, there were only 96 respondents in that subsample. With a sampling error of 10 percent, all we know is that for Independents, somewhere between 29 and 49 percent favored Bush, and somewhere between 21 and 41 percent favored Clinton. To say that Bush led Clinton among Independents is not supported by the data. Bush's lead was, in fact, statistically insignificant (i.e., it could have occurred by chance). When reading reports about the politics of those under 30, the gender gap, the politics of the religious right, and similar topics that involve the analysis of subgroups, one should pay special attention to sample size. A difference of 5 or 6 percent can be quite *meaningful* in a subsample of 300, and quite *meaningless* in a subsample of 50.[7]

Applied Sampling and Surveys of Public Opinion

Using a large barrel of marbles and a table of random numbers, we drew a "perfect" sample. That is, the sampling method fit perfectly with the mathematics of sampling theory. When we sample humans we cannot draw a perfect sample. Although a marble cannot refuse to tell us if it is red or green, a person may refuse to be interviewed. Sampling theory does not allow for refusals. Consequently, surveys of public opinion only approximate the underlying theory of sampling. If these deviations from theory are modest, opinion polls can and do work well. But there are many instances in which sampling theory is ignored (or those conducting the polls are ignorant). If the poll simply concerns political opinions (favor/oppose abortion, approve/disapprove of tax reform, keep/ abolish the 55 mph speed limit), there is no reality test. The survey may have been done badly and be considerably off the mark, but how would one know?[8] On the other hand, pre–election day surveys have a reality test: election day. In these surveys, sampling mistakes have, in several dramatic cases, cast opinion pollsters in a highly unfavorable light.

In the previous chapter we discussed the prescientific straw polls that were used to gauge candidate fortunes prior to 1936. The best-known of the commercial publications conducting straw polls was the *Literary Digest*. The *Digest* accurately forecast the winner (if not the exact percentage points) of each presidential election between 1920 and 1932. In 1936, as in previous years, it sent out some 10 million postcard ballots "drawn from every telephone book in the United States, from the rosters of clubs and associations, from city directories, lists of registered voters, [and] classified mail order and occupational data" (*Literary Digest*, Aug. 1936, 3). About 2.2 million returned their postal ballots. The result was 1,293,699 (57 percent) for Republican Alf Landon and 972,867 (43 percent) for President Franklin Roosevelt. On election day, Roosevelt not only won but won by a landslide, receiving 62.5 percent of the vote and carrying every state except Maine and Vermont. The *Literary Digest* was not only wrong; it was wrong by 19.5 percent. On November 14, 1936, the *Literary Digest* published the following commentary:

WHAT WENT WRONG WITH THE POLLS?

None of Straw Votes Got Exactly the Right Answer—Why?

In 1920, 1924, 1928 and 1932, the *Literary Digest* Polls were right. Not only right in the sense they showed the winner; they forecast the actual popular vote with such a small percentage of error (less than 1 percent in 1932) that newspapers and individuals everywhere heaped such phrases as "uncannily accurate" and "amazingly right" upon us. . . . Well this year we used precisely the same method that had scored four bull's eyes in four previous tries. And we were far from correct. Why? We ask that question in all sincerity, because *we want to know.*

Why did the poll fare so badly? One reason that can be discounted is sample size. The *Digest* claims to have polled 10 million people (and received 2.2 million responses). Thus a large sample is no guarantee for accuracy. Rather, their sampling procedure had four fundamental defects. First, the sample was drawn in a *biased* fashion. The *Digest* clearly did not use random selection or anything approaching it. Even though questionnaires were sent out to ten million people, a large part of the sample was drawn from telephone directories and lists of automobile owners— during the Depression, a decidedly upper-middle-class group, predominantly Republican in its political sentiments. In other words, the *Digest* did not correctly specify the population. A second factor contributing to the *Digest*'s mistake was time. The questionnaires were sent out in early September, making impossible the detection of any late trend favoring one candidate or the other. Third, 1936 was the year that marked the emergence of the "New Deal Coalition." The *Digest* had picked the winner correctly since 1920 using the same methods as in 1936, but in 1936 voting became polarized along class lines. The working class and the poor voted overwhelmingly Democratic, while the more affluent classes voted predominantly Republican. Since the *Literary Digest*'s sample was heavily biased in the direction of the more affluent, it is not surprising that their sample tended to favor Landon. Finally, there was the problem of self-selection. The *Digest* sent out its questionnaires by mail. Of the 10 million they mailed, only a little over 2 million responded—about 22 percent. Those people who self-select to respond to mail surveys are often quite different in their political outlooks from those who do not respond. They tend to be better educated, to have higher incomes, and to feel more strongly about the topics dealt with in the questionnaire

(Dillman 1978). So even if the sample of 10 million had been drawn in an unbiased fashion, the poll probably still would have been in error due to the self-selection factor (Squire 1988).[9] One very fundamental principle of survey sampling is that *one cannot allow the respondents to select themselves into the sample.*

Despite the failure of the *Literary Digest,* several public opinion analysts did pick Franklin Roosevelt as the winner. Among them was George Gallup, who built his reputation on a correct forecast in 1936. In terms of percentage, Gallup did not get particularly close. He missed by almost 7 percent. But he got the winner right, and that is what most people remember. He was, in fact, closer in 1948 (off by 5 percent) when he made his infamous prediction that Dewey would beat Truman— that, too, is well remembered.[9]

The technique used by Gallup in 1936 and up until the Dewey-Truman disaster is called *quota sampling.* This technique employs the census to determine the percentage of certain relevant groups in the population. For example, what percentage is male, Catholic, white, and college-educated? Within these groups interviewers are then assigned quotas. They must interview a certain percentage of women, a certain percentage with less than high school education, a certain percentage of blacks, etc. But there are few, if any, constraints as to which specific individuals in these groups are to be interviewed. Once the interviews are completed, the sample is weighted so that it will be representative of the population on those variables. If 15 percent of the population is male, high school-educated, and making over $25,000 a year, the sample will be weighted to reflect those proportions. The principal problem with quota sampling is a variation on the problem of self-selection. The interviewer has too much opportunity to determine who is selected for the sample. An interviewer who must get a specified number of "female blacks" may avoid certain areas of town or may get the entire quota from a single block. There is a natural tendency to avoid shabby residences, long flights of stairs, and homes where there are dogs. Experience with quota samples demonstrates that they systematically tend to underrepresent the poor, the less educated, and racial minorities.[10]

Research on Gallup's misprediction in 1948 reveals he had too many middle- and high-income voters.[11] A second factor contributing to Gallup's mistake was that he quit polling two weeks before the election (Bradburn and Sudman 1988, 29).[12] When significant movement takes place, it often occurs just before the election. For example, in 1980 Jimmy Carter and Ronald Reagan were virtually tied even the weekend before the vote. A strong move toward Reagan over the weekend allowed him to pile up a substantial victory. To capture these changes, Gallup and other survey organizations now poll right up to the day of the election.

Contemporary Sampling Methods

We used simple random sampling (SRS) to illustrate the principles involved in drawing a scientific sample. However, SRS is seldom used in actual public opinion surveys. There is no master list of all Americans that could be sampled. Even if there were, the persons selected would be widely scattered throughout the country, making in-person interviews prohibitively expensive. For example, an interviewer might have to travel all the way to Kerrville, Texas, just to talk to one respondent. Rather, polls where respondents are personally interviewed use *multistage cluster samples*.

The first step in drawing a multistage cluster sample of the American electorate is to divide the country into four geographic regions. Within each region, a set of counties and standard metropolitan statistical areas (SMSAs) is randomly selected. To insure a representative selection of the national population, each county or SMSA is given a chance to be selected proportional to its population (probability sampling). National surveys typically include about 80 primary sampling units (PSUs). Once selected, the PSUs are often used several years before they are replaced. The reason is economic: Compact geographic areas save time and money. Interviewers are expensive to train, but once trained they can be used over and over.

About 20 respondents are chosen within each PSU. First, four or five city blocks (or their rural equivalents) are randomly selected. Then, four or five households are sampled within each block.[13] It is at the household level that the continued use of probability methods becomes most difficult. Ideally the interviewer obtains a list of all persons living in the household and samples from the list. And indeed, some academic polls (such as the General Social Survey and the National Election Studies) attempt to meet this ideal. Most survey organizations, however, abandon probability methods at the block level and rely on some type of systematic method for respondent selection. The problem is that specific individuals are hard to locate. Interviewers are given a randomly drawn starting point and then instructed to stop at every nth household. The interviewer first asks to speak to the youngest man of voting age; if no man is at home the interviewer asks to speak to the youngest woman.[14] If both refuse or no one is home, the interviewer goes to the next adjacent dwelling. Each interviewer has a male/female quota and an age quota, but this is not a *quota sample* because the interviewer cannot choose who gets into the sample.

Multistage cluster samples work well and are an efficient compromise given the expense involved in a simple random sample approach. The drawback is that cluster samples have a greater sampling error than SRS, as would be expected since the respondents are "clustered" into 75 to 100 small geographic areas. A simple random sample of 1,000 has a 3 percent sampling error. Gallup reports that its national samples (cluster samples) of 1,000 have a 4 percent sampling error.[15]

In recent years, in-person surveys have increasingly been replaced by telephone surveys. The principal advantage of the telephone is its low cost. It also frees one from having to use clusters, as the physical location of a respondent is irrelevant in a phone survey. However, there are disadvantages as well. Nationwide, it is estimated that 20 percent of all phone numbers are unlisted. In some areas, like Los Angeles, unlisted numbers are estimated as high as 62 percent.[16] The solution to this problem is to use a random-digit- dialing scheme. A ten-digit phone number is composed of an area code (the first three numbers), an exchange (the next three), a cluster (the next two), and the two final digits. If one knows the geographic assignment of area codes, exchanges, and clusters by the phone company (which will usually provide this information for a fee), a population can be defined and sampled. In large cities (for example, Houston, Texas), there are approximately 10,000 of these seven-digit codes (if we limit ourselves to Houston we can ignore the area code). The following is an example:

496-78__ __

The first five digits would be randomly sampled from the population of 10,000. Then the last two digits would be chosen from a table of random numbers or with a computer program that generates random digits. These methods allow persons with unlisted numbers to get into the sample. On the negative side, calls are made to a large number of non-working numbers. But the sample is quite representative. Once the household is selected, it is then necessary to sample residents within the household. Sophisticated methods to insure random selection have been developed by statisticians, but they require an enumeration of all household members by age and sex—information many respondents are unwilling to provide over the phone. A simple alternative is the "next (or last) birthday" method. Interviewers ask to speak to the person who has the next birthday. This technique gives a good approximation of random sampling within the household (Lavrakas 1987).

Another problem with telephone surveys, although it applies to in-person surveys as well, is refusal. The telephone, however, particularly lends itself to abuse, as persons selling aluminum siding, upholstery, or "can't miss" real estate deals will sometimes attempt to gain a respondent's confidence by posing as a pollster. The sales pitch comes later. A study by the Roper Organization showed that 27 percent of a national sample had experienced these sales tactics (Turner and Martin 1984, 73). People, especially in large cities, are becoming wary of those claiming to be taking polls. It is currently estimated that the refusal rate for telephone surveys is 34 percent (Rothenberg 1990). However, the refusal rate is only slightly lower for in-person surveys.[17] Refusals are of consequence only if those who decline the interview are systematically different on the *questions of interest* from those who consent to the interview. However, in an extensive analysis of nonresponse from both the NES and the GSS, Brehm (1993) argues that nonresponse is neither random nor inconsequential. Typically overrepresented in NES and GSS samples are the elderly, blacks, women, the poor, and the less-educated. Underrepresented are men, young people, whites, and the wealthy. Brehm goes on to argue that this bias in response rates results in some biased substantive inferences.

Finally, the exact percentage of households with telephones is a question open to debate. It is certainly high, but how high? The 1990 Census reports that 95 percent of all households have phone service, although in five states the percentage falls below 90 percent, with Mississippi being the lowest at 87 percent. The Census also reports that 43 percent of homes without telephones are found in tracts where the median income is less than $20,000.[18] Thus, those without phones are found among the least affluent segments of society. This "lumpen proletariat" is one population subgroup that rarely finds its way into any survey, regardless of methodology.

Reputable studies of public opinion will provide an account of their sampling procedures. The better journals will usually have an insert labeled "How the Poll Was Conducted," which includes a discussion of sample size, dates of the interviews, sampling methods, weighting methods, sampling error for the entire sample, sampling error for key subgroups, and notice that beyond sampling error other types of errors can occur due to the practical difficulties of polling.[19]

2-2 Question Wording

It should surprise no one that in survey research, as in everyday life, the answers received are often dependent on the questions asked. This reality has both an upside and a downside for opinion polling. The upside is that people are sensitive to the way survey questions are phrased. That means they are paying reasonably close attention to what they are being asked, and their answers can be taken seriously. If changes in question wording had no impact, the opinion poll would likely be too blunt an instrument to be of much use. The downside is that since the distribution of public opinion can be a function of question wording, incorrect or inappropriate inferences about its true nature are easily possible. Not all variations in question phrasing affect the distribution of responses. But in some cases they clearly do. In this section we will review some of the aspects of question wording that can affect the distribution of opinion.

Multiple Stimuli. Many questions have more than one stimulus to which respondents may react. Such questions are not faulty, but rather are often a necessary requirement for measuring opinions on complex topics. Examples of commonly used single-stimulus questions are: "Generally speaking, do you consider yourself a Democrat, an Independent, a Republican, or what?" or "Do you approve or disapprove of the way President Clinton is handling his job?" But suppose we were interested in public support for the First Amendment right of free speech. We could ask people to agree or disagree with the statement, "I believe in free speech for all, no matter what their views might be." In 1978, 89 percent of opinion-holders agreed (Sullivan et al. 1982). But that tells us little other than in the abstract there is a near consensus on a fundamental principle of the American Creed. However, real controversies over free speech do not occur in the abstract, but in concrete circumstances. Thus we might ask, "Suppose an admitted Communist wanted to make a speech in your community. Should he be allowed to speak or not?" In 1991, only 68 percent of opinion-holders said the person should be allowed to speak. If the admitted Communist was teaching in a college, 43 percent said he should be fired. It is quite clear that in specific circumstances, people are responding to both the "free speech" stimulus and "Communist" stimulus. As we shall see, the level of support for free speech is a matter of considerable controversy (see Chapter 6).

There are many less obvious instances of multiple stimuli that can affect the distribution of opinion. One way is to preface the question with the name of an authoritative or admired person or institution. Consider the responses of white Americans to different phrasings of a question about the controversial policy of minority set-asides (Sniderman and Piazza 1993, 113).

Form A	**Form B**
Sometimes you hear it said there should be a law to ensure that a certain number of federal contracts go to minority contractors. Do you favor or oppose such a law?	The Congress of the United States — both the House of Representatives and the Senate — have passed a law to ensure that a certain number of federal contracts go to minority contractors. Do you favor or oppose such a law?

Form A		Form B	
Favor law	43%	Favor Law	57%
Oppose law	57	Oppose law	43
	100%		100%

Invoking the symbol of the "law" in this question transforms the policy of set-asides from one backed by a minority of white respondents to one back by a clear majority—a change that may not be trivial in the politics of affirmative action. The use of authoritative symbols will also provide a cue for the uncertain, decrease the "don't knows," and raise the percentage of those favorable and unfavorable among those who know little or nothing about the issue in question (Smith and Squire 1990).

Framing Effects. By framing effects we mean the effect the previous content of the interview might have on a specific question. For example, respondents usually desire to be consistent in their answers. When asked in 1980 if "the United States should let Communist newspaper reporters from other countries come here and send back to their papers the news as they see it," 55 percent said yes. But if the question is preceded by one that asks whether "a Communist country like Russia should allow American newspaper reporters to come in and send back the news as they see it," then 75 percent favor letting Communist reporters into the United States (Schuman and Presser 1981, 27). Since most answered "yes" to allowing American reporters in (Communist) Russia, it is obviously inconsistent to bar Communist reporters in the U.S. Returning to the abortion issue, general support for abortion will increase if a specific item with a high level of support is asked first. Thus if respondents are asked if abortion should be permitted "if there is a strong chance of serious defect in the baby" (84 percent say yes), general support for abortion is 13 percent greater than if the specific abortion item is not asked first (Schuman and Presser 1981, 37).

Other examples of framing effects include the questionnaire placement of presidential popularity or presidential vote items. Incumbent presidents do worse on both if the question comes late in a survey as opposed to early. The reason is that content of the interview reminds respondents of troublesome aspects of the incumbent's presidency (Sigelman 1981). Pocketbook voting (voting on the basis of changes in one's personal finances) can be induced by asking questions about finances immediately before ascertaining vote choice (Sears and Lau 1983). Finally, pollsters sometimes provide information on somewhat obscure topics before asking opinions about the topic. Suffice it to say, the content of the information provided in the stem of the question can easily affect the answer given.

Balanced Arguments. If a question mentions only one side of a controversy, that side will often get a disproportionate number of responses. An example is: "Do you favor the death penalty?" Since only one option ("favor") is given, we might expect that option would be more frequently chosen than if the question is balanced—i.e., "Do you *favor* or *oppose* the death penalty?" The same is true for questions that use an "agree/disagree" format (called "Likert scales"). The common practice is to inform the respondent of both options.[20]

At best, however, agree/disagree questions never really present clues about the consequences of agreement or disagreement or the reasons one might choose a particular option. In the example below, providing balanced alternatives on a question about unemployment yields quite different results compared to an agree/disagree alternative (Cantril 1991, 126).

Form A		Form B	
Do you agree or disagree with this statement: Any able-bodied person can find a job and make ends meet?		Some people feel that any able-bodied person can find a job and make ends meet. Others feel there are times when it is hard to get along and some able-bodied people may not be able to find work. Whom do you agree with most?	
Agree	65%	Can make ends meet	43%
No opinion	10	No opinion	18
Disagree	25	Sometimes hard to get along	39
	100%		100%

If one wishes to describe the level of opinion, questions that present two polar alternatives are clearly superior to Likert-type questions (see the Appendix for examples used in the 1992 NES). Likert items are most useful for building scales or perhaps comparing subgroup differences. A single agree-disagree question is usually of little value for gauging the level of public opinion, although several taken in concert can often be quite useful (see Chapter 4 on abortion).

The Middle Position. The public seldom splits into polar camps on any issue, and even when a middle position in not offered, many will volunteer an intermediate alternative. When a middle position is offered in a question it is usually taken by many more people than when not offered. Schuman and Presser (1981, 166) demonstrate that when respondents are asked on political issues if they "are on the liberal side or the conservative side," 16 percent volunteer that they are "middle of the road." But if the "middle of the road" option is offered, it is taken by 54 percent. While there is little doubt about the consequence of offering a middle position (or an "unsure" or "undecided" option for issue questions), there is no consensus about the desirability of doing so. Some argue that most respondents do have a preference, albeit in some cases a weak one. Offering the middle alternative encourages certain respondents not to express their opinion.

Response Acquiescence. Often when people are asked whether they agree or disagree with an abstract statement, or one about which they know little, they tend to agree rather than disagree. This tendency is called "response acquiescence." It arises mostly because the public is ill-informed and may not have genuine opinions on many issues (see Chapter 3). We can illustrate this by using a 1986 study of attitudes toward pornography. Respondents were asked whether they agreed or disagreed that "people should have the right to purchase a sexually explicit book, magazine, or movie, if that's what they want to do." Evidently, people saw this statement as a referendum on individual rights, since an overwhelming 80 percent agreed with the statement. However, in the same poll respondents were also asked whether they agreed or disagreed with the opposite statement, that "community authorities should be able to prohibit the selling of magazines or movies they consider to be pornographic." Sixty-five percent agreed with this opposite view as well.[21] Overall, a large number of respondents agreed that the public had a right to purchase pornographic materials, and also agreed that the community has the right to stop people from purchasing the same material. The most likely explanation of this contradiction is response acquiescence. These examples indicate the danger of using single Likert-type items to measure the level of public opinion. The best strategy for dealing with response acquiescence is to use two or more items where half are worded positively and half negatively. That is, to support free speech the respondent must agree with one statement and disagree with another.

Filter Questions. Most people believe that good citizens should have opinions on current political topics. Thus, when interviewed by polling organizations, they have a tendency to offer opinions on subjects about which they know little or nothing. In an otherwise conventional survey of the Cincinnati area, Bishop et al. (1980) included a question asking respondents whether the nonexistent "Public Affairs Act" should be kept or repealed. Eighteen percent thought it should be kept; 16 percent favored its repeal. Given these findings on a fictitious issue, it should not be surprising that on real but somewhat obscure issues many will offer opinions on matters about which they have no true attitude.

One way to reduce this problem is through the use of filter questions. Respondents are read a question and response alternatives and then asked, "Where would you place yourself on this scale, or haven't you thought much about this?" Using the 1992 NES question that asks people to indicate on a 1-to-7 scale if they feel more or less money should be spent on defense, 12 percent of the sample indicated they had not thought enough about the issue to have an opinion. But that does not mean that all the remaining 88 percent have a "true" attitude. Another 29 percent took the middle position on the scale. It seems likely some taking this position have either no attitude or one that is poorly developed.

One danger in using screening questions is that some people with real attitudes, but hesitant to express them, may be filtered out of surveys. An alternative is to use branching questions, where those who say they are undecided or unsure are encouraged in followup probes to make a choice (T. Smith 1984; Krosnick and Berent 1993). But, of course, this strategy runs the risk of eliciting opinions where no true underlying attitude exists.

Conclusion. Variations in question wording can clearly influence the distribution of public opinion. That fact should be recognized and considered when using opinion data. Some questions are obviously biased (see next section). Read carefully the questions. What are the stimuli? Are authorities being invoked? Are inferences being made about the level of opinion from single Likert items? Are "no opinion" screens used on obscure issues? Are balanced questions truly presenting both options in a fair manner? All of these possibilities are cause for concern. Some types of inferences are more reliable than others. Multiple questions on the same issue can give insight into the range of opinion. But the most reliable strategy is to compare responses to the same question. Thus subgroup differences on the same question are usually quite meaningful. Even better is to compare change over time in response to the same question. Since the stimulus is identical, variation is likely due to a change in the public's view.

2-3 The Misuse of Surveys _____

Back before the advent of probability sampling, the media attempted to measure public sentiment by using "straw polls." The principal defect of straw polls, like those conducted by the *Literary Digest*, is the ability of respondents to "select themselves" to be counted in the poll. As a consequence, there is no way of assessing the sampling error. The factors by which a person gets into the sample are unknown. One might think that with the advent of modern survey methodology, straw polls would have disappeared. Not so. They are in fact alive and well—and most are as unreliable now as they were in the 1930s.

Modern Straw Polls

A natural poll that receives a fair amount of media play consists of letters to the President (the media also sometimes pick up on letters to Congress). When a national crisis occurs that is generally perceived as presenting the President in a poor light, the White House will frequently report that "the mail" is running 10 to 1, 5 to 1, etc. in favor of the President. When Special Prosecutor Archibald Cox was fired during the Watergate scandal, the Nixon White House reported that the mail was running more than 2 to 1 in favor of the President's actions. Many in the Senate and House of Representatives, on the other hand, reported that their mail was running overwhelmingly in opposition to the President's action. More recently, in response to the revelation that President Clinton's nominee for attorney general, Zoe Baird, had employed illegal aliens for child care, mail to U.S. senators was running more than 400 to 1 in opposition. On the other hand, an ABC/*Washington Post* poll done at the same time showed a more modest 58 percent opposed to her confirmation (Clymer 1993). Letters of this sort are basically meaningless as an indication of public sentiment. We know that those who "self-select" to write to public officials overwhelmingly tend to write to those whom they feel are sympathetic. If people like the President and support him in a controversy, they will write to the White House. If they are hostile, they will write to someone else, such as their senator or representative, or not at all.

Another common straw poll involves surveys sent out by public officials or various partisan organizations. These are sometimes published by the media, heralded in bold headlines as if they constituted a reasonable assessment of public opinion. For example, a story in the *Houston Chronicle* carried the following headline: "Survey Here Shows Opposition to President's Energy Program." The "survey" turned out to be responses to 200,000 questionnaires mailed out by Houston area Republican Congressman Bill Archer. There were a total of 43,010 responses to this mailout, or about 22 percent (about the same response to the *Literary Digest* poll). The poll also reported that respondents favored production of the B-1 Bomber and retention of "right to work laws."[22] Suffice it to say, a survey of this sort measures virtually nothing. It is severely contaminated by self-selection. There is no way to compute sampling error, given the bias in the way respondents got into the sample. While the information might be valuable to Congressman Archer as an indication of what his attentive constituents think, it has little or no value as a measure of public opinion.

A variety of political organizations also attempt to assess public opinion by using mail surveys, often combined with highly biased questions. For example, a questionnaire in 1980 from the Republican National Committee, with a return deadline of September 29, 1980 (in time for use in the presidential campaign), included the following items:

- Recently the Soviet armed forces openly invaded the independent country of Afghanistan. Do you think the U.S. should supply military equipment to the rebel freedom fighters?
- Do you believe the U.S. should launch a new program to modernize and increase our Navy in view of the Soviet's massive naval buildup worldwide?

In April 1993, Ross Perot paid $190,000 to *TV Guide* to have a 17-question survey inserted in the magazine (Kolbert 1993). The questions were clearly slanted in a fashion to reflect his personal views on American politics. For example:

- Should we eliminate foreign lobbyists completely—no loopholes—and make it a criminal offense?
- Should laws be passed to eliminate all possibilities of special interests giving huge sums of money to candidates?

Given the highly loaded questions it should come as no surprise that, in the first example, critics of Mr. Carter would be more likely to complete this questionnaire and return it than those who are undecided or supporters, or supporters of Mr. Perot, in the second example, would detect the appropriate response to his questions.[23] These polls have many of the same defects as the mail surveys that are periodically conducted by *Playboy* and *Penthouse* about sexual habits.[24] There is a great likelihood that those willing to divulge information about their sex lives differ in important regards from those who are unwilling. Mail surveys are not always meaningless, but they must be conducted with great care by people with specialized training. Most that are done correctly are published in academic journals and rarely show up in the popular media.

Regrettably, television, including highly regarded network news programs, has gotten into the straw poll business. Television journalism is a combination of news and entertainment, and often in the competition for ratings, entertainment takes precedence over hard news. That was certainly the case in 1992 when CBS News ran a program immediately following President Bush's State of the Union message, called "America

On Line." The idea was to provide program viewers with an 800 number that they could call and respond to a short survey (mostly about the state of the economy). More than 24 million citizens attempted to call, of which about 315,000 got through. Simultaneously another "scientific" poll was being conducted, also for use on the program.[25] However, the anchors frequently referred to the call-in poll as though it was a representative survey. The poll was introduced by Dan Rather as "taking the public pulse." Based on call-in results, Connie Chung reported that "53 percent were worse off [financially] than four years ago. It's important here to note that this is quite dramatic." She explained to Dan Rather that only a month ago a periodic CBS News poll had found only 30 percent claiming to be "worse off." According to Chung, "This does not bode well for President Bush on his night of the State of the Union." Of course, the 53 percent to which Chung referred was meaningless as a measure of public opinion. Although not mentioned on the show, it was later revealed that the companion "scientific" survey showed only 32 percent "worse off" than four year ago (Tierney 1992).

Following harsh criticism from the professional polling community, the executive director of ABC News vowed that call-in polls would not be used in the future due to their nonrepresentative nature (*New York Times* 6 July 1987, 15). That promise, however, was not kept. Call-in polls are now a regular feature on television news programs, including ABC's Nightline (Brady and Orren 1992).[26] The program host usually introduces these polls with a disclaimer that "we don't pretend the results are scientific, but here's what we found." Viewers should treat that statement as the equivalent of "certain bored people with strong feelings on some subjects are willing to pay a long-distance charge to register their views in a poll that means nothing. Here are the results."

2-4 Interpreting Scientific Surveys _____

Polls that are correctly executed do not always "predict" the actual election day winner. Polls taken at the same time will sometimes show conflicting numbers. Occasionally the numbers will swing wildly over a short period of time. These characteristics do not necessarily mean the polls are defective, but they do require explanation.

Preelection Surveys

The media tend to attribute more accuracy to preelection polls as "predictors" of the election day outcome than even the best-designed

FIGURE 2–1 Two-party candidate margins in final preelection polls by survey house

Points	1980 Reagan over Carter	1984 Reagan over Mondale	1988 Bush over Dukakis	1992 Clinton over Bush
25 points		Black/USA Today (25)		
		NBC (24) Time (24)		
20 points		New York Times/CBS (21)		
		Gallup (18)		
		Actual Margin (18)		
		Gallup/Newsweek (17)		
15 points		ABC/Washington Post (14)		
		Harris (12)	Gallup (12)	Gallup/USA Today/CNN (12)
			Black/CNN/USA Today (10)	
			Washington Post/ABC (10)	
		Roper (10)	CBS/New York Times (9)	
10 points	**Actual Margin (10)**		**Actual Margin (8)**	Washington Post (8)
				NBC/Wall Street J. (8)
				CBS/New York Times (8)
	NBC/Associated Press (7)			ABC (7)
				Harris (6)
5 points	ABC/Harris (5)		Harris (5)	**Actual Margin (5)**
			NBC/Wall Street J. (5)	
	Gallup (3)			
	CBS/New York Times (1)			
0 points				

*Source:*s Michael R. Kagay, "Why Even Well-Designed Polls Can Disagree," in Thomas Mann and Gary Orren, eds., *Media Polls in American Politics* [Washington D.C.: Brookings, 1992]; Robert M. Worcester, "A View from Britain: You Can Do Better," *The Public Perspective*, 4 [November/December, 1992].

43

polls can possibly deliver. First, an obvious point. Preelection polls refer to sentiment at the time they are conducted, not on election day. The "horserace" analogy commonly used to discuss elections is, in this case, appropriate. The horse that is ahead going into the stretch is not always the horse (or the candidate) that wins. But even given the overall trend, there are still "house effects."[27] By house effects are meant variation in survey results due to idiosyncratic ways in which different survey organizations conduct their polling. For example, there is surprisingly great variation in the way the candidate choice question is asked in presidential elections.[28] Thus we frequently find the polls at some variance with one another during the campaign due to question wording effects. Even the final polls, taken just before election day, may differ. We see these house effects in Figure 2-1.

Presented are the final polls between 1980 and 1992, as reported by the major survey houses. Note in 1980 the systematic underestimate of the Reagan vote that appeared in all surveys. We know there was a major move toward Reagan the weekend before the vote. The likelihood is that in 1980 the movement continued after the last polls were taken, leading all polls to err on the low side of the Reagan vote. We see the same effect in 1992, with all the surveys overestimating the Clinton share of the vote. Although not shown, they all also underestimated the Perot vote.[29] The reasons are probably the same as for the Reagan underestimate. In other years, polling houses are more or less evenly distributed on both sides of the actual vote. It is, however, somewhat surprising to see how large the margin of error is in some instances. These are very reputable survey houses polling on the weekend (and often on into Monday) before the election. But as noted previously, the important point for historical memory is getting the winner right. Rarely since 1948 has a major survey house forecast the wrong winner in a presidential election.

Nevertheless, the reason why the polls can differ so much over the course of the campaign, up to and including the weekend before the election, merits explanation. Typically 15 percent or more of the electorate is undecided during a presidential campaign (the figure is much higher for lower-level races), winding down to 5 to 8 percent a few days before the balloting. Survey houses differ in the way they handle these undecideds.[30] While common sense might dictate a simple reporting of candidate preferences plus undecideds, most media polls do not follow that strategy. If voters claim to be "unsure," they are pressed in a followup question to indicate which candidate they "lean to." Voters who maintain they are in fact really "undecided" must be quite firm in their conviction in the face of pressure to make a choice. The inevitable result of this strategy is a sizable swing in candidate preferences, mostly accounted for by those forced to make a choice when their initial reaction was "undecided" (Crespi 1988; Moore 1992).

Another practice common to media polls is allocating the "undecideds" to one candidate or the other. If the undecideds *are not* split, there is an implicit assumption that either they will not vote, or will vote in proportion to those who have decided. As one approaches the election, there is often a momentum that favors one of the candidates—the undecideds do not split 50/50. This flow of the undecideds was one reason Truman beat Dewey (the last Gallup Poll showed that 19 percent of the electorate was undecided). It is also the reason that Richard Nixon squeaked out a win of less than 1 percent over Hubert Humphrey in 1968, when the polls had shown Nixon with a 15-point lead in the final weeks of the campaign. And it is the reason Ronald Reagan soundly defeated Jimmy Carter in 1980, when polls showed the contest to be very close, and why Ross Perot performed better than almost all preelection polls indicated.

If undecideds in preelection polls do not split evenly on election day, how then is one to allocate them before the election? There is no one correct answer for all circumstances. Sometimes the undecideds are reported as just that—"undecided." However, the poll will then underestimate the percentage of the vote going to a candidate who has momentum. Sometimes undecided respondents are asked to rate candidates on a 0 to 10 scale. The undecideds will be allocated to the candidate they like best. If there is a tie on that question, party identification is used to assign the undecideds to a candidate.[31] Other polls exclude the undecideds altogether and base their preelection forecasts only on those voters willing to make a choice.[32] In 1992, the Gallup Poll, in particular, engaged in some very dubious practices in assigning the undecideds. On the weekend before the election, it assigned all the undecideds in its tracking poll to Clinton, causing Clinton's lead to grow from 2 points on Friday to 12 points on Monday. Gallup made this decision based on electoral history, which suggested that most undecideds in a presidential election vote for the challenger. But in 1992, rather than moving to Clinton, the undecideds moved to another challenger, Ross Perot (Morin 1992). The error resulting from projecting the historical vote patterns of a two-person race to a three-person race was a major embarrassment for the Gallup Organization.[33]

Allocating undecideds in a contest that pits a black candidate against a white candidate causes particular problems, and polls in a number of races have greatly overestimated the proportion of the vote going to the black candidate. Studies of a number of such races now suggest the best strategy is simply to assign all the undecided voters (who normally are almost entirely white) to the white candidate. What seems to be operating is a cross-pressure, in which some white Democrats are reluctant to vote for a black candidate, and declare to pollsters that they are undecided. On election day, however, they vote Republican (Morin 1991).

Perhaps the most fundamental problem with pre–election day polls as election day predictors is an inability to define the population properly. Recall that a random sample must be drawn from a finite population. But it is impossible to define the election day population. Only a little over one-half of adult Americans vote in presidential elections. No one has yet determined a method that, with any degree of accuracy, predicts who will vote. Yet it is those election day voters who constitute the population, not adult Americans or even registered voters. In 1984, a preelection survey conducted by the Roper Organization asked a national sample of those over 18 if they were "almost certain to vote" or "probably won't bother" to vote in the upcoming election for President (Roper 1985). The results were:

Certain to vote	78%
Probably will vote	11
Unsure	12
	101%

Actual turnout in 1984 was 53.2 percent.

The problem in accurately assessing turnout is linked to social desirability. People want to be good citizens, and so they say they will vote. Even after the election, respondents will tell interviewers they have voted when in fact they have not. In 1978, the Center for Political Studies at the University of Michigan did a "vote validation" study in which they checked poll records to see if those who said they voted did in fact vote. Fifty-five percent of their sample claimed to have voted, but the official record showed that only 43 percent had actually cast their ballot (Katosh and Traugott 1981, 521). Clearly, then, pollsters must employ "educated guesswork" in place of science to define the population. Turnout patterns are fairly constant from one election to another, but they do change, and that change can often spell the difference between victory and defeat.

Without an agreed-on population, poll-takers use a cornucopia of methods for estimating "likely voters." Most pollsters ask a series of screening questions designed to identify likely voters (such as past voting behavior, interest in the election, strength of candidate preference, demographic characteristics, etc.), although occasionally the only screen is for registered voters (see below for an example). Those polls that do screen employ a distinctive methodology. Generally speaking, no two polls use the same screening questions, and consequently no two polls look at exactly the same population (Crespi 1988, Ch. 4).

Screens are of consequence for poll results. The tougher the screen in terms of weeding out potential nonvoters and those with weak candidate preferences, the greater the support for Republican candidates. For example, in surveys taken between August 26 and 31, 1992, a *Washington Post*/ABC News Poll had Clinton leading Bush by 19 percent, while a Lou Harris Poll had Clinton ahead by only 2 points. The *Washington Post* Poll used an easy "registered voter" screen—that is, the interviewer simply asked the respondent if he or she were registered. The Harris Poll used a battery of "tough" screens to identify "likely voters" and weed out nonvoters. The survey with the tougher the screen not unexpectedly showed a higher proportion of voters favoring President Bush (Lipset 1992). On the week before the election, the Gallup Poll changed its screen from the "easy" registered voter question to a much tougher "likely voter" screen. This change in the definition of the population cut about 4 points from Bill Clinton's margin over George Bush in the CNN/USA Today tracking poll conducted by Gallup. There is lively debate over whether this surge by Bush was an illusion due to the change in the screen (and thus a change in the definition of the population), a real gain by the President, or both (Hugick and Molyneux 1993; Erikson 1993; Ferree 1993). But the important point is that the type of screen can have an important consequence for a poll result.[34]

It is, by the way, the use of screens to define likely voters (plus weighting factors) that allows a pollster working for Democratic candidate Smith to say his client is ahead while the pollster working for Republican candidate Jones says her client is ahead. Neither has "faked" the numbers; rather they disagree on the probable composition of election day voters. The Republican poll-taker sees a big turnout among affluent whites; the Democratic poll-taker sees an atypically high minority turnout. As one prominent pollsters observes:

> I think there is a little bit of Julia Child in every pollster. There is an impulse to cook things in a way most favorable to [your] candidate. People do not want to carry bad news. So there is a tendency, if you're a Democratic pollster, to weight black respondents at their proportion of registered voters even though there is a lot of historic data that the black turnout is disproportionately lower.[35]

Election Day Exit Polls

A recent innovation in opinion polling is use of the exit poll. Representative precincts are selected within an electoral district, and voters are interviewed immediately after leaving the voting booth. These polls are commissioned by the news media so they can "project" the winner of a contest early on election day, and understand the demographic and issue correlates of the vote choice. Prior to 1990, all three networks conducted their own exit polls. There was often a lively competition among them to see which could be the first to "call" the election day winner. The expense of this operation led the networks, along with CNN, to pool resources and create a single polling unit, Voter News Surveys (VNS), which now does all the election day exit polling. Consequently, all networks now rely on a single source for exit poll information, which has somewhat diminished the "news value" of an immediate presentation of the results.

Exit polls could usually project the winner of a statewide election by 3:00 P.M., even though the polls do not normally close until 7:00 P.M. The media have, however, agreed not to release the results of exit polling in a specific state until the polls in that state have closed. But when the winner is forecast in the East Coast and Midwestern states in a presidential election, the polls will remain open for several hours on the West Coast (due to different time zones). The polls were still open in 11 states when CBS News first projected that Vice-President Bush had won the 1988 presidential election (*New York Times* 10 Nov. 1989, 17). In 1980, Jimmy Carter actually conceded the election to Ronald Reagan based on network projections while voting was still in progress in the West. The effect on West Coast voters of learning these election results has been the subject of lively controversy.

The claim is that voters in the West, having heard the election winner projected by the networks, will be less likely to go to the polls. While it is true these voters cannot affect the outcome of the presidential contest, there are many other contests on the ballot that could be affected by a drop-off in voter participation. Research on this question is mixed. Based on a study of the 1980 election, John Jackson concluded that the exit polls and Carter's early concession resulted in a turnout decline of 6 to 12 percent—to the detriment of down-the-ticket Democrats—in those states where the polls were still open.[36] The data show conclusively that those who had heard the early projections were more likely to abstain from voting than were those who had not heard these projections. However, this simple relationship begs the question of cause and effect. Was the turnout differential due to those hearing the projection not voting? Or is the explanation for the fact those who *did not* hear the projection voted in greater numbers than those did hear explained by the fact they were occupied at the voting booth when the projections were made?

There have been many calls for the media to voluntarily restrain from projecting the winner until voting is finished in all states. Congress has held hearings on the subject, and there are numerous calls for legislation requiring the polls to stay open for the same hours in the contiguous 48 states. Some states have tried to make it difficult for exit pollsters to do their work by restricting how close they can get to the voting booth. Such laws have been invalidated by federal courts. The networks argue that any government-imposed limitations on exit polls would constitute censorship and violate the First Amendment.

2-5 Conclusion

During the 1930s, 1940s, and 1950s, public opinion polls received little attention from the mass media. Reporters saw pollsters as potential competitors—given the technical nature of their subject, they might want a byline of their own. Those fears have now largely subsided, although, as we noted in the chapter's introduction, poll-bashing is still a frequent phenomenon in the media. Polls are ubiquitous, and commentary on public opinion is fair game for all. Attempts to mislead deliberately occur, but they are not frequent. Rather, the key to understanding polls is a realization that the numbers do not speak for themselves; they require interpretation. Among the keys to that interpretation are how the sample was selected, how the questions were phrased, an appreciation for the context in which the survey was conducted, and a comparison to other surveys taken at the same time or an analysis of trends over time.

Notes

1. VRS stands for Voter Research and Surveys, a nonprofit organization that conducts exit polls for the three major television networks plus CNN.
2. For a detailed discussion of the growth of the polling business, see Ladd and Benson (1992).
3. The quote from Nixon comes from *Time* magazine, reported in Crespi (1989, 27).
4. Strictly speaking in terms of statistical theory, the poll would be repeated an infinite numbers of times, which would yield a percentage between 42 and 48.
5. National samples are usually larger than state or local samples because one other factor that affects sampling error is variation, and there is likely to be more variation in attributes measured nationally, as opposed to those in a geographically smaller area. Also, those conducting national samples are often interested in looking at subgroups (e.g., blacks or women). The larger the sample, the lower the sampling error when doing a subgroup analysis.

6. The data are from a 1992 post-election survey in Texas done by the Public Affairs Research Center at the University of Houston.

7. From a technical standpoint, the real question is whether or not the differences are statistically significant. A subsample of 50 showing a larger difference than for our example may surpass commonly accepted levels of statistical significance.

8. One's suspicions are aroused, however, if polls on the same topic at about the same time with similarly worded questions show quite different results.

9. Lest we complacently assume the polls inevitably get more accurate, it should be noted that the Gallup organization, in a poll for CNN and *USA Today*, mispredicted the 1992 vote by a greater margin than it mispredicted the 1948 vote (an error of 6 vs. 5 percent). But as in 1936, Gallup got the winner right in 1992, so its wide-of-the-mark forecast will likely be forgotten.

10. While quota samples have been abandoned by major survey houses in the United States, virtually all surveys done in Great Britain and many other European countries rely only on quota samples. In fact, all 56 preelection polls done prior to the 1992 British general election were based on quota samples. That election was, of course, a major embarrassment to British polling—on the order of Gallup's famous 1948 misprediction that Dewey would beat Truman. And, like Gallup in 1948, the misprediction of a close election by British pollsters (the Conservatives won easily by a margin of 7.6 percent over Labour) can be attributed to the inherent shortcomings of quota samples (Jowell et al. 1993).

11. In his book *The Superpollsters* (1992), David Moore interviewed a number of those who worked as field staff for Gallup during the days he used quota samples, and provides an interesting firsthand account of the hazards and biases of allowing the interviewers leeway in selecting respondents.

12. It should be noted that Gallup was not the only national pollster to mispredict the 1948 election. The other well-known national polls, the Crossley Poll and the Roper Poll, both had Dewey ahead of Truman. One suspects that the same sort of sampling errors that afflicted Gallup afflicted these other polls as well, since they used essentially the same methodology (Bradburn and Sudman 1988, 29).

13. For a more detailed discussion of sampling by the NES or GSS, see the sampling appendix that is usually included with each codebook.

14. Interviewers usually ask for the youngest male or female because they are the least likely to be home. However, if a sufficient number meeting specified age and sex distributions are met, interviewers will then ask for the oldest male or the oldest female.

15. The exact size of the sampling error will depend on the number of clusters and the size of each cluster (Sudman 1976, Ch. 4).

16. This information comes from *The Frame* (March 1993), published by the commercial sampling house Survey Sampling, Inc., of Westport, Connecticut.

17. For more information, see Groves and Kahn (1979) and Lipset (1980) for a discussion of refusal rates.

18. *The Frame*, March 1993. The other states falling below 90 percent are New Mexico, Arkansas, West Virginia, and Kentucky.

19. A good example—an insert on "How the Poll was Conducted"—can be found in the *New York Times*, 6 June 93, section A, page 14.

20. The evidence is that using only "agree" or "favor" in a question as opposed to a balanced form of the question often makes no difference. Nevertheless, it sometimes makes a difference, and it is easy to write balanced questions using these types of formats (Schuman and Presser 1981, 181–82).

21. A 1986 *Time*/Yankelovich Survey, cited in "Opinion Roundup," *Public Opinion*, Sept./Oct. 1986:32.

22. Reported in the *Houston Chronicle*, 8 Oct. 1977:3. More recently, in another mail survey by Congressman Archer, the *Houston Chronicle* ran a front-page story asserting "Bush's popularity Falls in Own Houston District." The story reported that only 43 percent of the residents in his old highly Republican district approved of his job performance when national approval rates were around 50 percent. Archer mailed out 250,000 questionnaires and received 18,000 in return (stamps were not provided) (Bernstein 1992). Most likely the low ratings were due to those in the hard-pressed oil industry self-selecting to vent their frustration. In the 1992 election, Bush carried the district by a wide margin.

23. In the case of the Perot poll, CNN conducted a poll in which half the sample was asked the Perot version of the question (80 percent said "yes") and the other half was asked a more neutral version, which read "Should laws be passed to prohibit interest groups from contributing to campaigns, or do groups have the right to contribute to candidates they support?" In this latter version, only 40 percent said laws preventing contibutions should be passed (Kolbert 1993).

24. Another example of this type of survey are those done by pop psychologist Shere Hite. Hite has published a number of books on the sexual and romantic relationships between men and women. In her most recent book, *Women and Love, a Cultural Revolution in Progress* (Knopf, 1987), she mailed out 100,000 questionnaires to women selected from the mailing lists of a variety of women's organizations. She received 4,500 responses (4.5 percent). Given the self-selection problem (women most likely to respond were those who had unsatisfactory romantic relationships), some of the "findings" were quite surprising. For example, Hite reported that 75 percent of the women in her study married more than five years had extramarital affairs. A survey by ABC News/*Washington Post*, using conventional sampling methods, found 7 percent of women reported extramarital affairs. The ABC poll was reported in the *Houston Chronicle* (27 Oct. 1987, p. 2, section 1).

25. This "scientific" poll was a panel back from a survey of 2,800 respondents that CBS/*New York Times* had conducted two weeks previously. These respondents were also provided with a (different) 800 number and asked to call back immediately after the State of the Union address. The response rate from the orginal panel was only 43 percent, casting considerable doubt on the validity of the "scientific" survey used in the program (Frankovic 1992).

26. For a discussion of the continued use of call-in polls by "Nightline" and other news organizations, see Cantril (1991, 144–46). Call-in polls have

even found their way to PBS, where in February 1992, MacNeil/Lehrer Productions produced a three-part series, "America on Trial." Proponents of varying agendas made their case in a courtroom-style setting. After the program, viewers were asked to respond as "jurors" on the question of the evening and dial one 800 number to record a "yes" or another 800 number to record a "no" (Cantril 1992).

27. For a good analysis of house effects on other errors in preelection polling, see Crespi (1988).

28. For a list of the way the major polling firms ask this question, see Crespi (1988, Ch. 5.).

29. "The Polls in 1992: A Roper Review," *The Public Perspective 4* (November/December 1992, 11).

30. The option of "unsure" is usually not offered to respondents. Rather, they are asked to choose between or among the candidates (Moore 1992).

31. This practice of pushing undecideds to make a choice is defended by Frank Newport, editor-in-chief of the Gallup Poll, in the following words: "[I]f pollsters allow voters the explicit option to call themselves 'unsure' about their vote, the number of reported undecideds would jump. All major polling organizations, however, eschew this structure because it would make polling less valuable and less interesting. Most voters, when asked in which direction they lean, have a preference and are willing to express it. It would not be very instructive . . . to allow large numbers of voters to claim they are undecided through the election season. We would miss the dynamics of change, we would be unable to tell how well the candidates were doing in response to events, and publicly released polls would be out of synchronization with private, campaign polls" (Letter to the Editor, *New York Times*, 6 Nov. 1992, section A).

32. Irving Crespi, "Letter to the Editor," *New York Times* (7 Sept. 1988, section A).

33. In the words of Thomas Mann of the Brookings Association, coeditor of *Media Polls in American Politics* (1992): "Gallup comes away from this election with its reputation tarnished. Some of their behavior is inexplicable. They will have some explaining to do to the polling community" (quoted in Morin 1992).

34. The same is true for the number of callbacks. If a respondent cannot be located on the first call, it is standard practice to make another two or three attempts to contact the person before replacement. Research by Gallup has shown that the more callbacks used by a survey house, the more Republican the sample. In other words, substitution of the appropriate respondent by a new respondent biases the sample in a Democratic direction. This finding means that "overnight" surveys, in which only one call is made to a specific person, may have some serious biases (Cantril 1992, 102).

35. The quote is from Harrison Hickman, of Hickman and McWheter, a polling firm that works predominantly for Democrats. See Edward Walsh, "Polls Are Telling Us More, But Are They Telling It Like It Is?" (*Washington Post* 13 Apr. 1987, natl. ed., p. 37).

36. For arguments that exit polls do affect turnout, see Jackson (1983) and Delli Carpini (1984). For a study arguing there is no effect on early projections, see Epstein and Storm (1984).

CHAPTER 3

Microlevel Opinion: The Psychology of Opinion Holding

In theory, democracy works best when the people actively attend to public affairs. Ideally, people would direct policy-makers toward the problems most deserving of attention and actively monitor their deliberations. Although people would disagree among themselves, opinions would be soundly reasoned and logically consistent. In this best of all worlds, preferences would transcend conflict among self-interested parties, to reflect a concern for the general welfare.

In actuality, public opinion falls considerably short of this ideal. As early survey researchers explored the nature of public opinion, they found several reasons for pessimism. For instance, respondents often express preferences so thoughtless as to arguably be too shallow for consideration as meaningful opinions. The opinions that people do hold sometimes seem like unconnected preferences in no logical relationship to one another. Where predictability exists, opinions often flow from disturbing prejudices rather than thoughtful consideration. Often it appears that political leaders find it all too easy to manipulate political symbols in such a way as to fool a politically gullible mass public.

Although recent discussions of the capabilities of mass opinion vary in their theoretical perspectives, they find some significant reasons for optimism. (Compare Page and Shapiro 1992; Sniderman et al. 1992; Kinder and Herzog 1993; and Zaller 1992.) Many ordinary people do stay politically informed and can be considered to be politically sophisticated. Actually, it can seem remarkable that people hold political opinions at all. Why, we might ask, do people bother to develop and maintain political opinions when the time spent on politics might be better spent dealing with our private lives? Since most of our political attention is as passive spectators watching helplessly on the sidelines, why do we bother to pay attention and invest in our opinions? Indeed, a strong argument can be made that if the main purpose of following politics is to affect political outcomes, staying informed and thinking about politics becomes a losing investment (Downs 1958).

Since many people are sufficiently political to ignore such advice, political opinions must be of some benefit to the people who hold them. It has long been recognized that holding political opinions serves several positive psychological functions (M. B. Smith et al. 1956). For instance, opinions serve a social function, as when people learn to agree with the prevailing views within their preferred social groups. Opinions can serve a direct psychological function as when political opinions follow directly as an extension of personality. An often cited example is the person who seeks an ordered and disciplined personal environment, being more susceptible to authoritarian political ideologies. Opinions can also promote economic self-interest, as when people develop political opinions consistent with their economic standing as rich or poor. Sometimes people develop elaborate ideologies to rationalize their economic standing, as when rich people adopt a conservative economic ideology to justify their hold on their wealth.

As one would expect, opinions often reflect self-interest, as when the rich adopt more conservative economic positions than the poor (see Chapter 7). But the pull of self-interest is far from universal, as people often derive opinions from values that have little if anything to do with obvious self-interest (Sears and Funk 1990). Examples of attitudes that do not reflect self-interest include concerns for justice and the plight of others, but also can include symbolic racism or even identifying with the values of one's aggressor. One revealing study examined the attitudes in differently affected school districts when a Texas court ordered tax-rich districts to pay more school taxes and tax-poor districts to pay less. While attitudes toward this decision generally reflected how one's district was affected, many liberals who had to pay more taxes favored the change and many conservatives who had to pay less were opposed— contrary to their economic interests (Tedin 1994).

While sometimes it may seem that people generate opinions in an arbitrary fashion, opinions usually have reasons behind them. Consider opinions about an issue like whether the government should spend more on welfare for the disadvantaged. People who favor less spending will argue the principles of limited government and self-reliance, or possibly verbalize concern about people falling into a welfare "trap." People who favor more spending will cite egalitarian arguments and express sympathy for the immediate needs of the poor (Feldman and Zaller 1992).[1]

This chapter examines public opinion at the microlevel of the individual citizen, usually when observed as a survey respondent. We will examine first the extent of political knowledge and the depth of opinion-holding. Then we will explore the core values and beliefs that sometimes hold opinions together. For politically sophisticated respondents, it is possible to summarize core political values in terms of position on the liberal-conservative ideological spectrum. Finally, we explore a source of political orientation that is adhered to by sophisticates and nonsophisticates alike. This is the respondent's party identification, or relative allegiance to the Democratic or Republican party.

3-1 Political Attention and Opinion-Holding _____

When a survey informs us regarding public opinion on some issue, underlying the reported division of opinion is a considerable diversity in terms of attention and caring about the issue at hand. At one extreme we find highly attentive citizens who follow public affairs closely and hold informed (if diverse) preferences regarding even complicated questions of public policy. These citizens vote regularly, and vote based on informed policy decisions. Moreover, they make their views known to their elected leaders even during the time intervals between political campaigns.

At the other extreme are many citizens who can correctly be described as "apolitical," meaning that they are virtually disengaged from politics. They ordinarily pay no attention to the political news in newspapers and television, and do not vote. Their interest in politics might be perked up only by unusual events, such as the threat of war or a politician's sex scandal. But by their passivity, they collectively forfeit their influence on policy outcomes.

Most people are in between these most attentive and most inattentive extremes. People vary in their attention to the world of government and politics for several reasons. Cognitive ability (intelligence) certainly is helpful for understanding politics and holding political opinions, but it may be an overrated factor. When people are politically inattentive, it would be far too much a leap to assume that they lack the mental capacity to follow public affairs, or that politics is too complicated for ordinary folks to figure out. Whether one follows politics closely is less a matter of intelligence than it is personal taste, similar to the choice of whether to follow certain sports, like football or baseball. And just as sporting events are more fascinating and comprehensible to regular followers of the sport, so too is following politics easiest for those who have invested in knowledge about the political world. For those who choose not to invest in an understanding of politics, following current political events is a considerably more difficult task (Zaller 1992).

Just as it is misleading to describe public opinion by focusing on the typical citizen, it can be misleading to assume that a citizen's attention level regarding one aspect of politics extends to all others. People vary not only in their taste for public affairs but also in regard to which aspects of public affairs engage their interest the most. For instance, some people focus on national politics but ignore their local political environment, while some do the reverse. Some people are "issue specialists" who become members of the attentive public only when issues dear to their interests enter the public agenda. For some issues, they hold strong opinions and make their views known. On others, they react with indifference.

Political Knowledge

In late 1983, United States armed forces conducted a surprise invasion of Grenada, a tiny nation that most Americans had never heard of. Within a few days of the invasion, a CBS/*New York Times* poll found 63 percent of Americans able to identify Grenada as an island in the Caribbean. This was a remarkable amount of learning for a nation often scolded for its lack of knowledge of geography. But of course this event was unusual. Other political events can attract near universal attention, but only if they contain the necessary elements of human interest and drama—if not the U.S. going to war, then a hostage drama or a sex scandal. Complicated political matters often get ignored by much of the general public. For example, when a controversial presidential appointment consumes the attention of Washingtonians "inside the beltway," polls suggest that most Americans tune out. With rare exception, even the best-known Cabinet members, Supreme Court justices, senators, and political columnists will be anonymous to most Americans.[2]

Polls conducted over the years occasionally quiz their respondents about their levels of political knowledge. The results of these knowledge surveys show levels of ignorance that often appear shocking when observed for the first time. Table 3.1 presents an information scale, showing the percentage of American adults who can correctly answer a variety of factual questions about government or politics.

The information varies from civics book knowledge to simple information about foreign governments. Without an exact benchmark of what, exactly, is a passing grade, we let the table speak for itself regarding the degree of public absorption of the political news that dominates the front pages of daily newspapers and the lead stories of network television news. The good news is that knowledge of politics has at least not declined over the years; the bad news is that with the growth of education levels and access to the mass media, knowledge *should* be increasing (Delli Carpini and Keeter 1992).

Public knowledge does improve when an issue is consistently in the news. The U.S. involvement in Nicaragua's civil war in the 1980s pro-

TABLE 3.1 The Level of Information Among the Adult U.S. Public

		Year	Source
96%	Know the President's term is 4 years	1989	D&K
94%	Know the capital city of U.S.	1946	AIPO
83%	Aware of right to a jury trial	1987	Hearst
78%	Know what the initials FBI stand for	1949	AIPO
74%	Can name U.S. vice-president	1989	D&K
73%	Can name state's governor	1989	D&K
74%	Know meaning of term "wiretapping"	1969	AIPO
72%	Know states cannot prohibit abortions	1989	D&K
70%	Can name their mayor	1967	AIPO
69%	Know office held by Ted Kennedy	1988	NES
68%	Know the President is limited to 2 terms	1970	NES
63%	Know China to be Communist	1972	NES
60%	Know President nominates federal judges	1992	NES
58%	Know law's constitutionality decided by Supreme Court	1992	NES
58%	Know *Roe* vs. *Wade* about abortion rights	1989	D&K
57%	Know Republicans are more conservative party	1992	NES
55%	Can name at least one of state's U.S. Senators	1989	D&K
52%	Know there are two Senators from their state	1978	GSS
52%	Know Democrats control House of Representatives *(since 54)*	1990	NES
50%	Can name President of Russia (Yeltsin)	1994	T-M
46%	Can identify first ten amendments as Bill of Rights	1989	D&K
37%	Know job held by Yasser Arafat	1988	NES
34%	Can name the current secretary of state	1978	GSS
30%	Know term of U.S. House member is 2 years	1978	GSS
26%	Can identify Tom Foley as Speaker of House	1992	NES
25%	Can name both U.S. Senators from state	1989	D&K
23%	Know the two nations involved in SALT	1979	CBS/*NYT*
16%	Can identify Nelson Mandela as black South African leader	1990	NES
8%	Can name Chief Justice of U.S. Supreme Court	1987	CBS/*NYT*

Source: AIPO: American Institute for Public Opinion (Gallup); NES: National Election Studies; GSS: General Social Survey; CBS/NYT: CBS News/*New York Times* polls; Hearst: Hearst Corporation; D-K: National Survey by Della Carpini and Keeter (1992); T-M: Times-Mirror.

vides a case in point. Back in 1983, only 29 percent knew that the United States backed the rebels and not the government in Nicaragua. By mid-1986, after years of headlines about the controversial funding of the Contra rebels, this figure had increased to 46 percent. Following the publicity of the "Iran-Contra" scandal, the figure "soared" all the way to 54 percent in mid-1987 and 66 percent in early 1989 (Sobel 1989). After many years of publicity, finally a majority of Americans had absorbed the most rudimentary facts about American involvement in Nicaragua. On the other hand, years of controversy about whether the U.S. should support the Contras evidently went over the heads of almost half of all Americans.

One concern about the public's low attention to politics is that potentially what polls show to be the views of the mass public can differ greatly from "informed" opinion. There are two ways of looking at this problem. On the one hand, those who believe that informed opinion should carry greater weight can argue that poll results are contaminated by the counting of passive, uninformed opinions. On the other hand, those who believe that people should have equal influence can argue that poll results can be a useful corrective to the perhaps one-sided views of the assertive minority who make their views known. The differences between informed and uninformed opinion that are known to exist are generally attributed to the greater education and income of those who are more knowledgeable.

We present some examples from the 1992 National Election Study survey. For this task, we introduce a summary index of political information. We score respondents on the basis of their knowledge of candidate policy differences, which studies show to be a good measure of relevant political information (Luskin 1987; Zaller 1992). Details of this index are presented in the Appendix to this book. When we use this index, we compare voters at two information extremes. High-information respondents are the 22 percent (29 percent of voters) who correctly saw Bush to the right of Clinton on five separate issues. Low-information respondents are the bottom 36 percent (29 percent of voters), whose knowledge of candidate differences on issues appears so impoverished that their evaluations of candidate positions approached the "guess" range.

TABLE 3.2 Opinion by Level of Political Information, 1992

Opinion	High Information	Low Information	Difference
Increase U.S. aid to Russia	46%	19%	+ 27%
Reduce defense spending	80%	58%	+ 22%
Give government aid to minorities	41%	24%	+ 17%
Legalize all abortions	56%	39%	+ 17%
Equal role for women	92%	82%	+ 10%
Oppose death penalty	24%	21%	+ 3%
Support national health insurance	61%	61%	0%
Increase domestic spending	48%	62%	− 14%
Guarantee job, good standard of living	36%	43%	− 7%
% Liberal (of ideological identifiers)	46%	31%	+ 15%
% Democratic (of party identifiers)	52%	62%	− 10%

Source: NES, 1992 election data. Percentages represent percentages among opinion-holders. For measurement of high- and low-information respondents, see the Appendix.

Table 3.2 shows some differences in opinion-holding by knowledge-ability in the National Election Study's 1992 survey. For each of several issues, the most striking difference between the opinions of high- and low-knowledge respondents is on the two foreign policy items of defense spending and helping Russia. The more knowledgeable were more "liberal" in terms of supporting Russian aid and cuts in defense spending. Evidently, the more knowledgeable were the first to learn and accept the new consensus among elites that the Cold War had ended and that the U.S. needed to ally with the new Russian Republic. Some other issues showed modest tendencies for liberal opinion to increase with knowledge, perhaps an indication of greater acceptance of liberal social policies among the most politically sophisticated. But there is no general rule. On domestic spending and a guaranteed standard of living, two issues where the poor and less educated have an interest in liberal spending policies, the least knowledgeable are the most liberal.

Depth of Opinion-Holding

Chapter 2 presented some examples of how seemingly minor variations in the framing and wording of survey questions can provoke major variations in survey results. Such phenomena could not occur were not people often ambivalent about their political convictions. On a given political issue, some survey respondents can call from memory long-term convictions that they have held on the particular subject. Many, however, can offer no more than the top-of-the-head casual opinions of the kind sometimes known as "doorstep" opinions. One consequence is a disturbing degree of response instability when people are interviewed more than once, in what is called a "panel" survey. Many panelists who offer opinions in successive interviews change their position from one side to the other—seemingly inconsistent with the traditional notion of an attitude as an enduring predisposition. The implications are important for understanding public opinion.

Table 3.3 shows some examples of response turnover, from a special (pilot) National Election Study survey in 1989. The issues shown varied from the hotly debated (abortion, death penalty) to the technical and obscure (funding the Stealth bomber, building a new Alaska pipeline). Respondent views were measured in the summer and again in the fall of 1989. The questions were part of framing experiments, in which different subjects were randomly assigned different ways in which the questions were framed. Different subjects received different framing conditions, which sometimes also varied for the same respondent over time. Still, the exact question asking for an opinion was the same for all respondents for all issues. Respondents received no filter to encourage nonresponses, and over 90 percent offered opinions to each question.[3]

TABLE 3.3 Turnover of Opinion Response on Selected Issues, 1989 NES Pilot Study

Death penalty				Stealth bomber			
		Summer 1989				Summer 1989	
		Oppose	Favor			Oppose	Favor
Fall 1989	Oppose	19%	5%	Fall 1989	Oppose	41%	8%
	Favor	5%	73%		Favor	9%	42%

Abortion				More welfare spending			
		Summer 1989				Summer 1989	
		Legal	Restricted			Favor	Oppose
Fall 1989	Legal	34%	5%	Fall 1989	Favor	35%	11%
	Restricted	6%	53%		Oppose	11%	43%

Affirmative action				New Alaska oil pipeline			
		Summer 1989				Summer 1989	
		Favor	Oppose			Oppose	Favor
Fall 1989	Favor	13%	8%	Fall 1989	Oppose	36%	10%
	Oppose	5%	74%		Favor	12%	42%

More gun control				More cooperation with Russia			
		Summer 1989				Summer 1989	
		Favor	Oppose			Favor	Oppose
Fall 1989	Favor	59%	7%	Fall 1989	Favor	38%	10%
	Oppose	13%	21%		Oppose	13%	39%

More spending to fight AIDS				More aid to Nicaraguan Contras			
		Summer 1989				Summer 1989	
		Favor	Oppose			Oppose	Favor
Fall 1989	Favor	48%	8%	Fall 1989	Oppose	49%	11%
	Oppose	15%	29%		Favor	10%	30%

Sources: NES, 1989 pilot study data. In some instances, framing of question varied with respondent and with wave.

Table 3.3 shows from 13 to 22 percent switching sides between interviews just a few months apart. As discussed below, analysts agree that almost all of such switching represents not true opinion change but rather some sort of response "error." As one would expect, more response error appears for obscure issues such as Alaska pipelines and Stealth bombers which people typically do not think much about than for salient moral issues like abortion and the death penalty.

The setup of Table 3.3 enhances the observed stability because multiple respondent choices are collapsed into two alternatives. Responses appear less stable when a middle ground is included. Table 3.4 presents the abortion example again, this time with three alternatives.

Whereas in Table 3.3 the various choices for restrictions on abortion were combined as one, for Table 3.4, we separate out the extreme "right to life" position that abortions should never be permitted or permitted

TABLE 3.4 Opinion Consistency on Abortion, 1989

	Summer 1989		
	Never permitted, or Only if Rape, incest, or Woman's Life in Danger	Other Than if Rape, Incest, or Woman's Life in Danger, After Need Established	Always Permitted as Matter of Personal Choice
Fall 1989			
Never permitted, or Only if Rape, incest, or Woman's Life in Danger	31%	6%	1%
Other Than if Rape, Incest, or Woman's Life in Danger, After Need Established	6%	12%	4%
Always Permitted as Matter of Personal Choice	2%	5%	34%

Source: NES, 1989 pilot study.

only under exceptional circumstances from the more moderate or middle position that abortions "should be permitted . . . but only after the need has been clearly established." The turnover table now shows 25 percent changing their position from one survey to the next, with many respondents finding the middle position attractive. Notably, however, virtually no respondent switched from pro-choice to pro-life or vice versa.[4]

If the amount of turnover of responses to the abortion question seems high, consider that abortion positions are probably the most stable of political attitude responses, rivaled perhaps only by party identification (Converse and Markus 1979; Wetstein 1993). Less morally charged issues show considerably less response stability. Typical is the turnover of responses to the NES's "guaranteed living standard" question between the preelection and postelection surveys in 1984, shown in Table 3.5.

Only a minority of the respondents (40 percent) had a sufficiently firm attitude to take the same side consistently (pro/pro or con/con) in both interviews. A few (10 percent) changed sides completely from one interview to the next, and others (14 percent) took no position in either interview. The remainder (35 percent) took sides in one interview but not in the other.

The most studied patterns of response instability are from two four-year three-wave panels as part of the National Election Studies

TABLE 3.5 Opinion Consistency on Government Guarantee of a Job and Good Standard of Living*

	Preelection Response, 1984		
	Government Should Guarantee Job and Good Standard of Living	In Between, No Opinion	Government Should Let Each Person Get Ahead on Own
Postelection Response, 1984			
Government Should Guarantee Job and Good Standard of Living	14%	9%	4%
In Between, No Opinion	8%	14%	7%
Government Should Let Each Person Get Ahead on Own	6%	12%	26%

Cell entries represent percentage of the entire sample.

Source: NES, 1984 election data.

(Converse 1964; Converse and Markus 1979). In a "1950s" panel, the same respondents were interviewed at two-year intervals, in 1956, 1958, and 1960. The NES "1970s" panel interviewed the same respondents in 1972, 1974, and 1976.

One important fact from the NES panel studies is that the time interval between panel waves has little bearing on the observed amount of response stability. For instance, the degrees of response turnover to questions on abortion and guaranteed living standards asked four years apart in the NES 1970s panel are only slightly larger than the amount of response turnover shown in Tables 3.3 and 3.4 for the same issues when the same question was asked only a few months apart.

This evidence suggests that response change does not represent true change in underlying attitudes. If people were really changing their minds frequently, long time intervals would produce greater decay of initial positions. While scholars agree that response instability generally does not indicate true attitude conversion, they disagree in what the unstable responses mean. One position, developed by Philip E. Converse, holds that people who change positions usually have no position but instead respond randomly. This "nonattitude" explanation has been challenged by other scholars, who prefer a "measurement error" explanation. While the details of the opposing interpretations are too complicated to receive full treatment here, we can present brief sketches of the competing points of view.

The "Nonattitudes" Explanation

After analyzing turnover patterns from the 1950s panel, Philip Converse (1964) proposed that virtually all respondents who change their position over time hold no true convictions, but instead express random responses or "nonattitudes." The strong evidence for infrequent true change is that response instability varies little with the time between surveys. Surveys four months or four years apart yield about the same amount of response turnover. If people were actually changing their minds, observed opinions would be more stable over the briefer time interval.

If the nonattitude thesis is correct, most observed response change is random error, as if changers are simply flipping coins. Just as coins can be flipped heads one time and tails the next, they can also be flipped consistently heads or tails both times. Thus a further implication of the nonattitudes thesis is that many consistent responses are random responses that appear stable only by chance. On one notorious issue from the 1950s panel, the abstract "power and housing" question (whether "the government should leave things like electric power and housing for private businessmen to handle"), Converse reached a startling conclusion (1964, 293). He estimated that less than 20 percent of the adult public held meaningful attitudes on this issue even though about two-thirds would venture a viewpoint on the matter when asked in a survey.

Many have found the implications of the "nonattitudes" explanation to be quite disturbing. In a democracy, public officials presumably respond to the policy preferences of the public, enacting these preferences into law. But if large segments of the public do not really have coherent preferences or preferences at all, why should elected officials heed their views? How, in fact, could they?

The "Measurement Error" Explanation

If the "nonattitudes" explanation is correct, the reason why many people give unstable responses to opinion questions is that these individuals lack the political sophistication necessary to form crystallized opinions. But contrary to this prediction, response instability varies little if at all with measures of political sophistication or political knowledge (Achen 1975; Erikson 1979; Feldman 1989). The disturbing level of instability found for surveys of the general public is also found for

subsamples representing the sophisticated and informed. If even politically sophisticated respondents respond with a seeming random component, what is to blame? It probably is not a lack of capability on the
part of the respondents.

For this reason, a "measurement error" explanation has been proposed
to account for response error (Achen 1975; Erikson 1979). This explanation does not challenge the evidence that most response instability represents error rather than true change. But by the measurement error
explanation, the "blame" for the response instability is placed not so
much on the capabilities of the respondents, as on the survey questions
themselves. This is not to say that survey researchers do not know how
to ask good questions. Rather, even the best survey questions will produce some instability from respondents who hold weak or ambivalent
attitudes about policy issues. Some inherent limitations in the survey
enterprise make measuring attitudes an imprecise task. These include
ambiguities in question wording, the problem of investigator-defined responses to closed-ended questions that may not be congruent with the
way respondents frame issues, and the problem of respondents having
to give immediate answers to perhaps 100 or more questions with virtually no opportunity for reflection or considered judgment. By this "measurement error" interpretation, the public is viewed neither as highly
opinionated nor as largely void of meaningful opinions. Instead the interpretation suggests that people generally—whether sophisticated or
not—have opinions sufficiently ambivalent that that they cannot be estimated with total reliability by simple survey questions.

As an example, consider a question about the appropriate level of
welfare spending. When prompted to think about the matter, a respondent might recall the plight of the poor, or possibly arguments why welfare is wasteful or self-defeating. When interviewed one day, this respondent might recall the "liberal" arguments in favor of welfare and
respond accordingly; next time when asked, the respondent might focus on the conservative arguments against, and respond accordingly. If
interviewed still a third time, the respondent might go either way. This
sort of variation does not represent any true change in the underlying
attitude, which can be described as a rather constant level of ambivalence. But this variation does not represent random responding of the
"nonattitudes" variety either. It represents "error," in the sense that the
response depends on the momentary activation of liberal or conservative stimuli (Zaller 1992; Zaller and Feldman 1992).

Implications

We would like to think of a survey response as measuring an exact
attitude. In the case of a dichotomous (either/or) response, we would

like to think that in some fundamental way, the response (e.g., picking the liberal or conservative alternative) represents on which side of a precise dividing line the respondent truly belongs. Unfortunately, it does not work this way. Responses are at best probabilistic functions of long-term attitude dispositions. For example, a person's long-term attitude on the "guaranteed standard of living" question might be such that the person gives the "liberal" response to the survey question 70 percent of the time. Another more conservative respondent might respond "liberal" only 15 percent of the time. Both of our hypothetical respondents display some ambivalence about guaranteed living standards, but still may represent ideological extremes. Our hypothetical voter who responds liberally 70 percent of the time and the one who gives the liberal response 15 percent of the time may be near the high and low percentile score in terms of liberal thinking on the particular question, but in actuality these extremes are not far apart.

Another implication of research on response stability is that while there may be only modest variation among people in their true underlying attitudes, these underlying attitudes are quite stable. Consider our hypothetical individual whose true attitude on the chosen issue is a 70 percent probability of choosing the liberal alternative to the particular question, and presume that this places the individual at the 80th percentile of liberalism on the issue (the respondent is more liberal than 80 percent of citizens). In two or four years, our respondent should still be near the same 80th percentile. Stimuli in the environment might cause minor variations in probabilistic responses, for example, with a conservative mood swing lowering everybody's probability of a conservative response. But our hypothetical respondent would still be more liberal than 80 percent of citizens.

Of course if peoples' attitudes are as stable as just described at the *micro*level, could we expect opinion trends at the *macro*level? We will see in the next chapter that net public opinion on an issue often is very stable over time. We will see interesting exceptions, however, and these occur when the electorate responds in a uniform way to one-sided environmental stimuli.

3-2 Liberal-Conservative Ideology and the Organization of Opinions _____

When a person expresses viewpoints on a number of political subjects, we might expect that these opinions would be connected to each other in some pattern. One expectation is that peoples' opinions would be connected by logical consistency with the person's core political

values. For instance, a person who believes strongly in individual responsibility would be inclined to respond negatively toward government help for the inner cities or toward the government guaranteeing
a job and a good standard of living. A person with strong egalitarian
values would be expected to respond in an opposite fashion. To take another example, a person committed to traditional social values probably would oppose abortion rights and oppose gays serving in the military. A person with a strong belief in individual choice would take the
opposite view.

We could try to account for opinions in terms of how people weight
political values such as individual responsibility, equality, tradition,
and individual freedom. When we describe peoples' core political values in this way, we begin to describe the person's political ideology. In
the broadest sense, a person's ideology refers to any set of beliefs about
the proper order of society and how it can be achieved. People with
strong ideologies use their personal ideology as guide for understanding the political world.

As a convenient shorthand, observers often prefer to reduce ideology
to the single dimension of the left-right ideological continuum, classifying peoples' political values simply according to their relative liberalism vs. conservatism. The left-right ideological distinction between
liberals and conservatives has considerable meaning when describing
the opinions of political elites, or politically active people. For instance,
delegates to national political conventions clearly understand ideological labels and tend to polarize as consistent liberals or conservatives
(Herrera 1992; Jennings 1992). Because the ideological liberal-conservative continuum holds lesser meaning to those near the bottom of the
sophistication ladder, the importance of liberal-conservative ideology
within the mass public has been a matter of uncertainty and controversy.[5]

A standard poll question is to ask respondents their ideological identification, usually with the three choices of liberal, moderate, or conservative. As discussed in Chapter 2, one-fourth or more will decline to
classify themselves ideologically given the choice of "not interested." Of
those who choose, almost half will choose the "moderate" or "middle-
of-the-road" alternative when offered.

Ideally, ideological classification would be a convenient way to measure peoples' core political values and to summarize their political views
over a variety of issues. In practice, the result is mixed. The most politically sophisticated segment of the public approximates the ideal. For
them, ideological identification goes a long way toward describing their
political convictions. But when less sophisticated people respond to the
ideological identification question with a response of liberal, moderate,
or conservative, we can be less sure of what the response means. At worst,

the response can represent some idiosyncratic meaning known only to the respondent or perhaps a doorstep opinion made up on the spot.

Liberal and Conservative Terminology

What do the terms "liberal" and "conservative" actually mean? At the philosophical level, political thinkers with reputations as liberals and conservatives differ in several ways. Conservatives view society as a control for humanity's worst impulses; liberals view the human condition as relative to the quality of society. Conservatives consider people to be inherently unequal and due unequal rewards; liberals are egalitarian. Conservatives venerate tradition, order, and authority; liberals believe planned change brings the possibility of improvement.[6]

Of course people who are liberal or conservative in their practical politics need not strictly adhere to the particular philosophy associated with their ideological label. Nevertheless, we can see the implications of these philosophic distinctions at work in the common applications of the ideological labels to particular political points of view. Conservatives are more afraid than liberals of "big government," except on matters of law-and-order and national security; during the Cold War era, conservatives were the more anti-Communist in their rhetoric. Conservatives are more likely to see harmful consequences of government help for the disadvantaged, while liberals see the benefits. Conservatives tend to be moralistic; liberals are more permissive.

These kinds of relative distinctions are familiar to people who follow politics closely. But the language of ideology holds lesser meaning for the mass public as a whole. One test is whether the individual can both identify the Republicans as the more conservative party and offer a plausible definition of the term "conservative." Roughly half the public passes this test of understanding of ideological labels (Converse 1964; Luttbeg and Gant 1985).

What do people think of when they hear the terms "liberal" and "conservative?" Table 3.6 summarizes the responses from the 1984 NES study of how people describe liberals and conservatives.

For this exercise, respondents were asked, "What sort of things do you have in mind when you say that someone's political views are liberal?" and similarly, "What sort of of things do you have in mind when you say that someone's political views are conservative?" Respondents were allowed up to three responses to each question, six overall. They averaged between two and three responses to the two questions, with 75 percent giving at least one response.

As typical for other years, the spend-save distinction was the one used most often to explain ideological labels (liberals spend and conservatives save). Also prominent were economic principles (e.g., socialism vs.

TABLE 3.6 Perceived Meaning of Ideological Labels, 1984

Question:　"What sort of things do you have in mind when you say that someone's
political views are liberal?"
"What sort of things do you have in mind when you say that someone's
political views are conservative?"

Type of Mention	Example	Percent Who Mention
FISCAL PRINCIPLES	L's for socialism; C's for free enterprise	13
SPEND/SAVE	L's wasteful; C's thrifty	28
CHANGE	L's look to future; C's look to past	26
PERSONALITY	L's are open-minded; C's are moralists	16
SOCIAL VALUES	L's care; C's are uncaring	16
ROLE OF GOVERNMENT	L's favor federal control; C's for states' rights	6
RACE	L's help blacks; C's do not	4
ECONOMIC GROUPS	L's for poor; C's for rich	11
GROUPS, GENERAL	L's/C's for people like me	8
ECONOMIC ISSUES	L's for minimum wage; C's are against	22
SOCIAL ISSUES	L's for abortion; C's are against	10
FOREIGN POLICY ISSUES	L's are isolationist; C's are interventionist	12
ISSUES, OTHER	L's/C's for the farm program	4
PHILOSOPHY, OTHER	L's/C's for freedom	4
LABELS	L's/C's are extremists	2
	N = 978	

Source: Adapted from NES, 1984 election data analysis by Kathleen Knight, "Ideological Conceptualization and Ideological Meanings in the American Mass Public: 1966 to 1984." Paper delivered at the 1986
American Political Science Association Convention.

free enterprise), postures toward change, personality distinctions (e.g.,
open-minded liberals vs. moralistic conservatives), and social values
(caring liberals vs. tough-minded conservatives). All these are reasonable, broad distinctions. Many responses, however, dealt with peripheral
matters, such as which groups liberals and conservatives support or liberal and conservative positions on narrow policy issues.

　　When survey respondents are asked to classify themselves on the liberal-conservative spectrum, their answers tend to correspond to their
policy positions. Some examples of the relationships between ideological
self-placement and positions on specific issues are shown in Table 3.7.

TABLE 3.7 Ideological Preferences and Opinions on Selected Policy Issues, 1992

Belief	Support Among Self-Declared Liberals	Support Among Self-Declared Conservatives
The government should provide "more services even if it means an increase in spending"	73%	32%
The government should guarantee "that every person has a job and a good standard of living"	55%	21%
Favor "government insurance plan which would cover all medical and hospital expenses for everyone"	82%	27%
The government "should make every effort to improve the social and economic position of blacks"	55%	18%
The U.S. "should spend less on defense"	85%	65%
"Aid to [Russia] should be increased"	36%	32%
"Women should have an equal role in running business, industry, and government"	96%	81%
Always permit abortion "as matter of personal choice"	72%	36%
"Homosexuals should be allowed to serve in U.S. Armed Forces"	70%	45%
"Oppose death penalty for persons convicted of murder"	35%	15%

Source: NES, 1992 election data. Reported figures are percentage of opinion-holders only.

Self-declared liberals in fact take positions considerably more liberal than do self-declared conservatives.

This tendency is even clearer when issue positions are summed over several issues. Table 3.8 shows that, as measured by their composite stands over ten separate issues, people who are very liberal identify as liberals and people who are very conservative overwhelmingly identify themselves as conservatives. It may also be noted that people who cannot identify themselves as liberal, moderate, or conservative tend to cluster in the center of the political spectrum as measured by their stands on specific issues.

Use of Ideological Language

Although the ideological terms are within the vocabularies of a large share of the American public, few actually employ them to defend their choices of party or candidate. For each National Election Study, respondents are asked what they like and dislike about each major party and presidential candidate. The profile of responses to these questions in 1956 is reported in the classic study of American voting behavior, *The American Voter* (Campbell et al. 1960, 216–49). The researchers were interested not only in the individuals' image of the parties and candidates but also in the conceptual sophistication of the responses. Respondents who spontaneously and knowledgeably evaluated the parties and candidates in terms of their placement on the liberal-conservative spectrum were labeled as "ideologues."

TABLE 3.8 Correspondence of Ideological Self-Ratings and Summary of Positions on Ten Issues, 1992

Ideological Self-Rating	Summary Position on Ten Issues*				
	Very Liberal	Liberal	Center	Conservative	Very Conservative
Liberal	66%	31%	16%	8%	1%
Moderate	17	25	26	22	18
Conservative	7	18	29	42	65
Don't Know	11	26	30	28	16
	100%	100%	100%	100%	100%
(Percent of total sample)	(8%)	(25%)	(32%)	(28%)	(7%)

*See the Appendix for construction of ten-item summary scores. The full distribution of scores is shown in Figure 3–1. The categories here are: Very liberal -10 to -6, Liberal -5 to -2, Center, -1 to +1, Conservative +2 to +5, and Very Conservative +6 to +10.

Source: NES, 1992 election data.

Thus began a search for "ideologues" within the electorate that continues to hold a central place on the research agenda of public opinion analysts. In some respects, *The American Voter*'s label "ideologue" was unfortunate, because in popular usage it holds a negative connotation: the ideologue as ideology-driven fanatic. As used in the sense of *The American Voter,* however, the ideologue is a political sophisticate whose central view of political actors is in terms of their place on the ideological spectrum. The ideologue's own political perspective could be moderate, extremist, or anywhere in between.

Even with a generous definition of what the ideologue response would demand (to include what *The American Voter* calls "near ideologues"), only 12 percent of the 1956 respondents fit the ideologue category. A typical ideologue response was that of an Ohio woman who, when asked what she liked about the Democratic party, answered, "Nothing, except it being a more liberal party, and I think the Republicans as being more conservative and interested in big business." A weaker ideologue response was given by a Texas man: "I think the Democrats are more concerned with all the people . . . they put out more liberal legislation" (Campbell et al. 1969, 232).

An added 42 percent of the 1956 sample expressed their likes and dislikes about the candidates (Eisenhower and Stevenson) and parties in terms of the groups they represented. Farmers often expressed their political likes and dislikes in terms of "group-benefits" (e.g., "I think [the Democrats] have always helped the farmers"; Campbell et al. 1960, 236). Most group-benefit responses were class-related, evoking the notion that Republicans favor big business while the Democrats favor the "little person."

Still another 24 percent of the 1956 respondents referred to the "nature of the times" the different parties are associated with when in power. Nature-of-times voters were guided by perceptions of past performance, such as which party brought economic prosperity or which party kept their promises. Finally, 23 percent were found to offer no issue content whatsoever when asked to describe their partisan likes and dislikes. Typical was the North Carolina man who answered as follows (with interviewer questions abbreviated):

(Like about the Democrats?)	" No, Ma'am, not that I know of."
(Dislike?)	" No, Ma'am, but I've always been a Democrat, just like my daddy."
(Like about the Republicans?)	" No."
(Dislike?)	" No." (Campbell, et al. 1960, 246)

This distribution of how people conceptualize partisan politics may be interpreted to mean that Americans are not very ideological, and in one sense this would be correct. The authors of *The American Voter* account for the scarcity of ideologues in terms of the public's "cognitive limitations," particularly a lack of intellectual ability to think in terms of ideological abstractions (Campbell et al. 1960, 253). But our knowledge that many citizens know the liberal-conservative terms and can apply them to issue positions suggests the alternative interpretation that the American public does not find the ideological terms particularly useful to describe their partisan likes and dislikes. Now many political scientists see *The American Voter* judgment as overly harsh. Although the authors did not realize it at the time, the 1956 presidential election was probably the least ideological of all modern campaigns, conducted essentially as a referendum on President Eisenhower's first term. Because the 1956 campaign was not conducted at an ideological level, 1956 respondents were not prompted to explain their likes and dislikes about parties and candidates in terms of ideological nuances. They chose easier criteria of group representation and the nature of the times. In later elections, ideology and policy issues played greater roles. The 1964 (Johnson vs. Goldwater) and 1972 (McGovern vs. Nixon) campaigns were particularly ideological. As ideological cues became more visible, the proportion of the public who could be labeled ideologues increased considerably.[7]

Table 3.9 enumerates the electorate by "level of conceptualization" for each presidential year, 1956 to 1988, based on NES surveys. In recent presidential elections, the electorate has divided roughly equally into the four levels of conceptualization. To summarize: At the top level, "ideologues" view parties and candidates in terms of their ideological and policy differences. At the second level, "group-benefits" people see party and candidate differences in terms of the differences in the groups they represent rather than the policies they offer. At the third level, "nature of the times" people evaluate parties and candidates only by past judgments of party and candidate performance. At the bottom, "no-issue-content" types seem unresponsive to political cues.

As we have seen, a greater proportion of the electorate can utilize the ideological language than are classifiable as ideologues. One explanation is that many individuals can use ideological labels without pursuing much ideology. For instance, many at the "group-interest" level identify with liberals or conservatives as a group with which they share a common interest, much as some may feel about teachers or labor unions (Tedin 1987).

Some people learn to associate terms like "liberal" and "conservative" with groups and symbols rather than specific policies (Conover and Feldman 1981). A person might associate the term "liberal" with "black" or "feminist" or the term "conservative" with "the middle class"

TABLE 3.9 Levels of Political Conceptualization, 1956–1988

	1956	1960	1964	1968	1972	1976	1980	1984	1988
Ideologues	12%	19%	27%	26%	22%	21%	21%	19%	18%
Group benefits	42	31	27	24	27	26	31	26	36
Nature of the times	24	26	20	29	34	30	30	35	25
No issue content	22	23	26	21	17	24	19	19	21
	100%	99%	100%	100%	100%	101%	101%	99%	99%
Number of cases	1,740	1,701	1,431	1,319	1,372	2,870	1,612	2,257	2,040

Source: Paul R. Hagner and John C. Pierce, "Correlative Characteristics of Levels of Conceptualization in the American Public: 1956–1976," *Journal of Politics,* 44 (Aug. 1982): 779–809; updates compiled by Paul Hagner and Kathleen Knight.

or "business" (Miller et al. 1991). These cues may serve to simplify politics and provide an informational shortcut (much like party identification), even if in most instances they are unaccompanied by a high degree of ideological sophistication. If one knows a candidate for public office is a liberal, or a policy is characterized as liberal, one need seek no further information to make a judgment. The labels can be used to minimize the costs of gathering information.

Ideology as Liberal Conservative Consistency

One might suspect that many people are actually quite liberal or quite conservative in the views they express, even when they do not choose these terms to describe their political orientation. Figure 3-1 shows one distribution of the American public's liberal-conservatism "scores" as measured by their cumulative responses to ten opinion questions in the 1992 NES survey. A person with all liberal opinions would score at -10, whereas a person who expresses conservative outlooks on all ten issues would score at +10. Most respondents were near the midpoint of the scale (0), indicating that their liberal and conservative viewpoints balanced each other out.

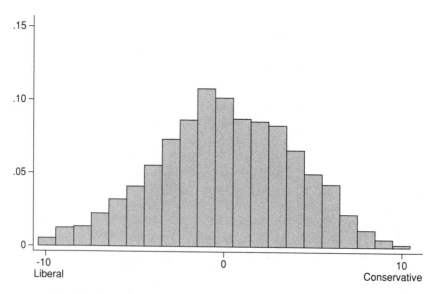

Fig. 3-1 Distribution of 10-issue composite opinion scores, 1992.

Since over a series of issues most people give some liberal and some conservative positions, there is a temptation to label the public as political moderates. But these voters in the center cannot be grouped together as sharing the same moderate ideology, because they differ greatly in their pattern of responses on individual issues. For instance, one voter with balanced liberal and conservative views may be liberal on social welfare issues and civil rights but conservative on foreign policy and law and order, while another with equally balanced views professes exactly the opposite opinions. Still a third person may have an overall score that is neither very conservative nor very liberal for the reason that he or she expresses few opinions at all.

It is sometimes argued that if ideology influences peoples' opinions, opinions on two separate issues should be predictable from one another since both are "constrained" by the opinion-holder's ideological perspective. Table 3.10 shows some 1992 examples of the search for ideological constraint.

For a pair of issues, an individual is more likely to offer consistently liberal or conservative positions if the issues are logically related or share some common content. The top row of Table 3.10 presents several examples: In Table 3.10a, people's opinions regarding government involvement in health care are predictable from their general views on domestic government spending. In Table 3.10b, people's opinions regarding government help to provide jobs and a good standard of living show consistency with their views on government aid for minorities. In

TABLE 3.10 Correlations Between Opinions on Selected Issues, 1992

	(a) Increase domestic spending			(b) Guaranteed job, living standard			(c) Legalize all abortions	
		Pro	Con		Pro	Con		Pro	Con
National health insurance	Pro	44%	18%	Federal aid to minorities	Pro 23%	8%	Equal role for women	Pro 49%	39%
	Con	12%	26%		Con 14%	55%		Con 2%	10%
	Gamma = .70			Gamma = .83			Gamma = .70		

	(d) Legal abortions			(e) Gays in military			(f) More domestic spending	
		Pro	Con		Pro	Con		Pro	Con
National health insurance	Pro	33%	31%	Guaranteed living standard	Pro 25%	14%	Cut military spending	Pro 39%	31%
	Con	15%	21%		Con 33%	28%		Con 17%	13%
	Gamma = .00			Gamma = .19			Gamma = -.05		

Source: NES, 1992 data. See the Appendix for the full text of opinion questions.

Table 3.10c, people's opinions on abortion appear consistent with their views on whether women deserve an equal role with men in business and government. Each example shows many exceptions, however, of individuals holding a liberal position on one issue but a conservative position on the other.

When issues are not closely related in terms of content, liberal-conservative consistency tends to fade. Table 3.10d shows one cannot predict an individual's position on abortion from the individual's position on national health insurance. Table 3.10e shows a similar lack of predictability for the issue pair of a guaranteed living standard and gays in the military. Of course, for neither of these pairs is there a requirement of logical consistency. But consider also the relationship between domestic spending and military spending, shown in Table 3.10f. Seemingly people should gravitate to ideologically consistent choices of either more domestic spending and less military spending (liberal) or less domestic spending and more military spending (conservative). Table 3.10f shows instead a slightly negative correlation. Many people favor either more spending for both domestic and military purposes or less spending for both.[8]

The low levels of ideological constraint within the general public reflects very real variations in ideological sophistication. Liberal-conservative opinion consistency is quite high among those most knowledgeable about politics, such as people identified as "ideologues" (Stimson 1975; Knight 1985). We can illustrate from those respondents classified as most knowledgeable in the 1992 NES survey. Among this select "high information" group, opinions on different issues are rather highly correlated, even for pairs of issues in which no correlation is evident for the public at large. Our illustration is the following relationship between opinion on medical care and on abortion, among the knowledgeable:

		Legal Abortions		
		Pro	Con	
National Health	Pro	41%	20%	
Insurance	Con	15%	24%	Gamma = .54

We see that with the accumulation of a high level of political information, people tend toward consistently liberal or consistently conservative positions, even on this pair of unrelated issues for which there exists virtually no correlation for the general public. A broader illustration is to compare the high-information group and the low-information group in terms of their distributions on the composite ten-item liberal- conservative scale. Figure 3-2 shows the results.

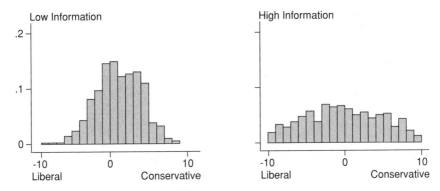

Fig. 3-2 Composite Opinion by Information Level.

The informed show some gravitation toward the liberal and conservative poles. The uninformed are very highly clustered in the center of the spectrum.

Despite the fact that the most knowledgeable are the most responsive to liberal vs. conservative distinctions, we should not insist that use of the liberal-conservative dimension is a requirement for political thinking. Liberal-conservative consistency is not the only possible ordering principle for political opinions. On foreign policy, for example, core values regarding the morality of warfare and ethnocentrism appear to be important (Hurwitz and Peffley 1987). More generally, people can make their opinions consistent with their own personal ideologies and need not apply the notion of liberal vs. conservative ways of thinking. Consider abortion attitudes, which until recently did not correlate much with conventional liberal-conservative orderings as measured by other policy opinions. As Kristen Luker states: Attitudes concerning abortion result from "beliefs and attitudes about motherhood; about sexuality; about men and women; about the role of children; and more broadly, about such global things as morality and the role of rational planning in human affairs" (Luker 1984, 31).

Summary

The public is mixed in its understanding and usage of ideological language and thinking. Most citizens do not engage in the ideological thinking of the sort found among political elites. But ordinary citizens often use ideological labels in at least a limited way as part of their political vocabulary. Many, however, do not even do this. Perhaps for as much as half the electorate, the liberal vs. conservative component of political discourse is nothing more than a confusion of background noise. The fact that there is little ideological consistency to people's issue positions demonstrates that few people use their ideological position as a cuing devise to arrange their responses to the political world. The kind of attitudinal constraint that motivates people toward consistently liberal, conservative, or moderate political viewpoints is reserved for a relatively small, politically active segment of the public.

In our effort to understand public opinion, we should not ignore this politically sophisticated segment of the American public, which does follow government and politics in terms of the liberal-conservative continuum. Thinking about politics in liberal vs. conservative terms is sophisticated not because it is preferable to hold ideologically extreme convictions or to view the political world through a distorted lens. Rather, to have the liberal-conservative spectrum as a political frame of reference is necessary to understand the language of politics as it is practiced by political elites. Many ordinary Americans do follow this ideological discussion.

3-3 Party Identification and the Organization of Political Opinions

So far, we have ignored partisanship as a way of organizing political opinions. More than on the basis of ideology, Americans divide on the basis of their party identifications. Whereas ideological identification may be of particular relevance only for a select segment of the public, people at all levels of sophistication appear to hold meaningful party identifications. Whereas the pollster's ideological identification question is intended to summarize the person's political values, party identification represents the person's net evaluation of the Republican and Democratic parties. It is relatively easy to prefer one party over the other without considering nuances of ideological placement.

For most people, party identification is a central aspect of political identity. Compared to ordinary political opinions, people's party identifications are quite stable over time, both before and after adjustment for measurement error (Green and Palmquist 1991). For instance, when interviewed during two successive presidential campaigns four years apart, most respondents persist with their original basic identification as a Democrat, Independent, or Republican. Only a small percentage of respondents switch party identification from Democratic to Republican or vice versa. Those who switch generally move in and out of the Independent category rather than "convert" from one side to the other.

As discussed in Chapter 5, the source of one's party identification is often the political values that were transmitted in the family during childhood. At the other end of the causal chain, party identification is the best predictor of how people vote. Following the sequence through, we find that people vote for the party with which their parents had identified.

Survey researchers normally ascertain party identification by asking respondents whether they consider themselves Democrats, Independents, or Republicans. Republican partisans may then be asked whether they consider themselves "strong" or "not so strong" (often translated as "weak") Republicans (or Democrats). Classifying on strength plus partisan direction makes four categories of partisans. Meanwhile, Independents are sometimes asked whether they "lean" toward one of the parties. The Independents can be classified as Republican leaners, Democratic leaners, and pure Independents. Pure Independents typically make up no more than about 10 percent of a national sample, suggesting that few citizens are purely neutral when it comes to partisanship. Altogether, there are seven potential categories of party identification, on a scale from "strong Democrat" to "strong Republican." Usually, however, the three-category classification is sufficient. Except where otherwise indicated, this book will employ the simple three-category division of party identification as Republicans (strong plus weak), Democrats (strong plus weak), and Independents (pure plus partisan leaners).

Party identification can be a handy cue by which to orient the remainder of one's political beliefs. An alert Republican, for example, would learn that a good Republican is supposed to subscribe to conservative positions on certain issues and would respond accordingly. At the same time, we might expect that the rare event of a partisan conversion results when the convert becomes aware that his or her ideological views are out of alignment with his or her partisan heritage. These causal processes could not occur, however, unless people were aware of the Democratic vs. Republican differences on the issues of the day.

Perceptions of Party Differences

As we will see in Chapter 11, Democratic and Republican leaders are ideologically different, with the Republicans generally conservative and Democrats generally liberal. In other words, at the leadership level the usual party stereotypes are true. Here, we can ask: To what extent does the public perceive these party differences?

TABLE 3.11 Public Perceptions of Party Differences on Issues, 1988 and 1992

Perceptions of Which Party is More in Favor of...	Democrats	Republicans	No Difference, Don't Know, No Interest
More domestic spending (1992)	53%	12%	33%
National health insurance (1988)	43%	8%	50%
Guaranteed living standard (1992)	42%	8%	50%
Aid to minorities (1988)	44%	8%	48%
Equal role for women (1988)	31%	11%	58%
Cooperation with Soviet Union (1988)	27%	15%	57%
Cut defense spending (1992)	53%	16%	31%

Source: NES data. The measures of perceived party differences are based on respondents' ratings of the two parties on seven-point scales.

The periodic NES national surveys have monitored the public's perceptions of the parties' policy positions. Table 3.11 summarizes these perceptions for three questions asked in 1992 and four others from the 1988 NES survey but not asked in 1992.

On most issues, about half saw the Democrats as the more liberal party. Very few guessed incorrectly that the Republicans were the more liberal. Thus, among those people who see party differences, the direction of the perception is almost always that the Democrats would pursue what are regarded as liberal policies and the Republicans the opposite.

Interestingly, the public's perceptions of party differences on issues have been growing over the years. As recently as the early 1960s, the public saw party differences only in terms of social welfare issues. The public image of the parties as distinct on social welfare issues goes back to the New Deal era of the 1930s, when the parties began to develop opposite philosophies toward the role of the federal government in the economy. Until about 1964, party differences on issues outside the social welfare sphere were not sharply focused at the leadership level, such as congressional and presidential politics. It is no surprise, therefore, that before the 1960s people generally did not see either party as more liberal or conservative on civil rights or foreign policy issues.

Nowadays, Americans generally perceive the Democrats as the more liberal party, not only on social welfare issues but on civil rights, foreign policy, and even social issues like gay rights. This happened largely because the parties became more polarized at the elite level. Public perceptions simply followed the behavior and the rhetoric of party leaders. The biggest change occurred with the ideological Goldwater election of 1964 (Carmines and Stimson 1989). Senator Goldwater, the 1964 Republican candidate, campaigned as a forthright conservative. By opposing the Civil Rights Act of 1964, he altered the

Republican image on civil rights. By his tough posturing about the Soviet Union, he made the Republicans appear to be the most belligerent on foreign policy. His Democratic opponent, President Johnson, was able to exploit Goldwater's image as an extreme conservative. Goldwater lost the election in a landslide, but he and his supporters made a long-standing imprint on the Republican Party.

Events after 1964 added to the growing perceptions of party differences. In 1972, it was the Democrats' turn to run a candidate targeted as an ideological extremist. President Nixon successfully tagged his opponent, Senator George McGovern, as the candidate of "amnesty, abortion, and acid." This unfair label helped to generate the impression that the Republicans were the party of conservative reasonableness on social issues and that the Democrats were the party of liberal permissiveness. The Reagan and Bush presidencies also accentuated the perception of party differences on issues. The perception of the Democrats as the party of liberalism and the Republicans as the party of conservatism continued into the 1990s.[9]

Party Identification and Policy Preferences

On most issues, the views of Democratic and Republican identifiers diverge in predictable liberal vs. conservative ways.

TABLE 3.12 Party Identification and Policy Opinions, 1992

	Percent Liberal of Opinion-Holders					
Issue	Strong Democrat	Weak Democrat	Independent	Weak Republican	Strong Republican	Gamma
Domestic spending	88	71	55	32	24	.55
National health insurance	81	76	65	49	33	.45
Living standards	61	35	37	21	15	.47
Aid to minorities	48	43	27	17	17	.39
Women's role	89	89	88	89	78	.14
Abortion	53	53	49	42	31	.18
Death penalty	33	25	19	12	10	.33
Aid to Russia	23	27	29	28	42	−.13
Military spending	76	74	73	65	45	.23
Gays in military	70	63	61	53	36	.27
Mean	*62*	*56*	*50*	*41*	*33*	
Liberal identifiers*	70	59	42	19	5	.63

*Liberals as percentage of liberal plus conservative identifiers.

Source: NES, 1992 election data. For the full text of the opinion questions, see the Appendix.

Some examples from 1992 NES data are shown in Table 3.12. Although the differences among "weak Democrats," "Independents," and "weak Republicans" are slight, the policy differences between "strong Democrats" and "strong Republicans" generally are rather sharp. Following historical tradition, party differences are greatest on social welfare issues. On one issue, aid to Russia, Republicans are slightly more liberal, perhaps because friendship with Russia was an idea associated with Republican presidents.

Figure 3.3 displays the difference between Democratic and Republican identifiers in terms of scores on the composite ten-item index of liberalism-conservatism.

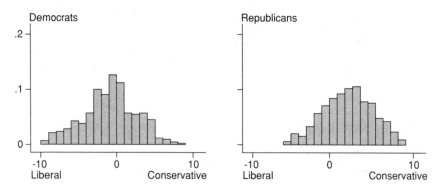

Fig. 3-3   Composite Opinion by Party Identification

In terms of their net ideological direction, most Democrats are left of center and most Republicans are right of center, but there are many exceptions. In fact, the reader might be surprised by the proportions of the public who appear as conservative Democrats and liberal Republicans. Clearly, ideology and partisanship are not the same thing.

The correlation between partisanship and ideological direction sharpens if we isolate informed citizens. Figure 3-4 repeats the ideological comparison of Democrats and Republicans, this time separately, for voters at the low and high end of the information scale.

Among low-information voters, there exists almost no correlation between partisanship and ideology; among this set, Democrats are only barely to the left of Republicans on average, with considerable overlap. But among high-information voters, virtually all Democrats are to the left of center and virtually all Republicans to the right. In other words, find an informed voter and partisanship follows ideology, or perhaps it is the other way around.

Issue differences between Republican and Democratic identifiers have grown in response to the perception of widening party differences.

While Democratic identifiers have been somewhat more liberal than Republicans on social welfare issues since the 1930s, only recently have Democratic identifiers become more liberal than Republican identifiers on other issues. As with perceptions, differences in Democratic and Republican views showed their greatest increase around the time of the ideological 1964 election. Before that time, Democrats in the electorate were not identifiably more liberal on civil rights, foreign policy, or social issues. Of course, they had no reason to be, since people saw the two parties as differing only on the social welfare dimension.

What causes the consistency between political opinions and party identification? Do people learn their political opinions from their party identifications, or do political opinions shape party identifications? Undoubtedly both causal processes are at work, but their relative contributions can only be roughly estimated.

Because party identification can be such a strong and stable attitude, some have argued that partisanship drives policy opinions more than than the reverse (Campbell et al. 1960, Ch. 6; Luttbeg 1981). Often, when parties realign their positions on an issue, their supporters will follow. Consider, for example, the opinions of partisans after

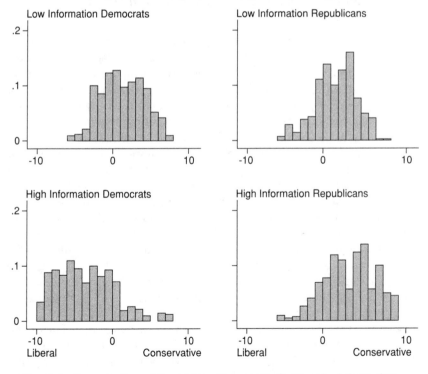

Fig. 3-4 Democratic and Republican Composite Opinion, by Information Level.

Republican President Nixon initiated the thaw in U.S. relations with with the People's Republic of China in the early 1970s. Republicans abandoned their hostility to "Red China" faster than Democrats.[10] Similarly when President Reagan initiated a new friendship with the Soviet Union, Republicans were the quicker to think the Cold War over.[11] And when in early 1991 many congressional Democrats balked at supporting Bush's intervention in the Persian Gulf, the split in war opinion between Democratic and Republican rank and file widened noticeably (Zaller 1992, 104–05).

While partisanship influences people's perceptions of the world and shapes their opinions, often it is party identification that changes when initial partisanship and issue positions get out of alignment (Markus and Converse 1979; Page and Jones 1979; Franklin and Jackson 1982; Jacoby 1989). Some who become ideologically disaffected from their home party become Independents (Luskin et al. 1989). Those who go all the way and shift from one party to the other often display the ideological zeal of true converts.

Party Identification: Psychological Identification or Running Tally?

Political scientists still do not fully understand party identification. *The American Voter* (Campbell et al. 1960, Ch. 6) presented one influential interpretation: that one's party identification is essentially a psychological attachment or "affective orientation" to one's favorite party. By this view, party identification can approach blind loyalty, as when people find reason to support their party's position and vote for its candidates long after they have rational reasons for doing so.

Some scholars, however, emphasize the more rational aspects of party identification. By this view, people learn a party identification based on what Morris Fiorina (1977a) calls a "running tally" of their partisan decisions. For example, the voter who finds repeated reason to vote Republican will begin to call himself or herself a Republican—not so much out of psychological attachment as by way of learning a convenient shorthand rule for deciding how to vote. If reasons develop for this voter to vote Democratic instead, he or she will not blindly continue down the Republican path in the face of contrary evidence. Instead, this voter will vote Democratic or even change partisanship in response to the new running tally.

Both interpretations of partisanship carry some validity. For example, many partisans persist in voting loyally for their party even when their party no longer represents their views on issues. But many partisans casually change their allegiance when circumstances seem to warrant it. Perhaps our question should be whether by forming a standing decision to vote Democratic or Republican, people enhance or detract from their ability to vote rationally. We will address this question in later chapters.

Notes _____

1. Analysts must be sensitive to the accuracy of the reasons people give for their opinions. For instance, people can recall their position on some matter but not the original reasons, and then rationalize their choice with new reasons that may not have had any bearing on their choice. There now exists a lengthy literature on how people store and retrieve political information when making or remembering political judgments. For some recent examples, see Lodge and Stroh 1993 and Wyer and Ottati 1993.

2. Two examples show the relative anonymity of Washington personalities among the public at large. When Edwin Meese was appointed attorney general by Reagan in 1991, one-quarter admitted to having heard the name. Of the remainder, one-quarter could not remember anything about him. Overall, most did not identify Meese as the new attorney general (Robinson and Clancey 1984). As a second example, a 1993 Times-Mirror survey asked respondents to evaluate several supposedly well-known newspeople.

   While the national sample had little difficulty rating television celebrities such as network anchors, many respondents had difficulty with the one person on the list whose primary role was in print rather than broadcast journalism. This person was George Will, the well-known conservative columnist. Slightly more than half failed to rate Will, including 41 who said they did not know who he was.

3. Sample sizes represent 500+ respondents. The fact that the responses shown in Table 3.3 are part of a framing experiment is not a source of serious distortion. In some instances, different framing in the two waves enhances response turnover. Yet this contamination appears slight. For issues in which some respondents were given variable framings and others the same framing, the effect of this difference in stimulus appears to have been but a few percentage points. Where some respondents repeatedly received an elaborate framing of the underlying arguments for the two points of view while a control group got none, responses were more stable when respondents received framing.

4. The abortion question was actually asked three times in the 1989 NES pilot study. The pilot respondents were first asked their abortion views in late 1988, as part of the regular NES 1988 election survey. Over three waves, only 26 percent took a consistent pro-life position and only 27 percent took a consistent pro-choice position. An even smaller 5 percent were consistently in the middle, but 42 percent took the middle position in at least one wave.

5. As a practical matter, the single dimension of liberal-conservative ideology is a better measure of underlying political values than specific values measured individually. Zaller (1992, 26) states the case nicely: "There is. . .a tendency for people to be fairly consistently 'left,' 'right,' or 'centrist' on such disparate value dimensions as economic individualism, opinions toward Communists, tolerance of nonconformists, racial issues, sexual freedom, and religious authority. The correlations among these different value dimensions are never so strong as to suggest that there is one and only one basic value dimension, but they are always at least moderately strong, and among highly aware persons, the correlations are sometimes quite strong. And, of course, there are also moderately strong correlations between people's self-descriptions as liberal or conservative and their scores on the various value measures.

6. For discussions of the origins of liberal-conservative terminology, see Kerlinger 1984 and Rotunda 1986.

7. On the increase in ideologues in 1964, see Field and Anderson, 1970; Pierce, 1970; Nie et al. 1976, 110–22; and T. Smith 1990. Some studies (Nie et al., Smith) define ideologues far more generously than we do here, to include any mention of the liberal-conservative language.

8. Correlations between opinions appear to have increased since the early readings in the 1950s. The greatest jump occurred at the time of the ideological 1964 election (Nie and Anderson 1974; Nie et al. 1976). Some scholars believe this increase is largely illusory, the result of better questions asked by survey researchers (Sullivan et al. 1978; Bishop et al. 1978).

9. Although the public has become more aware of party differences, the significance of this change is open to dispute, particularly since many people— in fact about half—apparently do not see party differences on topical issues even today. For differing interpretations, see Pomper (1972), Margolis (1977), and Wattenberg (1986).

10. For instance, between 1966 and 1971, the percentage of Democratic opinion-holders who told Gallup they favored U.N. admission for China rose from one-third to nearly half. Meanwhile Republican support rose from 1 in 4 to a clear plurality in favor of admission.

11. For instance, in 1984 (pre-Gorbachev) and 1988, "strong Democrats" (with opinions) increased their support for cooperation with Russia by four percentage points. "Strong Republicans" (with opinions) increased their support by 24 points (source: 1984 and 1988 NES data).

CHAPTER 4

Macrolevel Opinion: The Flow of Political Sentiment

Public opinion specialists begin their investigations of survey data by analyzing the "frequencies," or the percentaged divisions of opinion for the sample. The frequency distributions reflect the content of public opinion at the moment of the poll. When a particular survey question has been repeatedly asked in the past, the latest frequencies also provide information about the opinion trends.

Frequency distributions must be interpreted with caution because, as we saw in Chapter 2, responses are often influenced by question wording. When the polls show a certain percentage favoring a particular response to a question, we need some anchor, some reference point, by which to measure the significance of the finding. One way is to compare the frequencies for one question with those for slightly different but related questions. This comparison allows us to see what distinctions the mass public makes in the kinds of policies it is willing to support. A particularly useful anchor is to compare answers to the same question over time. If the public displays a different level of support for some policy today than one year ago or five years ago, then we may have located a potentially important change in public opinion.

Unfortunately, the data that would allow for the accurate assessment of trends in public opinion are often not as available as one might expect. Commercial pollsters naturally ask questions that are of current interest to their media clients. As popular interest fades, those questions are often not repeated. Academic polling units are more concerned with the continuity and comparability of questions over time, but even they are not immune to the wax and wane of topical issues. Thus, questions dealing with civil liberties were frequently asked in the "McCarthy era" of the early 1950s, when many people thought our basic personal liberties were threatened. Such questions were not asked again until the early 1970s. Questions about race relations were seldom asked prior to the 1960s, when the aspirations of the black minority were given little thought by white politicians, press, and public. Even when the polls monitor opinions on the same issue over time, they often vary question wording so it is difficult to separate real change from question wording effects.

In the following sections we present an overview of macrolevel public opinion, or what polls tell us about the content of public opinion both today and in the past. Poll trends are often described in ideological or partisan terms, as if the public's frame of reference is shifting on the liberal-conservative or Democratic-Republican continuums. We begin by first examining opinion on specific policy issues that have been polled over the years, searching for liberal or conservative trends that might be specific to the issue at hand. Second, we consider the possibility of general ideological movement. Third, we examine changes in the distribution of party identification over the years. And fourth, we consider one important partisan question well-known for its volatility: the President's approval rating.

4-1 Trends in Policy Opinions _____

For convenience, most policy questions can be divided into four general domains: social welfare, civil rights, foreign policy, and social issues. Social welfare controversies pertain to the distribution of wealth and government efforts to help the disadvantaged; civil rights refer to the quest for equality under the law; foreign policy obviously refers to views about the U.S. role abroad, and social issues usually involve differences over lifestyles or "moral values," such as abortion, prayer in the public schools, or capital punishment.

Social Welfare Issues

From the New Deal to the present, the American public has been receptive to government programs to accomplish economic welfare objectives. In fact, on social welfare legislation, mass opinion has often been well ahead of congressional action. For example, the earliest polls revealed an overwhelming majority (89 percent) in favor of "old age pensions" prior to the adoption of the Social Security Act in 1936 (Cantril 1951, 521). A majority also supported the right of workers to organize and bargain collectively before the 1941 Wagner Act enacted these principles into law (Page and Shapiro 1992, 136). Majority approval has continually been found prior to each increase in the federal minimum wage (Erskine 1962b, 26; Gallup Poll Index, Sept. 1985, 17).

It has long been noted that the American public is ideologically conservative, but programatically liberal (Free and Cantril 1968). Abstractly, in terms of ideological identification, Americans are more conservative than liberal (see Table 4.6), but when it comes to specific social welfare programs they usually are supportive. For example, when asked in 1992 (NES) if the government should "provide fewer services, even in areas such as health and education, in order to reduce spending," or should the government "provide many more services, even if it means an increase in spending," 39 percent chose more services and spending, 31 percent chose fewer services and spending, with the remainder taking the middle position.[1]

Table 4.1 shows that very few Americans want reductions in federal spending for a wide variety of social programs. The most frequent preference, in fact, is not to reduce spending or even to keep spending the same, but to increase spending, as we see, for social security, health care, aid to the homeless, loans and grants to college students, as well as other programs. Despite occasional rhetoric to the contrary, the services provided by government to its citizens are very popular.

Of course, there are limits to the public's enthusiasm for social welfare programs. Most notably, Americans clearly make the classic distinction between the "deserving poor" (those who have fallen on hard times through no fault of their own) and the "shiftless poor," who would rather receive a government handout than hold a job.[2] Thus, in the mid-1980s one poll showed that 88 percent of those with opinions agreed that the government ought to help those "who are unable to support themselves," while at the same time 91 percent agreed that "too many people on welfare could be working" and 94 percent said, "[t]oo many people on welfare get money to which they are not entitled" (Page and Shapiro 1992, 125). This distinction can be seen most graphically by large changes in poll numbers when slight changes are made in the way questions are phrased. For example, in a question-wording experiment,

TABLE 4.1 Opinions on Selected Federal Welfare Programs, 1992–1993

Should spending increase, decrease, or stay the same for:	Increase	Stay the same	Decrease
Social Security¨	46%	46%	8%
Improving and protecting health¨	74%	18%	8%
Improving educational system¨	69%	25%	6%
Welfare¨	17%	26%	57%
Assistance to the poor¨	65%	23%	12%
Protecting the environment¨	59%	32%	9%
Food stamps˙	17%	53%	30%
Aid to college students˙	61%	31%	8%
Aid to homeless˙	73%	21%	6%
Research on AIDS˙	62%	30%	7%

˙NES, 1992.
¨GSS, 1993.

one-half of the 1993 GSS sample was asked their view on spending "for assistance to the poor." Sixty-four percent said the government should increase spending.[3] The other half of the sample was asked for their views on spending "for welfare." Only 17 percent said the government should increase spending. More than a mere illustration of question-wording effects, this experiment reflects a belief among Americans that the government should help those who cannot help themselves, but that those who can work and do not merit little sympathy. There is a widespread belief among the American public that people who receive financial assistance ought to work for their money, even if the work they do is of little use.

Health Care. As we noted earlier, the public has frequently been out in front of elected officials on many innovations in social welfare policy. This has certainly been the case with regard to health care. Since the 1930s, opinion polls have consistently shown the public favors some form of government intervention. In 1937, a Gallup Poll showed that over 70 percent favored the notion that "the federal government should provide free medical and dental care for those who cannot pay." During the 1950s and 1960s, 60 to 65 percent supported the principle of the government paying the medical bills of the elderly, which was enacted into law in 1965 with Medicare (Erskine 1975). In 1975 and 1985 Roper Polls, 76 percent and 73 percent respectively thought adequate medical care was a "right" to which citizens were entitled. Similarly, since at least 1977, a majority has favored "national health insurance, financed by tax money, and paying for most forms of health care" (Shapiro and Young 1986). By 1993, 62 percent were in favor (CBS/*New York Times* 1993). But these sentiments do not necessarily mean the public wants "socialized medicine" or the government directly running health care. Most Americans seem to prefer a mixed system, with private insurance available, perhaps subsidized by the government or employers, with the state acting only as the provider of last resort (Page and Shapiro 1992, 131). Using the NES 7-point medical care question, where Point 1 represents a "government health insurance plan which would cover all medical and hospital expense," and Point 7 meaning expenses would be "paid by individuals through private insurance," slightly more people favor government over private insurance, but with a measurable movement since 1970 away from the extremes toward a middle position in which both the government and private sectors are involved in health-care funding (Mayer 1992).

Taxes. The public often appears to want to have its cake and eat it too. While it wants a plethora of public services (as seen in Table 4.1), it does not want to pay for them. For instance, it wants universal health care and access to the marvels of high-tech medicine, but with little or no increase in taxes (Taylor 1993, 21).

Regardless of how the question is phrased, a majority of the public invariably concludes that taxes are too high. When asked in 1991 if federal taxes were too high, about right, or too low, 58 percent responded "too high." When asked if "taxes in this country are reasonable or unreasonable," 77 percent said unreasonable. When asked if "you and your family have reached the breaking point in the amount of taxes you pay, or not," 66 percent say they have reached the breaking point (Mayer 1992, 444–45).

The public's desire for more services and less taxes suggests a general resistance to accepting tradeoffs. Sometimes people compartmentalize their thinking about taxes and services. One way to avoid the mental discomfort of dealing with an unpleasant reality is to keep issues mentally separate, and not make connections among them. For analysts who see a "rational public," the contradictions and inconsistencies of the public's demand for more services but lower taxes are among the most difficult to explain.[4]

Anti-tax sentiment has fluctuated over time. The question about "too high" federal income taxes has been asked since 1947. For this question, the least anti-tax sentiment was in March 1949, when only 49 percent thought taxes were too high. With new taxes to pay for the Korean War, the number quickly shot up to 73 percent in March 1952. It then declined gradually, dropping to 49 percent in 1961. The costs of the Vietnam War helped push the figure upward again, to 73 percent in 1969. After the war, anti-tax sentiment declined through the mid-1970s, only to rise again in the late 1970s as part of an overall anti-government right turn. With the Reagan tax cuts of 1981, sentiment that taxes were too high declined to 55 percent by 1988, where it essentially has remained (Page and Shapiro 1992, 162–63).

Civil Rights

Discerning the true attitudes held by white Americans on civil rights issues has proven to be a difficult and controversial task. Taking easy issues first, polls clearly show at a minimum that Americans have rejected the prevalent "white supremacist" ideology that pervaded mass attitudes as recently as a few decades ago. Poll data from the 1930s and 1940s suggest that perhaps a majority of white Americans once believed blacks to be intellectually inferior and undeserving of equal status with whites. In 1939, a Roper Poll found 76 percent of white respondents agreeing that "Negroes" had generally "lower" intelligence than white people (Page and Shapiro 1992).[5] As late as 1944, just 44 percent believed that "Negroes are as intelligent as white people" (Erskine 1962a). But only 12 percent of whites, in a March 1994 Harris survey, agreed with the stereotype that blacks have less native intelligence than those from other races.

In the analysis of public opinion on racial issues, it is common to distinguish between questions concerning the goals or ideals of the civil rights movement, and government action to actually implement those goals into public policy. The public is more supportive of the abstract goals of the civil rights movement than their implementation. For example, when asked in 1985 if black and white children should go to the same or separate schools, 93 percent of whites preferred the ideal of both races "going to the same schools" (GSS). But when asked if the government in Washington "should see to it" that black and white children attend the same schools, or if this is "not the government's business," just 43 percent of whites supported implementation of the ideal by government action (NES 1992).

We see a somewhat similar pattern in the trends over time. Whites have become much more liberal on questions concerning the ideals of the civil rights movement, but not on the implementation of these ideals. In terms of ideals, endorsement of fair employment practices for blacks rose from 42 percent in 1944 to 96 percent by 1972 (Smith and Sheatsley 1984, 15–16). In 1958, only 37 percent of white respondents indicated they would vote for a well-qualified black candidate for president, but by 1993, 89 percent would do so (Niemi et al. 1989; GSS 1993). In 1944, 45 percent said Negroes should have as good a chance as white people to get a job; by 1972, a near-consensus of 97 percent shared that belief (Page and Shapiro 1992, 69).

Figure 4-1 presents trends in white support for integrated schools, both in terms of principle and implementation. First, consider the question of whether white and black children should attend the same or separate schools. In 1942, just 30 percent said "same school" and 66 percent said "separate schools." Figure 4-1 picks up the series in 1956, when the trend had moved 19 points in a liberal direction to 49 percent for "same school." By 1985 (the last year the question was asked), 93 percent of the white public favored the ideal of black and white children attending the same school. Thus from 1942 to 1985, there was a 62 percent increase in white support for integrated schools, perhaps the largest change in public opinion for which we have data.

Figure 4-1 shows a different trend, however, on the question of whether the "government in Washington should see to it" that black and white children go to the same schools. When framed in terms of possible federal action, there is less support for the integration posi-

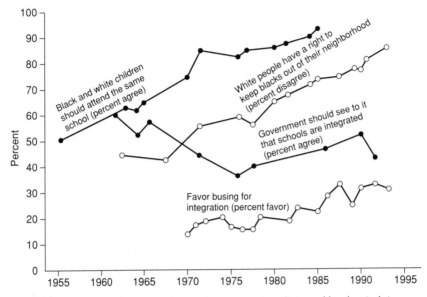

Fig. 4-1 Support for school integration, open housing, and busing to integrate public schools (Source: NORC, Gallup and GSS surveys)

tions, with white Americans more in favor of government action in the 1960s than in the 1970s and later. While opposition to racial discrimination is almost universal, attitudes about government intervention are anything but consensual.

Still, not all implementation trends are conservative. Figure 4-1 shows that in the case of busing, whites have become more supportive. While busing remains generally unpopular there is, nevertheless, a steady liberal trend amounting to a 19 percentage point increase in support over a 20-year period. Perhaps busing is not as threatening now as it was in the past. Few white children are actually bused of out their neighborhoods, and the magnet school approach, which often requires busing, has generally met with approval.

Finally, Figure 4-1 shows that whites have increasingly rejected the right to keep blacks from their neighborhoods. Note, however, that it was not until 1972 that a majority of whites settled on that view. By 1993, the number disagreeing that white people "had a right" to keep blacks out of their neighborhood had grown to 84 percent.

Affirmative Action. Certainly the most controversial issue in the implementation of civil rights is "affirmative action." Whites are overwhelmingly nonsupportive, as seen from responses to the following NES questions in 1988 and 1992:

Some people say that because of past discrimination it is sometimes necessary for colleges and universities to reserve openings for black students. Others oppose quotas because they say quotas give blacks advantages they haven't earned. What about your opinion — are you for or against quotas to admit black students?

	For	Against	Unsure
1988:	33%	58%	9%
1992:	23%	71%	6%

Some people say that because of past discrimination, blacks should be given preference in hiring and promotion. Others say that such preference in hiring and promotion is wrong because it discriminates against whites. What about your opinion — are you for or against preferential hiring for blacks?

	For	Against	Unsure
1988:	19%	75%	6%
1992:	13%	84%	3%

White attitudes on affirmative action are very firmly held. In a series of experiments designed to see if respondents could be "talked out" of various positions on race-related issues, Sniderman and Piazza (1993) had considerable success on a variety of social welfare issues, but little success on affirmative action. They also found a correlation between negative stereotypes about blacks and attitudes about affirmative action. One might infer that such negative stereotypes lead to an opposition to affirmative action. But Sniderman and Piazza (1993, 97–104) present evidence for the reverse effect as well—that opposition to affirmative action leads to a negative stereotyping of blacks. One-half of a sample was selected randomly and asked if they agreed or disagreed with a variety of stereotypes about blacks—they are irresponsible, they are lazy, they are arrogant. These questions were then immediately *followed* by a single question about affirmative action in employment. The other half of the sample was asked the same questions about blacks, but they were immediately *preceded* by the question about affirmative action in employment. The data show significantly higher percentages of negative stereotypes about blacks for the sample getting the affirmative action question preceding as opposed to following the racial stereotype questions. Sniderman and Piazza (1993, 109) concluded that "[a]ffirmative action is so intensely disliked that it has led some whites to dislike blacks—an ironic example of a policy meant to put the divide of race behind us in fact further widening it."

How does one explain the lack of support among whites for specific remedies to solve the problem of racial discrimination in the face of their overwhelming support for the ideals of racial integration? Two explanations are commonly debated: race per se and the politics of race. The first of these, the "symbolic racism" argument (Sears and Kinder 1971), holds there has been very little change in whites' attitudes about blacks, which remain mostly hostile. When asked opinions about policy questions with racial implications, whites are more likely to respond to the racial symbol (e.g., "black") rather than the policy content of the question. However, over the years public expression of racist sentiment became increasingly unfashionable. Outright racial discrimination also became illegal. Consequently, people learned it was socially unacceptable to express overtly racist opinions. Instead, racial hostility is expressed indirectly by a glorification of traditional values such as "the work ethic" and "individualism," in which blacks and some other minorities are seen as deficient (Sears 1986). Thus some of the apparent liberal trend in racial attitudes is not real change but simply reflects the need to express "socially desirable" opinions. Opposition to implementation, usually on grounds other than race, is simply disingenuous.[6]

A rival explanation is simple, straightforward politics. Sniderman and Piazza (1993, 107) argue that "the central problem of racial politics is *not* the problem of prejudice" (italics in the original). The agenda of the civil rights movement has changed from one of equal opportunity to equal outcomes. No fair-minded person could find consistency between the American Creed and denial of voting rights, segregated universities, workplaces, and lunch counters, and confinement to the back of the bus. But in the eyes of many, the new civil rights agenda of racial quotas and affirmative action very much clashes with the principle of equal treatment for all. Its implementation also requires an activist, expansionist government. Anti-statism, manifested as hostility to federal power, is a long-standing tradition in American politics. The political explanation holds that inconsistencies with the American Creed, and concerns about the power and trustworthiness of the federal government, prevent many whites (particularly conservative whites) from translating an abstract commitment to racial equality into support for specific federal policies (Sniderman et al. 1992).

Foreign Policy

Scholars often depict public opinion on questions of foreign policy as being particularly shallow and without meaningful content. Typical is the observation by Light and Lake (1985, 94) that "public opinion polls show that people do not follow foreign affairs closely and often do not know enough about the specifics of a particular issue to form opinions." As applied to most citizens on most foreign policy issues, one cannot easily object to this statement. However, an important foreign policy matter can easily grab the public's attention and profoundly affect the popularity of the President or the outcome of the next election.

Foreign policy opinions are subject to more abrupt changes than are domestic policy opinions. If "abrupt" change is defined as 10 or more percentage points over a single year, abrupt changes are twice as likely on foreign policy as on domestic issues (Page and Shapiro 1989). The explanation is straightforward: There are simply more dramatic events on the international scene than on the domestic scene. Few domestic occurrences have the impact of the Cuban missile crisis, the Iran hostage crisis, the invasions of Grenada and Panama, and the war in the Persian Gulf.

Internationalism vs. Isolationism. One volatile indicator of foreign policy sentiment is mass preferences for an internationalist vs. isolationist posture in foreign policy. Prior to World War II, American opinion was strongly isolationist. In 1937, 70 percent of opinion-holders said U.S. entry into World War I had been a mistake (Free and Cantril 1968, 62). That same year, 94 percent of opinion-holders said the United States should "do everything possible to keep out of foreign wars" rather than "do everything possible to prevent war. . . ." Between 1939 and late 1941, the percentage who said they would vote in favor of entering the war against Germany rose only from 13 to 32 percent. Support for war with Japan a month before Pearl Harbor was even lower, with just 19 percent endorsing the view that "the United States should take steps to keep Japan from becoming too powerful, even if this means risking a war with Japan" (Hero n.d.).

But once the U.S. was involved in World War II, internationalist sentiment increased sharply. By June 1943, 83 percent said the United States would have to play a larger part in world affairs than before the

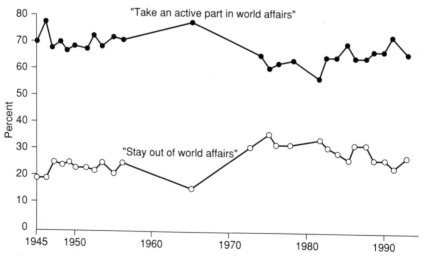

Fig. 4-2   "Do you think it would be best for the future of this country if we take an active part in world affairs, or if we stayed out of world affairs?" (Gallup, NORC, GSS).

war (Page and Shapiro 1992, 176). Figure 4-2 tracks post–World War II internationalist vs. isolationist sentiment as monitored by the question of whether the U.S. should "take an active part" or "stay out" of world affairs.

The high point of internationalist sentiment occurred in the mid-1960s, just before full American involvement in the Vietnam conflict. Poll results such as these helped to convince the makers of American foreign policy that the American public would put up with a long and protracted war in Vietnam. Of course they were tragically mistaken. The public turned against the war, and internationalist sentiment took a sharp decline. In August 1965, 24 percent thought it was a mistake sending troops to Vietnam; by December 1967, this number had risen to 45 percent, and as American involvement faded, it increased to 61 percent in May 1971 (Niemi et al. 1989, 71). By 1975, the proportion who wanted the United States to "stay out of world affairs" surged to 36 percent. The proportion has changed little since then (see Figure 4-2).

Defense spending. One source of frequently shifting opinion is public perception of the adequacy of defense spending. Figure 4-3 shows a roller coaster of changing beliefs regarding whether the United States is spending "too little on the military, armaments, and defense."

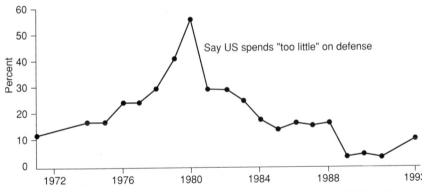

Fig. 4-3 Percent who say the United States is spending "too little" on the military, armaments, and defense. (Roper, GSS)

Beginning in 1978, large segments of the public began to believe that U.S. defenses were underfunded. This conservative trend resulted in part from the Soviet Union's invasion of Afghanistan in 1979, which President Carter denounced as "the worst threat to world peace since World War II." In protest, he withdrew American participation in the 1980 Moscow Olympics. Also in 1979, American hostages were held in

Iran, and the United States seemed powerless to get them back. Following a renewed military buildup under both Carter and Reagan, the citizenry became reassured that America's defenses were again strong. As the 1980s progressed, support for increased defense spending retreated to the level of the early 1970s. Finally, with the collapse of the Soviet Union, we see support for an increase in defense spending falling to record lows.

Russia and China. Since the end of World War II, the most relevant foreign policy question has been how the United States conducts its foreign policy in relationship to the Soviet Union (now Russia and the Independent States) and China. Mass attitudes toward these nations have generally followed the lead of American foreign policy. During World War II, when the Soviet Union and the United States were allies, favorable attitudes toward the USSR grew until, at war's end, 55 percent said, "Russia can be counted on to cooperate with us once the war is over." This trust, born of wartime camaraderie, soon evaporated, and by October 1946, the percentage who thought Russia could "be trusted to cooperate with us during the next few years" dropped to 28 percent. By the late 1940s, most Americans thought it was more important "to stop Soviet expansion in Europe and Asia than avoid a major war." During the Korean War and in the early 1950s, a majority said they expected war with Russia during their lifetime (Hero n.d.).

The chill of the Cold War reached its nadir in the early 1950s. As can been seen from Figure 4-4, in 1953 and 1954 only 2 percent of the public said they "like" the Soviet Union.[7]

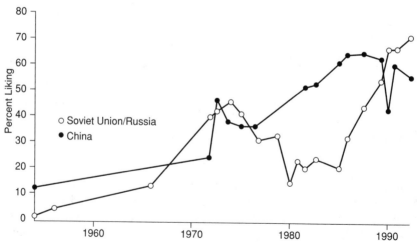

Fig. 4-4   Percent who "like" Russia/Soviet Union and China (Gallup and GSS)

But beginning in the late 1950s, Americans gradually began to warm to the world's other superpower. By 1973, with the Vietnam War winding down, liking of the USSR surged to 45 percent. Then following the 1979 Soviet invasion of Afghanistan and, later, President Reagan's rhetoric about the Soviet Union as the "evil empire," a new chill set in. A new melt then appeared with demise of the Soviet Union, the implementation of *glasnost* by Mikhail Gorbachov, and friendly overtures to the West by Russian President Boris Yeltsin.

Americans' attitudes toward China have also responded to events. Back in the 1960s and earlier, the United States did not even recognize the Chinese government and vigorously opposed "Red China's" membership in the United Nations. As late as 1964, only 14 percent of the public favored UN membership for China (even the year it was admitted, 1971, a majority of Americans still opposed membership). Public sentiment toward China gradually warmed (see Figure 4-4), except for a temporary plunge in 1990 following the crackdown on student protesters in Tiananmen Square. By 1993, favorable sentiment toward China, while on the increase, fell for the first time behind favorable sentiment toward Russia. By that index, Russia forged slightly into the lead.

Social Issues

In recent years, a new set of concerns called "social issues" have appeared on the American political agenda. In their broadest context, these issues involve conflicts between the forces of change and the forces committed to maintaining "traditional moral values." Examples of social issues include prayer in the public schools, decriminalization of marijuana use, government restrictions on pornography, and tolerance for gay lifestyles. Recent opinion on these issues is shown in Table 4.2.

On social issues, the public is generally thought to be rather conservative. Many but not all the divisions shown in Table 4.2 support this perception. One obvious limitation on the public's social conservatism is a willingness to support sex education in public schools. At the other extreme, most Americans oppose a complete ban on school prayer.

Even on school prayer the public's conservatism should not be exaggerated. Consider, for instance, responses to a 1992 NES survey, in which respondents were offered four choices: a full prayer ban, allowing a moment of silence, a nondenominational prayer, or a Christian prayer. Most (51 percent) preferred the "mild" solution that schools offer a moment of silence. Only 10 percent wanted schools to set aside time for recitation of Christian prayers.

Because most of the social issues presented in Table 4.2 are relatively new on the public agenda, it is difficult to establish trend lines of any length. Nevertheless, there are some trend data available. In the case

TABLE 4.2 Opinion Distributions on Social Issues (of Opinion-Holders)

		Liberal	Conservative
Marijuana:	Do you think marijuana should be made legal or not?"	23% [Yes]	77% [No]
Gay rights:	Should there be laws to protect homosexuals against job discrimination?*	60% [Yes]	40% [No]
Pornography:	Should there be laws against the distribution of pornography whatever the age?"	58% [No]	42% [Yes]
Sex education:	Do you favor sex education in the public schools?*	88% [Yes]	12% [No]
Prayer in schools:	By law, [should] prayer be allowed in public schools (1992)?*	11% [No]	89% [Yes]

Sources: *NES, 1992. **GSS, 1993.

of the legalization of marijuana, support peaked at 30 percent in 1978, declined to 16 percent in 1987, but by 1993 had risen to back to 23 percent. For pornography laws, the trend has been stable at least since 1973, with those favoring laws against its distribution ranging between 57 and 62 percent. The same stability occurs for sex education and prayer in the public schools. Opinion in these two areas has been more or less constant for the last 20 years (Niemi et al. 1989; NES 1992; GSS 1993). Despite public concern about AIDS, there seems to be a general increase in support for gay rights. Those favoring a law protecting homosexuals against job discrimination went up by 6 percent (meaning a 6 percentage point increase) between 1988 and 1992. Other surveys also show an increasing tolerance among the public for gay lifestyles.

Law and Order. One set of issue opinions that show a decidedly conservative trend are those dealing with law and order. Opinion on the death penalty (which had trended liberal from the 1930s to the 1960s) provides the clearest example. As can be seen in Figure 4-5, support for the death penalty for convicted murderers rose from around 50 percent in the 1950s and 1960s to over 70 percent in the 1980s and 1990s. Figure 4-5 also shows considerable public sentiment for the view that the courts do not deal harshly enough with criminals. By 1993, 81 percent endorsed that position, up 32 percentage points from 1965.

Figure 4-5 also shows that increases in support for the death penalty and beliefs that the courts do not deal harshly enough with criminals roughly track increases in violent crime. Some (e.g., Meyer 1992) claim that trends such as the growing support for the death penalty are a direct response to real changes in the violent crime rate.[8] But statistically, cause and effect is not clear. Political rhetoric and media attention

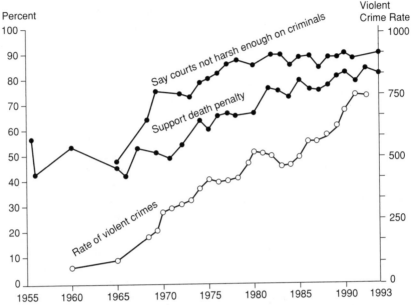

Fig. 4-5 Law and Order Opinion and the Rate of Violent Crime (Source: Niemi, Mueller and Smith[1989], GSS [1989–1993], Stanley and Niemi [1992])

to crime are likely the strongest immediate causes of public harshness toward criminals. Regardless, elected officials have clearly reacted to changing opinion, with legislatures mandating stiffer sentences for criminals, which in turn has led to considerable overcrowding of the nation's prisons.

Women and Politics. If law and order questions have shown a strong conservative trend, opinion about the appropriate role of women in politics shows an equally strong liberal trend. From Gallup and GSS, we have data spanning fifty years on the question of whether the public would vote for a qualified woman for president—the ultimate nontraditional role. As shown below, we see a strong leftward flow of opinion on this issue, beginning with the advent of the women's movement in the late 1960s.[9] The trend then abated somewhat in the late 1970s with the defeat of the Equal Rights Amendment and the organization of opposition to legal abortion, and then began another leftward move in the late 1980s.

Would Vote for a Qualified Woman for President

1937	1945	1949	1955	1958	1963	1967	1969	1972	1975	1978	1983	1991	1993
33%	38%	50%	52%	54%	55%	57%	59%	70%	78%	79%	83%	87%	91%

Over the decades, the public shifted from general opposition to the idea of a woman president to a general consensus accepting the idea in principle. Other opinion indicators on the role of women show a similar pattern. Since 1972, the NES has been asking respondents if women should have "an equal role with men in running business, industry, and government" or whether a "woman's place is in the home."[10] In 1972, 47 percent choose the "equal role" opinion. By 1980 it was 60 percent, and by 1992 it was 75 percent.

Abortion. The most salient of the social issues in the 1980s and 1990s is abortion. Currently, large segments of the public feel strong cross-pressures on this issue. It is clear that many Americans believe abortion is a morally serious matter. For example, in 1989, when asked if they "favored abortion used as birth control," a majority said "no" by a margin of 80 to 13 percent. A majority (57 percent) also agreed that "abortion is murder." But Americans are strongly resistant to government interference in their personal lives. Thus we find in the same survey 51 percent of the public endorsing the statement, "I am in favor of abortion because every woman has the right to control her own body" (Schneider 1989).

The public debate on abortion stresses the extremes, with the "pro-life" advocates demanding an end to all abortions, and the "pro-choice" advocates demanding abortion upon request. But most Americans favor neither polar position. In a 1993 Gallup survey, 32 percent said that "abortion should be legal in any circumstance," and 13 percent said "abortion should be illegal under all circumstances." The majority, 51 percent, said that "abortion should be legal only under certain circumstances."

Fortunately, we can discover the circumstances under which the public feels abortion should be allowed. Since 1965, the General Social Survey has been asking respondents if "you think it should be possible for a pregnant woman to obtain a legal abortion . . ." and then six different circumstances are specified. We can group these circumstances into "traumatic" and "elective," with traumatic being external circumstances beyond the woman's control (Cook et al. 1992), including danger to her health, damage to the fetus, and rape or incest. Elective reasons include personal and economic considerations, such as if a married woman wants no more children, the family cannot afford more children, or if an unmarried pregnant woman does not wish to marry the father. Opinion on these items has been remarkably stable since the *Roe v. Wade* decision in 1973 (Cook et al. 1992). Compared to other time series of similar length, its variation is trivial (Stimson 1991, 82). Public support for abortion rights in traumatic and elective circumstances for 1993 is:

Traumatic Abortion		Elective Abortion	
. Defective fetus:	79%	. Married, does not want children:	45%
. Health danger:	86%	. Cannot afford children:	47%
. Rape/incest:	79%	. Does not want to marry:	46%

Obviously, circumstances are crucial for the public's willingness to support abortion. Less than an absolute majority favor abortion for any of the elective reasons, while support is overwhelming in traumatic circumstances.[11] However, only about 7 percent of all abortions are done for traumatic reasons (Torres and Forest, 1988).

Given these mixed feelings, it is therefore not surprising to find that only a minority of the public favors reversing *Roe v. Wade* (which in some states would effectively outlaw abortions). When asked by Gallup in March 1993 if the *Roe* decision should be overturned, the public was opposed by a margin of 55 to 38 percent. But in the same poll, 80 percent favored a law requiring parental notification before a pregnant teenager under 18 could get an abortion. And in January 1992, Gallup reported that over 70 percent of the public favored a law requiring physicians to inform patients about alternatives to abortion, notification of husbands if a married woman wants an abortion, and a 24-hour waiting period before the procedure. It seems clear that the public wants abortion kept legal, but with regulations and restrictions.

Despite the long-term stability of the six-item GSS abortion series, recent years have seen a shift in favor of the pro-choice position that abortions should be generally legal. In the Gallup series for abortion being "legal in all circumstances," support rose from 24 percent in 1988 to 32 percent in 1993. Similarly, in the NES series, agreement that "a woman should be able to obtain an abortion as a matter of personal choice" rose from 36 percent in 1988 to 46 percent in 1992.

Many politicians who once took hard-line stands against abortion have since retreated, apparently believing the tide of public opinion has turned in favor of abortion rights. Pro-choice advocates became much more active as they responded to the Supreme Court restrictions on abortion in cases like *Webster v. Reproductive Health Services*. The threat of even further restrictions may be one reason for the increase in liberal sentiment on the abortion issue. Pro-life advocates have not, however, conceded the contest over public opinion. Some evidence indicates that anti-abortion attitudes are more intensely held than pro-abortion views, and politicians are known to pay greatest attention to those with the strongest convictions.[12]

4-2 General Ideological Movement _____

   The preceding section has shown various trends on specific survey items. For a particular issue, opinion might become more conservative over time, or more liberal, or, as often the case, just stays the same from one survey reading to the next. If there is a general ideological trend from the data we have examined, it would seem to be lost in the details. A challenging question is whether the public regularly undergoes changes in its "ideological mood." Conceivably, one could detect general currents of opinion that sometimes flow in the liberal direction and sometimes in the conservative direction. We do know that any general ideological movement cannot be large. From one year to the next, net opinion on any issue will rarely change more than a few percentage points. And large movements generally are responses to events unique to the issue, such as when defense spending preferences once fluctuated in response to the momentary intensity of the Cold War.

   This emphasis on the electorate's ideological stability may seem contradicted by the fluctuation in presidential election results. One might think, for example, that Clinton's 1992 victory represents a surge of support for liberalism, or that the earlier victories for Reagan and Bush represented an earlier surge for conservatism. Such claims, however, are greatly overstated. While candidate ideologies matter in elections (see Chapter 9), the electorate's ideological movement from one election to the next is slight.

   One way to locate trends in liberalism or conservatism on the part of the public would be simply to record changes in the degree to which people call themselves liberals or conservatives. As shown in the previous chapter, self-rankings as liberals or conservatives are sometimes questionable for the reason that many people lack adequate understanding of these terms. At a minimum, however, changes in how people describe themselves ideologically should reveal shifts in how fashionable are the terms "liberal" and "conservative."

   In polls taken between the late 1930s and the mid-1960s, respondents remained about evenly divided between self-declared liberals and self-declared conservatives. But then a conservative shift began, so that by 1970, conservatives clearly outnumbered liberals, in some polls by as much as 2 to 1. This change is puzzling, since the public's stands on issues did not in obvious fashion become more conservative at the same time. Why did the liberal label go into disfavor so suddenly in the late 1960s?

   To some extent, the sudden shift toward "conservatism" reflected an increased public concern about issues on which people saw themselves as conservative (e.g., law and order issues) and less public concern about issues on which people saw themselves as liberal (e.g., New Deal social welfare issues). Also, in the changing 1960s, opponents of civil rights legislation frequently justified their position in terms of conservative ideology rather than opposition to the equal-opportunity goals of the civil rights movement. Finally, the mid-1960s were a time when much liberal legislation (Medicare, federal aid to education, major civil rights protection) was enacted. As policy became more liberal, people's ideological frame of reference changed: To be a liberal was to seek even more liberal policies rather than simply supporting the new status quo.

In any case, the growth of conservative self-identification in the late 1960s was a one-time event. Table 4.3 shows the distribution of the electorate's ideological self-identification since 1976. Compiled from CBS/ *New York Times* surveys, the table is notable for the absence of any trend. In terms of ideological identification, the electorate showed the same distribution in the Carter years of the late 1970s as the Reagan-Bush 1980s and the early Clinton years of the 1990s. Most people choose the "moderate" option, with conservatives outnumbering liberals about 34 to 22 percent.

TABLE 4.3 Ideological Identification of the U.S. Public, 1976–1993

Question: "How would you describe your views on most political matters? Generally do you think of yourself as liberal, moderate, or conservative?" Don't know/no answer responses are excluded.

Year	% Liberal	% Moderate	% Conservative
1976	25	39	36
1977	23	45	32
1978	25	40	35
1979	23	41	36
1980	20	47	33
1981	20	44	36
1982	20	45	34
1983	21	45	34
1984	21	47	33
1985	21	45	33
1986	21	45	35
1987	23	43	34
1988	20	45	34
1989	22	42	36
1990	23	43	34
1991	23	43	34
1992	22	45	34
1993	22	44	35

Source: Pooled surveys by CBS News/*New York Times*. Yearly readings are composites of multiple surveys.

A second way to monitor changes in general liberalism/conservatism is to carefully estimate movement by combining responses to multiple survey items containing left-right political content. Two ambitious sets of estimates have been reported which somewhat contradict both each other and the trend (or, recently, lack of it) in ideological identification. After assessing a variety of political and social issues, Tom Smith (1990) argues that opinions became gradually more liberal between World War II and the mid-1970s, and then leveled off in a "liberal plateau." James Stimson (1991) made a similar investigation, restricted to a narrower set of strictly policy opinions. Stimson's research shows a more oscillating movement of what he calls the electorate's ideological "mood."

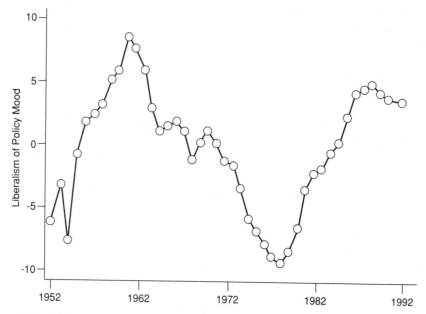

Fig. 4-6 Public's Policy 'Mood,' 1952–1992. *Source:* James Stimson.

Stimson's updated findings are shown in Figure 4-6. Stimson's mood index shows an increase in liberalism in the 1950s and early 1960s, followed by a decline in the late 1960s and 1970s, followed again by a liberal surge in the 1980s, perhaps leveling off in the 1990s. The scale shown represents movement on the scale of percent liberal (among opinion-holders). Thus, the maximum difference in "mood" is between 8 points more liberal than average (1962) and 9 points less liberal than average (1979). Thus, mood may move noticeably when sufficient measurement effort is applied, but the range of movement is rather small.[13]

4-3 General Partisan Movement _____

From an electoral standpoint, one of the most important indicators is the distribution of party identification among the categories of Democrats, Republicans, and Independents. The conventional view among political scientists regarding trends in party identification is that macrolevel partisanship is quite stable except for the rare shock of a "partisan realignment." Partisan realignments are precipitated by political parties making major changes in their policy orientations. As parties' policy images change in fundamental ways, the electorate can respond with surprisingly large shifts in party identification.

Two crucial realignment periods occurred around the time of the 1896 election and then again in the early 1930s. The 1896 realignment is evident from the fact that geographic voting patterns that had been stable for decades suddenly became disrupted and never returned to normal. In its 1896 convention, the Democratic Party accepted much of the platform of the Populists, a rising third party of economic protest, and nominated William Jennings Bryan, whose campaign for president featured the inflationary policy of "free silver." This new issue division attracted fresh adherents to the Democratic cause but panicked a greater number into leaving. Consequently, the Republicans became the dominant political party until the 1930s (Burnham 1970, 119–20; Sundquist 1973, 183–217).

The New Deal realignment of the 1930s came in response to Franklin Roosevelt's early social welfare policies. Roosevelt was first elected in 1932, as the electorate demanded change at the top with the onset of the Great Depression. Once in office, Roosevelt's policies, known as the "New Deal," greatly expanded the role of the federal government to deal with the national emergency. People tended to align their partisanship anew based on their preferences for or against Roosevelt's economic liberalism. Although no polls were available until 1936, trends in election outcomes and voter registration clearly showed a major electoral shift in favor of the Democratic Party (Ladd 1970; Sundquist 1973, 183–217). To some extent, the electorate's division into Democrats and Republicans even today can be traced back to the New Deal realignment.

If there were polls in the 1920s, they would have shown a Republican dominance in partisanship. By 1937, when a national poll asked the party identification question for the first time, the Democrats predominated. In 99 percent of national polls conducted between 1937 and the present, Democrats outnumbered Republicans. On paper at least, the Democratic Party has a decisive edge in identification.

As discussed in Chapter 3, individual-level party identifications are quite stable over time, as individuals rarely change their party preference. Still, when people do change partisanship (even if momentarily), they move in one-sided fashion in response to events. Figure 4-7 shows the annual readings of party identification in the Gallup Poll since 1945. The graph shows regular movement in the proportions Democratic, Independent, and Republican. The partisan landscape changes via gradual evolution as well as realignment shocks.

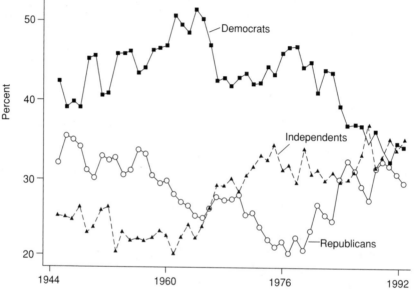

Figure 4-7 Party Identification by Year in Gallup Poll, 1945–1993

One obvious trend is the surge of Independents in the 1960s and 1970s. Until about 1965, polls would typically show only about 21 or 22 percent as political Independents. By the late 1970s, the proportion calling themselves Independents regularly registered at 35 percent or more. Over the same period the proportions of partisans who called themselves strong Democrats or strong Republicans declined, signaling a general weakening of party ties. Some observers call this trend beginning in the mid-1960s a general "dealignment," as people seemingly disengaged from formerly strong party ties.

A second observable pattern of Figure 4-7 is one that has only recently become recognized. This is a regular shifting of the fortunes of the two parties in terms of party identification. The Democrats enjoyed two major peaks in terms of identification, around 1964–65 with the landslide election of Lyndon Johnson and the early Jimmy Carter period around 1977. Since the late 1970s, the Republicans made significant gains in identification until by the early 1990s, they were only a few points behind the Democrats in identification.

Close investigation of these trends show that party identification tracks both the electorate's evaluation of the President and economic conditions (MacKuen et al. 1989). Reagan's popularity, for instance, helped the Republicans gain in the 1980s. Some observers even saw the Republicans the possible beneficiary of a new realignment in the 1980s. However, with the reversal of party fortune signified by Clinton's presidential victory in 1992, the Democrats' lead over the Republicans has increased once again.

Movement of party identification bears almost no resemblance to movement of ideological mood or ideological identification. Net partisanship (or macropartisanship) is an evaluative response to the general competency of the party controlling the White House rather than a judgment about policy direction. As these judgments change, we find party identification moving more in the aggregate than does ideological identification or any typical indicator of policy preference.

4-4 Presidential Approval _____

Without a doubt, the most closely watched political indicator in the U.S. is the President's approval rating. Unlike the other macrolevel attitudinal indicators we have discussed, presidential approval shows fluctuations so large as to attract general attention from both politicians and the general public. The President's approval rating takes on importance because it is widely believed to measure the President's degree of political support at the moment, and is also thought to be an important component of "presidential power." It may also provide a general guide regarding the President's prospects for reelection (Lewis-Beck and Rice 1982; Brody and Sigelman 1983).

While many polling organizations ask some variant of the "presidential approval" question, the standard measure is Gallup's question, asked regularly for over fifty years. When the Gallup Organization polls the American public, it regularly asks its respondents whether they "approve" of the President's performance, "disapprove" of the President's performance, or have no opinion. Attention generally focuses on the percentage (of all respondents) who "approve" of the President's current performance.

Gallup's sampling of presidential approval began with some sporadic monitoring of Franklin Roosevelt back in the late 1930s, when public opinion polling was in its infancy. However, regular readings of Roosevelt's approval rating were interrupted by World War II. But beginning with Harry Truman, presidents have been monitored in terms of their public approval on virtually a continuous monthly basis. This data base provides enough information that, in general terms at least, we now know which kinds of circumstances increase a president's popularity and which lead to its decline. Figure 4-8 depicts the history of presidential approval polling, from Truman to Bush.

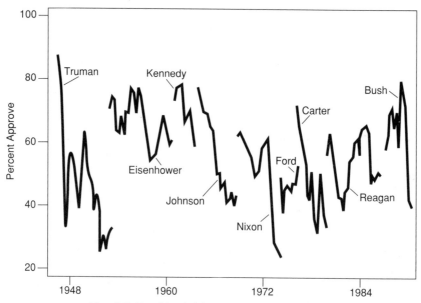

Fig. 4-8 Presidential Approval, Truman to Bush

All presidents enjoy some time above 50 percent approval; and most have unhappily spent some time below the 50 percent baseline. Presidents Truman, Nixon, and Carter all spent time below the critical 30 percent approval level. Three sources account for most variation in a president's approval rating. These are a "honeymoon" effect, a "rally-round-the-flag" effect, and the effect of the economy.

The Honeymoon. Every president starts the term with a rather high level of political support, with approval ratings in the 70 percent range not unusual at the beginning of the term. Then, as the president's term unfolds, the approval rating undergoes a gradual but inevitable decline. It is not surprising to find that presidents start out with an aura of goodwill, with even supporters of the defeated opponent offering their approval. The more interesting question is why does this honeymoon eventually fade? Some say the reason why presidents lose support over time is that they cannot please all segments of society all the time. Eventually, so this theory goes, the President must upset the expectations of some supporters, and this disillusionment creates a spiral of declining approval (Mueller 1973). Indeed, one might imagine a general rule that political support decays over time, with leaders inevitably becoming less popular the longer they govern. The implication is that no matter what presidents do to solve national problems, their political support will continue to erode.

A second interpretation is more optimistic. A president's early loss of popularity is best considered as a retreat from a starting point that was artificially high at the outset, rather than erosion of a natural base (Kernell 1978). About a year into a presidency, the President's popularity reaches its natural, lower, equilibrium level. By this second year, a president's popularity level will converge toward the middle range of about 50 percent. From this point on, approval is as likely to rise as it is to fall. The approval rating will continue to vary around the usual average of about 50 percent, as a function of actual events that reflect sometimes positively and sometimes negatively on the President's stewardship.

The basic reason why presidents begin with an artificially high approval rating is that newly elected presidents start out free of criticism—either from other politicians or from the media. This hiatus from criticism arises in part because the President has just proved his popularity at the ballot box. It also arises because the new president is a blank slate; the new president has conducted few official acts to be second-guessed. Instead of criticizing a new president, politicians and the media respond with words of support. Ordinary citizens take their cue from these expressions of goodwill—they, too, express approval (Brody 1990).

As a presidential term evolves, however, the President must take actions that are subject to second-guessing and criticism from the media and from political opponents. The result is a natural decline in support. But after the first year, a new president's popularity generally stabilizes at a more natural level. Still, popularity will continue to move in response to how the President is perceived to cope with events and the task of national leadership. We examine next some sources in this variation.

Rally-Around-the-Flag. From time to time, public attention is focused on some foreign policy event—perhaps an unexpected crisis or a major treaty or U.S. intervention in some foreign land. In the past, most of these were related to the Cold War. Early examples include the Soviet shooting down of a U.S. spy plane (the Francis Gary Powers U-2 incident) in 1960; the Cuban missile crisis in 1962; and seizures of U.S. ships by Communist foreign governments in 1968 (the *U.S.S. Pueblo* by the North Koreans) and in 1975 (the *Mayaguez* by the Cambodians). However, not all salient foreign policy events are anxiety-provoking. Examples would include events such as major treaties (e.g., Nixon's Moscow Treaty of 1972), "summits" (starting with Eisenhower's Geneva summit conference with Soviet leaders in 1955), and peace efforts such as Johnson's bombing halt (1968) or Carter's Camp David accords (1978) establishing the foundation for peaceful relations between Israel and Egypt.

What these events have in common is a focus on foreign policy. Generally, major foreign policy events are followed by a short-term surge in support for the President—what is called the "rally-around-the-flag" effect. These are "special moments" when eyes turn to the President, and the media and national politicians are seen to unite behind the President.[14]

Going to war is a special case. In the short term, wars traditionally result in the showering of approval on the President. One example comes from the early days of polling. While Roosevelt's approval ratings in the late 1930s were no more than respectable (typically in the mid-fifties), entry into World War II saw his numbers rise into the seventies. More recent wars show similar patterns. Truman gained 9 points following the start of the Korean War in 1950. Johnson gained 8 points following a major escalation of the Vietnam War in 1966. Lesser conflicts, such as Johnson's 1965 invasion of the Dominican Republic and Reagan's invasion of Grenada, also were followed by surges in presidential popularity. The biggest gain from a war certainly was George Bush's popularity surge to Gallup's record high of 87 percent in March 1991 following the brief Gulf War against Iraq.

But the political rewards from wars and invasions can be short-lived. The Johnson administration, for example, certainly miscalculated regarding the American public's taste for a prolonged war in Vietnam. Johnson fell in a few short years from the seventies to the low thirties in approval. During Korea, Truman declined even further—into the twenties, as did Carter during the Iran-hostage crisis. Both Truman and Johnson declined to seek reelection, and Carter was defeated in 1980. Bush's unique popularity after the Gulf War shows what a short successful war can do to presidential popularity. But Bush's approval decline in the war's aftermath (from 67 percent in August 1991 to 46 percent by January 1992) provides still a new lesson. The political benefit from any presidential success may be short-lived.

The Economy. It is common knowledge that the President's approval rating rises and falls with the state of the economy. When unemployment or inflation rise, the President is blamed. When these indicators of economic gloom decline, the President is praised. Naturally, the approval numbers reflect these tendencies. It is as if the electorate reads the state of the economy as a sign of the President's competence.

The exact mechanism by which the electorate converts economic perceptions into presidential approval has been the subject of considerable scholarly investigation. The simplest mechanism would be the straightforward response of personal "pocketbook" considerations—that when people face good economic times they support the President, and when they face hard times they do not. By this interpretation, presidential approval would track the economy in direct response to the electorate's collective personal economic experience.

Consider, however, that most people, most of the time, know that they do not owe their current economic fortune to the President. If the economy is thriving, a person who just got fired or laid off is not likely to blame the President for his or her personal misfortune. Similarly, if the economy is clearly troubled, a person who earns a big raise and promotion is not likely to attribute this good fortune to the President.

But people do recognize the state of the general economy as having some relevance to their personal economic well-being. Consequently, citizens reward or punish the President not on the basis of their particular personal circumstances, but from their perceptions of the national economy. Such responses are called "sociotropic," since people respond to how society is faring rather than how they personally are doing economically (Kinder and Kiewiet 1979). But the motive is still largely personal. People care about the national economy because they personally can be affected.

Sociotropic evaluations of presidential performance tend to be "prospective" rather than "retrospective." That is, people update their evaluations based on prospects for the economy's future rather than evaluating the economy's recent performance. We know this because statistically presidential approval tracks consumer expectations about the nation's economic future rather than consumer evaluations of current conditions (MacKuen et al.1992).

The basis for these prospective economic evaluations by the public is mostly the current state of the economy. Everything else being equal, the electorate's forecast is predictable from current or recent conditions. But the electorate is also sensitive to signs of the future that are independent of the past, such as what economists call "leading economic indicators." It works this way. When economists look into their crystal balls, they are reading leading indicators. The trend of these indicators gets reported in the newspapers and on the evening news. In this way, knowledgeable people learn how the economy will behave before it happens. They do so not because they have special economic intuition; they learn about the economic future because they learn what economists say will happen before it happens.

Figure 4-9 shows how public perceptions of the economic future coincide with presidential approval.

Fig. 4-9 Presidential Approval by Consumer Expectations, Eisenhower to Bush

This graph shows quarterly approval from 1954 (Eisenhower's second year) through 1992 (Bush). Overlaid with presidential approval is the best economic indicator of presidential approval. This is the net national response (positive minus negative answers) to the question:

> Looking ahead, which would you say is more likely—that in the country as a whole we'll have continuous good times during the next five years or so, or that we will have periods of widespread unemployment or depression, or what?

This item measures economic expectations as part of a battery of the "Index of Consumer Sentiment" produced by the Survey Research Center at the University of Michigan. Clearly, from Figure 4-9, surges of consumer optimism coincide with surges of presidential approval.

Summary. We have accounted for variation in presidential popularity in terms of three factors: the early-term "honeymoon," international "rally points," and the economy, especially in terms of expectations about the economic future. Referring again to Figure 4-9, one can see not only the contribution of economic expectations but also the honeymoon and rally events. Whether the President's approval is higher or lower than the overlaid variable of expectations marks whether approval is greater or less than expected on the basis of the economy alone. One can readily see the honeymoon effect. Early in each term, approval exceeds the amount one would anticipate based on economic expectations alone. Some rally points are visible. For instance, we see two upward bumps in approval during the Kennedy administration, following the Bay of Pigs invasion and the Cuban missile crisis. Carter has two upward bumps due to the Camp David Accords and the early Iran hostage crisis. Reagan's approval record shows a mid-presidency bubble of abnormally high approval in the afterglow of the Grenada invasion. This is followed by a decline in popularity due to Reagan's Iran-Contra scandal.

Still, we have not accounted for all the bumps and wiggles of presidential popularity. Note in particular the steep descent by Johnson, presumably due to the prolonged Vietnam War. Nixon took an even bigger nose-dive, soon after he won a landslide victory for his second term. This of course was the result of the Watergate scandal, compounded by an economic recession. Nixon abandoned his presidency in the face of near-certain impeachment for his complicity in the Watergate coverup. The fast fall by Ford at the start of his term was the response to Ford's presidential pardon of Nixon for possible Watergate crimes. Finally, note the upward bump early in Reagan's first term, evidently the sympathy response to Reagan's survival against an attempted assassination.

4-5 Conclusion: What Moves Public Opinion?

We have seen that public opinion has changed dramatically on many issues since reliable public opinion data has become available. Large shifts have sometimes occurred over short periods of time, or moves have been incremental over the years, but have aggregated to a fundamental reversal in American political sentiment.

The most important reason for abrupt change in public opinion is response to political events of the time. In this chapter we reviewed many such instances, like the demand in the late 1970s for greater defense spending in response to foreign policy setbacks and elite rhetoric about a weakened military capacity, or the conservative trend on law and order in response to rhetoric about the increasing crime rate. Incremental change, however, is more complex to explain. Cohort replacement is certainly one factor. Almost 50 percent of the American electorate is replaced every 20 years (Abramson 1983, 54). When we see dramatic change in support for the ideals of the civil rights movement between 1960 and 1980, it is important to understand that only about one-half of those comprising the adult population in 1960 were still part of that population in 1980. The new 50 percent enter the electorate often socialized to a different set of political values. Thus, the change that appears in support for the ideas of the civil rights movement does not necessarily mean that people have changed their minds, although that may have happened as well. Finally, the effects of modernization have certainly impacted upon the political opinions of the American public. Included here are demographic trends such as rising levels of education, the decline of the rural population, and the growth of large cities, as well as the increasing penetration of the national mass media to all sectors of society. Students of comparative politics argue that these trends have a long-term liberalizing effect on the populations that experience them (Dahl 1989).

Notes

1. Responses to the services and spending question are based on a 7-point scale (see Appendix), where 1–3 are combined at one end, 4 is the midpoint, and 5–7 are combined at the other end.
2. See Charles Murray, *Losing Ground* (1985, Ch. 1), for a discussion of the deserving and nondeserving poor. One survey showed that 37 percent believed people were poor because of "lack of effort," 29 percent said circumstances beyond his or her control, with the remainder saying both played a role (Mayer 1992, 90).
3. See Smith (1987) for a report on this experiment using earlier data.
4. For an attempt to salvage rationality in public opinion given the inconsistencies on taxing and spending, see Page and Shapiro (1992, 161–62).
5. Most whites in this 1939 sample claimed that blacks were born with less intelligence.
6. According to this view, the racially prejudiced find a respectable outlet to express their views on symbolic issues such as the busing of school children for racial balance. It has been demonstrated, for example, that the most vocal opponents of busing often are nonparents with little direct stake in the matter (Sears et al. 1979).
7. The question reads: "You will notice that the boxes on this card go from the highest position of 'plus 5' for a country which you like very much, to the lowest position of 'minus 5' for a country you dislike very much. How far up the scale and how far down the scale would you rate the following countries?" The plus scores are combined for the positive rating and the minus scores are combined for the negative rating. In October 1953, 72 percent of the public gave Russia a "minus 5"; by 1991 that figure had dropped to 10 percent.
8. Mayer (1992, 270) shows that a simple equation, in which the murder rates for five years previous are used to predict current support for capital punishment, is quite accurate in forecasting opinion on this issue. A 1-unit increase in the murder rate (measured in murders per 100,000 population)

yields a 4.5 percent increase in support for the death penalty. Murder rates explained 77 percent of the variance in support for the death penalty. It might also be noted that states with the highest rates of murder and non-negligent manslaughter convictions also have the highest number of per capita executions (Nice 1992).

9. The National Organization for Women (NOW) was started in 1966, and the National Women's Political Caucus was formed in 1971.

10. Respondents place themselves on a 7-point scale in answering this question. Responses 1–3 were combined to indicate preference for an equal role of men and women in government and society.

11. Additional information can be gained though various combinations of six abortion items. Thus 76 percent of the public favors abortion for all three of the traumatic reasons, while only 7 percent oppose abortion in all three of these instances. For elective abortion, 37 percent of public say they favor abortion for all three reasons, while 47 percent say they oppose abortion for all three of these circumstances.

12. For example, in a Harris Poll conducted from July 7 to 11, 1989, voters who favored and opposed *Roe v. Wade* were asked, "If a candidate for political office stood for most of the things you believe in, took a stand on abortion that you disagreed with, you would certainly not vote for that candidate . . ." Of those who favored *Roe v. Wade*, 12 percent said they would certainly not vote for the candidate; of those who opposed *Roe v. Wade*, 23 percent would certainly not vote for that candidate.

13. A question that is not yet fully answered is what causes the small shifts in the electorate's ideological mood. Durr (1992) has argued that statistically, mood follows the economy—good times lead to liberal moods and bad times cause the electorate to turn conservative. Another interpretation is that mood responds to changes in policy, so that liberal policies (such as during the 1960s) cause mood to turn conservative while conservative policies (such as during the 1980s) cause mood to turn liberal (Wlezien 1994).

14. We discuss the psychology of these rally events in Chapter 8.

CHAPTER 5

Political Socialization and Political Learning

Just as one learns to read and write, and what is fashionable in clothing, one learns about politics. A considerable portion of this learning occurs before the individual is old enough to enter the voting booth. Children, for example, tend to share the same partisan preference as their parents. A central premise of political socialization holds that what one learns as a preadult affects one's later political life. This assumption is crucial, for there is little reason for interest in the reaction of preadults to their political environment, except insofar as it affects their adult attitudes and behaviors.

To "socialize" someone means "to make social, make fit for life in companionship with others" (Random House Dictionary). Thus, one perspective on political socialization focuses on the learning of attitudes, values, and acceptable forms of behavior necessary to fit into the political order. It is the learning or failure to learn the lessons of being a good citizen, as defined by the political status quo (Easton and Dennis 1969). Another perspective treats the field more akin to generic political learning. The emphasis is on individual political development rather than on molding the person to fit with the political community (Jennings and Niemi 1974). In this chapter we shall discuss both these perspectives on the socialization of citizens to political life.

5-1 The Preadult Years: Socialization to Citizenship ____

Every political system attempts to indoctrinate its children to accept and support the ongoing political order. From the perspective of systems theory, Easton and Dennis (1969, 5) advance the hypothesis "that the persistence of some kind of [political] system may in part be dependent upon the success of a society in producing children most of whom acquire positive feelings about it." But socialization is more encompassing than just encouraging the young to identify with the regime, and inculcating a benevolent view of the authorities. It is the transmission of the political culture from one generation to the next.

From a systems perspective, the purpose of socialization is to maintain a stable political order. According to Easton and Dennis (1969, 31):

> If the socialization process raises children who upon reaching adulthood have among themselves conflicting aspirations, conceptions of the rules of the system, attitudes toward compliance, and feelings about authority, it is assumed that this will probably build social and political cleavages into the system and that instability will result.

Of course, if political training results in a total commitment to socially acceptable beliefs, the forces for change and improvement in society would be greatly diminished. For instance, if socialization were a complete success, the change we have seen in the status of women and minorities could not have occurred.

To analyze the development of preadult political orientations we shall divide the early years into four periods: preschool (ages 3 to 5), early childhood (ages 6 to 9), late childhood (ages 10 to 12), and adolescence (ages 13 to 18). These are approximate categories, for just as children differ in their physical development, they differ in their political development. In conclusion, we shall discuss the consequences of socialization for citizenship.

Preschool

The dawning of political recognition begins before the child ever commences his or her formal education. Political impressions are often vague and inaccurate, but early awareness may lay the foundations for later political development.

Preschoolers frequently confuse political authority with religious authority. In a study of kindergarten children in California, Moore et al. report that when asked, "Who does the most to run the country," 30 percent responded "God" or "Jesus." Perhaps the most important public figures for the young child are the President and the police officer. One school of thought contends that both these officials play a major role in shaping the child's attachment to the political order. Schwartz (1975) found that 90 percent of her preschool sample were able to recognize the "man in the picture" as being "the policeman," and 75 percent were able to answer correctly when asked, "What does the policeman do?" The responses most frequently given concerned regulating traffic, helping lost children, and "catching bad people." The children, for the most part, saw the police officer as a benevolent authority figure. Less visible was the police officer's punitive and prohibitive role. Fewer than 10 percent of the preschool sample recognized a picture of the incumbent president. When asked, "What does the President do?" only a few could give an accurate or specifically political characterization. The President is not viewed by these young children as being particularly benevolent, especially when compared to the policeman (Schwartz 1975, 236–37). This may be due simply to the President's lower visibility—a situation that, along with perceived benevolence, changes dramatically at the next stage of political development.

Public servants are not the only political symbols visible to the preschool child. Even at this early age, children manifest a sense of political community. When presented with a picture showing nine different flags, the vast majority were able to identify the American flag. When asked, "Which flag is your favorite?" 60 percent chose the American flag and another 19 percent identified the Liberian flag, which closely resembles the American flag (Schwartz 1975, 242–43). Thus preschool children both know and identify with the symbol of the American political community.

Early Childhood

With the onset of early childhood, the content of the young person's political world begins to expand rapidly. However, the increase in content is almost entirely in terms of feelings and affect. Political understanding and critical thought have yet to emerge. The young child now becomes very aware of the existence of the President. Government is personalized; that is, the child becomes aware of political authority by becoming aware of certain individuals—notably the President and the police officer. The young person sees these figures as possessing great power, and is aware that they stand above the family in the obedience hierarchy. Unlike adults, who often tend to be quite cynical about politics, the young child sees the President and the police officer (and political authority) as trustworthy, helpful, and benevolent. This outlook is illustrated by the following excerpt from an interview with a third-grade boy (Hess and Torney 1967, 42).

Q. What does the President do?
A. He runs the government, he decides the decisions we should try to get out of, and he goes to meetings and tries to make peace and things like that.
Q. When you say he runs the country, what do you mean?
A. Well, he's just about the boss of everything. . . .
Q. And what kind of a person do you think he is?
A. Well, he's an honest one.
Q. Anything else?
A. Well, loyal and usually pretty smart.
Q. Who pays him?
A. Well, gee, I don't know if anybody pays him; he probably doesn't get too much money for the job—I don't know if he gets any money.

Q. Why would he take the job?
A. Well, he loves his country and he wants his country to live in peace.

To a surprising extent, young children believe that the policeman and especially the President "would always want to help me if I needed it," that "they almost never make mistakes," and that "they know more than anyone." Reasoning from the "primary principle" and the "benevolent leader hypothesis," students of political socialization attach considerable importance to the idealization of authority by young children. According to the primary principle, "what is learned early in life tends to be retained and to shape later attitudes and behavior" (Easton and Dennis 1969, 9). According to the benevolent leader hypothesis, the image of the President (the most visible symbol of political authority) that is formed in early childhood has a direct effect on the formation of attitudes and beliefs about other political figures and institutions. There is a hypothesized "spillover effect" from this early view of the President to later perceptions of other political authorities. Because the President is favorably viewed, they too tend to be viewed favorably. It is believed, therefore, to be very significant that the child's introduction to politics is a very positive one. Later in life, when the individual is able to make critical judgments about politics, this early idealization builds what David Easton (1965) refers to as "diffuse support." It is a reservoir of goodwill toward the political system that is independent of any benefit the individual might receive. It helps legitimize the political order, and in times of political stress, the residue of this early idealization helps maintain a positive attitude toward government.

Late Childhood

Beginning about the age of 10 or 11, children start moving away from a personalized view of government to one based on a more sophisticated understanding. During this period the child learns the "civics book" norm of not always voting for the same political party, but for the best person. In a national sample, 49 percent of fourth-graders say a good citizen would join a political party and vote for its candidates instead of voting for the best person. But by the eighth grade, only 26 percent endorse this strategy (Hess and Torney 1967, 96). Views of what constitutes "good citizenship" also undergo change. Young children tend to see the good citizen as someone who is "helpful to others" and "always obeys the laws." But by late childhood, good citizenship is defined more in terms of adult conceptions: political interest, voting, and getting others to vote (Hess and Torney 1967, 37). Sigel and Brookes (1974, 110) investigated conceptions of democracy among fourth-graders. They found only 17 percent answered "yes" to the question, "Is a democracy where the people rule?"

("I don't know" was the most frequent answer.) They interviewed the same students two years later (then in the sixth grade) and found that 44 percent could respond correctly. However, definitions of democracy in late childhood and even through adolescence seldom include the right to criticize government. Only 54 percent of the eighth-graders in Hess and Torney's sample checked the option "you can say things against the government" as one possible definition of democracy. And fully 84 percent of eighth-graders agree that "the government usually knows what is best for the people." Such open acceptance of government and intolerance for dissent are generally regarded as unhealthy for democracy (see Chapter 6). But from a systems theory standpoint, one can ask, "Do not such attitudes indicate successful socialization?" Acceptance of government and intolerance for dissent surely promotes "system stability." It is implications such as these that have led to trenchant criticism of the systems perspective on political socialization (Connell 1987).

It is in late childhood that young people begin to separate individual from institutional roles. They begin to understand the difference between the office and the man or woman who holds the office. The presidency and the President are no longer seen as the same. Children also display the beginnings of critical judgment; they are sensitive to partisan and policy considerations. For example, those raised in Democratic households are more critical of a Republican president than children raised in Republican households. The President also becomes associated with certain policy positions (Weissberg 1974, 54). Still, political understanding is basically immature. Children will revert back to personalization if asked about something they cannot comprehend.

Adolescence

The major spurt in a child's political learning usually comes during adolescence. An important aspect of this growth is the ability to comprehend the abstraction of community interest apart from self-interest. Ideals such as community and society are usually beyond the grasp of 11-year-olds, but not beyond those who are 15 (Adelson and O'Neil 1966). By mid-adolescence the individual is in many ways politically beginning to resemble an adult. By the ninth grade, children have some ability to think along a liberal-conservative continuum. Adult levels of political efficacy are also reached by the ninth grade (Merelman 1971; Hess and Torney 1967). One orientation that shows surprisingly little growth is support for democratic values (free speech, minority rights, rules of the game, etc.). Merelman (1971, 79) finds no increase in support for democratic values between the ninth and twelfth grades. As we shall note shortly, many blame the failure of this development on the shortcomings of the public schools.

TABLE 5.1 Affect Toward Political Objects

	The U.S.	The Flag	Constitutional System	Congress	The Courts	Current Government
Very Negative	1%	3%	3%	6%	8%	24%
Negative	4	3	10	16	17	35
Neutral	8	13	20	32	27	19
Positive	31	22	36	31	31	17
Very Positive	57	59	32	16	17	5
	100%	100%	100%	100%	100%	100%

Source: Roberta S. Sigel and Marilyn B. Hoskin, *The Political Involvement of Adolescents* (New Brunswick, NJ; Rutgers UP, 1981): 73. Copyright © by Rutgers, the State University.

An orientation that begins in early childhood and, for the most part, continues unchanged through to adolescence is the positive view most preadults have of the political system. Despite "de-idealization," political shocks like the Iran-Contra scandal, and increased sophistication about most political topics, American adolescents retain a positive attitude toward the political order. But they can be quite negative about government officials. Presented in Table 5.1 are the views of high school seniors in 1974 (shortly after Watergate) toward the political community, the constitutional order, and the incumbent government (Sigel and Hoskin 1981, 73–75).

Note that less than a majority felt positively about the Congress (46 percent), the courts (48 percent), and the incumbent government (22 percent). But 59 percent were very positive about "the flag," and 57 percent were very positive about "the U.S.," with the negatives being minuscule. The "constitutional system" does not fare as well (32 percent very positive; a total of 68 percent either very positive or positive), but still the negatives are small. Obviously, there had been some erosion in the favorable image of government, but these high school seniors still moved into adulthood with a fundamental commitment to the ongoing political order.

Socialization to Citizenship and Its Consequences

The most dramatic findings in the citizenship literature are the extent to which children "personalize" government and the remarkable degree to which they idealize authority, notably the President. But do these findings really mean anything for adult political behavior? The theory of diffuse support, born of childhood idealization, is an appealing one, but difficult to verify empirically. The theory seems not to be general, since not all children idealize authority. Black (Greenberg 1970), Mexican-American (Garcia 1973), and Appalachian children

(Jaros et al. 1968) tend to see political authority as less benevolent than white children view it.

More importantly, during the Watergate era, even middle-class white children came to see the President as almost sinister. Several studies done during the Watergate scandal (1972–1974) showed a "dramatic decline" in the positive image of the President (Arterton 1974; Haratwig and Tidmach 1974; Dennis and Webster 1975; Hawkins et al. 1975; Rodgers and Lewis 1975). Christopher Arterton reports that, based on a Boston area sample, attitudes toward the President in fall 1973 "could only be described as wholly negative." The benevolent leader was transformed by Watergate into a "malevolent" leader. In the early 1960s, anywhere from 50 to 66 percent (depending on grade) reported the President was their "favorite of all" or "of almost all." By 1973, the range was 5 to 23 percent, with the older children (fifth-graders) being the least positive. Children in 1962 and 1973 were asked to "compare politicians" with "most people" in terms of power, selfishness, intelligence, honesty, and trustworthiness. The "spillover effect" of the President's image to other political authorities, which was positive in 1962, was negative in 1973. Particularly large differences between 1962 and 1973 exist on selfishness and trustworthiness. Fifty-four percent of the fifth-graders in 1962 thought politicians were less selfish than other people; only 19 percent thought so in 1973.

If the systems theory of childhood socialization is correct, we would expect to see substantial differences between those age groups that were in the fourth through the eighth grades between 1973 and 1975 and those that are both older and younger. Using a somewhat broader sweep, Delli Carpini (1986) reports that those socialized during the antiwar period of the late 1960s were somewhat more cynical as they entered the electorate than were those socialized earlier. However, using the 1992 NES, we find those between 28 and 34 (who would have been in grade school during Watergate) are no more or less trusting of government than other age cohorts.[1] However, we should not make too much of a weak test. As we shall see later, in some issue domains there is convincing evidence to support the persistence hypothesis.

5-2 The Agents of Preadult Socialization _____

Having traced the development of political attitudes through the preadult years, we shall now attempt to sort out the agents most responsible for this development. The family seems to be the most influential source of preadult attitudes, but it certainly is not the only source. Schools make an effort to indoctrinate children, and it seems unlikely that the effort is totally unsuccessful. Other possible agents of early political socialization include childhood friends and the mass media (see Chapter 8 for a discussion of the mass media). Finally, when important historical events occur, it seems likely they would leave an imprint on the young.

The Family

Political influence is a function of two factors: communication and receptivity (Williams and Minns 1986). Parents score high on both these dimensions. Children, particularly young children, spend a large amount of time with their parents. The opportunities for children to learn parental attitudes and for parents to exert influence on children is considerable. Also, in terms of receptivity, few bonds are as strong as the affective ties between parents and children. The stronger this tie and the more personal the relationship, the greater the ability to exert influence.

A common assumption is that the political attitudes of family members are highly similar. Since most family members appear to share the same party preference, it seemed logical to many investigators that the same pattern would hold for other political orientations. Evidence to support this belief came from a number of early studies (pre-1960) in which parents and children were not independently interviewed.[2] Children (normally students) would be interviewed and then asked to report the political attitudes of their parents. The parents themselves were not actually interviewed. We now know that this methodology grossly overestimates the amount of parent-child similarity on most political issues. In reporting parent attitudes, children tend to "project" their own attitudes onto parents, artificially inflating attitude correspondence. In actuality, the similarity in political attitudes between parents and their offspring since World War II could at best be described as moderate. Table 5.2, taken from a study by Kent Jennings and Richard Niemi, displays the relationships between a national sample of high school seniors and their parents on four policy issues.

Reading across the rows in the table we can see that the students are much more likely to be pro–school integration and pro–school prayer when their parents favor these positions. For example, of the pro-integration parents, 83 percent have children that also favor integration, but when parents oppose integration the percentage of children favoring integration drops to 45—a difference of 38 percent. This relationship weakens considerably for the question of an elected Communist being allowed to hold office and virtually disappears on the question of allowing speeches against churches. In the case of the latter, knowing the parent's attitude is of no use in predicting the student's attitude. Most students favor allowing speeches against churches regardless of

TABLE 5.2 Relationship Between Student and Parent Opinions on Four Policy Issues

Students	Federal Role In School Integration* Parents			Prayers In Public Schools* Parents			Elected Communists Can Hold Office Parents			Allow Speeches Against Churches Parents		
	Pro	Depends	Con	Pro	Depends	Con	Pro	Depends**	Con	Pro	Depends**	Con
Pro	83%	64%	45%	74%	62%	34%	45%	—	32%	88%	—	82%
Depends	7	17	14	3	8	7	1	—	0	0	—	0
Con	10	18	41	23	30	59	53	—	67	12	—	18
Total	100%	99%	100%	100%	100%	100%	99%		99%	100%		100%
	(961)	(202)	(453)	(1253)	(68)	(238)	(1337)		(1337)	(1376)		(523)
	Tau$_b$ = .34			Tau$_b$ = .29			Tau$_b$ = .08			Tau$_b$ = .08		

*Based on pairs in which both parents were "interested enough" to give a pro or con response.
**Ten or fewer cases

Source: M. Kent Jennings and Richard G. Niemi, The Political Character of Adolescence (Princeton, NJ: Princeton UP, 1974): 78. Reprinted by permission of Princeton University Press.

TABLE 5.3 Student Party Identification by Parent Party Identification

Student	Parents			
	Democrat	Independent	Republican	Marginals˙
Democrat	66%	29%	13%	(43%)
Independent	27	55	36	(36%)
Republican	7	17	51	(21%)
Total	100%	100%	100%	
Marginals˙	(49%)	(24%)	(27%)	100%

*The marginal totals present the proportion of parents and students that hold a particular party prefer-ence. For example, looking at the column marginals we can see that 49 percent of the parents call them-selves Democrats. Looking at the row marginals we can see that 43 percent of the students in the sample call themselves Democrats.

Source: M. Kent Jennings and Richard G. Niemi, *The Political Character of Adolescence* (Princeton NJ: Princeton UP, 1974): 41. Reprinted by permission of Princeton University Press.

what their parents think. One can infer that parents have little influ-ence on these latter two issues. Also, parents seem to have little influ-ence on more diffuse orientations like political efficacy and political trust. Relationships are very similar for the "legally elected Communist" and "speech against churches" issues (Jennings and Niemi 1974, 127–32, 146–47).[3]

In sharp contrast to the situation for issues is the case of party identification. Table 5.3 documents the widespread agreement be-tween parents and children on the question of party preference. Again, reading across the rows of the table, when we move from par-ents who are Democratic to those who are Independent to those who are Republican, the percentage of Democratic children drops dra-matically. The reverse holds for the case of Republican parents. When parents agree between themselves on partisanship (74 per-cent do agree), 76 percent of the adolescents follow the preferences of their parents. Interestingly, when parents disagree on partisanship (one is a Democrat, the other a Republican), the child is more likely to adopt the mother's partisanship than the father's (although the number of Independent children rises substantially, as one would ex-pect given the cross-pressures).[4] This generational continuity is im-portant because it helps maintain the ascendancy of the dominant political party. Since the New Deal, the Democratic Party has been preferred by a majority of Americans. As long as parents continue to socialize children successfully to their own party preference, the Democratic Party seems well placed to continue its favored position with the electorate.

However, there is clear evidence that parents are not currently as successful in transmitting partisanship as they were in the 1940s, 1950s, and into the early 1960s. In 1958, 79 percent of children with

Democratic parents and 72 percent with Republican parents adopted parental partisanship. By 1976 these figures had dropped to 62 percent and 56 percent, respectively. In 1992 it was 57 and 56 percent (NES). This failure of socialization is one of the causes of the current "partisan dealignment." The decrease in successful transmission is a function of an increasing conflict between parental partisanship and the issue preferences of the offspring. When these predispositions complement each other, transmission is successful. But when cross-pressures exist (e.g., parents are liberal Democrats but the offspring is anti-abortion, anti-affirmative action, opposed to gay rights), the response on the part of the younger generation is political independence (Carmines et al. 1987; Luskin et al. 1989).

Even with current declines, party identification is still passed on from parent to child with much more success than other political orientations. The best explanation seems to be that most political questions are remote from the day-to-day concerns of the family. Few parents hold their political opinions strongly, and few children have an accurate perception of those opinions. In this regard, party identification is unique. It is one attitude that is normally of some consequence to parents and highly visible to children. At election time, young children will often ask if "we" are Democrats or Republicans. Tedin (1974) demonstrated that while 72 percent of a sample of high school seniors were aware of parental party identification, no more than 36 percent were aware of parent attitudes on any one issue. But when issue attitudes were about as salient and well-perceived as partisanship, parent-child correspondence on those issue was about the same as for partisanship. A variation in this point is illustrated by Beck and Jennings (1991). They found that high school seniors first interviewed in 1965 who came from politicized homes were much more likely to share their parents' 1965 partisanship 17 years later, in 1982, than were students from nonpoliticized homes. Thus parents seem to have the potential to exert more influence on issue attitudes than they often do. Perhaps in an era like the Depression of the 1930s, when politics were polarized and certain issues were seen by many as being highly important, parents would use considerably more of their available resources to politically socialize the young.

The Peer Group

Like parents, the peer group enjoys considerable opportunity to influence attitudes and behavior. There are strong affective ties involved, and young people normally spend a substantial part of their time with friends. Parents and peers differ, however, at the point in the preadult's life when influence is greatest. Parents dominate the lives of their offspring until adolescence, then peers become increasingly important (Beck 1977). Despite the considerable attention paid to peer groups in the United States, there is relatively little research and (perhaps as a logical consequence) little agreement on the role of peers as an agent of political socialization. Some scholars argue that peer groups are the most important of all adolescent socialization agencies, while others assert that the influence of peers is largely redundant.[5] Peers are seen as simply reinforcing the lessons learned in the family and school. It is clear, however, that adolescent peers can be influential in areas involving the individual's status in the group. But these areas usually involve matters of taste in music, clothing, and hairstyles, rather than politics. In the Jennings-Niemi national study of parents and students, a subset of the students were asked to indicate their best friend of the same sex, who was then included in the sample. As expected, for party identification the correlation between students and parents greatly exceeded that between students and peers. On the other hand, in the case of changing the voting age from 21 to 18 (one had to be 21 to vote at the time of the survey), the student-peer correlation exceeded the student-parent correlation.[6] This is the pattern one would expect. Partisanship is learned during early childhood and is not a particularly "youth-oriented" issue. On the other hand, preadults were more likely to become aware of the 18-year-old vote issue during adolescence, and the issue is particularly relevant to high school seniors. We would, therefore, expect more peer influence in the latter instance. In situations in which parents and peers disagree on partisanship, the student is more likely to follow the parent. But when parent and peer disagree on the 18-year-old vote, the student is more likely to follow his or her best friend (Sebert et al. 1974). Thus peer-versus-parent influence seems to be issue-specific.

It is difficult to make any absolute assessment of peer influence, but it seems certain that even in adolescence, peers are not as important as parents. When politics are remote from one's day-to-day concerns, and when family social harmony as well as one's status in the peer group are only slightly affected by politics, parents probably have an advantage over peers in the socialization process. We have noted that one important precondition for influence is communication. Politics are more important to the 35-to-50-year-old group (the common age of parents with adolescent children) than to those under the age of 21 (Milbrath and Goel 1977, 114–16). If one assumes all other things are equal, adolescents are more likely to be aware of and receptive to parent attitudes simply because most contemporary political issues are more important to parents (Tedin 1980). But there are exceptions, like the 18-year-old vote in 1965. And there are certain to be others at other times, depending on the political climate.

The Primary and Secondary School

Many political theorists, practical politicians, political reformers, and political revolutionaries believe or have believed that the school is an instrumental agent in the political training of the young. Examples abound. After the 1917 Russian revolution, children were removed from the family (presumably still attached to the old order and unsympathetic to Communist values) and required to spend long periods of time in school for political retraining. The Allied Powers followed a similar policy after the defeat of the Nazis in World War II. The schools were "de-Nazified," and German youths were instructed in the principles of democratic government as defined by the West. The same beliefs are reflected in the fierce debate over a multicultural curriculum in American schools. The school is seen as the appropriate vehicle for instructing students in the values necessary for life in a multi-ethnic society.[7]

It is a popular assumption that some nations spend an inordinate amount of time politically "indoctrinating" their young. Usually singled out are Communist nations, most notably the Soviet Union prior to Gorbachev. One study showed, however, that in the 1960s American schools expended even more time on "political education" than did those in the USSR (Bereday and Stretch 1963). Regardless, it is important to understand that virtually all nations require the schools to devote considerable attention to building support for the political order and teaching obedience to political authority. This practice is certainly widespread, and from the standpoint of maintaining political stability and continuity, it is a necessity. One need only observe the difficulties encountered by nations in which primary loyalties do not reside with the national government. For example, in many nations ethnic loyalty comes before national loyalty. Political stability is highly dependent upon the ability of the agents of socialization to produce in children feelings as to the rightness, the oughtness, the legitimacy of the political order. In virtually all nations this task is assigned to the schools. They are the one agent of political socialization over which the government has considerable control.

There can be little doubt, as we noted in the section on childhood political development, that preadults in the United States generally learn the lessons of patriotism and obedience. What is not clear is the relative role of the family and school in teaching these orientations. In one major study of the public schools, Robert Hess and Judith Torney conclude that "[c]ompliance to roles and authority is the major focus of education in elementary schools (1967, 126). Most readers are undoubtedly aware of the patriotic rituals that characterize most classrooms—voluminous pictures of American heroes, the display of the American flag and proclaiming one's allegiance, singing of patriotic songs, "young citizen's leagues," and the emphasis on obedience to authority.

However, students of political education agree that teaching loyalty and obedience is only one aspect of political education. There are other goals as well, such as teaching political knowledge, political participation skills, and, particularly, the acceptance and support of democratic values. On these goals there is a consensus that education in the public schools does not fare well. For example, a Gallup survey showed that 61 percent of high school seniors said they were "not very" or "not at all" interested in politics.[8] In 1988, less than two-thirds of twelfth-graders were aware that it is legal to participate in a boycott, organize a recall election, or impeach legislators (Anderson et al. 1990). In terms of sophisticated political thinking, 50 percent of a sample of high school juniors thought the assertion, "The American form of government may not be perfect, but it's the best type of government yet devised by man" was a factual statement (as opposed to being a value statement). Levels of factual knowledge tend to be quite low. Anderson et al. (1990) report that only 61 percent of high school seniors recognized (in 1988) that having more than one political party was a fundamental difference between the U.S. and the USSR; only 58 percent knew the U.S. has a two-party system, and just 50 percent knew that the governor is a member of the executive branch.

Finally, support for democratic values tends to be low. One study of seniors found that 60 percent favored allowing the police and other groups to censor books and movies (Remmers and Franklin 1963, 62), and another reported that only 36 percent were in favor of allowing a legally elected Communist to assume office (Jennings and Niemi 1974, 65). Anderson et al. (1990) report that only 51 percent of high school seniors knew that the right to religious freedom is part of the Bill of Rights, and only 47 percent knew there is a constitutional ban on double jeopardy.

The thrust of the empirical research seems to indicate that schools have little if any effect on teaching of the democratic creed or political values in general. Variations among teachers seem to have little impact on students' political learning (Jennings et al. 1974, 210). Langton and Jennings (1968) showed that whether or not students had taken any civics courses was largely irrelevant to their levels of political knowledge, political interest, interest in political media, political discussion, political efficacy, civil tolerance, political trust, and participatory orientation. In a comprehensive examination of the effect of the curriculum, Jennings et al. (1974, 205) concluded, "[o]ur findings certainly do not support the thinking of those who look to the civics curriculum in American schools as a major source of political socialization. When we investigated the student sample as a whole we found not one case out of the ten examined in which the civics curriculum was significantly associated with students' political orientations." This finding was reconfirmed in 1988 by Anderson et al. (1990, 75), who found that the number of civics courses taken by high school seniors was unrelated to their average civics proficiency.[9]

But while few studies show any causal relationship between what is taught in the school and political orientations (Merelman 1980, 319–20), it is clear that education does predict support for democratic values—and not just when one contrasts the college-educated population to those without college. For example, the 1993 GSS shows that while only 40 percent of those with a grade-school education support free speech for an atheist, 68 percent of those with a high school education are supportive. Forty-one percent of those with a grade-school education would allow a homosexual to teach in a college, but 67 percent of those with a high school degree would be willing. Numerous other examples could be offered. It may be that a high school education simply "slots" people into social, economic, and political positions in which they have a greater opportunity to learn democratic norms. Or it could be that the school does have an impact, but we simply have not come up with the appropriate research designs to measure it.

College: Higher Education and Its Impact

Although most students are legally adults when they enter college, the college experience is for many a transition period between life with the family and being truly on one's own. Today almost one of every two high school graduates goes to college. At the turn of the century, most young people did not even graduate from high school, let alone contemplate attaining a college degree. Consequently, the proportion of the adult population with college experience has been rising steadily. For example, over the short span of time from 1950 to 1990, the proportion of adults with at least some college rose from 16 percent to 45 percent; the proportion with actual college degrees rose from 8 percent to 20 percent (1990 U.S. Census). The trend will undoubtedly accelerate, as a lagged result of the post–World War II educational boom. What are the political implications of the growth of the college-educated public? College generally has a liberalizing effect on noneconomic political opinions. Evidence in support of this view can be found in studies going back to the 1920s. College seniors are consistently found to be less conservative than entering freshmen.[10] An example taken from the mid-1970s is presented in Table 5.4. The obvious in-

TABLE 5.4 Ideological Self-Placement of College Students by Year in School

	Liberal	Moderate	Conservative	Don't Know
Freshmen	30%	44%	24%	2%
Sophomores	40	38	20	2
Juniors	41	29	22	2
Seniors	40	24	20	3
All Students	35	36	22	2

Source: The Gallup Opinion Index, Sept. 1975, 19.

ference is that students track to the left as they move through the years in college.

Three explanations are commonly advanced for these gains in liberalism: increased awareness, enlightenment, and indoctrination. None of these standing alone is entirely convincing. The *awareness* explanation is predicated on the fact that two of the stronger correlates of education are political knowledge and use of the media. Being informed about innovations and current events is directly related to education. One scholar advances the hypothesis that "thanks largely to wider personal contacts and greater exposure to the media of opinion, the better educated are the first to sense changes in the climate of opinion and quickly respond to new fashions in social thought" (Stembler 1961, 172). For example, in a study of support for the civil rights of women and blacks, one investigator found a large increase in support for women's rights occurring among the educated shortly after the media began devoting considerable attention to the issue. However, no parallel increase was found in support for black civil rights (which received no attention out of the ordinary), indicating that increased liberalism on women's issues was due to an awareness factor (Schreiber 1978). Currently, we see this pattern for "black" as opposed to "African-American" in terms of the preferred identifier for members of this racial group. Among blacks in the mass public, the college-educated are most likely to prefer "African-American." And the media (much influenced by the college-educated) have moved steadily to favor the newer label (Smith 1992). Since conservatism has an important status quo component and liberalism has an important change component, a critic might argue that the *awareness* explanation is confusing becoming liberal with simply becoming trendy.

A second argument asserts that education leads to "enlightenment," which in turn leads to liberalism. According to William Stephens and C. Stephen Long (1970, 17):

> Students learn in school. They become more sophisticated, knowledgeable, broadened, attuned to the world outside, and this is why they become more liberal and more politically aware. . . . Education promotes en-

lightenment; enlightenment promotes liberalism, political interest and participation.

This somewhat gratuitous statement presumes that with education the scales fall from one's eyes, enlightenment occurs, and the virtues of the more liberal political options become apparent. However, as we shall demonstrate in Chapter 7, education is not always a correlate of liberalism. On economic issues, the better educated tend to be more conservative. But it is probably true that as education increases, so does one's ability to think analytically and critically. The consequence is likely to be a rejection of stereotypes and prejudice, an increased tolerance of diverse lifestyles, and an increased liberalism across a variety of social issues.

A third explanation holds that the "liberal" college faculty *indoctrinates* students in the direction of their own political views. As Table 5.5 shows, college faculty members are decidedly more liberal than their students. Moreover, this table underestimates the liberalism of the relevant American professorate. Those disciplines that directly deal with government, society, and the human condition have the most liberal faculty. A 1989 Carnegie Commission survey (Boyer and Whitelaw 1989) showed that 70 percent of the social science faculty considered themselves liberals (compared, for example, to 41 percent among engineers), while only 15 percent labeled themselves conservative. When asked, students report that the college experience has a considerable influence on their values, and certainly the faculty makes an important contribution to the college experience.[11]

But the indoctrination explanation probably underestimates the ability of students to make independent judgments. As students become better educated, they become more adept at critical thought and conse-

TABLE 5.5 Political Orientations of College Students and Faculty, 1976–1989

Year	Liberal	Middle of Road	Conservative	
Students				
1976	38%	39%	23%	100%
1984	25	39	26	100%
1989		No survey conducted		
Faculty				
1976	44%	28%	28%	100%
1984	42	27	31	100%
1989	57	16	27	100%

Source: Ernest L. Boyer and Mary Jean Whitelaw, *The Condition of the Professoriate: Attitudes and Trends,* 1989 (New York: Harper and Row, 1989).

quently should be more resistant to indoctrination. When asked about changes in their political opinions, the most frequent reason students give is an "increased thinking about political questions."[12] Further, the degree of leftward movement among students varies across historical eras. Kesler (1979) demonstrates that students reported moving significantly to the left in 1969–70 (the height of anti-Vietnam War movement), but much less so in surveys done in 1961–63 and 1977–78. These historical effects cannot be explained by changed attitudes among faculty.

There is some evidence that the current crop of college students is more conservative than those of 10 or 15 years ago. Table 5.5 shows the political ideology of a representative sample of undergraduates and faculty in 1976 and 1984. Note there was a considerable move to the right on the part of students between 1976 and 1984. This move has not been matched by the faculty, who remained about as liberal in 1984 as they were in 1976. It seems clear that, at least in part, students were being socialized in a conservative direction by forces outside the university. While there was no change among the faculty between 1976 and 1984, observe that the faculty moved to the left between 1984 and 1989 (unfortunately, no comparable student survey was conducted in 1989).

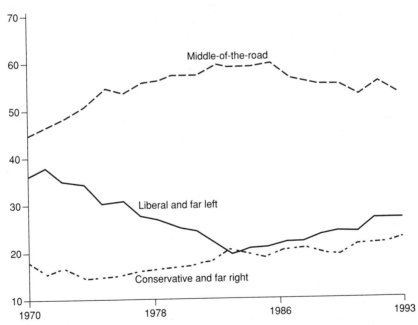

Fig 5-1. Ideological self-identification of college freshmen, 1970–1993. Source: Alexander W. Astin, *The American National Norms for 1991* (Los Angeles: University of California Press, 1991) 1993 data reported in *The Chronicle of Higher Education*, 26 January 1994, A31.

One explanation for the student data is that incoming freshmen are more conservative in the 1980s and 1990s than they were earlier. We see evidence of this in the American Council of Education's survey of college freshmen, reported in Figure 5-1.

Incoming freshmen were slightly more conservative in both 1985 (20 percent) and 1993 (24 percent) than in 1970 (18 percent). But the big movement among freshmen was a drift away from self-proclaimed liberalism toward being middle-of-the-road. In 1970, 38 percent called themselves liberals; in 1985 this dropped to only 21 percent, but recovered to 27 percent in 1993. The big surge in student preferences was for "middle-of-the-road" (up from 46 percent in 1970 to 58 percent in 1985 and 50 percent in 1993).

Most observers would agree that college has an impact on student political views. There are substantial differences between young people (18–22) in college and young people who do not attend college, as can be seen from data in two different periods presented in Table 5.6. However, not all these differences can be laid at the feet of the college experience. We know from panel studies (where respondents are reinterviewed over time) that many of the differences we see between those who choose to go to college and those who do not *already* exist before the individual ever sets foot on campus. In 1965, a national sample of high school seniors were interviewed and then reinterviewed in 1973. With this panel design, it is possible to compare those who went to college with those who did not, and to analyze the differences between

TABLE 5.6 Opinions of Youth Attending College and Opinions of Youth Not Attending College

Opinion	College	Noncollege
There is too much concern with equality and too little with law and order*	17%	42%
Patriotism is very important*	35	60
There should be more respect for authority*	59	86
Religion is very important*	38	64
Abortion should be allowed if pregnant woman does not want to marry child's father**	51	38
Would allow a Communist to speak in local community**	82	59
Federal government has too much power**	34	52
Would vote for a black for president**	92	83
Liberal in politics**	42	28

*1970 Gallup Poll reported in Robert Chandler, Public Opinion (New York: Bowker, 1972), 6–13.
**1988–1991 pooled GSS (18–22 year-olds, whites only).

these two groups in 1965, when they were still in high school. The data show both an effect for preadult socialization and an effect for education. In some instances the opinion differences between those college-bound and those not were already apparent when the respondents were seniors in high school. On questions of civic tolerance, the college-bound were already more liberal than their noncollege age cohorts. But by 1973 these differences had increased even further. Thus, there seems to be both a self-selection factor at work as well an impact of higher education. On the other hand, there was little difference in 1965 on questions of prayer in the public schools and support for racial integration. By 1973, however, there were substantial differences between those with a college degree and those who had not been to college, leading to an inference that college had caused opinion change in a liberal direction (Jennings and Niemi 1982, 257–60).

5-3 Political Generations _____

When we speak of "political generations," we are talking about a group of people who have been socialized by the same historical events during their formative years. Of course, "the sixties generation" is the best-known recent incarnation of the idea that certain age groups hold opinions that sharply distinguish them from others. Another frequently discussed age group is "the Depression generation," those persons who were in their impressionable years during the Great Depression of the 1930s. Currently there is much commentary on the politics of "the baby boom generation," those people born between the end of World War II and 1964. When one speaks of a "generation gap," the common understanding is that the young and old differ in their political outlooks. There are, in fact, many nontrivial differences of opinion between persons of varying ages (see Chapter 7, Table 7.7 for examples). Two explanations receive the bulk of the attention: life-cycle effects and generational effects. The unit of analysis for these discussions is the "age cohort," which is persons who fall into the same age group at a particular point in time.

A *life-cycle effect* exists when people's political views are influenced by maturation. As a reference point, assume each new political generation enters political life with identical political attitudes. Then, any difference across generations would be due to aging. When we find, as we often do, that the young are more liberal than their elders, these age differences would be explained by life-cycle effects. The implication is that the young, having few responsibilities, can afford to be idealistic. As they age, however, they take on the responsibility of raising a family, paying a mortgage, and holding down a full-time job. The effect is nicely captured in a comment about partisan politics by Winston Churchill: "Those at 18 who are not socialist have no heart; those at 40 who are still socialist have no head." In addition, it is often noted that learning continues throughout life, but reevaluation seems more frequent early in life than later (Dawson et al., 73–92). Certain predispositions become reinforced over time, as people are more likely to expose themselves selectively to political stimuli with which they agree than to those with which they disagree. The life-cycle concept assumes a process that is similar for all age groups over time. It has been asserted, for example, that as one gets older, political parties of the right become more attractive. This assertion (which we shall investigate shortly) posits an independent effect of aging on partisan predispositions.

A *generational effect* exists when a specific age cohort is uniquely socialized by a set of historical events. The logic of generational analysis dictates an interaction between age and experience. The usual assumption is that certain events in history make an indelible imprint upon the young (defined approximately as the 17-to-26-year-old cohort). It is argued that a generation's singular personality is shaped when its members leave the family and step out into the world on their own. Those that are younger remain shielded to a certain extent from the trauma of external events by the family. Those who are older are better equipped to resist its influence by their previous life experiences. For a distinct political generation to exist, something of historical consequence must have happened during their "impressionable years" (about ages 17 to 26).[13] It is difficult to imagine anything occurring in the 1950s that would have distinctively stamped a generational cohort. On the other hand, one can easily conceive of the Vietnam War era (1965–1972) or the Great Depression of the 1930s as defining unique generations.

To complicate matters further, strong political shocks can affect young and old alike, such as when the Cold War ended, all age groups relaxed their interest in further defense spending. Such general shocks are usually called "period effects."

Generations and Party Identification

Much of the research on generational politics has concerned change in party identification. Generational effects are most important in the *direction* of party identification (Republican, Independent, Democrat), but variation in the *strength* of partisanship (strong partisan, weak partisan, Independent) responds more to life-cycle effects.

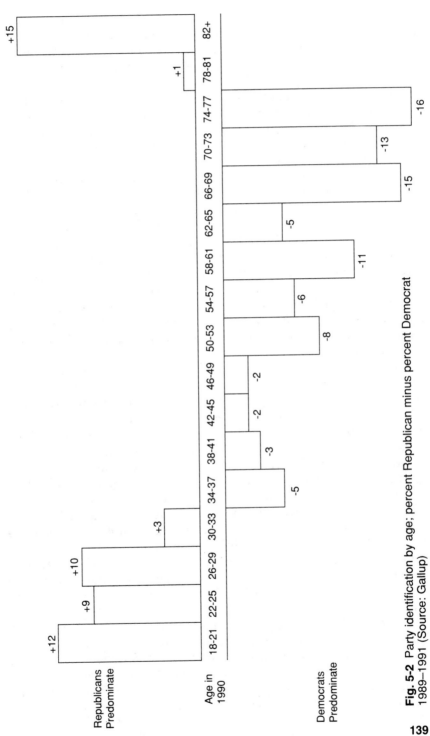

Fig. 5-2 Party identification by age; percent Republican minus percent Democrat 1989–1991 (Source: Gallup)

Partisanship is often imprinted on a political generation by historical events. We can see examples in Figure 5-2, which simply displays the relationship between age and the direction of party identification from an accumulation of Gallup Polls between October 1989 and March 1991 (N=12,600).[14]

Note, for example, that voters in their impressionable years during the 1930s Depression are now the most Democratic age cohort in the electorate. But note also the partisanship of those in their impressionable years during the boom years of the 1920s, when Republicans were ascendant. These citizens, in their eighties in 1990, were the most Republican age cohort. The difference in partisanship between those age 74 to 77 in 1990, and those over 82, illustrates the profound effect of being socialized in the "Roaring Twenties" vs. the "Great Depression." Finally, the young are more Republican than their elders (save those over 80), having been socialized under the beleaguered President Carter or the optimistic years of the early Reagan administration. However, as Democratic fortunes have improved, the young, being highly impressionable, have become increasingly less Republican. Thus, among 18-to-21-year-olds in 1985, the Republicans held a 10-point advantage; among those 18 to 21 years old in 1991–1992, the advantage had dropped to 6 points, and in 1993 it was only 3 points.[15]

Although not depicted in Figure 5-2, the 1960s generation (socialized between 1965 and 1973) also uniquely responded to the events of the time. If we look at a very special subcohort, those college graduates who protested the Vietnam War, and compare them to college graduates who did not protest, we find a strong, persistent generational impact. Jennings (1987) has made this analysis using a subset of the Jennings-Niemi parent-child panel. The panel contained 129 college graduates who had protested the war and a matching sample of college graduates (about twice as many) who had not been war protesters. These two groups differed little when they were in high school. Protesters "to be" were 39 percent Democratic; nonprotesters were 38 percent Democratic. By 1973, the two groups had shifted in opposite directions, with the protesters 48 percent Democratic and the nonprotesters 27 percent. By 1982 these percentages had changed little. The antiwar movement had clearly left its partisan mark on those who were actively involved.

But not all age differences in partisan direction are generational. Some scholars see a life-cycle effect: a tendency for the electorate to become more Republican as it ages (Abramson 1983, 124; Delli Carpini 1986, 208–11; Knoke and Hout 1974, 700–13). For example, the parents in the socialization panel showed a slight Republican increase (39.5 percent in 1965 to 43.3 percent in 1973), although no Republican increase was evident among their children, who were then entering adulthood. Thus there is some support for the contention made by the authors of *The American Voter* that Republicanism, because of its "air of respectability, conservatism, and social status," may have an increasing appeal to people as they mature (Campbell et al. 1960).

Life-cycle effects are particularly operative for the *strength* of partisanship. Any survey will show that young adults have weaker partisan attachments than their elders. For example, the 1992 NES data showed 41 percent of those over 55 claiming to be "strong" partisans, compared to only 17 percent under 30. Similarly, only 29 percent of those over 55 were Independents, compared to 48 percent of those under 30. With figures such as these, one might forecast a general decline in partisanship as older cohorts with firm partisanship exit the electorate and get replaced by younger cohorts with weaker partisan attachments. But this does not happen—at least under equilibrium conditions—since each new generation acquires stronger partisan attachments as it ages. Under equilibrium conditions, the electorate's net partisan strength is stable, with each age cohort showing the same strength of partisanship as previous cohorts at the same point in the life-cycle. This picture of equilibrium fits the data for an earlier period, from at least 1952 (and perhaps earlier) to about 1965 (Converse 1976; Cassel 1993).

However, the development of partisan intensity is strongly susceptible to the shock of historical events that defines political generations. Earlier we saw the directional change in party identification among war protesters. For most youth of the late sixties, the partisan impact of the Vietnam years was a profound drop in the strength of partisanship. Those cohorts in their impressionable years after 1965 have been much more likely to call themselves Independents and much less likely to show increases in the strength of their partisan attachments over time. Thirty-six percent of the younger generation in the Jennings-Niemi socialization study were Independent in 1965, rising to 48 percent in 1973 and then declining to 43 percent in 1982. Even with the decline, this generation stands out in its unwillingness to adopt a party preference (Jennings and Markus 1984, Table 2).

In the case of the socialization panel (with the same persons being interviewed in 1965, 1973, and 1982), the number of Independents among the 1965 high school seniors had actually increased by 1973. But between 1973 and 1982 there was a fairly substantial move away from Independence toward partisanship. The increase in partisanship was found mainly among those who voted. Those who did not vote tended to remain Independents. Thus one aspect of age that may lead to the acquisition of partisanship is simple learning based on experience. Even though the 1965 seniors seem to have increased their partisanship, they also seem, due to generational effects, unlikely to reach the level of partisan intensity of their parents (Jennings and Markus 1984).

Generations and Issues

Is there evidence of a generational effect on issue positions? Delli Carpini made an intensive study of the 1960s generation and isolated a number of instances in which this generation differed from surrounding age cohorts. What we would expect among this generation, of course, is a leftist bent to their political ideology. For the most part, Delli Carpini finds that the generation of the 1960s was more supportive than other cohorts of government involvement in the issues of race, civil liberties, economics, and social concerns. But the differences were not large, and as the generation has aged, its distinctiveness has begun to erode. There is a pull toward the political center that is exerted by society as one moves through the life-cycle (Delli Carpini 1986, 120–38).

If lasting effects of the sixties generation are to be located, they would most likely be found among the subcohort of sixties antiwar activists. A failure to find generational effects would be a severe setback for the generational thesis. An analysis was performed by Jennings (1987) using the sample of college graduates who protested the war and the matching sample of college graduates who were not protesters. An advantage of the panel approach is one can look back to high school and see if the differences are explained by self-selection. On many issues there were substantial generational effects. In 1965, while in high school, the protesters (to be) were 8 percent less favorable to prayer in the public schools than the nonprotesters, but 17 years later they were 30 percent less favorable than the nonprotesters. The protesters were 13 percent more supportive of a federal role in school integration in 1965, but 43 percent more supportive in 1982. But on many other issue orientations, the once very liberal protesters began to move in a conservative direction. While 83 percent of the protesters considered themselves "liberals" in 1973, only 63 percent did so in 1982. Declines of at least 20 percent also occurred on questions of government responsibility for providing jobs, legalization of marijuana, rights of accused, helping minorities, and equality for women. The protesters were still considerably more liberal than the nonprotesters in 1982, but they had lost at least some of their distinctiveness.

By 1982, the protesters' attitudes had been shaped by both generational and life-cycle effects. Their experience as antiwar protesters stamped them with an indelible liberal print, while life-cycle effects pushed them back in a conservative direction. Furthermore, their liberalism has been eroded by exposure to the conservative ethos of the

1980s. Opinion change resulting from this exposure is an example of a "period effect," a concept we will explore directly.

Period Effects on Political Attitudes

The events that shape those in their impressionable years can also affect older citizens as well. When historical events influence all age groups, the result is known as a "period" effect. To some extent, all citizens are influenced by the periods of time through which they live. One specific example of a period effect was the impact of Vietnam and Watergate on political trust, as trust in government decreased among all age groups.

While the magnitude of an event's impact may be diminished for citizens beyond the formative years of young adulthood, these older citizens add the force of numbers to their response. The notion of period effects also serves as a reminder that political socialization through adulthood is more than a gradually increasing conservatism of outlook or a hardening of political partisanship.

Generations and Political Realignment

The responses of new generations of young voters are particularly relevant to the understanding of partisan realignments. The U.S. has periodically undergone a partisan realignment. During realignments, the pace of partisan change quickens, with unusual numbers of voters changing their partisanship in response to new issues and events. The most recent realignment occurred during the 1930s, in response to the Depression and New Deal, and featured dramatic gains for the Democratic Party. Since the 1960s, pundits have occasionally forecast the next realignment to be around the corner. Such forecasts became quite frequent in the early 1980s, when observers commonly expected that a Republican realignment was imminent.

There is reason to believe that when a new realignment arrives, the vanguard will be young voters. Young voters lack strong partisan attachments, so they are particularly susceptible to political trends. (Note in Figure 5-2 their reaction to the Carter and early Reagan years.) Moreover, young voters who have come of political age since the mid-1960s have shown an unusual degree of partisan independence. Many of these "young" Independents now face middle age. Perhaps they are still waiting for the right political party or movement to represent them.

The idea that young voters lead realignments is labeled the "mobilization" theory of realignment, because it involves the mobilization of new voters. However, period effects could also create realignments, with both new voters and old voters showing equal rates of partisan conversion. If events are strong enough to cause a realignment, they may be strong enough to convert both old and young from one party to another. This view is known as the "conversion" theory.[16]

Will young voters lead the next realignment? Predictions based on the 1930s realignment are difficult, because that realignment happened just as public opinion polling began. We saw, however, that the Depression cohort, who began voting in the 1930s, even today leads other age groups in allegiance to the Democratic Party. But young voters in the 1930s were not numerous enough to account for a massive realignment by themselves. Examining early Gallup Polls and *Literary Digest* Polls (see Chapter 2), Erikson and Tedin (1981) found evidence of considerable voter conversion during the realignment era. Realignments, it seems, are events of such force that even older generations of voters find the pressures difficult to resist.

5-4 The Persistence of Political Orientations _____

At the outset of this chapter, we noted that a key assumption justifying the study of political socialization is that orientations formed early persist over time. There is a good deal of evidence that many important political predispositions do endure over a considerable time span. There is also a good deal of evidence that people continue to learn and adjust their political perspective in response to their adult environment and the events in their lives.

It is important to understand that when we speak of persistence, what mostly persists are core values and predispositions rather than specific opinions on issues of the day. Thus overarching values, such as partisanship, liberal-conservative orientation, or racial attitudes, tend to persist, while trust in government or attitudes about defense spending tend to be more fleeting. Regarding persistence, two major points merit elaboration. First, political attitudes are very malleable through "the impressionable years." The basics of political socialization are not completed by the end of grade school, as some argue (Hess and Torney 1967). Second, after the impressionable years, political orientations harden considerably. Change still occurs, but stability markedly increases.

It is the persistence of early childhood orientations that are most questionable. One can ask if children below the eighth grade really have meaningful political attitudes at all. Vaillancourt (1973) found the responses of these children to questions about the idealization of government authority were highly unstable, suggesting attitudes were weak or nonexistent. Kolson and Green (1970) demonstrated that young children were very prone to response acquiescence. In addition, the grade-school children that so idealized government in the late 1950s and early 1960s became cynical and disillusioned in the 1970s as a result of the Vietnam War and Watergate, indicating that early childhood socialization had little staying power. While Greenstein (1965) found that 60 percent of his fourth-grade sample identified as Republicans or Democrats, Jennings and Niemi (1982) demonstrated that partisanship was highly malleable into early adulthood.

There is considerable evidence that much political learning takes place during the impressionable years, and once those years have passed, the stability of core political values increases greatly. Perhaps the most dramatic example of persistence is the Bennington study originated by Theodore Newcomb. Young women (16-to-20-year-olds), mostly from conservative homes, matriculated at Bennington College, which in the 1930s had an avowedly liberal faculty. Students were first interviewed between 1935 and 1938, then reinterviewed in 1960, and again in 1984. The data thus stretch over almost fifty years. Among the key findings were that the Bennington experience moved the students considerably to the left during their impressionable years. Using a number of items to create a scale of "liberal-conservative" political orientations and a panel design, Alwin et al. (1991) found a high level of persistence over a fifty-year period. The authors concluded that 60 percent of the variance in 1984 political predispositions could be predicted from the predispositions in the 1930s when the students were attending Bennington, whereas the remaining 40 percent reflected attitude change (Alwin et al. 1991, 265). The shorter Jennings-Niemi three-wave panel demonstrates a similar point. The attitudes of the student cohort were more susceptible to change between 1965 (when the students were 18) and 1973 (when they were 26), than between 1973 and 1982 (when they were 35). Thus the correlation between student partisanship in 1965 and their partisanship in 1973 is .40, but is .57 between 1973 and 1982. The correlation between civic tolerance in 1965 and 1973 is .34, but is .52 between 1973 and 1982 (Jennings and Markus 1984).[17] Once the filial generation had passed through their impressionable years, their attitudes stabilized. The cohort data presented in Figure 5-2 makes the same point using a different methodology. Those respondents in adolescence and early adulthood during the "Roaring Twenties" (before the Great Depression) are markedly different in partisanship from those who spent their impressionable years during the Great Depression—despite the fact that more than fifty years had passed since they were adolescents and young adults. Much more evidence can be marshaled to support the general proposition of openness and change during the impressionable years, followed by a stabilizing and persistence of core political attitudes (see Sears 1991 for a review).

5-5 Conclusion _____

In this chapter we focused mainly on the preadult sources of political learning. Some political learning takes place in childhood, although "the impressionable years" seem to be the most important. While attitudes crystallize in later adulthood, political learning still takes place as individuals respond to their environment and life events. Even partisanship, the most stable of political predispositions, responds in adulthood to issues and political personalities (Markus 1979; Fiorina 1981; MacKuen et al. 1989). But generally speaking, political change in adulthood is incremental. It is the impressionable years that offer the greatest potential for a radical break with the past.

Notes _____

1. To make this a fair test so there would not be possible overlap, we looked at the levels of trust in government among those between 28 and 34, and compared them to those between 18 and 24 and those between 42 and 50. A one-way analysis of variance revealed no difference. The trust items used are those reported in Chapter 6, Figure 6-1.
2. Many of the studies are reviewed in Hyman (1959).
3. Another explanation for low relationships is measurement error. Dalton (1980) corrects for measurement error and finds a substantial increase in parent-adolescent relationships using the Jennings-Niemi data.
4. Following the conventional wisdom, the evidence indicates that when wives and husbands disagree on party preference, wives are more likely to change in the direction of the party preference of their husbands. However, most data on this issue are taken from the 1960s and 1970s (Weiner 1978).
5. The former point is made by Harvey (1972, 601); the latter point is made by Silbiger (1977, 174).
6. For party identification, the student-parent correlation was .66; the student-peer correlation was .26. For the 18-year-old vote, the student-parent correlation was .08 and the student-peer correlation was .29.
7. Recently, the New York public schools attempted to mandate, beginning in the first grade, a set of curricular materials requiring that "classes should include references to lesbians and gays in all curricular areas." School Chancellor Joseph Fernandez told the *New York Times* that "our schools are the single most important front in the battle against discrimination." District 24 refused to implement the curriculum. Chancellor Fernandez suspended the board and assumed its powers. Fernandez himself was shortly dismissed, and the gay and lesbian parts of the curriculum were moved forward to the sixth grade (Wolf 1993).
8. "Gallup Survey: Six of Ten Teenagers Show Little Interest in Politics, Politicians," *Houston Post* 19 Oct. 1977.

9. The only effect was for those who had taken no civics courses in high school, as opposed to those who had taken less than one-half year or more. There was no difference among those who had taken less than one-half year, one-half year, between one-half and one year, one year, and more than one year.

10. See the summary of the extensive literature on this point in Feldman and Newcomb (1969); even a research project sponsored by William F. Buckley's journal, *The National Review,* came to the conclusion that "[a]ttending college still makes it more likely that a student's thinking will be deflected leftward"; see Kesler (1979). For a view challenging the notion that education leads to liberalism, see Jacob (1956).

11. A 1969 poll for CBS News asked students: "Which of the following events, if any, have had a great effect on your life and values, which have had a moderate effect, and which have had little or no effect?" Sixty-six percent of the college students said the "college experience" had a "great effect." This was the highest percentage of nine possible options (Kesler 1969).

12. On the question of the influence of college on political attitudes, 42 percent attributed their change in attitudes to either "lectures or course readings" or "personal contact with faculty" (Kesler 1979, 1488).

13. There is no agreement about exactly what ages constitute the impressionable years, other than that they extend from adolescence through to early adulthood.

14. These data were kindly provided to us by Professor Everett Carl Ladd of the University of Connecticut and the Roper Center.

15. Gallup surveys reported in *The Public Perspective,* September/October 1993, p. 12.

16. The best statement of the mobilization theory is found in Andersen (1979); an argument for the conversion hypothesis is found in Erikson and Tedin (1981); for a critique, see Campbell (1985); see Erikson and Tedin (1986) for a response. For a somewhat different approach to generations and changes in party identification, see Beck (1974).

17. It is important to distinguish here between absolute continuity and relative continuity. By absolute continuity, we mean those who were strong liberals at Time #1 are strong liberals at Time #2. By relative continuity, we mean those who were the most liberal at Time #1 are the most liberal at Time #2, but they may not have maintained their exact position on the scale. Correlation coefficients measure relative continuity, so what we are talking about in this section is the tendency, over time, for the most liberal respondents at Time #1 to be the most liberal at Time #2, not that they maintain the exact position on issues between time points. It would be unreasonable, for example, to think that, in the Bennington study, respondents would maintain the same issue positions over a fifty-year period.

CHAPTER 6

Public Opinion and Democratic Stability

In a democracy, public opinion is important because it can influence the decisions that political leaders make. In previous chapters we have discussed the level of public opinion on questions of public policy. Certain other types of political orientations are particularly important because the extent of their existence may influence the functioning of democratic government. In this chapter we shall analyze attitudes and predispositions considered by many as necessary to maintain a democracy, as well as examine the degrees to which Americans appear to hold these attitudes.

Ideas about what is vital for the functioning of democratic government can be divided into four groups. First, there should be widespread support for the rules of democracy. An apt analogy here is the rules of the road for driving an automobile. If most people did not accept the rule that one must stop when the light is red, chaos would ensue. The rules of democracy involve guarantees that the civil liberties of all shall be protected—that majorities rule, but minorities have rights.

Second, democracy's stability may rest on a social consensus regarding values and goals. Disagreements must not be so fundamental that neither resolution nor compromise can be gained by institutionalized procedures. Too great a division may overtax even the best procedures for resolving conflict. Contemporary examples include the Protestant-Catholic division in Northern Ireland, the Christian-Muslim division in Lebanon, the Tamil (Hindu)-Sinhalese (Buddhist) conflict in Sri Lanka, and the Serb-Croat-Muslim division in Bosnia.

Third, if people are to accept government decisions, they must believe that their political actions can be effective and that they can trust the government to respond to their interests. If political alienation becomes sufficiently intense and widespread, it may pose a threat to democratic stability.

Fourth, in coping with personal anxieties and needs, certain personality types find comfort in blaming others. Alternatively (or simultaneously), some seek a solution to their problems in a strong leader. When such personalities are common, minority rights become very fragile, and the stability of democracy can be threatened.

6-1 Support for Democratic Values _____

One of the great threats to any political system, democracies included, is the desire on the part of those who hold political power to maintain it, and to work their will free from constraints imposed by others. Ambition in political leaders is not, in and of itself, an undesirable trait. But history is strewn with examples of those in government warding off competition by the expeditious route of eliminating it. Consequently, democracies must anticipate that leaders may not suffer criticism gladly, and may not want to share or give up political power if there is a way to avoid it. One solution to this problem, developed by the framers of the American Constitution, was to build in a series of mechanisms designed to protect the rights of those outside government who aspire to political influence from those on the inside who hold political power. But constitutions can only go so far in making good on these protections. One need only witness the ineffectiveness of "constitutionalism" in a country like Lebanon. As Judge Learned Hand (1959, 144) once observed, "Liberty lies in the hearts and minds of men and women; when it dies there, no constitution, no laws, no court can save it." Some commitment to democratic values on the part of both political leaders and the public seems essential.

In using the term "democratic values," we are referring to procedural norms. These norms do not refer to the substance of legitimate political conflict, such as the desirable tradeoff between inflation and unemployment, but to the "rules of the game" in which that conflict takes place. One important set of procedural norms is found in the Bill of Rights. Here Americans are guaranteed the right to criticize government (free expression), freedom from unreasonable search and seizure, protection from self-incrimination, a speedy and public trial, free exercise of religion, and so on. Two related democratic values of great importance are majority rule and minority rights. At regular intervals the population is mobilized into opposing camps. Each camp proclaims its own virtue and criticizes the opposition. An election is then held, and the winners take control of the government. The losers remain free to rouse popular hostility toward the new leaders, in the hope of embarrassing them and ultimately replacing them in office. This procedure is normally the way decision-makers are chosen in the United States. One therefore hopes to find an understanding among the electorate that these are the methods that should be employed to select public officials.

As shown in Table 6.1, survey evidence does, in fact, demonstrate that when democratic values are stated in the abstract (e.g., "public officials should be chosen by majority vote"), there is an overwhelming positive consensus of support for them. But note that these assertions are very general, with no reference to any specific person or group.

TABLE 6.1 Support for Democratic Values Stated in the Abstract

Statement	Democratic Response	Uncertain Response	Undemocratic Response
People in the minority should be free to try to win majority support for their opinions.	89%	9%	2%
Public officials should be chosen by majority vote.	95	3	2
I believe in free speech for all, no matter what their views might be.	85	7	9
No matter what a person's political views are, he is entitled to the same legal protections as anyone else.	93	4	3

Source: John L. Sullivan, James Piereson, and George E. Marcus, *Political Tolerance and American Democracy* (Chicago: U of Chicago Press, 1982), p. 203.

These statements basically constitute an official American political ideology—the sort of lessons that are taught in a variety of both political and nonpolitical contexts by the family and the school, and reinforced by the mass media.

However, when statements about the rules of the game have a double stimulus, with references both to democratic principles and to unpopular groups, support for these rules declines.

Relevant evidence is presented in Table 6.2, in which the statements are two-pronged. Each refers to a democratic norm plus some specific group or activity. For example, in the statement "Members of the Ku Klux Klan should be banned from running for public office," individuals are asked to respond to both the norm of free elections and feelings about the Klan.

One interpretation of these data is that public support for procedural rights is less than ideal. In the case of elections and the Ku Klux Klan, 70 percent would ban a Klan member from running for public office. The pattern in Table 6.2 is clearly one of a lack of enthusiasm for the values of democracy when items refer to protests, demonstrations, or unpopular groups, such as American Communists. But, as we shall detail shortly, others argue that research on democratic values and civil liberties is plagued by question-wording artifacts that make it extremely difficult to determine the true level of support for these principles.

A Growth in Democratic Tolerance?

Table 6.3 shows the change over time in Americans' tolerance of some selected unpopular groups.

TABLE 6.2 Support for Democratic Values, By Specific Application

Statement	Democratic Response	Undecided	Undemocratic Response
[Should] people who want to overthrow the government by revolution [be] allowed to hold public meetings to express their views? (GSS 1990)	57%	5%	38%
Should a judge ever be allowed to ban the press from covering a criminal trial? (CLS 1978–79)	36	28	36
[Should] a person who believes that blacks are genetically inferior be allowed to teach in a college or university? (GSS 1993)	43	4	53
Should x-rated movies be totally banned for sale to adults? (Gallup 1985)	54	3	43
If the police suspect that drugs, guns, or other criminal evidence are hidden in someone's house, should they be allowed to enter a house without first obtaining a search warrant? (CBS 1970)	66	2	32
If a man is found innocent of a serious crime, but new evidence is uncovered, do you think he should be tried for the same crime again? (CBS 1970)	38	4	58
Forcing people to testify against themselves [prohibited by the Fifth Amendment] is (never justified/may be necessary) (CLS 1978–79)	40	26	35
If a person is suspected of a serious crime, do you think the police should be allowed to hold him in jail until they can get enough evidence to charge him? (CBS 1970)	38	3	58
If someone is suspected of treason or other serious crimes, he should not be entitled to be released on bail (Gibson 1987)	21	14	65
Members of the Ku Klux Klan should be banned for running for public office (Gibson 1987)	23	7	70
People ought to be allowed to vote even if they can't do so intelligently (McClosky 1958)	48	N/A	52
[It is]...a good idea for the government to keep a list of people who take part in demonstrations (Harris and Westin 1979)	25	26	50

Sources: John Sullivan et al. *Political Tolerance and American Democracy* (Chicago: U. of Chicago Press, 1982); CBS: Robert Chandler, *Public Opinion* (New York: Bowker, 1972); Herbert McClosky, "Consensus and Ideology in American Politics," *APSR*, 58 (June 1964); CLS: Herbert McClosky and Alida Brill, *Dimensions of Tolerance* (New York: Russell Sage Foundation, 1983); Louis Harris and Alan F. Westin, *The Dimensions of Privacy* (Stevens Point, Wis.: Sentry Insurance, 1979); James L. Gibson, *Freedom and Tolerance in the United States* (NORC: unpublished codebook).

TABLE 6.3 Public Tolerance for Advocates of Unpopular Ideas, 1954–1993

	Person Should Be Allowed to Make a Speech			Person Should Be Allowed to Teach in College			Person's Book Should Remain in the Library		
	1954	*1972*	*1993*	*1954*	*1972*	*1993*	*1954*	*1972*	*1993*
An admitted Communist	28%	52%	71%	6%	39%	91%	29%	53%	70%
Someone against churches and religion	38	65	73	12	40	54	37	60	70
Someone who favored government ownership of all the railroads and large industries	65	77	*	38	56	*	60	67	*
Someone who believes that blacks are genetically inferior	*	61**	62	*	41	45	*	62	67

*Question not asked
**GSS, 1976.

Sources: 1954 data is from Samuel Stouffer, *Communism, Conformity and Civil Liberties* (New York: Wiley, 1954); 1972 and 1993 data are the GSS.

One point attracts immediate attention. There has been a substantial increase in political tolerance between 1954 and 1993. Or at least that is one possible interpretation of Table 6.3. Note, for example, that tolerance of a Communist teaching at a college or university has grown from 6 percent in 1954 to 39 percent in 1972 to 70 percent in 1993. A simple conclusion is that the American public has become more tolerant. A common explanation for this change is that increases in exposure to social and cultural diversity lead to increases in support for democratic norms. Two changes of consequence for this explanation are rising levels of education and the move from rural to urban areas. The proportion of people who have been to college has more than doubled since the 1950s (Ladd 1993, 21). Educated people are more likely to understand the importance of protecting democratic liberties, if only in their own self-interest. Also, social and cultural diversity, such as that found in the city, brings individuals into contact with people who are not like them. They learn that those who are different are not always dangerous (Williams et al. 1976).

A less obvious explanation for the rise in support for democratic values holds there has been little "real" change between 1954 and 1993; rather, what we see is nothing more than an artifact of the question. That is, the groups used in 1954 to elicit tolerant or intolerant responses are not as threatening currently as they were in 1954. At the time of the 1954 survey, the climate of opinion in the United States was strongly influenced by the scare tactics of the ultra-right-wing junior senator from Wisconsin, Joseph McCarthy. He claimed to have proof that Communists had infiltrated the American government, and more than a few people believed him (Goldstein 1978). The groups identified in the 1954 survey are those usually associated with the left— Communists, atheists, and socialists. Tolerance may appear to have gone up simply because these groups no longer pose the danger that many once thought.[1]

In an ambitious project, Sullivan, Piereson, and Marcus (1982) devised a test to determine if the increased tolerance one sees in Table 6.3 is real or simply an illusion. They suspected that support for the civil liberties of a specific group was largely driven by emotion rather than considered judgment. If someone liked atheists, that person would have no problem allowing them the right of free speech. It takes no tolerance to "put up with" someone with whom one agrees, who is promoting a political agenda with which one concurs. On the other hand, the same person might heartily dislike members of the Ku Klux Klan and be quite willing to deny them free expression. The acid test for tolerance, according to Sullivan and his colleagues, is putting up with those whose ideas one finds repugnant. In other words, they

TABLE 6.4 Levels of Tolerance Using Content-Controlled Items

Item	Percent Tolerant Least-Liked Group
Members of the [least-liked group] should be allowed to teach in public schools	19
The [least-liked group] should not be outlawed	31
Members of the [least-liked group] should be allowed to make a speech in this city	50
The [least-liked group] should not have their phones tapped by our government	63
The [least-liked group] should be allowed to hold public rallies in our city	32

Source: James Gibson, *Freedom and Tolerance in the United States* (NORC: unpublished codebook, 1987).

suspected that support for procedural rights depended on whose ox was being gored.

Sullivan et al. (1982, 60–63) devised a "content-controlled" question in which respondents were given a list of groups and asked which one they liked least (with an option to supply a group not on the list). Respondents were then queried as to whether they would "put up with" (i.e., be tolerant of the procedural rights of) their least-liked group.

As Table 6.4 demonstrates, tolerance using a least-liked approach does not seem to have improved much since 1954.[2] For example, only 18 percent would allow a member of their least-liked group to teach in the public schools. These levels of tolerance are not much different from the 1950s. If true, this finding has disturbing implications. It calls into question the inherent willingness of Americans to embrace one of the pillars of democratic thought: tolerance. It also seems to offer little hope for improvement. The early studies showed a strong relationship between education and support for democratic values. One might suppose, then, as aggregate levels of education increased, so would political tolerance. However, the revisionist thesis holds this is not the case, since Americans are no more tolerant now than they were during the McCarthy era of the 1950s. Thus improvements in the general level of education, according to this viewpoint, are not the answer to what is seen as a dangerously low level of support for democratic values.

Not surprisingly, this general line of research has been subject to substantial criticism. Among the most telling is a claim that the questions used are inherently incapable of determining the "true" level of support for democratic values. The questions are flawed because by their very nature they have double stimuli—support for a general principle and reactions to an unpopular group or political act. Further, these stimuli are not balanced. A very strong stimulus (one's *single most* disliked group) is contrasted to a much weaker stimulus (abstract democratic values).

In the typical survey setting, in which respondents must give answers in a few seconds, it is not unexpected that the strong stimulus frequently overwhelms the weaker one (or first comes to mind). Most people know whom they like and whom they do not. Coming to grips with an abstract principle is more difficult (Brady and Sniderman 1985; Kuklinski et al. 1991; Zaller and Feldman 1992). Thus, initially, the strong stimulus dominates. But, importantly, Chong (1993) demonstrates that people can be easily talked out of their antidemocratic positions. Or, if simply allowed to ramble during in-depth interviews, they will often change their minds or come down on both sides of the issue. Chong argues that people have great difficulty reconciling their desire to support the principles of democratic procedure with their fears and apprehensions about unconventional groups or political activities. Thus, support for democratic values is mostly determined by how the question is framed. If it is made clear to respondents that a "constitutional right" is involved, they tend to support democratic principles regardless of how unpopular a group or activity may be. But if the democratic principle in the question is abstract, most people react to the unpopular group or act rather than the underlying principle (Kuklinski et al. 1991; Chong 1993). While this research may cast doubt on claims that the public is hostile to democratic values, it nevertheless tends to support the argument that the public is at best ambivalent about them. The in-depth interviews show that respondents can be talked out of the democratic response about as easily as the reverse.

The Theory of Democratic Elitism

If the public is as equivocal or nonsupportive of democratic values as many believe, how does democracy in the United States survive? American colleges and universities contain substantial numbers of atheists (Gibson and Bingham 1985, 15). In 1993, 28 percent of the public would not allow atheists to teach in these institutions (GSS). Why has there been no mass movement to root out the nonbelievers? Beyond the obvious observation that what people say has no one-to-one link with actual behavior, the most influential accounting for this circumstance is "the theory of democratic elitism" (McClosky 1964; Rose 1964; Stouffer 1955). The theory was spawned by the observation that support for democratic values is not evenly spread throughout the population. Three groups are regarded as being particularly relevant: those with little or no political interest, the educated and politically alert, and elected and appointed public officials. These groups differ in their levels of commitment to democratic values, with the low-interest group being the least committed and public officials being the most committed. For example, Nunn and his associates (1978) demonstrated that 83 per-

cent of a community leader sample could be classified as "more tolerant" compared to only 56 percent of a comparable mass sample. Data
from the 1993 General Social Survey show that while 70 percent of the
mass public would support free speech for a Communist and 67 percent
would support free speech for a militarist, several samples of elite
groups show that well over 90 percent of the respondents demonstrate
a firm (verbal) commitment to democratic values (Gibson and Bingham
1985; McClosky and Brill 1983).

Perhaps the most important predictor of support for democratic
norms is education. Several investigators have presented data showing
that the better educated tend be more supportive of democratic procedures than those with less education (Stouffer 1955; Nunn et al. 1978).
The 1993 General Social Survey shows that only 41 percent of those
with a grade-school education would allow a homosexual to teach at a
college or university, while 88 percent of those with a college education
would do so. In addition, some go even further and argue that within
categories of education, political elites are more tolerant than the public. One author inferred from the Stouffer data (part of which is presented in Table 5.3) that the "differences between leaders and the community at large does not seem due simply to education, since 79 percent
of the college-educated leaders are among the more tolerant as compared to 66 percent for the general college-educated population"
(Kornhauser 1970, 67). According to the theory of democratic elitism,
political leaders are more tolerant than their education alone would
predict because of their exposure to the democratic values that perme-
ate the American elite political culture (McClosky 1964; McClosky and
Brill 1984). The system works, therefore, because those who are least
attached to democratic values are very unlikely to be active or influential in politics. On the other hand, those most committed to democratic
tolerance are the ones who have the most influence on actual political
outcomes because of their high interest and high levels of political participation. Proponents of democratic elitism can point to countries like
Argentina, where government has been very unstable, and find confirmation of their theory in the fact that educated political activists in
that nation are very low in their support for democratic values (Dahl
1971, 139). That American political elites score very high on these values is then interpreted as an explanation for democratic stability in the
United States. In the words of one of the more influential writers on the
subject: "Democratic viability is . . . saved by the fact that those who are
the most confused about democratic ideas are also most likely to be politically apathetic" (McClosky 1964, 365).

However, once they are actively engaged, the masses can pose a substantial threat to democratic values. One common explanation for the
repression that occurred in the 1950s during the McCarthy era is that

demands on the elites for repressive action were made by a mass public feeling threatened by American Communists.

Considerable criticism has been directed at the theory we have just discussed. Any explanation of democratic stability that portrays political activists and office-holders as saviors and common people as potential saboteurs of democratic government will be found immediately suspect by many. Reanalysis of the Stouffer data by Robert Jackman (1972), for example, casts considerable doubt on the claim that political influentials are more supportive of democratic values than are others who share their education, sex, region of origin, and other distinguishing characteristics. The Sullivan et al. (1982, Ch. 8) least-liked-group analysis, which found that political activists were more tolerant than nonactivists, seems to confirm this position. But the relationship was spurious, caused by other factors being related to both support for democratic values and tolerance.

Critics note that despite the survey evidence, the actual record of tolerance for democratic rights by the mass public has not, in the view of most people, been unduly alarming. On the other hand, one can point to certain elite behaviors that many find to be dangerously undemocratic. Among examples of this are the internment of Japanese-Americans during World War II, the failure of political elites to respond critically to violations of traditional norms of free speech and due process by Senator Joseph McCarthy, and the events surrounding the break-in at the Watergate by persons in the employ of the President of the United States.

In the case of the McCarthy era, James Gibson (1988) has correlated the tolerance scores of the mass and elite samples from the 1954 Stouffer survey, aggregated by state, with an index measuring repressive legislation passed by the states during that period. He found no evidence of demands for the repression of American Communists emanating from the mass public, but did find evidence of a link between intolerant state elites and repressive state legislation.

A different type of critique holds that the survey evidence supporting the elitist theory is itself invalid. Mary Jackman (1978) argues that the better-educated simply learn what are socially desirable and "appropriate" answers to questions about democratic tolerance. Evidence for this claim can be seen in the 1993 GSS survey, in which a surprisingly high 43 percent of the college-educated *would not* allow someone who believed blacks are genetically inferior to teach at colleges or universities. They have apparently learned that it is now socially chic to condemn racists, even though their rights of free expression are no different than those of the Ku Klux Klan or any other group. But this learning is of a very superficial sort, according to Jackman. When it comes to endorsing the ideals of the civil rights movement, the well-educated are considerably more supportive of these ideals than those with less education. However, in demanding *applied* situations (such as government action to benefit racial minorities), the well-educated are no more likely to be supportive than are the less-educated. (For more detail, see Chapter 7.) Jackman and Mulha (1984) stress that education does not so much increase tolerance as it increases the ability of those in the privileged class to develop sophisticated rationales for their privileged position.

Finally, cognitive psychologists (and their followers in political science) claim that the better-educated and more politically aware have a greater store of democratic (vs. nondemocratic) "considerations" to sample from memory when being interviewed. Thus they have a greater probability of giving democratic responses (Zaller and Feldman 1991; Chong 1993). That does not, however, necessarily mean they are more committed to democratic principles.

Pluralist Intolerance

In another approach to reconciling an intolerant public with continuing democratic government, Sullivan et al. (1982) offer a theory of "pluralistic intolerance." While the public may be quite intolerant, their data show no consensus as to what group should be suppressed. There was a great deal of diversity among the groups Americans like least. In the Sullivan et al. (1982) 1978 survey, the least-liked group was American Communists at 29 percent, followed by the Ku Klux Klan at 24 percent; Gibson's (1987) more recent survey reverses this order, with the Klan at 32 percent and American Communists at 24 percent.[3] Since there is no agreement on what groups to suppress, elites receive mixed signals and consequently have the freedom to act on the basis of their (presumably democratic) preferences. In other words, with no intolerant consensus, there is no demand for political repression against any one particular group.[4]

The theory of pluralistic intolerance is based on a simple linkage model. When a group is very unpopular among the mass public, political repression will occur. This linkage receives some support in comparing the early 1950s to the late 1970s. In the 1950s, intolerance was focused on Communists and people of the political left. Repression of those persons has been amply documented (Goldstein 1978, Ch. 6). On the other hand, intolerance is currently unfocused and repression much less evident. However, the direction of causation here is very much open to question. It is possible that both the policy of repressing the left during the McCarthy era, and mass public opinion concerning Communists and the like, was determined by political elites.[5] In fact, a common interpretation of mass-elite linkage is that elite opinion and behavior shape mass opinion, not the reverse (Parry 1969). The danger in focused intolerance at the mass level may be that demagogic elites can find a receptive audience to fuel an antidemocratic political movement.

Intolerant Beliefs and Intolerant Behavior

While many seem to agree that support for democratic norms is important, investigators can do little more than speculate about the impact of these values on stable democracy. Gibson (1992) finds the less tolerant tend to perceive lower levels of political freedom, and that in some circumstances personal intolerance inhibits political discussion. But such consequences are hardly threats to the political order. It is important to appreciate that behavior has multiple causes, of which attitudes are only one. (See Deutscher 1973.) For example, a person would probably look for group support before attempting to prevent an atheist from speaking or before removing books by a Communist from the public library. The perceived likelihood that one's actions might be challenged also influences whether or not persons will act on their beliefs. Thus, translating antidemocratic beliefs into behavior may be considerably more difficult than translating a preference for a political candidate into the behavior of casting a vote for that candidate.

6-2 Political Consensus _____

Clearly, a democracy will be more stable if citizens agree, or are in consensus, over basic values and goals. Some conflict over issues is inevitable in a democracy, because public policies generally cannot benefit or penalize all persons or groups equally. Intense or severe political conflict, however, is undesirable because it may threaten the stability of democracy. Robert Dahl defines intensity of conflict as a function of the extent to which each side sees the other as enemies to be destroyed by whatever means necessary (Dahl 1971, 335). As issues become more intensely debated, the language of conflict becomes harsher; opponents are accused of acting out of less than honorable motives, and tactics that were once regarded as illegitimate are given serious consideration. The Protestant-Catholic split in Northern Ireland and Muslim-Christian split in Lebanon are classic examples of a political division that makes democratic government and the protection of civil liberties virtually impossible.

The United States has clearly experienced political conflict, but unlike many other countries, there has not been significant controversy over a number of fundamental issues. Evidence from several surveys indicates that: (1) the broad elements of the constitutional order are widely endorsed; (2) there is a consensus that defects should be remedied by legal processes of change; (3) most people are satisfied with the economic order, with 94 percent agreeing that we "must be ready to make sacrifices if necessary . . . to preserve the free enterprise system"; few want to nationalize large corporations; big business is widely accepted; labor unions are less popular, but few want to see them eliminated; (4) Americans believe that opportunity exists for personal achievement—the doors of success are open for those willing to work; and (5) most people are content with their lot. Americans believe the United States is the best place in the world to live.[6] NES data (1988) show that 85 percent say they feel extremely good or very good when they see the American flag fly; 92 percent profess extreme or very strong love for their country; and 94 percent are extremely or very proud to be an American.

Traditional sources of cleavage that have posed problems in other countries have, for the most part, been moderate in the United States. Among the most important of these are class, regionalism, and religion. Particularly important is the fact that political attitudes are only weakly related to these divisions. (See Chapter 7.) Regional differences (at least currently) also tend not be intense. The American public is very mobile. The Bureau of the Census reports that in a typical year, 20 percent of the population moves, with about one-third moving a considerable distance. Even the South, on the question of race, is beginning to lose some of its uniqueness. Religious antagonisms, too, do not lead to severe issue conflicts. One reason is that religious preference is only slightly related to social class. One's religion does not determine one's opportunities or economic well-being. The low salience of these conflicts is evidenced in that 94 percent of opinion-holders (Gallup 1983) said they would vote for a Jew for President, 89 percent (GSS 1993) said they would vote for a black, and 94 percent (Gallup 1983) said they would vote for a Catholic.

Two issues, however, have proved to be very divisive—race and (until its termination) the Vietnam War. Violence and antidemocratic behavior have accompanied attempts to resolve each. The race issue, of course, has existed since the beginning of the Republic, and has been the principal threat to the survival of democratic rights in the United States. Recent violent manifestations of this cleavage were the urban riots that occurred in virtually every city between 1965 and 1968, then again in several cities in the 1990s in response to several high-visibility assault and murder trials in which victim and accused were of different races. Today there still exists a wide gap between the opinions of whites and blacks on a substantial range of issues. These differences are most pronounced on questions of what constitutes fair treatment for blacks (again, see Chapter 7), but exist in other domains as well.

The possibility for conflict between the races is intensified by the fact that socioeconomic differences reinforce issue disagreements. Most blacks are working class and many are unemployed, while a considerably greater proportion of whites belong to the more affluent sectors of American society.

While blacks clearly have some specific policy grievances and tend to view partisan politics from a different perspective than whites, blacks do not reject the central tenets underlying the American political system. In 1981, 76 percent of a national sample of black respondents thought the United States had a special role to play in the world; 86 percent said that the United States was the best place in the world to live (Gallup 1986); and in 1988 (NES), 87 percent of blacks were "extremely proud" or "very proud" to be Americans. Less than 3 percent were "not proud at all."

Unlike the race issue, which threatens to polarize Americans along racial lines, the Vietnam War polarized along ideological lines. Disagreement on this issue was so intense that it resulted in a number of actions at the fringe of legality and some that went considerably beyond. There were demonstrations, riots, occupation of buildings, violence (police and hard-hats vs. protesters), and the shooting of unarmed demonstrators. As a counter to the perceived threat of leftist protesters, the government engaged in a number of illegal practices, such as wiretapping and surveillance.

The Vietnam War caused the display of many traits that are characteristic of intense political conflict. The stakes were high, there were substantial numbers on both sides with strongly held beliefs, and there was no compromise acceptable to competing sides. While relatively few were directly affected by the war, a very vocal minority was outraged over the notion of American boys being required to fight and sometimes die in someone else's civil war. Another sizable minority saw the war resisters as traitors. Compromise was extremely difficult; both sides were committed. In addition, the North Vietnamese would accept only one solution—total American withdrawal.

While attitudes about the war posed a very serious cleavage, there were two factors that served to diminish its polarizing effect. First, the entire population was not divided into two extreme camps. Rather, after 1968, the majority tended toward the middle position. They viewed the war as a mistake, but did not want it ended by an immediate withdrawal or an all-out military attack. There also existed "cross-cutting cleavages." Extreme conflict becomes more threatening when an individual's attitudes and group memberships reinforce each other. An example would be a very high proportion of "doves" who were college-educated, under 30, white, Democratic, pro–affirmative action, pro-abortion, anti–big business, and religious agnostics. However, attitudes toward the Vietnam War were not highly associated with other attitudes or with group membership. Doves were not necessarily pro-abortion, college-educated, or under 30. Rather, views on the war cut across these divisions. The existence of cross-cutting cleavages served to mute the intensity of the conflict.[7]

6-3 Political Support: Trust and Efficacy _____

A common assumption is that the political system works better when citizens give it their support than when they are "alienated," or es-tranged from government. The two most prominent dimensions of po-litical support are political trust and efficacy (Craig 1993). Trust is the affective component of support. Those high in trust are satisfied with the procedures and products of government. The opposite of trust is po-litical cynicism, or the evaluation that the political system is not pro-ducing policies according to expectations. Efficacy is the cognitive or be-lief component of support. It is the extent to which a person believes his or her political activities will influence government. Trust relates to an assessment of government output, and efficacy relates to the conse-quences of one's input.

Political Trust and Democratic Stability

No government has the complete trust of all its citizens. However, many argue that it important for democratic government to maintain some minimal (usually unspecified) level of trust among its citizens. One argument is pitched at the normative level. If the distinctive character of democracy is the substitution of voluntary consent for coercion, it is a matter of no small moral shortcoming when citizens withdraw trust out of a conviction that government is not acting in their best interests (Tussman 1960; Sabine 1952; Gamson 1968). Others make claims of a more practical bent. Levels of trust are thought to affect the leadership strategies available to political decision-makers. Leaders must be able to make decisions and commit resources without first consulting those per-sons who will be affected by the decisions and called upon to supply the resource materials. According to William Gamson (1968, 45–46), when trust is high, "the authorities are able to make new commitments on the basis of it and, if successful, increase such support even more. When it is low or declining, authorities may find it difficult to meet existing com-mitments and govern effectively." Thus, in 1964, the government could draw on its "credit rating" with the electorate and send troops to fight an overseas police action in Vietnam with little public debate.

That sort of freedom was certainly constrained after 1972. Weatherford (1987) argues that levels of trust are particularly important in the economic area, where the government needs maneuvering room to pursue long-term policy goals. For example, if inflation becomes entrenched, the government must sometimes call upon citizens to endure the pain of recession for the promise of stable prices at a point in the indeterminant future. Citizens must have faith in the fairness and competence of governing institutions, and not demand a premature accounting based on a short-term appraisal of costs and benefits.

If trust drops sufficiently low, some contend, it can lead to social disruption. Disruption may serve as an impetus to needed reform, or it may threaten the stability of an existing regime. At the very least, a portion of state resources will have to be diverted to cope with the disturbances. Almond and Verba (1965, 354) write that insufficient trust is particularly dangerous when the system is not performing in an adequate fashion, as, for example, during an economic depression. Lipset (1960, 69) provides evidence from the 1930s that when many democratic governments had ceased to be effective, those that had induced a sense of trust were able to withstand the strain, while those not so advantaged (such as Austria, Germany, and Spain) succumbed to antidemocratic movements. Arthur Miller (1974, 951) has flatly asserted, "A democratic political system cannot survive for long without the support of a majority of its citizens."

Levels of political trust may serve as a barometer indicating how well government is performing. It is, therefore, no surprise that scholars have paid considerable attention to the fluctuations in trust over time.[8] Presented in Figure 6-1 are the trends, between 1958 and 1992, in three items that measure trust in government. The data for 1958 reflect the tranquillity of the Eisenhower years. After 1964, trust began to decrease at a steady pace until 1980. Common explanations include the government's handling of the civil rights movement, the Vietnam War, Watergate, the pardon of Richard Nixon, and the economic and foreign policy problems associated with the Carter administration. Arthur Miller (1974 and 1983) has shown that the decrease comes about equally from the dissatisfied left and the dissatisfied right. For example, cynics on the left tended to think the government had moved too slowly on civil rights; cynics on the right felt it had moved to rapidly. Miller concluded that disenchantment of this sort with government policies (outputs) is the primary reason for the decline in trust between 1964 and 1970.

Between 1972 and 1974 there was another very sharp decline in trust, particularly on questions concerning beliefs that "the government will do right" and "the government is run for a few big interests." The most plausible explanation is Watergate. Daily accusations of

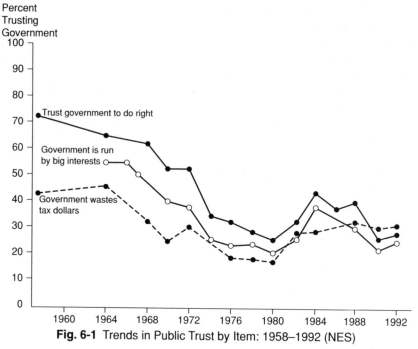

Fig. 6-1 Trends in Public Trust by Item: 1958–1992 (NES)

break-ins, slush funds, wiretapping, extortion, coverups, etc., are not designed to encourage enthusiasm for government. But even after President Nixon left office there was no immediate decline in cynicism. In fact, trust did not rebound until Ronald Reagan took office and proclaimed it was "morning in America." At that point, Republican trust increased, as one would expect once the GOP captured the presidency. But, contrary to expectations, it also increased among Democrats. The explanation for this seems to be economic. Democrats, who apparently expected the worst with the election of Ronald Reagan, were pleasantly surprised to find the worst did not occur. They responded with a moderate increase in political trust. The Reagan administration's attack on big government also helped boost levels of trust. By 1984, trust had rebounded considerably, although it was nowhere close to the levels of the late 1950s and early 1960s. Following its 1984 peak, trust declined again, mostly in response to the Iran-Contra scandal (Miller 1991). Republicans also seem have responded to the breaking of the "read my lips—no new taxes" pledge by George Bush. Between 1990 and 1992, their belief that the government wastes tax money increased by 10 percent (NES 1990, 1992).

There is general agreement that satisfaction/dissatisfaction with governmental performance is the source of variations in political cynicism. There is considerable disagreement, however, over what it all means.[9]

Does a decline in trust indicate withdrawal of allegiance from the political system as a whole, or is it simply dissatisfaction with the performance of office-holders? The basic distinction here is between *criticism* (defined by Webster as "judging with knowledge and propriety") and *cynicism* (defined as "fault finding, captious criticism") (Baloyra 1979, 987). Obviously, the latter is more serious than the former. Loyalty to the political order does not necessarily preclude criticizing the policies and procedures of those currently holding public office. Based on an analysis of survey data by presidential pollster Patrick Caddell, President Carter delivered a major address on July 15, 1979, in which he spoke of a "crisis of confidence" that "threatens the very fabric of our society." According to Caddell, there was a crisis of confidence in American institutions resulting from the successive shocks of the civil rights movement, Vietnam, and Watergate, and not from the performance of the Carter administration *per se* (Caddell 1979).

The evidence, however, seems to indicate that the trust items reported in Figure 6-1 covary with dissatisfaction over the policy outcomes generated by incumbent office-holders. In the 1976 NES, respondents were asked in a straightforward fashion whether they thought the lack of trust in government was due to the individuals in office or if there was something more seriously wrong with government in general. Sixty-eight percent thought the problem resided with incumbent political officials. In 1978, the NES added several new questions to the trust index, which were designed specifically to resolve the issue of trust in the regime vs. trust in the authorities. The items used the same wording as the standard questions, but substituted "President Carter," "the Carter Administration," or "the U.S. Congress" for "the government in Washington." Although ambiguities remain, one study concluded, "the basic political trust index has a very substantial component that evaluates political authorities (Abramson and Finifter 1981, 301).[10] It now seems clear that low trust (at least as seen since the mid-1960s) does not mean a rejection of the political order. The controversy has now shifted as to whether dissatisfaction with political personalities leads to declining trust, or is it dissatisfaction with policy outputs that leads to declining trust. The evidence currently favors the latter (Miller 1991).

Another issue concerns the effects of low political trust on the day-to-day operations of government. How far must it decline before it makes a difference? One obvious observation is that in the mid-1970s, when trust was at its nadir, the process of government did not operate with any appreciable difference from the 1950s. The weapons of war were still being built, pensions were paid, and the garbage was collected. On some of the items reported in Figure 6-1, the level of trust had fallen below 30 percent. One author speculates that the support of 15 percent of the population is enough (Wright 1976, 269). But the social location of the group is important. In the United States, support is highest among the white, non-Southern, non-Jewish, middle-aged upper middle class. The trust of this group, it has been argued, may be the key to democratic stability.

Political Efficacy and Democratic Stability

The concept "political efficacy" was originally developed in the early 1950s to explain variations in voting turnout. The four questions used to measure it have been repeated frequently and over a longer period of time than almost any other social indicator of the survey sort. Efficacy can best be described as a belief that one can influence the political process. It is a feeling that an active citizen can play a part in bringing about social and political change, and that one's input counts (Campbell et al. 1954, 187). Since it was first developed, the concept has been generalized to account for a wide variety of political activities. In the most comprehensive study of political participation to date, Sidney Verba and Norman Nie (1972, 88) found a strong association between efficacy and their overall index of political participation—16 items. Their study, in addition, generally shows that the higher the sense of political efficacy, the greater the likelihood that one will participate in political activities of a relatively demanding sort. Conversely, a low sense of efficacy is one of the factors normally associated with political apathy (Verba and Nie 1972, 133).

Given its wide use and long history, the original four-item efficacy scale has been the subject of an extensive methodological review. It is now apparent there are serious problems with items as they were originally developed. One item ("officials don't care") seems a better measure of trust than efficacy. One other item ("voting is the only way") has proven highly unreliable (Acock et al. 1985). In recent years, however, considerable work has gone into constructing a reliable and valid measure of political efficacy (Niemi et al. 1991). The downside is that studies of efficacy and its consequences tend to be noncomparable because different questions are used. Plus, it is no longer possible to compare changes in the indicators over time.

Aside from its association with participation, political efficacy plays an important role in theories of democratic stability. Theorists of "participatory democracy" are concerned with the effect political participation has on individual character development. They see an elevated sense of efficacy as a desirable consequence of political activity; a belief that one can and should be self-governing is an important aspect of a meaningful existence (Pateman 1970, 45–46). A related perspective can be found in the five-nation study by Gabriel Almond and Sidney

Verba (1965), *The Civic Culture*. They see a strong sense of political efficacy as a key element in forming the ideal political culture in a stable democracy. Almond and Verba view the ideal citizen as believing in the success of his or her political actions (efficacy), believing that he or she is obligated to participate (citizen duty), but being rather inactive politically in actual practice. While they concede that "unless there is some control of government elites by nonelites, it is hard to consider a political system democratic." The authors also argue that elites must have the power "to initiate and carry out policies, adjust to new situations, meet internal and external challenges," and generally make authoritative decisions (Almond and Verba 1965, 476). Thus, low participation gives government room to operate, but the public's strong confidence in the potential effectiveness of their participation assures that political leaders will act in a responsible fashion. In the civic culture, citizens have a reserve of influence. They may not constantly monitor the activities of decision-makers, but the potential to act is there if needed. It is this potential that plays a major role in holding public officials accountable (Almond and Verba 1965, 346–47).

Citizen Roles: Combinations of Trust and Efficacy

It should come as no surprise that political efficacy and trust are related to one another; that those who feel they can influence government also tend to trust it (Walker and Aberbach 1970; Abravnel and Busch 1975). Presented below are four possible linkages between efficacy and trust:

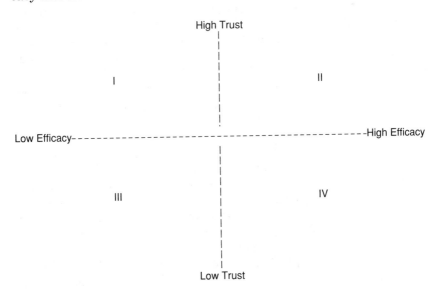

Our principal interest is in persons characterized by quadrant IV, because of their potential for violence and antidemocratic behavior. But first we shall briefly describe the other three types. Type I is the loyal subject, high on trust but low on efficacy. They rarely participate, believing that government will act responsibly in looking out for their personal interests. Type II is the combination many would consider to be the ideal democratic citizen: a person with a very positive outlook on the political order, politically attentive and involved—but within the limits of accepted social convention. Type III individuals, cynical and believing there is no hope of any political action that might improve their lot, are classic examples of the politically alienated. They are hostile, suspicious, and mistrustful of government, but lack the self-confidence to take action. Individuals from quadrant IV, cynical and efficacious, can be mobilized for political activity, but it may of a volatile and unconventional sort. It is often argued that the numbers of these persons must be minimized to maintain democratic stability. According the 1992 NES, 22 percent of the American public scored in both the top 25 percent in efficacy and bottom 25 percent in trust.[11] Thus, there would seem to be a substantial segment of the population that could be mobilized for active opposition to the government given appropriate circumstances. It might be noted, for example, that the low trust/high efficacy group voted about 10 percent more for Perot than the rest of the population.[12]

Considerable research has been conducted into the behavior patterns of those low on trust but high on efficacy. Shingles (1981), in a reanalysis of the Verba/Nie participation data, finds the combination of low trust and high efficacy overcomes the disadvantages of low income and low education in motivating political participation. This combination was a particularly important antecedent of black political activity. The data set, however, allowed only for examination of *conventional* political behavior. The research on *unconventional* political behavior has been of two sorts. One approach has been to look at the "predisposition" to engage in unconventional or violent behavior. Abravanel and Busch (1975) find, for a sample of college students, that Type IV respondents are likely to employ "nontraditional" forms of exerting political influence. Schwartz (1973) reports a repudiation of "conformist" modes of political participation among both students and urban blacks. The most sophisticated and extensive analysis of unconventional political behavior has been carried out over a 25-year period by Edward Muller and his colleagues. In a variety of research settings, Muller has demonstrated that collective violence most likely occurs among those distrustful of or alienated from government, who also believe that their actions (oftentimes violent) will get them what they want.[13]

Although there is little doubt about the reliability of these relationships, there is considerable uncertainty about the links between these attitudes and behavior. Those studies that investigate "predispositions" are subject to the same criticism we made earlier (see Section 6-1) about the linkage between statements of intent and political action. The studies of riot participants raise the question of the direction of causation. The respondents were interviewed after the riots were over. Did the attitudes cause the behavior, or did participating in the riot lead to a change of attitude? One could well imagine someone feeling considerably more efficacious after than before a violent outburst. Also, there is the possibility that riot behavior may be motivated by narrow or local grievances (for example, refusal of a supermarket chain to cash a check), but later justified by indicating the entire political order. The linkages between efficacy, trust, and political action are provocative, but not all agree they provide a satisfactory explanation for nonconventional political participation.[14]

6-4 Personality and Public Opinion _____

Individual political opinions can have their roots in the entire spectrum of human existence. Why, for instance, most personal injury attorneys oppose tort reform seems fairly obvious. They do not think the financial limitations on insurance claims proposed by insurance companies and their soulmates are in the best interest of the legal professional or in the best interest of the average American. It is not as easy to understand why some people are adamantly opposed to the fluoridation of drinking water, while others accept it as a desirable form of preventive medicine. One explanation that received considerable attention is that certain attitudes and behaviors are possibly influenced by personality.[15]

Although there is no agreed-upon definition, we shall follow Eysenck and define personality as "the more or less stable and enduring organization of a person's character, temperament, intellect, and physique which determines his unique adjustment to his environment."[16] The basic element is the enduring, abstract perspective that a person uses to order the world and meet personal needs, for example, constructing a self-image in which one is an attractive and socially useful individual.

While trait psychologists have tried to associate personalities with specific attitudes and behavior, most researchers interested in personality dismiss such efforts as simplistic and naive. Rather, they pursue investigations across a wide range of attitudes and beliefs. As might be expected, such extensive and time-consuming assessments for each individual result in few persons being evaluated. The most frequently cited studies of personality and political behavior usually examine fewer than 30 persons. Such groups can in no way be considered a meaningful sample of any segment of the population. If the dynamics of personality and behavior noted in these limited groups were universal or identical to those of other people, as is sometimes claimed, these works would be more definitive. But their primary contribution is insight into the psyches of people other than ourselves, and the comfortable feeling that we know them personally, as opposed to the formality of a tabular presentation of one thousand faceless survey respondents. One study, however, that combines both a clinical and a survey perspective is *The Authoritarian Personality*.

The Authoritarian Personality

Influenced by events in Germany during Hitler's rule, a group of psychologists from the University of California at Berkeley began a systematic investigation into the personality structure of individuals particularly susceptible to anti-Semitic and Fascist political appeals. Was there something about the personality of some individuals that led them to actively support or passively sympathize with a program of genocide against Jews, homosexuals, and gypsies, and the replacement of democratic government by dictatorship (as happened in Germany between 1932 and 1945)? The study was completed in 1950 and has had a profound influence on all branches of the social sciences (Adorno et al. 1950).

The thesis of the book is straightforward. Prejudice, suspicion, distrust, and hostility are manifestations of attempts to resolve deep-seated psychological conflicts. At the heart of these conflicts is a highly ambivalent and tense orientation toward authority. Authoritarians are very submissive to those above them in the social order and very condescending toward those below. As depicted in German folklore, they are like a person on a bicycle—above they bow, below they kick. While such persons are outwardly very deferential, they in fact harbor considerable hostility toward authority. This hostility, however, is mostly unconscious, and authoritarians are only intermittently aware of the hate side of this love-hate amalgam. Rather, negative feelings are repressed by primitive ego defensive mechanisms. Authoritarians are extremely servile toward authority, driving from consciousness the malice they feel toward those above them. But repression has its costs, and the tensions created seek some alternate outlet. To compensate for feelings of personal weakness, authoritarians present a very tough facade. They are very critical of those they see as beneath them, particularly those who are different, such as members of minority groups (Greenstein 1969, 106–07). Other characteristics of the authoritarian syndrome include: (1) conventionalism, a rigid adherence to conventional middle-class values; (2) anti-intraception, opposition to the tenderhearted, subjective, and imaginative; (3) superstition, a belief in mystical determinants influencing one's fate; and (4) ethnocentrism, a strong attachment to one's own group and hostility to outgroups (Kirscht and Dillehay 1967, 5–6).

Authoritarianism is thought to originate primarily with childhood family relationships. Persons displaying the syndrome often describe parental affection as being given only as a reward for good behavior. Their parents employed rigid, punishment-oriented disciplinary practices, as opposed to discipline based on love withdrawal. Family roles were clearly defined in terms of dominance and submission. According to Adorno and his colleagues, "Forced into submission to parental authority, the child develops hostility and aggression which are poorly channelized. The displacement of a repressed antagonism toward authority may be one of the sources, and perhaps the principal source, of his antagonism toward outgroups" (Adorno et al. 1950, 482).

The implications of *The Authoritarian Personality* for public opinion and democratic stability became obvious to students of politics soon after its publication. One of the first tasks investigators set for themselves was to determine the political correlates of authoritarianism. (Are authoritarians prejudiced toward minorities? Do they hold antidemocratic political beliefs? And so on.) This undertaking was greatly aided by the fact that *The Authoritarian Personality*, unlike other such studies, provided a ready-made paper and pencil test to measure the extent to which the syndrome exists. This instrument, the California F- (for fascism) scale, has become virtually synonymous with authoritarianism. Typical agree/disagree items from the F-scale are (Adorno et al. 1950, 167):

- What young people need most of all is strict discipline by their parents.
- Most people who don't get ahead just don't have enough will power.
- Sex criminals deserve more than prison; they should be whipped in public or worse.

Investigators soon discovered some very severe methodological problems with the F-scale. Among the most difficult to resolve has been response set. All twenty items in the original F-scale were worded in a positive direction (to agree was authoritarian). As we indicated earlier, people with low education tend to be "yea-sayers," making it difficult to separate the effects of education from the effects of personality when all questions in a scale suffer from response set. One solution is to reverse some of the items so that disagreeing with the question is the authoritarian response. While this strategy has merit, it is less than a completely satisfactory solution.[17] Also, one essential requirement of a personality measure is that it not be contaminated by political content. It is now generally agreed that the F-scale is biased in the direction of right-wing authoritarianism. For example, one item from the F-scale states: "Homosexuals are hardly better than criminals and ought to be severely punished." Such a question may tap both personality traits and right-wing political outlooks. Consequently, the F-scale might not be sensitive to authoritarians of the left (such as American Communists).

There have been two important attempts to deal with the problem. The first, by Milton Rokeach (1960), was the development of a new measure: the "dogmatism" scale, which Rokeach claimed could tap authoritarianism of both the left and the right. Currently this dogmatism scale is one of the most frequently used measures of authoritarian tendencies (although it still suffers from response set, since to be "dogmatic" is to agree with scale items). The second solution was simply to recognize the problem and reformulate the concept as "right-wing authoritarianism." Bob Altemeyer (1981 and 1988) argues that authoritarianism naturally leads to right-wing political views because authoritarians feel compelled to support the conventional as well as traditional authority. Thus, for example, research in the former Soviet Union shows that authoritarians (using Altemeyer's scale) tended to be more supportive of the old Communist regime than nonauthoritarians (McFarland et al. 1992).

Due to methodological problems, research on authoritarianism is looked on with some suspicion. Because of the ease of administering the various pencil-and-paper instruments, there have been literally thousands of published pieces that employ authoritarianism as a variable. Many of these have been poorly done or are little more than "crass empiricism." The field is poorly integrated, since many studies are contradictory or noncomparable. Despite these problems, the question of the relationship between authoritarianism and political opinion has merit. It is slippery, elusive, and hard to measure, but as Meleon and his associates have recently observed, "the general concept of authoritarianism was, and still is, valid. Nearly all the hypothesized relationships between authoritarianism and antiminority tendencies, conservatism, and antifeminism, have been confirmed over the years" (Meleon et al. 1988, 416).

Furthermore, there *are* studies indicating an authoritarian effect that meet commonly accepted standards for scientific inquiry.[18] For example, in one investigation a persuasive message was presented in several different forms to a number of different groups. Those scoring high on the F-scale were particularly likely to change their attitude when the message was delivered by a high-status source. The effectiveness of the message increased further when its content suggested change in a prejudiced direction (Harvey and Beverly 1961, 125–30).

The research on democratic values discussed in section 6-1 has found authoritarianism (measured with Rokeach's dogmatism scale) to be related to political intolerance. Sullivan et al. (1982, 155) found "large and significant" differences (in the predicted direction) between those scoring high and those scoring low on the D-scale with regard to the toleration of respondents' least-liked group, as did McClosky and Brill (1983, 342) using the traditional F-scale. Gibson and Tedin (1988) report similar findings in a study of tolerance for gay rights. They found dogmatism contributed to an intolerance for gays by reducing support for norms of democracy.

Recently there has been a revival in research linking authoritarianism to racism. The correlation between these constructs is one of the most enduring in the social science literature. John Ray (1988, 673) has written that "[d]espite all the other failures of their theory, Adorno et al. would appear to have succeeded in at least one of their basic aims—to find something that would predict who is a racist who is not." Most recently, Sniderman and Piazza (1993) have shown that authoritarian values among whites lead to the negative stereotyping of both Jews and blacks. These groups are so different from each other in terms of educational accomplishment, material success, intact families, as well as other characteristics that factual considerations could hardly explain why the same people who hold negative stereotypes about Jews also hold them about blacks. Rather, the explanation is authoritarian values. It is not the actual characteristics of blacks, any more than it is the actual characteristics of Jews, that evoke prejudice and dislike. Rather, it is the ethnocentric dimension of the authoritarian personality—the generalized hostility toward outgroups—that is part of the syndrome.

One particularly interesting study on authoritarianism involved the classic experiment developed by Stanley Milgram (1969) to measure obedience to authority. In this experiment, a naive subject ("the teacher") was required by the study director ("the authority figure") to administer an electrical shock each time "the learner" failed to perform a rote memorization task satisfactorily. The teacher is not aware that the learner is in league with the person running the experiment, and is in fact receiving no shock at all. However, each time the learner fails the task, the authority figure (the experimenter) orders the teacher to shock the learner at an even higher level of voltage. As the shocks presumably become stronger, the learner cries out in pain. The object is to see how long the teacher will obey the authority figure and continue to administer the shocks. One disturbing feature of this study is that many subjects will continue to administer the shocks until the learner is in an apparent state of unconsciousness. Alan Elms administered the "teachers" the California F-test before conducting the Milgram experiment. He found that those who scored high on authoritarianism were highly reluctant (as predicted) to disobey the authority figure and terminate the experiment. Elms (1972, 113) explains:

> The relationship between obedience and some elements of authoritarianism seems fairly strong; and it should be remembered that the measure of obedience is a measure of actual submission to authority, not just what a person says he's likely to do. Too much of the research on authoritarianism . . . has been on the level of paper and pencil responses, which don't necessarily get translated into behavior. But here we have a realistic and highly disturbing situation. . . . So it does look as if those researchers in the late 40s had something, something which can be translated from abstract tendencies into actual authoritarian behavior: submitting to the man in command, punishing the weaker subordinate.

Is There a Democratic Personality?

Considerably less attention has been paid to the possibility that there might exist certain personality traits that promote support for democratic principles. Much of what has been written is either speculative or consists of inferences based on intensive interviews with small samples. Writers like Lasswell, Lane, and Inkeles talk about the democratic character as being warm, outgoing, high in self-esteem and ego strength, flexible, and tolerant of ambiguity (Lasswell 1951; Inkeles 1961; Lane 1962). One characteristic of this literature is a rather cavalier tendency to portray the democratic personality as the "healthy" personality and the nondemocratic personality as having psychological maladjustments.

It is misleading to talk about a democratic personality as if it were a distinct psychological type. But there may be certain personality traits that elicit support for democratic values as these values interact with particular environmental situations. The emphasis on environment is important, because personality traits that encourage support for democratic principles (the accepted norm) among citizens of the United States probably encouraged support of totalitarian communism (the accepted norm) among citizens of the former Soviet Union. In other words, there are personality types that work well within the given rules of the political game—whatever those rules might be. It is not surprising, therefore, that many politicians who were successful when communism was the accepted norm in the Soviet Union are also successful under the norms of democracy in Russia and the Independent States (for example, Boris Yeltsin, President of Russia).

6-5 Conclusion _____

There seem to be two fundamental prerequisites for the existence
and maintenance of democratic rights and freedoms. One is economic
and the other is psychological. In the case of the former, considerable
research indicates that some minimal level of economic affluence and
development is necessary before a democracy can operate successfully.
If people must worry about feeding themselves and their children, concern about democratic government will be a low priority for most.
Beyond simple sustenance, the most relevant factor associated with
economic development is communication networks. Without sufficiently developed channels of communication, interests cannot be articulated and aggregated; conflicting groups cannot exchange information on goals and desires.[19]

But once a minimal level of economic development has occurred, psychological factors become important. It has been demonstrated that after a certain "threshold," the most economically developed nations are
not necessarily the most democratic (Neubauer 1967). We have analyzed a number of political attitudes commonly thought to affect the
stability of democracy. All may be of consequence, but none alone, or
even in combination, provides a total explanation for the continued protection of democratic values in the United States. America has perhaps
been most fortunate in that there have been few intense group or issue
cleavages dividing the population. As long as some modest consensus
exists, and most of the population has a minimal degree of economic security, the system seems able to tolerate a wide variety of personality
types, a relatively low level of trust in government, and considerable
lack of enthusiasm (although perhaps not outright hostility) for procedural democratic norms.

Notes _____

1. One bit of evidence for this thesis is the rather substantial increase for
   the civil rights of Communists that occurred between 1988 and 1993. In
   1988, 60 percent would allow an admitted Communist to speak; in 1993,
   it was 71 percent. In 1988, 45 percent would an admitted Communist; in
   1993 it was 61 percent. And in 1988, 59 percent would allow an admitted
   Communist's book to remain in the library; by 1993 it was 70 percent.
   Changes for other groups are not nearly as large, so the explanation
   must be that with the fall of the Soviet Union, Communists do not seem
   so dangerous.

2. However, Sullivan, Piereson, and Marcus (1982, 67) concede that tolerance may have increased somewhat between 1954 and 1978, but not as much as the items in Table 6.3 would lead one to believe.
3. This data is a module in the 1987 GSS.
4. A point first noted by Herson and Hofstetter (1975).
5. For another critique of the theory of pluralistic intolerance, see Gibson (1986) and Sniderman et al. (1989).
6. Surveys are taken from Robert A. Dahl (1966, 40-41), Ladd (1989, 365-369), Dahl (1982, 286-98); Ladd (1981, 7-12), and the 1988 and 1992 NES.
7. Much of our discussion of the Vietnam War draws on Dahl (1982, Ch. 26).
8. The literature on political trust is voluminous. Among the better, more recent studies are Shingles (1981), Miller (1991), and Weatherford (1992).
9. A good discussion can be found in Citrin (1974); see also the exchange between Patrick Caddell and Warren Miller in *Public Opinion* (Oct./Nov., 1979).
10. Recently, Eber and Lau (1990) have argued that both Miller and Citrin are right. There are some people who view the "stuff" of politics in terms of people and some who view it in terms of issues. The latter will be become alienated when policies are not to their liking, the former when the performance of office-holders is not to their liking.
11. Using the 1992 NES, V6105 through V6108 were used for the efficacy scale; V6120 through V6123 were used for the trust scale.
12. High efficacy/low trust respondents in the 1992 NES survey voted 27 percent for Ross Perot for president.
13. Muller's most recent research on the trust/efficacy dimension is reported in Finkle, Muller, and Opp (1989).
14. For a review of the psychological theories of unconventional political behavior, see Finkle and Rule (1975).
15. For a recent review of the field, see Greenstein (1992).
16. Cited in Sniderman (1975).
17. For a further elaboration, see Herzon (1972).
18. For a review of many of these studies, see Kirscht and Dillehay (1967); for a more recent apprisal of authoritarianism and public opinion, see Duckitt (1989).
19. This thesis was first developed by Lipset (1959).

CHAPTER 7

Group Differences in Political Opinions

People often think of themselves as belonging to specific groups. This "group identification" may influence political opinions, as people see certain policies as being beneficial to the group with which they identify. Thus, we would not be surprised if blacks were more favorable to affirmative action than whites, or people with high incomes more opposed to social welfare programs than those living near the poverty line. However, not all group differences are the result of calculated self-interest. Many political opinions are based on "sociotropic" considerations—that is, on the well-being of the nation as a whole rather than on the individual or the group (Kinder and Kiewiet, 1981). Life experiences can also shape different political outlooks. For instance, individuals with college educations differ sharply from those without on a variety of noneconomic issues, such as abortion. Growing up in the South once virtually insured an allegiance to the Democratic Party, even for conservative whites.

In this chapter we explore the validity of generalizations made about group differences in public opinion. Most of these differences we find to be correct, but sometimes overdrawn. We also find that group differences change over time, and that generalizations that were true in the past may be more or less so today.

7-1 Socioeconomic Class and Political Opinions _____

Since a great many issues in political life concern the distribution of benefits within society, the rich and the poor often seem to have quite different economic interests. The "haves" and the "have nots" are expected to disagree, for example, on questions involving taxation and government services.[1] In most European democracies the major political battle lines are drawn between working-class parties and parties of the middle class. As indicated by the fact that the United States has never had an appreciable socialist movement, America has escaped the more extreme forms of class polarization and conflict. There are, nevertheless, class differences on many political issues.

How does one measure economic or social class? One possibility, called subjective social class, is simply to ask people into which social class they fall—the poor, working class, middle class, upper middle class, or upper class. About 97 percent in the 1992 NES willingly place themselves in one of these categories, with 51 percent identifying as working class, 38 percent as middle class, and 11 percent as upper class.[2] An alternate to the subjective approach is to use the objective indicators of occupation, income, and education. Each indicator has its problems. The connections among the three are often far from perfect. Many blue-collar workers have greater incomes than white collar-workers. Also, education is an imperfect predictor of income, because many with college degrees often have lower incomes than skilled manual workers. We could focus on income, but the same dollar amounts buy quite different life-styles in various parts of the country. A $30,000-a-year income in rural Montana might allow a pleasant middle-class life-style, while one might have to struggle to live on that amount in New York City.[3] People's subjective class identifications actually are quite predictable from education, income, and occupation (Jackman and Jackman 1983). Still, analysts worry about how accurately survey respondents perceive their social reality. We will proceed by employing what we see as the most appropriate indicator for the question at hand, with a sensitivity to the difficulties and imperfections of measuring socioeconomic class.

Class Differences on Social Welfare

Income is more concentrated at the upper levels of society in the United States than is the case for any other Western democracy (Phillips 1991, 9). In 1990, the richest 10 percent of Americans received 44 percent of the total family income.[4] The recent trend has been for an even greater concentration at the top. The Congressional Budget Office reports that from 1962 to 1983, there was no change in the total percentage of private wealth held by the top 1 percent, but between 1983 and 1989, it jumped from 31 to 37 percent. According to conservative analyst Kevin Phillips, "[n]o parallel upsurge of riches has been seen since the late nineteenth century, the era of the Vanderbilts, Morgans and Rockefellers" (Phillips 1991, 10).

Yet, by European standards, cleavages along class lines in the United States are rather muted. Perhaps one reason is a belief among Americans that the opportunity to succeed financially is readily available to those with the energy and ability. For example, one poll found only 12 percent saying there is little or no chance of becoming rich in the U.S. if one is willing to work hard. When a British sample was asked a similar question, 63 percent said they did not think they had a chance to become rich if they really wanted to.[5]

Typically, the poor in the United States are more favorable to social welfare programs designed to raise living standards than are the more well-to-do. They are even more favorable if the program affects them directly. To take an early example, Gallup found in 1949 that 57 percent of the poor favored government action to improve the lot of the poor, compared to 28 percent of the prosperous.[6] This pattern has continued through the years and is reflected again in the 1992 National Election Study. Respondents were asked if government should provide more services in the areas of health and education, even if it meant an increase in government spending. Among opinion holders, 63 percent of the self-identified working class favored this position, 49 percent of the middle class, and only 38 percent of the upper class. Table 7.1 shows the relationship between subjective social class and beliefs that the government should spend more money on programs such as student loans, child care, Social Security, aid to the homeless, or science and technology.

For most of these programs the working class is the most likely to favor increased government spending. But there are interesting variations. The greatest difference among the classes is on increased funding for Social Security, unemployment, and child care. Obviously, the working class has real concerns about the well-being of their children when they are away from home and for their own financial security after retirement. On the other hand, there is only a slight difference on spending for student loans, which benefit all classes. And in the case of science and technology, the middle and upper classes are more likely to want spending increased. The opinions on these spending increases

TABLE 7.1 Opinions About Spending on Selected Government Programs by Subjective Social Class

Percent wanting government spending increased on	Working Class	Middle Class	Upper Class
Homeless	76	71	59
Poor	62	51	35
Social Security	57	42	27
Unemployment assistance	43	28	35
Child care	57	47	44
Food stamps	18	15	15
Student loans	63	60	55
Science and technology	39	45	51
Aid to former Soviet Union	15	17	27

Source: NES, 1992.

seem predictable from one's station in life. Social Security and unemployment are of much more concern to the working class than the more
affluent classes. On the other hand, the middle and upper classes are
potential beneficiaries of increasing spending on science and technology, and consequently support spending increases.

The effects shown in Table 7.1 are, for the most part, quite modest.
However, if we compare actual recipients of program benefits with nonrecipients, we find the differences increase dramatically. Cook and
Barnett (1992, 150) report that 75 percent of those receiving AFDC (Aid
to Families with Dependent Children) favored increasing AFDC spending, compared to only 32 percent of nonrecipients. The same is true for
food stamps, with 53 percent of recipients favoring an increase compared to 24 percent for nonrecipients. The same pattern holds for
Medicaid, Social Security, and unemployment insurance.

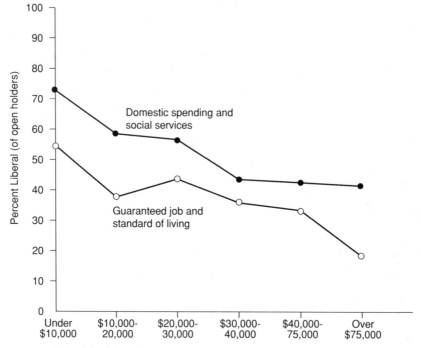

Fig. 7-1 Social Welfare Opinion by Family Income, NES 1992 (Whites Only)

For the 1992 NES, Figure 7-1 shows how family income, an objective
indicator of social class, is related to opinion on the issues of increasing
domestic spending and services, and support for a government-guaran-
teed job and good standard of living. (Nonwhites are excluded here in
order to show the effect of income independent of race.) We would expect for reasons of simple economic self-interest that those in the lower-
income categories would be supportive of public policies designed to

promote employment and fund social programs, with a commensurate lack of support among the more financially secure. As one goes from poor to affluent, one does in fact see a decline in the percentage of people holding liberal positions on these economic issues.

But as Shingles (1989) demonstrates, the usual effect of income on domestic policy opinion can be nullified by the person's party identification, particularly at the highest income levels. For illustration, consider the views of white respondents in the 1992 NES survey making more than $75,000. Reflecting their wealth, this group contained more than twice as many Republicans as Democrats. Among the wealthy white Republicans with opinions, only 11 percent said the government should provide more services and increase spending. But 90 percent of wealthy white Democrats with opinions chose this position over reducing services and taxes. And while support for a guaranteed job and standard of living was a mere 4 percent among wealthy white Republicans with an opinion, it rose to 35 percent among wealthy white Democrats opinion holders.

Class Differences on Noneconomic Domestic Issues

On noneconomic issues, liberalism tends to increase rather than decrease as one goes up the status ladder. Typical are the relationships between social class and opinions on equality for women, abortion, gays in the military, and rights of the accused, shown in Table 7.2.

While the differences are not large, they are consistent. Reading the table across, we see that support for women's equality rises as one moves up the status ladder, as does support for abortion, gays in the military, and rights of the accused. Similar relationships between status and opinion are found when people are asked about whether Communists, socialists, or atheists should be granted the full range of civil liberties. Among whites, high-status respondents express less racial prejudice than do low-status respondents (Sheatsley 1966; Hahn 1968; Campbell 1971; Hamilton 1975; Kinder 1986; Sniderman and Piazza 1993).

TABLE 7.2 Opinions on Noneconomic Domestic Issues by Social Class

Opinion	Working Class	Middle Class	Upper Class
Favor equal role for women	85%	89%	93%
Oppose law requiring women to notify father before abortion	29%	37%	54%
Allow gays in the military	56%	59%	67%
Support rights of the accused˙	39%	41%	47%

Source: NES, 1992.
*NES, 1976.

TABLE 7.3 Joint Effects of Income and Education on Selected Issues, Whites Only

		Education		
		Less than High School	High School Graduate	College Graduate
For legal abortions in all circumstances				
Family income	Low	36%	41%	79%
	Medium	39%	44%	62%
	High	*	53%	58%
For more domestic spending				
Family income	Low	57%	63%	69%
	Medium	54%	50%	53%
	High	*	53%	30%
For aid to minorities				
Family income	Low	26%	28%	52%
	Medium	16%	22%	40%
	High	*	15%	33%

Source: 1992 NES election data. Percents are based on opinion-holders, among white respondents. For full text of opinion questions, see the Appendix.
*Too few cases for analysis.

On issues outside the economic realm, status differences are complicated by the role of education. We saw in Chapter 5 that educational achievement promotes political tolerance and political liberalism. This liberalizing effect of education, however, is almost entirely limited to noneconomic issues. If we separate the effects of income and education on political attitudes, we find different patterns for economic and noneconomic issues. On noneconomic issues, high education but not high income is associated with liberalism. On economic issues, high income is negatively related to liberalism while education is not.

Table 7.3 shows some relevant examples. This table indicates that within each of the three income categories, liberal opinions on the noneconomic issue of legalized abortion increase with educational attainment. Notice, for example, the large differences in support for abortion in the low-income group with varying amounts of education. Only 36 percent of those without a high school degree support abortion, moving to 41 percent for high school graduates and 79 percent for college graduates. The reverse pattern can be seen for the economic issue of domestic spending. As family income goes up, individuals become more conservative on domestic spending. But for people who have the same income, differences in education have a lesser impact. The third issue—aid to minorities—taps both the economic dimension of financial aid and the noneconomic dimensions of attitudes toward minorities. On this issue one can see the joint liberal effect of higher education (which affects the noneconomic part of the issue) and the conservative effect of income (which affects the economic part of the issue). Thus we see that among those of low income, college graduates are most favorable to aid for minorities. But among college graduates, those with the highest incomes are the least favorable.

Class Differences on Foreign Policy

The major class difference in foreign policy attitudes is that people in the lower educational strata are more ready to take the "isolationist" position than the more "internationally minded" high-status groups. People of higher status and education are most in favor of such internationalist policies as foreign aid, detente with Communist nations, and support for continued U.S. financial aid to the United Nations. In Chapter 4, Figure 4-2, we presented time series data on whether the U.S. should take an active role in world affairs or stay out of world affairs. This item has shown very large class differences. For example, in 1948, 92 percent of the college-educated favored taking an active role, compared to only 59 percent of those with a grade-school education (Page and Shapiro 1992, 179). The class difference on this and similar items has changed little in the ensuing forty-plus years, as can be seen in Table 7.4.

The college-educated are more internationalist and less likely to see communism as the worst of all possible governments. Based on data such as these, academics and others frequently argued during the Cold War era that the less educated, presumably less attentive public should be mostly ignored. They simply did not have the grasp on world affairs to appreciate the necessity for an activist role in world affairs by the United States. But Page and Shapiro (1992, 181) argue that isolationism among the lower classes may well be rational. Given their precarious economic circumstances, the less affluent are understandably more concerned about feeding their families than dispensing foreign aid or protecting American investments abroad.

We might expect that high-status people would be more willing to support military action abroad, as it is in some ways a logical extension of internationalism, just as isolationism implies keeping the troops at

TABLE 7.4 Education and Internationalism

	Less than High School	High School Graduate	College Graduate
Take active role in world affairs	48%	66%	86%
Pull out of United Nations	19%	12%	6%
Communism worst kind of government	63%	49%	36%

Source: GSS, 1993.

TABLE 7.5 Education and Opinion on U.S. Involvement in Foreign Conflicts

Issue	Less than High School	High School Graduate	College Graduate
U.S. should be willing to use military force to solve world problems (1992)	24%	21%	25%
U.S. should expand the Vietnam War (1968)	39%	40%	41%
U.S. should be more involved in Central America (1986)	19%	21%	25%
The Persian Gulf War was worth it (1992)	48%	56%	61%

Source: NES.

home. The accumulation of survey evidence shows only a slightly greater tendency on the part of those with high economic status or high education to support American military adventures. When asked in 1992 how "willing the United States should be to use military force to solve world problems," we see from Table 7.5 almost no difference by education among those who responded "extremely willing" or "very willing."

In the case of Vietnam, back in 1968, support for the war among the college-educated may seem surprising because the most visible war opponents were found on college campuses. Only if we refine the educational index to isolate the small segment of people with graduate degrees or four-year degrees from the most prestigious universities do we find disproportionate antiwar sentiment at the top of the educational ladder (Rosenberg et al. 1970, 54–65). During the mid-1980s, the United States was deeply involved in guerrilla war in Central America. Again, the better-educated show only a slight tendency to be the most supportive. Finally, we see the better-educated somewhat more likely to agree that "all things considered the [1991 Persian] Gulf War was worth the cost."

We must be careful in extracting significance from the class differences on questions of foreign policy, as the "no opinion" rate increases dramatically as one goes down the status ladder. Quite understandably, lower-status people are more concerned with the economic issues of day-to-day living than more abstract questions of foreign policy. We may particularly suspect that poor people and those with little education often grope for what they perceive to be the "official" policy when asked to give their foreign policy views (Ladd 1970). For example, such tendency may be at least a partial explanation for why the less-educated were the most opposed to letting "Communist" China into the United States. The better-educated had the advantage of knowing the idea of China's admission was gaining respectability. They are more able to identify the official government position on international issues. Thus, when governmental opposition to a nuclear test ban treaty flip-flopped in the early 1960s, the polls showed that the more educated respondents changed accordingly, while those with less education remained stable (Rossi 1965). Such a pattern would only occur if considerable sophistication was required in order to follow changes in the official line or in main currents of thought.

Class Differences in Voting and Party Preferences

Since the years of Franklin Roosevelt's presidency, the relationship between economic class and party preference has reflected class differences on economic issues. In the 1930s, Roosevelt's efforts to expand the federal government's role in order to combat the economic effects of the Great Depression caused a "partisan realignment" of the American electorate. With the high salience of economic issues, the poor and working class were given a solid push toward the Democratic Party, and the more affluent clearly came to side with the Republicans. This basic partisan division of the electorate remains today, although in a weaker form, largely because new issues (most notably race) tend to undercut the link between class and partisanship established some sixty years ago. The Republicans have very

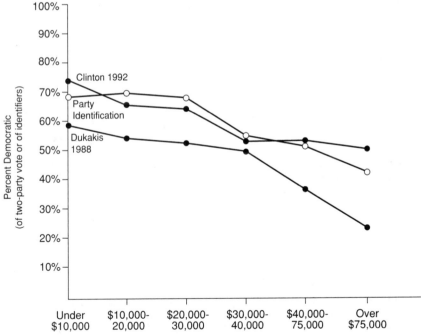

Fig. 7-2 Party Identification 1992, Vote 1988 and 1992 by Family Income (Source: NES)

effectively used race as a "wedge issue," most notably in 1988, to split off working-class whites from the New Deal coalition, which has served to weaken class voting. In 1992, Bill Clinton sought to recapture the "Bubba vote" by running as a "New Democrat"—shorthand for the Southern, more conservative wing of the party. For example, Clinton favored the death penalty, an important conservative symbol. If the Clinton campaign strategy was successful, we might expect to see an increase in class voting as wayward elements of the New Deal coalition returned to the party.

Figure 7-2 shows presidential voting in 1988 and 1992 (along with party identification) as a function of family income (for whites only).[7] Class voting was clearly different in 1992 than in 1988, but it is difficult to argue that class voting was greater. Somewhat ironically, Clinton's relatively conservative campaign seems to have helped him at both ends of the class spectrum, as he did better than Dukakis among both high- and low-income earners. He did particularly well at the low end, where many "Reagan Democrats" apparently returned to the fold. He also did better than Dukakis among the higher-income groups. Blacks show a much smaller class bias in their voting than do whites. In 1988, Bush got 10 percent of the black vote, but still only 15 percent among those earning over $50,000 (Bolce et al. 1992).[8] As has been the case in recent elections, 1992 could hardly be described as a polarization between rich and poor.[9]

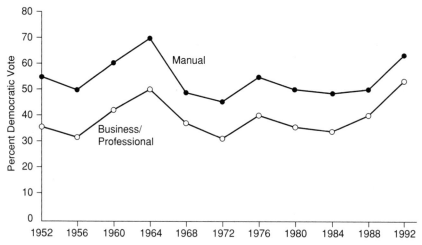

Fig. 7-3 Presidential voting (two party vote) by occupation. (Source: SRC/CPS/NES surveys reported in Harold Stanley and Richard Niemi, *Vital Statistics on American Politics* [Washington, DC: CQ Press, 1990], pp. 98–99.); NES 1988, 1992

Party identification in 1992 shows a clear class bias among white citizens.[10] We see that the Democrats hold a substantial advantage over the Republicans for individuals making under $30,000. It is only when family incomes exceed $40,000 that partisanship splits about evenly, and only among those making over $75,000 a year (21 percent of the white electorate) do Republicans have an advantage. Again, income has little influence on black partisanship. A total of 6 percent identify with the Republicans, but that number increases to only 11 percent for those making over $50,000 (Bolce et al. 1992).

Figure 7-3 traces the relationship between class and presidential voting, going back to 1952.[11] For simplicity of comparison, the voters are split into only two occupational categories—manual and business/professional.[12] According to this measure, class voting was greatest prior to 1964, and has closed somewhat since then. The data lend little credence to the class polarization thesis. Class differences in the 1980s did not widen, because there were few class-polarizing issues on the political agenda, and many issues that cut across class lines. Reagan's aggressive foreign policy and many of his social policies were popular among the working class, which took the edge off their disenchantment with his economic polices. Bush's use of mostly symbolic issues in 1988 (Willie Horton and the flag allegiance themes) again appealed to working-class whites, and dampened class polarization. Clinton, of course, did better among working-class whites, but class voting was reduced by his atypically strong showing among those in business and professionals.

Despite the fluctuations in the degree of class voting over the years, class differences in party identification have remained reasonably constant from the 1930s through the 1990s. Among identifiers, blue-collar workers have never been under 60 percent Democratic since 1939. However, professionals are now more Democratic in their two-party voting (61 percent) than any time since 1939, and in 1992 were only slightly less Democratic than blue-collar workers. In apparent compensation, those in the "business" category moved sharply toward the Republican Party in the 1980s, and in 1992 Clinton received only 47 percent of the two-party vote among this group.

The fact that class conflict has never dominated American politics to the extent it has in Europe may have been one long-term source of the stability of the American political system (Ladd 1970). But a further decline in the political importance of the traditional class-related issues may augur something quite different from a period of political tranquillity, for the increasingly important racial and social issues obviously could intensify political conflict in years to come.

7-2 Race and Political Opinions_____

The most profound political division between groups in the United States is between blacks and whites. In 1968, the Kerner Commission (U.S. National Advisory Committee on Civil Disorders 1968, 1) concluded that "Our nation is moving toward two societies, one black, one white—separate and unequal." While progress has surely been made since that date, there is a wide gulf between blacks and whites on most political issues, particularly on those involving discrimination and its remedies. Of course, blacks are not the only racial or ethnic minority in America. The proportion of Hispanics and Asians is growing at a rapid rate, and the former will soon outnumber blacks as the largest minority group in the United States. However, neither group has the distinctive political opinions that characterize the black population.

Blacks, Whites, and Political Opinions

Until the late 1970s, the central division of opinion in the United States concerning the role of blacks was the very issue of a racially integrated society. In a 1964 NES survey, respondents were asked if they favored "strict segregation" of the races, "desegregation," or "something in between." Not surprisingly, 73 percent of blacks favored desegregation, while only 6 percent favored segregation, with 21 percent favoring something in between. In the case of whites, about equal numbers chose strict segregation (25 percent) as desegregation (27 percent), with the remainder choosing something in between. But by 1978 (the last year this question was asked), only 5 percent of whites favored strict segregation—about the same as among blacks (6 percent). In 1964, the NES shows 74 percent of whites thought civil rights leaders were "pushing too fast" compared to 11 percent among blacks. But by 1980 the percentage had dropped to 40 percent among whites, with blacks remaining essentially unchanged.

By the late 1970s, the political agenda on race shifted to the question of whether the government should actively help blacks move into the economic mainstream through preferences in education and employment, or whether blacks themselves were responsible for their economic well-being. We can compare the distribution of these sentiments among blacks and whites using an NES question asked in 1974 and 1992 as to whether the government should "make every effort to improve the economic and social condition of blacks and other minorities" or whether they should help themselves.

	Whites		Blacks	
	1974	*1992*	*1974*	*1992*
Government should help blacks	25%	19%	63%	42%
Unsure	26	26	25	24
Blacks should help themselves	50	54	12	33
	101%	100%	100%	100%

There are substantial differences between blacks and whites on this issue in both 1974 and 1992. But the trend for both racial groups is in a conservative direction. While there has been a 6 percent drop in support among whites for government assistance to blacks and other minorities, there has been a larger 21 percent drop among blacks. The fact that blacks and whites have moved in the same direction suggests a declining belief among both racial groups in the ability of government to solve problems—including those that may stem from the consequences of America's past racial practices.

In recent years, much of the debate over racial policies has shifted to the arena of affirmative action. Given the dual emphasis in the American political tradition on equality and individualism, many well-intentioned citizens appear caught in a dilemma. First, there is a recognition that blacks historically have not had the same opportunities as whites, but there is a belief that educational opportunities and jobs should be filled on merit, without reference to race, sex, or religion.

As one would expect, blacks are more supportive of affirmative action than whites. In 1992, a NES survey asked respondents if they would favor a program in which a college or graduate school maintained a "quota," so that more minority applicants would get admitted than would otherwise be the case. Blacks were overwhelmingly favorable, but almost a quarter of all whites were favorable as well.

	Whites	*Blacks*
Favor educational quota	24%	70%
Undecided	5	8
Oppose Educational quota	71	23
	100%	100%

The current political agenda on affirmative action also includes racial preferences in hiring and promotion. In 1992, NES asked if due to past discrimination blacks should be given preference in hiring and promotion, or whether such preference is wrong because it discriminates against whites. Although there are again sizable racial differences, they are not as large as on the educational question. The reason is that many fewer blacks endorse compensatory action for jobs than endorse compensatory action for higher education. These data reflect a pattern seen in most questions on affirmative action. Both blacks and whites are considerably more favorable toward programs that create equality of opportunity than toward programs that mandate equality in outcomes.

	Whites	Blacks
Favor preferences for blacks in hiring and promotion	13%	53%
Undecided	4	5
Oppose preferences for blacks in hiring and promotion	83	41
	100%	100%

As we noted in Chapter 4, questions on affirmative action are very sensitive to question-wording effects, as many of the terms employed, such as "quotas" or "racial preferences," are politically charged, and the NES questions reported above may overstate the extent to which blacks and whites disagree on affirmative action. Sigelman and Welch (1991, 129) analyzed a large number of these questions and found, depending on question wording, that as high as 96 percent of blacks and 76 percent of whites favored affirmative action, or as low as 23 percent of blacks and 9 percent of whites were favorable. They also found that those affirmative action programs that get the most support from blacks also get the most support from whites. However, on all questions blacks were more favorable to affirmative action programs than were whites.

These opinion gaps are rooted in very large differences between blacks and whites about the continued existence of racial discrimination. For example, in 1987 one black citizen in four believed that half of the white American public shared the racial views of the Ku Klux Klan. Only a small sliver of whites shared this perception (Sigelman and Welch 1991). About four times as many blacks as whites perceived discrimination against blacks in education. Fifty-seven percent of blacks believed they got lower wages due to discrimination, while only 14 percent of whites believed such discrimination exists. Sigelman and Welch (1991, 59) write that blacks today "see racial discrimination as an everyday occurrence, not a historical curiosity." It is, therefore, not surprising to find blacks favoring government actions in their behalf.

When asked about changes among whites (in 1989) compared to five years ago, 44 percent of blacks saw an increase in antiblack sentiment nationally, but only 25 percent saw antiblack sentiment increasing in the area where they live (Sigelman and Welch 1992, 61). Why do blacks by a margin of almost 20 percent see things getting worse nationally rather than locally—where they have direct experience? The answer must certainly lie with the media, and its tendency to dwell on isolated, but sensationalist, racial incidents, such as Howard Beach,

TABLE 7.6 Race and Opinion on Selected Non-Civil Rights Issues

Issue	Whites	Blacks	Difference
Government should provide more services and increase spending	50	81	+31
Government should see that people have jobs and a good standard of living	34	68	+34
Oppose death penalty for those convicted of murder	17	41	+24
Favor laws to protect homosexuals from discrimination	59	70	+11
U.S. should have stayed out of 1991 Persian Gulf War	16	47	+31

Source: NES, 1992. Percents are of opinion-holders.

Bensonhurst, and the Rodney King case. By all reliable accounts, interracial violence is extremely infrequent. But, ironically, its very infrequency means it will get a disproportionate share of media coverage.

Even on issues that are tangential to civil rights, blacks are more likely than whites to take the liberal position. Some examples are shown in Table 7.6. Black vs. white differences are particularly strong on economic issues such as the pace of domestic spending, and whether the government should guarantee everyone a good standard of living. For whites, social class is a consistent correlate of opinion on these social welfare issues. However, for blacks there is no relationship. Upper-income blacks are about as supportive as lower-income blacks.[13] The reason for this nonrelationship is that greater income among blacks is related to greater racial identification (Tate 1993, 27–29). In other words, upper-income blacks are more likely to identify with their race than with their social class. Upper-class whites, on the other hand, are more likely to identify with their social class.

Blacks are also much less supportive of the death penalty than whites, perhaps because those on death row are disproportionately black. Note, however, that the death penalty is still supported by a majority of black citizens. Blacks are also less supportive of American military action abroad. For example, we see a sizable difference in support for American involvement in the 1991 Persian Gulf War. But this case is not an isolated example. Blacks were much less supportive of the Vietnam War than were whites, and have been less enthusiastic about other American military adventures, such as those involving the Nicaraguan Contras and military actions in Panama and Grenada. One area in which blacks have been more conservative than whites is on the issue of abortion. Black women are about twice as likely to have abortions than white women. But for all but one of the GSS surveys between 1972 and 1991, blacks were more opposed to abortion than whites (Cook et al. 1992, 46).[14] These differences, which were substantial in the early 1970s, have been closing gradually over the years, so that by the late 1980s the difference was typically around 5 percent, but sometimes as large as 10 to 15 percent, depending on the question. Much of this opinion gap has to do with differences in social background factors. Blacks compared to whites are less educated, more likely to have been raised in rural areas, and more likely to attend church regularly. These factors tend to depress support for abortion (Combs and Welch 1982).

Racial Groups and the Vote

In terms of the vote and party identification, there are major differences between blacks and whites. For instance, in 1992, 82 percent of blacks but only 39 percent of whites cast their vote for Bill Clinton. We present below the 1992 vote choice, as reported in VRS exit polls, for the four major ethnic groups in the United States.

1992 Vote	Asians	Blacks	Hispanics	Whites
Bush	55%	11%	25%	41%
Clinton	29	82	62	39
Perot	16	7	14	20
	100%	100%	100%	100%

We see Hispanics also voted heavily Democratic, although not to the same extent as blacks. The most Republican group in the 1992 electorate are Asians, but they amounted to less than 1 percent of the total vote cast in 1992. Like Hispanics, their electoral turnout is lower than their percentages in the total population.

The voting difference we see between blacks and whites is also found in terms of the underlying attitude of party identification. Among the adult white population, the 1992 NES shows 33 percent Democratic, 36 percent Independent, and 31 percent Republican. Among the adult black population, 69 percent are Democrats, 26 percent are Independent, and 5 percent are Republicans. Using the VRS exit poll for the 1992 presidential election, we can expand our analysis to include Asians and Hispanics. The data reported below are only for the 54 percent that voted on election day, not the overall adult population.

Party Identification	Asians	Blacks	Hispanics	Whites
Democrat	38%	77%	47%	35%
Independent	28	14	19	23
Republican	34	9	33	42
	100%	100%	100%	100%

Over time, American blacks have undergone a long-term reversal in their party allegiance. Between the Civil War and Franklin Roosevelt's presidency, most blacks who could vote opted for the Republican Party because it was the party of Lincoln. From the 1930s to the present, however, most blacks have supported the Democratic Party. Initially this shift was a response to economic issues rather than any consequential attempt on the part of the Democratic Party to remove racial barriers or explicitly pitch an appeal to blacks. Only in recent years could the Democratic Party be identified as the party with clearly greater sympathy for the civil rights cause. As a result of the Democrats' increasing image as the more "pro-civil rights" party, Democratic voting among blacks at the presidential level has changed from a tendency to near unanimity. The solidifying event was the 1964 election, in which President Lyndon Johnson took a strong stand in favor of the Civil Rights Act and Republican challenger Barry Goldwater opposed and voted against it in Congress (as an infringement on states' rights). The change over time is shown in Figure 7-4.

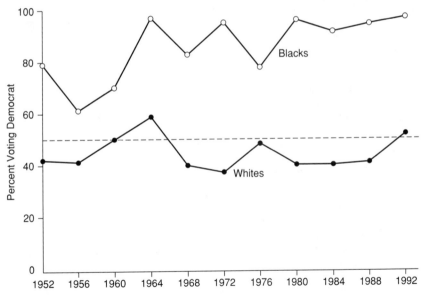

Fig. 7-4 Race and the Two-Party Presidential Vote, 1952–1992. Sources: Gallup Poll, 1952–1976, NES, 1980–1992

Clearly the black vote is a pivotal factor for the Democratic Party in presidential elections. In only one such election since World War II (1964), has the Democratic candidate received a majority of the total white vote.[15] Again, we find that the usual predictors of party preference among whites do not work in the case of blacks. Higher-income blacks are not more likely to be Republican, as is the case in the white population. In fact, black Republicans and black Democrats are remarkably similar, both demographically and in their policy preference Tate (1993).

TABLE 7.7 Age and Opinion on Selected Issues

	Percent Support Among Opinion-Holders		
	Under 30	Over 55	Difference
Economic Issues			
Government should cover all hospital and medical expenses˙	66%	61%	+5
Increase Social Security benefits˙	59	63	−4
Government should provide more services, even if it means increased spending˙	65	48	+17
Government should see to it that everyone has a job and a good standard of living˙	52	35	+17
Government should reduce income differences between rich and poor˙˙	67	51	+16
Social Issues			
Homeowners should not refuse to sell home to someone because of race or color˙˙	79	49	+30
Marijuana use should be made illegal˙˙	26	15	+11
Allow homosexuals to teach in college˙˙	79	56	+23
A woman should always be able to obtain an abortion as a matter of choice˙	50	38	+12
Men and women should have equal roles in business and government˙	93	78	+15
Foreign Policy/Military Issues			
Disagree U.S. should maintain a strong military˙	35	21	+13
Defense spending should be decreased˙	69	65	+4
U.S. is better off staying out of military conflict˙	29	32	−3
Wrong to send troops to Gulf War˙	19	25	−6
Liberal Conservative Ideology			
Ideological Identification˙			
Liberal	33	19	
Moderate	37	36	
Conservative	31	45	

*NES, 1992.
**GSS, 1993.
Percents are of opinion-holders only.

7-3 Age and Political Opinions _____

If one examines a breakdown by age of the scores of political issues that might interest the student of public opinion, three patterns stand out. On the majority of issues there are no meaningful age-group differences; on a sizable minority of issues, those older are more conservative than those younger, and on a small number of issues, the young are more conservative than their elders. There are at least three reasons why older cohorts might differ from younger ones. First, there may be composition effects in which (for example) younger cohorts are better-educated than those who have come before. Second, life-cycle effects in which the process of maturation results in greater responsibilities and consequently greater conservatism; and third, generational effects in which unique events and experiences lead to differing political outlooks.

The Politics of Age

To the list just mentioned we can add a fourth possibility—the politics of self-interest. For instance, in the early 1980s advocates for children blamed inadequate funding for programs benefiting youngsters on the political power of older Americans, whom they accused of greedily siphoning off more than their fair share of government dollars. In the 1990s, many have voiced concern that the Social Security and Medicare benefits enjoyed by older Americans will bankrupt the system before those currently paying the bill will be eligible to receive benefits. Issues such as these have raised the specter of intergenerational political conflict.

We see, however, from Table 7.7 that the largest generational differences are not on issues that might divide age groups in terms of their self-interest. On the issues of medical care and Social Security, the gap between older and younger citizens is insignificant. In an extensive analysis of age-based opinions, Christine Day concluded that "older people are nearly indistinguishable from younger adults on most issues—including aging policy issues" (Day 1990, 53). There is some tendency on more general economic issues for older Americans to be slightly more conservative than younger, as can be seen in Table 7.7. But it is on social issues, where society is in a state of flux, that we find younger cohorts consistently more liberal than older ones. The young are more receptive to new ideas since they are, for the most part, not committed to the old ones. This point can be illustrated using the 30 percent gap in the open housing item in Table 7.7. Very few under 30 have lived during a time when refusing to sell your home to someone because of race or color was legal. They are likely to simply take this prohibition for granted. Alternatively, those over 55 may recall when such practices were not only legal, but quite common. To endorse the more liberal position may mean changing an opinion that was once viewed as quite legitimate.

On foreign affairs, it is often thought that the young are more "dovish" than their elders. However, the evidence for this proposition is mixed. We see older cohorts slightly more likely to want a strong military and to oppose cuts in defense spending. But there is no difference on the general question of staying out of military conflicts, and the younger cohort is somewhat more supportive of U.S. involvement in the 1991 Persian Gulf War than those over 55. This latter finding is consistent with age differences in support for the Korean and Vietnam wars. Contrary to popular belief, in both instances it was the youngest age groups that were the most supportive of these wars. In the case of Vietnam, the highly visible protesters at prestige colleges were a small minority. Finally, in terms of ideological identification there is an equal split by age among the moderates, but the older age group is more likely to identify as conservative and the younger more likely to identify as liberal.

Most of the differences reported in Table 7.7 show the older generation to be more conservative than the younger. It is important, however, not to infer from these data that people get more conservative as they get older. In fact, based on an extensive analysis of archival opinion data, there is very little evidence to support the aging/conservatism hypothesis (Davis 1992, 281). Rather, a more convincing explanation is that the older generation has changed its views only modestly since its members were under 30, but the current under-30 generation has been socialized to more liberal opinions on these same issues.

7-4 Religion and Political Opinions

Compared with other nations, Americans are religious. Between 1974 and 1978, Gallup asked residents of nine nations to describe the importance of their religious beliefs.[16] As one can see from the following table, the United States stands out in the high proportion of its citizens who find religion to be very important.

	Very important	Fairly or not too important	Not at all important
United States	58%	37%	5%
Italy	36	58	6
Canada	36	55	9
Benelux	26	52	19
Australia	25	62	13
United Kingdom	23	52	20
France	22	56	20
West Germany	17	67	14
Scandinavia	17	67	13

More recent data, collected in 1991, comparing 14 nations shows that, next to Poland, the United States has the largest number of citizens who describe themselves as being at least "somewhat religious" (Greeley 1992).[17] Between 1952 and 1978, there was a sharp decline (from 75 to 53 percent) in the number of people who said religion was "very" important" in their lives. But as one might expect, given the public visibility of the religion/politics link since 1980, there has been a recent upsurge: In the 1990s, about 60 percent say religion is very important in their lives.[18]

Protestants, Catholics, Jews and "Nones"

In terms of religious preference, 64 percent of Americans are Protestant, 26 percent are Catholic, 2 percent are Jewish, and 8 percent profess no religious preference ("Nones").[19] On what basis would we anticipate religious denominations to differ politically? Although Protestants are a pluralistic group, we might expect they would be the most conservative. Until recently, they held higher-status jobs and enjoyed higher incomes than did Catholics (there is no difference today). But the fact that Catholic immigrants arrived more recently and were subjected to a certain amount of discrimination may have left traces of liberal sentiment. Also, doctrinal differences exist which might have political relevance. The Catholic Church has taken a strong position against birth control and abortion; mainline Protestant churches less so. Further, the Protestant focus on individual responsibility for one's own economic and spiritual well-being (the "Protestant ethic") may predispose Protestants to be conservative on economic questions and issues of affirmative action. The high-status, high-income occupations of Jews compared to other religious groups, plus their concern for the well-being of Israel, might lead us to anticipate that Jews would be the most conservative and internationalist of religious groups. Counterbalancing these forces is the unique history of the Jewish people as a persecuted minority, which drives them in a liberal direction, particularly on civil liberties.

Finally, a group that has received little attention, but now constitutes 8 percent of the population, are the "Nones." This category is a residual, consisting of atheists, agnostics, those indifferent to religion, and those believing in a Supreme Being but disenchanted with organized religion. We would expect them to be liberal, as to be unchurched is to be outside the American cultural mainstream. Such marginality tends to result in a liberal political outlook.

We shall limit our analysis to Northern whites, so as not to confuse the effect of denominational preference with region and race. The South is largely Protestant and conservative; blacks are largely Protestant and liberal. To contrast all four groups, we rely on the General Social

Survey pooled data set for the years 1989 to 1993. The GSS repeated many questions over several years. By combining the samples we can increase the sample size in small subgroups. While there are some variations in issue preferences from year to year, the large sample size allows for stable estimates in the case of Jews and Nones, which are a small percentage of the population.

Table 7.8 shows Catholics to be slightly more liberal than Protestants, but the margins are not large. Note that 23 percent of Protestants claim a liberal ideology, while Catholics are only slightly higher at 26 percent. (At the other end of the spectrum, 40 percent of Protestants and 31 percent of Catholics are conservative.) Jews and those with no preference are substantially more liberal than the two major religious groups, 51 and 44 percent, respectively. On economic

TABLE 7.8 Religious Denomination and Political Opinion, Northern Whites

Issue	Denomination			
Economic Issues	*Protestant*	*Catholic*	*Jewish*	*None*
Government should reduce income differentials	57%	55%	40%	50%
Government should improve standard of living	52	52	56	59
Government should help pay for medical care	76	81	74	80
Civil/Moral Issues				
Abortion allowed for any reason	40	39	80	71
Favor legalization of marijuana	16	16	38	47
Disapprove of prayer in public schools	35	41	88	73
Favor government aid to blacks	22	27	33	38
Men, women equally suited for politics	75	76	86	84
Foreign/Defense Issues				
Communism not worst form of government	49	48	68	69
Too much military spending	41	56	57	56
Take less active role in world affairs	59	54	43	46
Did the wrong thing in sending troops to 1991 Persian Gulf War*	12	16	29	28
Political Ideology				
Liberal	23	26	49	51
Moderate	37	43	36	30
Conservative	40	31	14	19
Party Identification				
Democrat	37	37	68	32
Independent	30	31	20	50
Republican	43	31	12	17

Source: GSS, 1989–1993. Percentages are of opinion-holders only.
*NES, 1992.

issues, there are modest differences, with Catholics being somewhat more liberal than Protestants, with Jews and Nones not being substantially different from the two major denominations. On foreign and defense policies, Protestants and Catholics differ only marginally. Jews are somewhat more internationalist than the other groups—as expected. But they were less supportive of the 1991 Persian Gulf War than the two major religious groups. Generally speaking, Nones are the most isolationist. Note that on the key issue of abortion, there is no difference between Catholics and Protestants—they are equally likely to endorse the statement that abortions should be allowed for any reason. Claiming a denominational affiliation is, of course, an easy response, and does not mean that people are actually religious. However, if we look at differences between Catholics and Protestants among those who attend church once a week or more, there is still almost no difference between the two groups. In the General Social Survey, six different questions are asked about abortion, and this pattern is more or less constant. On the other hand, Jews and Nones are much more supportive of abortion on demand than are Protestants and Catholics.

On less transitory opinions involving partisanship and voting, there are still differences between Catholics and Protestants, but they, too, are declining. Religious divisions were at their clearest in the 1960 presidential election, when the Democrats broke with tradition and nominated a Catholic, John F. Kennedy, for president. Among Northern whites, the breakdown of the 1960 presidential vote by religion was as follows:

Northern Whites	*Protestant*	*Catholic*	*Jewish*
Voting Democratic (Kennedy)	28%	83%	93%
Voting Republican (Nixon)	72	17	7
	100%	100%	100%

Almost three-fourths of the Protestant vote among Northern whites was for Nixon, while over 80 percent of the Catholic and Jewish vote went for Kennedy. In more typical elections, without a Catholic candidate, the religious division is smaller, but still present. Following are the presidential vote divisions among (northern white) Protestants, Catholics, and Jews in 1992.[20]

Northern Whites	*Protestant*	*Catholic*	*Jewish*
Voting Democratic (Clinton)	36%	48%	88%
Voting Republican (Bush)	43	30	7
Voting for Perot	21	21	6
	100%	100%	100%

The temporal stability of partisan differences between Protestants, Catholics, and Jews is shown in Figure 7-5.

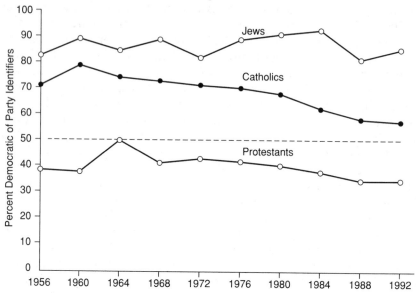

Fig. 7-5 Religion and Party Identification (Northern Whites only), 1956–1992
Source, NES

The figure shows the percent Democratic (among identifiers only) among Northern whites beginning in 1956. The most remarkable aspect of Figure 7-5 is the stability over time in partisan preference. Typically, Jews are about 80 percent Democratic, Catholics about 65 percent (and slowly declining), and Protestants about 40 percent. Of those declaring no religious preference, about 65 percent of those identifying are Democrats.[21] The long-term trend shows little loss of religious distinctiveness in party preference.

Many of the reasons advanced earlier to explain issue differences among the religions also apply to the differences we see in partisanship and voting. However, we should note that the Democrats have traditionally wooed the immigrant voters, most of whom were Catholic. The payoff of this policy for the Democratic Party has been the continued allegiance of many members of Catholic ethnic groups—the Irish, Italians, Poles, East Europeans, and Mexicans—who often continue to identify and vote Democratic despite having incomes that place them solidly in the middle class. One explanation for the continued Democratic voting among Catholics is that once American Catholics were less affluent than their Protestant neighbors—a condition that would naturally cause them to gravitate to the Democratic Party for economic reasons. But there is more than economics at work, because during the 1940s surveys showed that even affluent Catholics tended to be Democratic, much as affluent blacks do today (Berelson et al. 1954, 64–66). Perhaps the best explanation for the Democratic allegiance of Catholics is simply the socialization of partisanship from one generation to the next. Even though the social and economic reasons for remaining Democratic no longer exist, there is a family tradition of Democratic partisanship among Catholics. As we saw earlier, on issue positions Catholics are slightly more liberal than Protestants, but these differences are certainly not of the magnitude to prevent Catholics from comfortably embracing the GOP. Some analysts claim that Catholics are ripe for conversion to Republicanism. As evidence, it is noted that in countries where Catholicism is the major religion, its adherents are usually identified with the more conservative political parties. But minus a major realigning shock, partisan conversion rarely occurs.[22] If the Democratic Party is loosening its hold on Catholics, the process is likely to be gradual.

Protestant Denominations and Evangelicals

On most issues there is greater disagreement among Protestants of various persuasions than between Protestants and Catholics. Theological differences between denominations often show up as differences in political opinions. For example, the emphasis on personal salvation in the Baptist church and other "fundamentalist" groups seemingly makes their members conservative, while the more "worldly" involvement in social problems on the part of nonfundamentalist groups (Presbyterians and Episcopalians, for example) ought to make their members relatively liberal. Also, the theology of some fundamentalist Protestant denominations condemns departures from traditional life-styles, while more liberal denominations are more accommodating. Very sharp differences on these issues have been found between the political attitudes of Protestant clergymen of fundamentalist and nonfundamentalist churches, and among church members who are very politically involved. Wald and associates investigated the possibility that active membership in a specific congregation can have a direct effect on the political attitudes of parishioners. Based on a sample of 12 Protestant churches in a Florida community, they found parishioners from the more theologically conservative congregations were also more politically conservative, particularly on social issues. Wald et al. attribute this relationship directly to "messages from the pulpit and social interaction [among] the congregants" (Wald et al. 1989, 542; see Jelen 1992 for an extension of this research). Leege and Welch (1984), in a study of Catholic parishioners, came to a similar conclusion about the role of theology in political outlooks.

Recently, evangelical Christian groups have interjected a new dimension into American politics, due both to the uniqueness of their political beliefs and the grass-roots activism among their members. These groups are mostly Protestant, but they cut across denominations. There are two major evangelical subgroups that have been very politically active since the mid-1970s: the fundamentalists and charismatic/pentecostals. Fundamentalists emphasize personal experiences with the Holy Spirit (being "born again"), a literal interpretation of the Bible, and rejection of the Social Gospel (salvation through good works). "Charismatic" or "Pentecostal" Protestants are fundamentalists with a focus on the mystical, such as faith healing, prophecy, and speaking in tongues. Many in the fundamentalist movement are critical of charismatics, arguing their focus on spiritual gifts undermines the doctrine of the Bible's inerrancy. Fundamentalists tend to be more conservative on political issues than Pentacostals (Jelen 1993). Evangelicals currently comprise about 22 percent of the population and 48 percent of all Protestants (Wald 1992, 77). Comparatively speaking, they tend to be rural, Southern, less affluent, and less educated than the rest of the population (Reichley 1985, 312).

Table 7.9 presents evidence of how Protestant fundamentalists differ from more secular Protestants in their political views, according to the 1992 NES survey. The table is limited to white Protestants, as blacks tend to be more theologically conservative than whites, but more politically liberal due to their racial identifications. Fundamentalism is measured in terms of a variety of religious beliefs (such as being "born again"). The table contrasts the views of the 30 percent most fundamentalist with the 24 percent of Protestants most secular (or religiously indifferent) and the remaining 46 percent of 1992 white Protestant respondents) scored as in between.[23]

Overall, the evangelicals are very conservative, with almost all ideological identifiers choosing the conservative label vs. about half of the secular. As expected, it is on prayer in the public schools, civil rights, homosexuality, and, particularly, women's issues and abortion (the most salient topic on the New Right agenda) that one sees the largest differences. These differences are, for the most part, unaffected by controls for social background variables. It would seem no coincidence that membership in antifeminist groups tends to be heavily drawn from evangelical religions, while pro-feminist activists tend to be secular or belong to "worldly" denominations, although the possibility of self-selection can never be ruled out (Tedin et al. 1977). In the case of economic and domestic issues, the differences between evangelicals and the secular are smaller, and close considerably (though not entirely) when demographic controls are applied. On foreign affairs, fundamentalists are somewhat more favorable to increased defense spending, but there was no difference in attitudes about the 1991 Persian Gulf War. It seems apparent that the politics of the evangelical cause at the mass level is limited in its focus on social issues. Evangelical movements are not found only among Protestant denominations. They are also active within the Catholic faith. However, Leege and Welch (1991) find Catholic evangelicals differ from Protestants, with the former being noticeably more liberal.

Given their demographic characteristics, we might expect white evangelicals to favor the Democratic Party. They clearly did so in 1976, when their movement first gained national attention. In that year, evangelical Christians voted overwhelmingly for "born again" Democratic presidential candidate Jimmy Carter (Reichley 1985, 319–27). But since that time, fundamentalist Christians have been a mainstay of the Republican Party. In 1980, born-again white Christians gave Ronald Reagan 61 percent of their vote—a not insignificant proportion given the much greater tendency for others with similar background characteristics to vote Democratic. By the mid-1980s, most evangelicals were aware that it was the Republican Party that was most sympathetic to their social agenda. The 1992 Republican convention dis-

TABLE 7.9 Religious Fundamentalism and Political Views, White Protestants Only

Political Opinion	Religious Orientation		
	Secular	In Between	Fundamentalist
More domestic spending	48%	41%	32%
For national health insurance	63	56	38
Guarantee good standard of living	38	23	21
Permit all abortions	70	50	14
Against mandatory school prayers	67	60	51
Allow gays in military	68	59	32
Equal role for women	99	93	71
Fund more AIDS research	63	52	46
Cut defence spending	77	70	42
Oppose Gulf War	17	11	10
Increase aid to Russia	35	33	24
Percent Democratic (of party identifiers)	41	40	30
Percent Liberal (of ideological identifiers)	48	38	7
Percent for Clinton (of 1992 two-party vote)	57	49	23

Source: 1992 NES. Percentages are of opinion-holders only.

pelled any lingering uncertainty. Evangelicals are now among the most loyal of Republican voters.[24]

	% Republican 1988 Presidential Vote	% Republican 1990 House Vote	% Republican 1992 Presidential Vote
Catholic	52%	43%	36%
Jewish	36	26	12
White Protestant	66	57	46
White Evangelical	81	68	61

7-5 Geography and Opinions

People commonly think of American political opinion as differing along regional lines. The South stands out in particular for its political conservatism, particularly on civil rights. Outlandish fads (political and otherwise) are thought to start in the West, notably in California. The East is often characterized as being liberal (the land of Ted Kennedy and Mario Cuomo). There have been other regional stereotypes that once may have been valid, but seem less so today. The South, for example, was once the most internationally minded region in foreign policy, largely because of the cotton growers' interest in unrestrained trade with other nations. The Midwest at one time had the reputation, seemingly deserved on the basis of poll results, of being the most isolationist (or least internationalist) region of the country.[25] Typically, region is used as a surrogate for a common culture. A geographic area has a unique history (e.g., the Southern experience with slavery, the Civil War, and finally integration) which impacts upon the political outlook of its citizens.

Several factors, however, serve to undermine the impact of region. Americans are mobile (20 percent move each year) and dilute the native citizenry. The near universal penetration of the national media would also seem to have a homogenizing effect on regionalism. But we should not overstate the case. On many issues meaningful regional differences persist. Democratic partisans are still most frequently found in the South, but their partisan preferences do not translate into support for Democratic presidential candidates. In fact, the South in recent years has been the most Republican part of the nation in terms of presidential voting. In 1992, Clinton did best among voters from the East Coast (as did Dukakis in 1988).

Mayer's (1992, 200–205) analysis of 19 issue preferences by region shows that the South clearly stands out as the most distinctive. On virtually all social issues included in the GSS—school prayer, interracial marriage, allowing Communists to speak in one's community—the

South is distinctly conservative. The South is also uniquely conservative on foreign policy issues. Its residents wanted to spend more on defense and expressed the least favorable attitudes toward the former Soviet Union and toward communism as a form of government. But, as noted earlier, the South has historically not been atypically conservative on economic questions. If anything, the South today is more liberal on economic questions than the rest of the nation—although the differences are not large. It is, for example, the most willing region to increase spending on education and the least willing to cut back on welfare spending.

On the same issues that the South is uniquely conservative, the West is uniquely liberal. It is, in fact, substantially more liberal than any other region (including the Northeast) when it comes to abortion, interracial marriage, prayer decision in the schools, and the legalization of marijuana. For example, 69 percent of those in the South oppose the Supreme Court's decision to ban prayer in the public schools, contrasted with 48 percent in the West (Mayer 1992, 203). The West is also slightly more liberal on questions of foreign policy than the rest of the nation, but slightly more conservative when it comes to economic issues.

Finally, the stereotype of the East as a bastion of liberalism is certainly false. On social and foreign policy issues, it is a bit more liberal than the country as a whole, but only by a small amount. Economic preferences are mixed, with no clear pattern. Finally, the Midwest can be found mostly in the middle—somewhat more liberal than the South, but more conservative than the East or West.

But do regional differences have to do with regional culture, or are they simply compositional effects? Perhaps the South is less supportive of civil liberties because its residents have comparatively little education. While there is certainly some truth to this assertion, individual state culture makes a large contribution to one's partisanship and political ideology (Erikson et al. 1987). For example, with demographic factors controlled, living in Minnesota instead of Indiana results in a partisan difference of about the same magnitude as being in the lowest income category vs. being in the highest. There is something about state residence that impacts on partisanship and ideology beyond the fact that residents may differ in their religion, income, education, or union membership.

Other than state residence and regional groupings, the most common geographical division is one of cities, suburbs, small towns, and rural areas. It is generally thought that urban areas are sources of liberal and "nonconventional" political attitudes, with rural and small-town America being the bastions of conservatism. An analysis of GSS data by Yang and Alba (1992) focusing on nonconventional opinions, such as those toward the legalization of marijuana, the role of women in politics, and government regulation of pornography, shows the residents of urban areas are much more liberal on these domains than those living in small towns and rural areas. A study by Wilson (1985) also shows urban residence has a positive association with political tolerance—those living in urban areas were the most tolerant across all the target groups included in the General Social Survey. However, at least part of this variation is due to composition effects. City residents show up as more liberal in surveys because they have a large proportion of people with liberal group characteristics, such as blacks, Jews, and Catholics. Small towns and rural areas are conservative because they are predominantly Protestant and, outside the South, contain few blacks. But not all these urban/rural differences disappear when controls for composition effects are introduced. In fact, most remain statistically significant, although reduced in magnitude. One explanation, advanced by Fischer (1975), is an "urban subculture" theory, which holds that urban residents are more "nonconventional" in their political opinions because urban life provides a critical mass, meaning "the congregation of numbers of persons sufficient to maintain viable unconventional subcultures" (Fischer 1975, 1320). In other words, there is something about urban life—perhaps social diversity or the existence of support groups—independent of the social background of the residents, that makes them more liberal or nonconventional than those living in small towns and rural areas.

The Changing American South

The once distinctive South (the old Confederacy) is gradually losing its unique political character. The reasons are complex, but certainly involve the economic boom that began after World War II, migration (many blacks left the region in search of jobs, while many Northern whites moved into the region for the same reason), plus rapid industrialization of the region with attendant liberalizing consequences.

The result has been a gradual loss in Southern distinctiveness. On many political attitudes, the gap between the South and the rest of the nation has closed. In 1964, Southerners were 11 percentage points more conservative than other Americans, but in 1992 that gap was only 3 percent.[26] Southerners remain more traditional than the rest of the nation on issues like prayer in the schools, women's issues, and civil liberties, but again, the gap is narrowing. However, on social welfare questions, like government health programs and guaranteed jobs, there has historically been little difference between the South and the rest of the nation. The New Deal was popular among blacks and whites alike in the region. As noted earlier, if anything the South is now more liberal than the rest of the country on economic issues.

The uniqueness of the South is generally associated with two issues: a conservative stance on racial questions and overwhelming support for the Democratic Party. However, most surveys show only small differences between white Southerners and the rest of nation on race.

Table 7.10 shows the dramatic change by region among whites in response to the question of whether one favors the principle of black and white children attending the same school. In 1985, there is virtually no difference of consequence between whites in the South and whites in the rest of the nation on whether black and white children should attend the same schools.[27] For the 1992 NES question of whether the "federal government should see to it" that blacks and whites attend the sames schools, there is again almost no difference between the South and the rest of the nation.[28]

The initial attachment of the South to the Democratic Party goes back, of course, to the Civil War. But it was reinforced by economics. The South was long the poorest region of the country—a plus for the Democratic Party, given its image of providing jobs and benefits to the average person. As the national Democratic Party became increasingly liberal on civil rights, it became increasingly less attractive to many white Southerners. But the Republican Party benefited little. In response to the civil rights plank in the 1948 Democratic platform, South Carolina Governor Strom Thurmond ran as a "Dixiecrat" and took three states. The Republicans came up empty-handed. Nevertheless, presidential Republican voting has been a fixture in the South since 1948, and since 1968 it has given a larger proportion of its vote to the national Republicans than any other region.

TABLE 7.10 School Integration Opinion Among Whites, by Region and Education, 1956 and 1985

Favor Blacks and Whites Attending the Same School

	1956	1985
Non-South		
Less than high school	58%	86%
High school	67	98
Some college or more	79	99
South		
Less than high school	8%	67%
High school	20	93
Some college or more	30	98

Sources: 1956 data adapted from Howard Schuman, Charlotte Steeh, and Lawrence Bobo, *Racial Attitudes in America* (Cambridge, MA: Harvard UP), 78; the 1985 data are from the GSS.

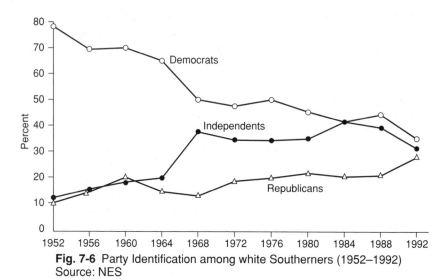

Fig. 7-6 Party Identification among white Southerners (1952–1992)
Source: NES

As can be seen in Figure 7-6, the major decline in Democratic Party identification among whites occurred following the presidential candidacy of Barry Goldwater in 1964. Goldwater voted against the 1964 Civil Rights Act on the ground that it violated states' rights. Since then, the decline has been gradual but steady. But Independents rather than Republicans have benefited more from the erosion of Democrat partisanship. However, Republican Party identification is particularly prevalent among young white Southerners (Wattenberg 1991). Those under 30 are more Republican than Democrat in their party leanings, while for those over 65, Democrats still predominate.[29] If this pattern continues, the Republicans will soon overtake the Democrats in terms of party preference among Southern whites.

7-6 Gender and Political Opinions _____

Since the early days of survey research, it was thought that there were few differences between the sexes in political opinions. Although women participated less than men, they were thought to be indistinguishable on questions of party and voting, with perhaps a few minor differences on issue positions. That situation changed in 1980, when considerable media attention was devoted to the gap between male and female voting for president. Women voted about equally for Reagan and Carter, but men gave Reagan 19 percentage points more than they gave Carter. Since that time, much attention has been devoted to the study of gender differences in political orientations. We now know the gender gap in voting to be a fairly recent phenomenon. Until 1980, there were either no differences, or women more than men tended to vote Republican. For example, women were more favorable to Dwight Eisenhower by a margin of 7 points in 1956, and had the 1960 presidential election been decided by women alone, Richard Nixon would have been elected president (Kenski 1988, 50). The gender gap that appeared in 1980 has continued in a weakened form through the 1992 presidential elections,[30] although it is frequently quite large in some state elections.[31] Coincidentally, the "gender gap" has also appeared as the key variable of party identification. The NES shows that in 1980, women were 3 percent more Democratic than men; in 1988, they were 10 percent more Democratic, and in 1992, the figure was 9 percent. This Democratic tendency is particularly noticeable among unmarried and well-educated women.[32]

In some issue domains, there have developed gender-based differences that are potentially of considerable import. A gender gap in political opinions may influence the public agenda in much the same way opinion differences between blacks and whites impact on the political process. Since women constitute a majority of the American electorate, even small gender differences can put substantial pressure on decision-makers.

Presented in Table 7.11 are gender differences in selected issue domains. Since the 1930s, surveys have shown that women are less prone to endorse violence and aggression in any form, be it at the personal level, capital punishment, or in foreign affairs. We see from Table 7.11 a 12-point gap on whether it was wrong to get involved in the Persian Gulf War. Before the war's culmination, this gap was typically 6 to 8 points higher, likely due to the uncertainty about its consequences and projected heavy loss of life. There was a similar gender difference in support for the Korean War and the Vietnam War, with women typically being about 8 to 10 percent less enthusiastic than men. Finally, there is a long-running series of questions dating back to the late 1940s relating to issues surrounding the development, testing, and possible use of nuclear weapons. Women have consistently been more dovish (or perhaps more compassionate and concerned with human life) than men. For example, in 1989 women were 16 percentage points more likely to believe that it was morally wrong to use the atomic bomb on Japan to end World War II (Brandes 1992). Miller (1988) argues that this gender difference on foreign affairs has important electoral consequences. When elections tend to turn on questions of human rights and issues of war and peace, the gender gap in voting increases, with women moving to favor Democratic candidates.

These differences on violence and aggression are probably due to an interplay between socialization and biology. Though not conclusive, there is some research showing that men have a greater predisposition to use force than women. Caldicott (1986) describes men as "insecure aggressors," while women are more nurturing and pacifist since "their bodies are built anatomically and physiologically to nurture life." Also, the socialization of young boys frequently emphasizes aggression (witness playground games), while such aggression is often discouraged in young girls (Miedaian 1991). Another possible explanation is that women are more risk-averse than men (Tedin and Yap 1993). For example, 31 percent of men favor building more nuclear power plants, but only 5 percent of women are favorable (1991 NES pilot).

There are also gender differences on compassion issues relating to jobs, education, income redistribution, and protection for the vulnerable in society. Women are generally more supportive of a compassion-

TABLE 7.11 Gender and Political Opinions

Opinion	Men	Women	Difference
Force, Violence, and Aggression			
Oppose death penalty for murder[b]	17%	27%	+10%
Want stricter gun control laws[c]	61	77	+16
Wrong to get involved in Persian Gulf War[a]	14	26	+12
Never bomb targets with civilians close[f]	19	39	+20
Compassion Issues			
Government see to good jobs/standard of living[a]	33	45	+12
Spend more on Social Security[b]	42	50	+ 8
Government should reduce income differences[a]	51	66	+15
Increase government services/spending[a]	46	63	+17
Gender-Related Issues			
Make French abortion pill legal[c]	61	49	−12
Favor abortion for any reason[b]	47	44	− 3
Men and women equally suited for politics[b]	78	79	+ 1
Men and women should have equal role[a]	88	87	− 1
Draft men only into the military[f]	35	52	−17
Civil Liberties/Rights			
Marijuana should be legalized[b]	29	20	− 9
Allow communists to speak[b]	75	67	− 8
Allow homosexuals to serve in the military[c]	47	68	+19
Favor preferential hiring for blacks[d]	12	14	+ 2
Women and minorities should be given preferential treatment for education/jobs[e]	10	10	0

Percentages are of opinion-holders only.
[a]NES, 1992   [d]NES, 1992, whites only.
[b]GSS, 1993.   [e]Gallup, 1989, whites only.
[c]Gallup, 1993.   [f]NES, 1991, pilot.

ate approach than men, but the differences are not large. Shapiro and Mahajan (1986) collected a large sampling of these issues and found the average gender difference to be only 3 percent. But on some issues, the differences are large, usually when questions address specific hazards vs. more general society-wide problems. For example, in addition to the difference in support for building nuclear power plants, there are substantial gaps on support for the 55 MPH speed limit, for state laws requiring seat belts, and for stiff jail terms for drunk drivers (Shapiro and Mahajan 1986, 51).

On civil rights issues, white men and white women usually do not differ. One exception is that women are considerably more supportive of gays in the military than men. But as we see from Table 7.11, even when women are the beneficiaries of special treatment, they are no more likely to support affirmative action than men. There are, however, consistent gender differences on civil liberties. On virtually every one of the 1993 GSS (Stouffer 1955) civil liberties items, men are more supportive than women. These differences are not limited to the United States, but show up in Western Europe and the former Soviet Union as well (Norris 1988; Tedin and Yap 1993; Tedin 1994). Controls for background factors reduce, but do not eliminate, these differences.

On most gender issues, there are few gender gaps. One exception is that by a margin of 17 points, women (compared to men) prefer to have only men drafted into the military (1991 NES pilot). However, on most other gender issues there are usually no differences between men and women, or differences that seemingly run counter to gender self-interest. In 19 successive readings of the General Social Survey (1972–1993), men have been more supportive of abortion than women by an average of 4 percent, although the difference has been as large as 10 percent.[33] The same is often true in other instances where the question of women's equality is directly addressed. For example, men were consistently more favorable to the passage of the Equal Rights Amendment than were women (Simon and Landis 1989, 275). One reason for this pattern is that on many issues that directly concern women, there is a greater gap among women than between men and women. Take, for instance, the label "feminist." Currently, 26 percent of women say they "think of [themselves] as a feminist" (NES 1992). Women accepting the label tend not to be "average"—rather, they are highly educated and affluent (Keene 1991). Their voting patterns are also atypical. Nonfeminists voted 44 percent for Bill Clinton, while feminists gave him 76 percent—a much greater gap among women than usually found between men and women.

We can see clearly the class division among women by looking at the NES question that asks if "women should have an equal role with men in running business, industry, and government," or if "women's place is in the home." Women disagree with each other on this question more than they disagree with men. The line of stratification divides working women and homemakers, and divides on level of education. On the equal role for women question, 68 percent of those who are working fall into the most egalitarian category (Option 1 on a 7-point scale; see Appendix), as opposed to 48 percent of the homemakers. Among working women with a college degree, 75 percent chose the most egalitarian option. At the other end of the spectrum, only 42 percent of homemakers with a high school degree or less chose this option. However, the trend over time is for both groups to increasingly choose the most egalitarian option.[34] Nevertheless, there are clearly life-style definitions and differences about what makes one an important and worthwhile person that split women on the issues at the heart of the women's liberation movement.

7-7 Conclusion

Group characteristics can clearly make a difference in how people see the political world. Belonging to a group is part of one's self-identification. Many groups have a vested political interest. Belonging to the upper social class encourages one to believe that through ones's own effort, success has been achieved, and government should be limited in its ability to spend tax money to aid those who have not been successful in life's competition. Race, sex, region, and age also intrude upon one's life in a fashion not entirely neutral, and consequently color the way one sees the desirable organization and ends of the polity.

Over time, certain group distinctions may increase or decrease in importance. For example, the distinction between urban and rural has declined with the rapid urbanization of society. Group distinctions that may increase in importance are between the young and the old, men and women, and service-sector employees vs. professionals. The potential may at some point replace traditional sources of voting alignments, such as partisanship or class. If that happens, the benefits that government bestows upon its citizens, as well as the obligations it demands, may also change.

Notes

1. When asked by Gallup in July 1988 if they belonged to the "haves" or the "have nots," 59 percent of Americans said they belonged to the "haves" and 17 percent said "have nots," with 15 percent saying neither or both and 9

percent unsure. When asked in March 1988, 41 percent of British respondents said they belonged to the "haves," while 37 percent said they were part of the "have nots."

2. We have combined lower-class, average-working, working, and upper-working into "the working class." "The middle class" combines middle and average-middle class, and upper-middle and upper are combined for "the upper class."

3. According to an April 1992 Roper Poll, it takes $25,300 for an American family to "just get by." It takes $35,800 to "live in reasonable comfort," and it takes $82,100 to "fulfill all your dreams." Bureau of the Census, *Current Population Reports,* 1990.

5. "Public Opinion and Demographic Report," *The Public Perspective* 4 (May/June 1993): 85.

6. "The Polls," *Public Opinion Quarterly* 12 (1949): 781.

7. Partisanship is percent Democratic of identifiers (Democrats plus Republicans, with Independents deleted). The vote is the two-party vote only.

8. In the 1992 NES survey, every black making over $75,000 (N=23) voted for Clinton.

9. The class base of the Bush vote pretty much mirrored the Clinton vote. Perot did best among the more affluent. He got only 15 percent among those making under $20,000. His best income group was those making $40,000–$75,000 from which he got 27 percent. However, he dropped to 17 percent among those making more than $75,000.

10. For Figure 7-2 we computed the percent Democratic of all Republican and Democratic identifiers, leaving out Independents, those preferring other parties, and the apolitical.

11. For an analysis over time of group-based divisions among Democratic and Republican voters, see Erikson et al. (1989).

12. A similar measure of class voting using a manual/nonmanual dichotomy was employed by Robert R. Alford (1963).

13. For blacks, the correlation between income and the "services and spending" item and the "good standard of living" item are nonsignificant. For whites, the correlations are .18 and .19, respectively.

14. In the 1993 GSS, blacks were more conservative than whites on three of the items, and whites were more conservative than blacks on three of the items.

15. Although Clinton received 53 percent of the white two-party vote in the NES survey, he received only 39 percent of the white vote with the Perot candidacy included. Among whites in the 1992 VRS Exit Poll, slightly more voted for Bush than Clinton.

16. Reported in Einstein (1981, 584). We have not reported the "don't knows," so the percentages may not add to 100 percent.

17. The nations are the USA, West Germany, East German, Britain, Netherlands, Hungary, Italy, Ireland, Poland, Northern Ireland, Norway, Israel, Slovenia, and New Zealand.

18. On April 17, 1992, Gallup reported 61 percent said religion was "very important in my own life"; on November 20, 1992, Gallup reported it was 59

percent, and on March 18, 1993, it was again 59 percent.

19. Based on combined 1990–1993 GSS data.

20. Our reports of religious divisions of the vote in 1960 and 1992 are from the National Election Studies.

21. The data for "Nones" comes from the GSS. In 1972, 70 percent were Democratic; in 1984, 68 percent; and in 1993, 71 percent.

22. For an example of conversions, see Erikson and Tedin (1981).

23. Table 7.9 is similar in form to a table presented by Miller and Wattenberg (1984). For the scale of religious orientation, each respondent received one point for each of the following: if they said religion was a guide to life, said religion was important to life, believed in the Bible's literal truth, rated "fundamentalists" favorably, claimed to be "born again," and described themselves as "fundamentalists" or "evangelical." We scored respondents at 0 or 1 as "secular," those with 5 or 6 points as fundamentalists," and the remainder of the white Protestant subsample as "in between". No attempt was made to distinguish between the fundamentalists and the charismatic or pentecostal subgroups.

24. Data are from exit polls as reported by *The New York Times.*

25. To take but one instance of one-time regional differences in foreign policy "isolationism," Southerners, when asked in 1945 whether the United States and Russia "should make a permanent military alliance," responded favorably by a ratio of greater than 2 to 1. At the other extreme, a slight majority of Midwesterners opposed such an alliance (Cantril 1951, 961). By the late 1950s, such disparities had largely disappeared (Key 1961a, 134).

26. Based on an analysis of responses about feelings toward conservatives (using a feeling thermometer) in the NES data, where 0 to 49 is negative, 50 is neutral, and 51 to 99 is positive.

27. Since almost everyone now endorses the general principle of white and black students attending the same school, the question has not been asked since 1985.

28. Outside the South, 46 percent with less than a high school degree favor integration compared to 49 percent in the South; for those with a high school degree, the numbers are 46 percent for the non-South and 39 percent for the South; and for those with a college degree, it is 42 percent for the non-South and 38 percent for the South.

29. White southerners under 30 are more Republican than Democratic by a margin of 28 percent (Wattenberg 1991).

30. In 1980, Reagan received 54 percent and Carter 35 percent among men; among women, Reagan received 46 percent and Carter 45 percent. In 1984, men voted 62 percent for Reagan, 38 percent for Mondale; women voted 54 percent for Reagan, 46 percent for Mondale; in 1988, men voted 57 percent for Bush and 41 percent for Dukakis; women voted 50 percent for Bush and 49 percent for Dukakis; and in 1992, men voted 41 percent for Clinton, 38 percent for Bush, and 21 percent for Perot; women voted 45 percent for Clinton, 37 percent for Bush, and 17 percent for Perot.

31. For example, the gender gap was 20 points in the 1990 election for governor of Texas (Tedin et al. 1991).

32. See Weisberg (1987) for a statistical demonstration using 1984 data.
33. Shapiro and Mahajan (1986) and our calculations from 1984–1991.
34. For the 1992 NES, for example, 68 percent of the college-educated women chose the most egalitarian option, and 27 percent of the homemakers with a high school education or less chose the most egalitarian option.

CHAPTER 8

The Print and Broadcast Media and Political Opinions

One's political beliefs are shaped by the political information one receives. This is an obvious statement of fact but an important one. In totalitarian political systems, the regime attempts to control the flow of information by controlling the national media. In democracies, the mass media are relatively free of government control. Indeed, one cannot imagine free democratic elections without a free flow of competing information in the mass media.

But the proper flow of political information requires more than simply the government allowing an unfettered mass media to print or broadcast free of political interference. What we read, see, or hear in the mass media is the product of the institutions that make up the newspaper, magazine, television, and radio industries. Within these institutions, individuals continually decide what to print or what to broadcast. For democratic citizens to be properly informed about public affairs requires that the news media provide a broad balance of information and viewpoints.

The importance of media content is indicated by the criticism and controversy that frequently surround the mass media. When people become disturbed by the course of political trends, the mass media and the people who run them provide convenient scapegoats. When the public appears to be mistaken or wrong-headed in its views, it is simple to blame the mass media for distorting the political messages that people receive. Or when the public appears fascinated with irrelevant sideshows instead of what we regard as serious issues of public affairs, it is easy to blame the mass media for emphasizing the wrong kinds of news stories.

Complaints about the influence of the media are not limited to conventional political issues. The content of what we watch on television is a particular target. With a certain ebb and flow, various critics accuse television of contributing to such trends as violence in society, sexism, lax moral standards, permissiveness about drugs, low SAT scores, and too much junk food. Political scientists register their own concern about some unwanted side effects from the introduction of television. Among the political trends that have been attributed to television are the decline of political parties, the drop in voter turnout, the superficiality of public debate, the ascendancy of slick media-oriented candidates, and the growth of public cynicism about politics.

Of course, just because a seemingly reasonable observer may lay a particular complaint at the doorstep of the mass media does not necessarily make the complaint valid. In this chapter we discuss the nature of the mass media, their possible biases, and their impact on public opinion.

8-1 The Mass Media and Their Political Content _____

For most Americans, the mass media intrude every day in multitudes of ways. About 80 percent of American households receive daily newspapers, and almost all contain at least one television set. Slightly more than half of American households are wired for cable television or "narrow-casting," which adds a new dimension. And Americans frequently listen to their radios (in the car if not at home). Add to this the many magazines available for us to read. In short, it is easy to argue that Americans suffer from information overload. Even though only a fraction of what we read and watch concerns politics and public affairs, the modern mass media are important for understanding the role of political opinions in modern democracy.

Newspapers

When the United States was founded as a nation, newspapers were already in place. But the newspapers of the early Republic were essentially forums for particular partisan points of view, rather than objective reports of the news. Also, early newspapers were not strictly "mass" media, since they were read mainly by small elite audiences. In the 1830s, newspapers were first brought to the masses in the form of the "penny press," as the early mass circulation newspapers came to be called. Newspapers of the penny press were cheap (1 cent) and willing to entertain the mass audience with human interest stories and sensational reports of crimes and disasters. They also introduced the first debate about the role of the mass media. Some observers saw the proliferation of mass circulation newspapers as the springboard for a truly democratic marketplace of ideas. Others saw the same phenomenon as debasing the currency of political discussion (Berkman and Kitch 1986, 1).

In any event, public demand for newspapers plus technological advances (e.g., the telegraph) allowed no retreat. By 1900, more newspapers were in publication than today. Many were strongly partisan, and many were sensationalistic purveyors of "yellow journalism." In the twentieth century the number of newspapers has dwindled to the point that fewer than 30 U.S. cities now enjoy competition from newspapers under different ownership. With this consolidation and the increased reliance on wire-service stories for newspaper copy, the bias in newspaper coverage—particularly of national and world events—has declined. Thus, the choices open to the newspaper consumer have decreased, while the objectivity of the product has increased. Beyond its local news coverage, the content of the typical reader's hometown paper is similar to that in the next town down the road. But of course the quality of the hometown coverage can vary. And certain "prestige" newspapers do provide unusually good coverage of world and national events. National political and business leaders pay close attention to the prestige newspapers (most notably the *New York Times, Washington Post, Los Angeles Times,* and *Wall Street Journal*). One recent trend is for some newspapers to become truly national. The *New York Times* and the *Wall Street Journal* now are generally available throughout much of the nation, as is Gannett's much different national newspaper, *U.S.A. Today.*

Radio and Television

Commercial radio and the first radio networks emerged in the 1920s. Commercial television became technically feasible by the late 1930s. However, World War II delayed the beginning of the television age until the late 1940s. Early radio had a major political impact, bringing to all American living rooms such events as the fireside chats by President Roosevelt and the horrifying reports of World War II. Early television also had its impact. For instance, Edward R. Murrow's reports on CBS's "See It Now" and the televised Army-McCarthy hearings (both in 1954) helped to destroy the mercurial career of demagogic Senator Joe McCarthy.

Early network television newscasts, however, did not amount to much. They were lightweight affairs, only 15 minutes long, without much interesting film coverage. The beginning of satellite communications in 1962 revolutionized television news, allowing instant coverage from around the world. Also in the early 1960s, network news shows became 30 minutes long. Soon thereafter they were telecast in color. Although there have been further technological advances, by the late 1960s network news telecasts took on the look that they have today.

Magazines

Magazines deserve mention also, because they play an important role in the formation of public opinion. At the top of the pyramid, small public affairs magazines that count their readers only in the hundreds of thousands (e.g., *Atlantic, New Republic*) try to influence the thoughtful opinion leaders. At the next level, newsmagazines (*Time, Newsweek, U.S. News & World Report*) each reach a few million readers a week. Newsmagazines are important molders of opinion. Perhaps correctly, President John Kennedy once asserted that *Time* was the most important influence on American public opinion (Halberstam 1979, 353). Kennedy's statement would be incorrect today, only because of the dominance of television. At the bottom of the magazine pyramid, mass circulation magazines like *People* and *Reader's Digest* also give important political cues to their readers.

Biased Media?

Although the news media pride themselves on the objectivity of their news coverage, they are not without their critics. From the left, some critics charge that because the media are business enterprises and depend on business advertising for profits, they unfairly favor the conservative viewpoint of the business community (Cirino 1972). From the right, other critics charge that because journalists tend to be political liberals, the media unfairly favor the liberal viewpoint (Efron 1971). Still other critics make more subtle observations. Some say that because the media try to appeal to the broadest possible audience, they constrict the flow of ideas to those in the "safe" middle range (Bennett 1980, 304–44.) Others see a structural bias to the journalist profession: Because journalists tend to be politically cynical and because they try to maintain the interest of their audience, the media sometimes give a particularly hard time to incumbent officeholders (Ranney 1976, 31–63; Hofstetter 1976). Still others offer the opposite complaint. They see newspeople as too uncritical of governmental officials, out of a need to protect their access to news sources (Hertsgaard 1988; Press and Verburn 1988).

Both newspapers and television news claim to present an objective account of the news. They differ, however, in their willingness to editorialize. Until recently, television stations were forbidden by the "fairness doctrine" of the Federal Communications Commission from overtly endorsing political candidates and from advocating particular points of view, unless they gave equal time to the opposite viewpoint. These strictures were substantially weakened in the late 1980s. Newspapers, however, traditionally endorse political candidates and advocate policy viewpoints and political causes. Although newspapers supposedly confine their advocacy to the editorial page, the publisher's bias sometimes extends to the news pages. For example, one study found that during the 1972 presidential campaign, newspapers that supported President Nixon's reelection bid gave the least coverage to the growing Watergate scandal (Bagdikian 1973).

In the 1992 presidential campaign, most newspapers (67 percent) chose not to endorse a presidential candidate. Of those that did, a slim plurality (18 vs. 15 percent) lent their editorial support to Bill Clinton rather than George Bush (*Editor and Publisher* surveys reported in Stanley and Niemi 1994). This preference for the Democratic candidate represented a break from newspapers' partisan tradition and may have been a sure sign that President Bush was in political trouble, since the usual pattern is for newspapers to support Republicans predominantly. For instance, in 1988, newspapers endorsed George Bush over Michael Dukakis by a ratio of over 2 to 1 (although, as in 1992, many remained neutral).

Two factors readily account for newspapers' proclivity for Republicanism and conservatism. First, newspaper publishers are businesspeople. Their conservative Republicanism is a natural reflection of the prevailing orthodoxy of the business community. Second, a newspaper's advertisers also represent the conservative business community. Although it has become rare for major advertisers to threaten newspapers because of their political positions, newspapers must depend on advertising as their major source of revenue.

TABLE 8.1 Views of General Public and Journalists on Selected Issues

		Public	Journalists
Consider self	liberal	23%	55%
	conservative	29	17
President Reagan	favor	56	30
	oppose	27	60
Sympathize with	business	33	27
	labor	32	31
Government should reduce income inequality	favor	55	50
	oppose	23	39
CIA aid to Nicaraguan Contras	favor	19	17
	oppose	44	76
Increase defense budget	favor	38	15
	oppose	51	80
Allow women to have abortions	favor	49	82
	oppose	44	14
Prayer in public schools	favor	74	25
	oppose	19	67
Death penalty for murder	favor	75	47
	oppose	17	47

Source: William Schneider and I. A. Lewis, "Views on the News," *Public Opinion,* 8 (Aug./Sept. 1985): 7. Reprinted with permission of the American Enterprise Institute.

The conservatism of newspaper publishers is balanced to some extent by the liberalism of working journalists. From a 1985 Times-Mirror survey, Table 8.1 contrasts some of the political opinions of U.S. newspaper journalists with those of the U.S. adult population. Most of the journalists surveyed identified themselves as liberal and expressed opposition to President Reagan. On most issues, the journalists' policy positions were more liberal than the general population's. The one exception is that newspaper journalists are not unusually liberal on economic issues. For instance, the 1985 Times-Mirror survey showed journalists to be more opposed than the general public to the government helping to redistribute income (Schneider and Lewis 1985).

The tension between the conservatism of newspaper publishers and the liberalism of newspaper journalists is illustrated by the political values of newspaper editors. Newspaper editors are more conservative than reporters. But they may be closer to the political liberalism of the reporters below them than the political conservatism of the publishers above them. For instance, one study disclosed ironically that while most newspapers endorsed Reagan for president in 1984, most of the editors of newspaper editorial pages voted for Reagan's opponent (St. Dizier 1986).

People employed in the radio or television broadcasting of news have not had their political opinions researched as carefully as those in the print media. One frequent observation about television reporters is that they do not hold exceptionally strong political views of any kind (Epstein 1974, 210–11). However, at the top reaches of television news—at the network level—both news reporters and managers tend to be more liberal than conservative, just like newspeople at the top levels of print journalism (Johnstone et al. 1976; Lichter and Rothman 1979).

Although some conservatives claim otherwise, there is no reason to believe in any sort of media conspiracy to promote liberal political doctrines. The reason why news employees show a liberal political tendency is not that conservative aspirants are pushed aside for their political views. To some extent, the political liberalism of journalists, especially outside the economic realm, simply reflects the "yuppie" values of young urban college-educated professionals—the class from which journalists are drawn. Another factor may be that journalism holds a special career attraction for people with liberal personality traits, much like a military career (for example) attracts conservative personalities.

In any event, a possible liberal "bias" to the preferences of newspeople would seriously matter only if the bias were to affect news content. In the newspaper industry, both the norms of objectivity and publishers' natural conservatism seem sufficient safeguard. In broadcasting, the norms of objectivity combine with the conservatism of station owners and network managers for the same purpose. When asked its views on the matter, the general public sees little bias. For instance, when a March 1993 survey in the *Los Angeles Times* asked the general public about possible media bias, 34 percent saw their favorite newspaper as liberal and 28 percent saw it as conservative. Television news was seen more liberal: 40 percent said network news was "liberal," while 19 percent said it was conservative.

Academic studies of network news coverage of presidential campaigns show that the networks attempt to achieve balance. Maura Clancey and Michael J. Robinson (1985a; 1985b) have analyzed television networks' coverage of recent presidential campaigns for *Public Opinion,* a journal published by the conservative American Enterprise Institute. They find that the networks devote equal amounts of coverage to both major party campaigns, and show no tilt toward one candidate or the other on policy issues. They find, however, that television reporters tend to give a negative "spin" to whichever candidate they cover. Television reporters may be particularly negative toward incumbents. According to Clancey and Robinson, the network reporters were most negative toward President Carter in 1980 and toward President Reagan in 1984. But in 1984 the reporters' spin decidedly favored Reagan over Mondale on the horse race (or "who is ahead?") aspects of the election. Television reporters repeatedly conveyed not only the fact that Reagan was leading in the polls, but also the powerful impression that Reagan's campaign was going well and Mondale's poorly.

The media show little inclination to challenge a popular president. Most observers of the Reagan presidency saw the American media as going relatively easy on the "Teflon" president, at least before the Iran-Contra scandal. The American public saw it this way too. In the 1985 Times-Mirror public sample, 30 percent saw the media as making Reagan look better than he was, while only 18 percent saw the media as making Reagan look worse than he was. The same respondents saw the media as treating the previous president, Jimmy Carter, quite harshly: 46 percent as worse than he was and only 6 percent as better than he was (Schneider and Lewis, 1985, 11). More recently, 71 percent of respondents in a Times-Mirror Survey in 1992 found press treatment of then President Bush as "fair," even as he was the subject of negative stories about the economy. In 1993, as Clinton was having his troubles with unfavorable stories, a lesser 51 percent of Times-Mirror respondents saw press treatment of Clinton as "fair."

Because they must appeal to wide audiences, the managers of the mass media are far more interested in upholding their reputations for objectivity and offending the least number of people than in promoting political doctrines. Thus, newspapers and television news programs rarely give serious attention to points of view that are known to be unpopular. The true "bias" of the mass media may be to reinforce those political values on which almost all Americans agree and to restrict the range of political debate to positions close to the political center.

Consensus on the News?

At least in theory, the news media have considerable discretion when deciding which events are newsworthy and which ones are not. Newspeople see themselves as exercising this discretion professionally and responsibly. When challenged as to why a particular story is included as news while another receives no coverage, the typical journalist will claim that the news media merely mirror what happens in society; that one story was newsworthy and the other not; and that newspeople themselves have little or no role in choosing what is news (Epstein 1974, 11–25). In practice, news selection often follows a hierarchical pattern, with journalists following the cues of others. For instance, network news programs often follow the lead of the day's front page of the major newspapers—the *New York Times,* the *Washington Post,* and the *Los Angeles Times* (Gans 1980; Showalter 1974). Many evenings, the three major network news shows share the same lead story (43 percent of the time). They run entirely different lead stories only 9 percent of the time (Foote and Steele 1986). National wire services (most notably the Associated Press) add to the uniformity of the news from different sources. Local newspapers and local newscasts have the major national or international news suggested to them—from the wire services or the network feeds.

Media managers and editors possess the power to act as "gatekeepers"—deciding which news to report. But when competing gatekeepers seek the same audience, they tend to make similar choices—so much so that competing news sources have been labeled "rivals in conformity" (Bigman 1948). Still, despite the inevitable similarity of the major stories reported, news managers and editors enjoy considerable discretion regarding lesser stories and features. For instance, Epstein (1974, 38) found that of 431 news stories presented in the network news over a six-week period, only 57 were reported by all three networks.

Luttbeg (1983) examined the news stories in 75 randomly selected daily newspapers and in 10 "select" or prestige newspapers, on seven scattered days in 1980–1981, representing one "composite week." Table 8.2 shows the stories that were most frequently reported in the first three pages of these newspapers. The striking feature is that even these top stories do not get universally reported. These eleven stories were the only ones that appeared in at least half of the sampled news-

TABLE 8.2 Top National and International Stories Covered by More Than Half of the Newspapers, for Seven Days in 1980 and 1981

Story	Date	Percent of Papers Covering	
		Sample Papers	Select Papers
Bush chosen Reagan's running mate	7/17/80	91%	100%
Polish strikes gain government support	8/24/80	68	88
OPEC increases prices again	5/26/81	67	71
Carter and Reagan set debate date	10/20/80	65	88
Plane crashes in Loveland, Colorado	4/18/81	65	67
Reagan vows no troops to El Salvador	3/4/81	63	63
Twenty-eighth Atlanta victim	5/26/81	61	14
Iraq-Iran war; Abadan cut off	10/20/80	58	63
Reagan lifts Soviet grain embargo	4/24/81	58	75
CORE reveals Atlanta suspect	4/24/81	54	38
Report on aborted Iranian hostage raid	8/24/80	54	63

Source: Norman R. Luttbeg, "News Consensus: Do U.S. Newspapers Mirror Society's Happening?" *Journalism Quarterly,* 60 (Autumn 1983): 486.

papers for the seven days examined. For the top five stories of each day, the 75 newspapers' average rate of coverage in the first three pages was only 41 percent. The average rate for the prestige papers was only slightly greater, 51 percent. For the three network newscasts, the average was 52 percent. These results suggest that the casual news consumer who relies on but one news source may miss about half of the day's five major news stories. To the extent there exists consensus on the news, it exists in thousands of local variations. And to the extent that print media shape public opinion, the opinion in one community must differ from that in another.

8-2 Mass Media Influence on Public Opinion _____

The first attempts to examine empirically the political influence of the mass media were the early studies of voting behavior: panel studies of voters in Erie County, Ohio, in 1940 and voters in Elmira, New York, in 1948 (Lazarsfeld et al. 1948; Berelson et al. 1954). These early studies presented a viewpoint regarding the influence of the media that has since become known as the "minimal effects" model of media influence. Perhaps because the researchers for these projects moved into voting research from market research, they expected to find campaign messages in the mass media (at that time, essentially newspapers and radio) to be quite influential on individual voters. They envisioned voters waffling in their choice of candidates somewhat in the way a consumer might change his or her choice of tooth-paste from purchase to purchase, depending on the effectiveness of the latest advertising.

These early researchers on presidential choice, however, made three discoveries that seemed to dismiss that mass media's influence. First, they discovered the anchor of partisanship. A substantial number of citizens interviewed as early as May of election year had already made up their minds how they were going to vote in November. This suggests that most voters had a "product loyalty" to one or the other of the two major political parties. Second, they discovered perceptual screening. To maintain their product loyalty, voters paid particular attention to the messages for the candidate whom they preferred. And they avoided exposure to campaign messages for the opposition, even misperceiving these messages when exposure was unavoidable. Third, they discovered the importance of personal conversations. When someone was about to change his or her viewpoint due to a persuasive message in the media, that person would often return to the original opinion after talking to others who shared that original opinion.

For these reasons, the messages on the mass media are less influential than they might appear. Because people's political views are anchored by their past beliefs, perceptual screening, and interpersonal communications, it is not likely that any particular revelation in the evening news will create massive changes in people's political likes and dislikes. To take one example, no event can compete for political shock values with the revelation in late 1986 that President Reagan was selling arms to Iran in the hope for the return of hostages. Yet there was no revolutionary turn in American public opinion. In one month, popular approval of Reagan's performance dropped about 20 percentage points, which perhaps defines the outer limit of how quickly public opinion can respond in the short run. Twenty percentage points is the greatest one-month drop in presidential approval ever recorded. Yet it may seem like not very much at all.

In recent years, researchers have explored beyond the minimal effects model. It is one thing to find that very real limits exist on the power of the mass media to influence citizens' political attitudes and beliefs. It is something quite different to argue that the role of the mass media is of little importance. As we will see, recent researchers do not search for evidence that people are helpless victims of their most recent exposure to propaganda in the mass media. Instead, they search for evidence of modest influence of the mass media on our political beliefs (e.g., Bartels 1993 and Finkel 1993). In this section, we explore some evidence of media effects on political attitudes.

Mass Media and Political Learning

During the Iran-Contra hearings of the summer of 1987, polls showed surprisingly strong interest in the testimony of Lt. Col. Oliver North and others who testified before the special Senate-House Committee. In fact, a surprising 71 percent reported that they watched or listened to some part of the live coverage of Oliver North's testimony (CBS News/*New York Times* poll, 9 July 1987). But the breadth of public comprehension was limited. For instance, one week further into the Iran-Contra hearings, only 33 percent of Americans could place Nicaragua in Central America (CBS News/*New York Times* poll, 16 July 1987).

This ignorance about the location of a key nation in the drama should not be a great surprise. But it also highlights an interesting puzzle. As we saw in Chapter 3, people generally are not very informed about political matters. Yet people regularly are exposed to political information in the mass media. As we know, people do read newspapers and watch television network news. How can understanding of public affairs be so low, given the information available?

News Comprehension. John Robinson and Mark Levy (1986, 87–106) asked people in a national sample whether they read or heard about each of a series of news stories that were prominently featured during the previous week. The researchers staggered interviews over four separate weekends in June 1983. Table 8.3 shows the proportions who recalled the various stories. As often noted, people readily learn stories with a strong human interest element. Thus, Robinson and

TABLE 8.3 Proportions of Respondents Aware of Selected News Items from Previous Week, 1983

	Percent Aware
Paul Volcker reappointed head of Federal Reserve Board	28%
Change in State Department officials	30
Supreme Court ruling on legislative veto	40
Developments at Geneva arms talks	42
"Stolen" debate briefing books	53
Western economic summit	67
Elections in Great Britain	67
Pope's trip to Poland	80
Disease called AIDS	80
Americans killed in El Salvador	85
Floods in Utah	89
Space shuttle flight	94

Source: John P. Robinson and Mark R. Levy, *The Main Source: Learning from Television News,* Chapter 4: "Comprehension of Week's News" (Beverly Hills, Calif.: Sage Publications, 1986), p. 91. Copyright © 1986 by Sage Publications, Inc. Reprinted by Permission of Sage Publications, Inc.

Levy's respondents were almost universally aware of flooding in Utah and a (successful) space shuttle flight. People are only slightly less likely to retain information about political stories highlighted in the news, but only if they involve uncomplicated or ceremonial types of events. Thus, about two-thirds of Robinson and Levy's respondents could recall reading or hearing about the recent British elections and the Pope's trip to Poland. The stories that people most readily avoid are the more complicated stories about government or politics. Thus, less than half of Robinson and Levy's respondents were able to recall the recent reappointment of Paul Volcker as chairman of the Federal Reserve Board or the recent Supreme Court decision restricting Congress's use of the legislative veto.

Processing the News. Doris Graber (1984) tried a unique approach to understanding how people learn from the mass media. She conducted several in-depth interviews with a small sample of 21 residents of Evanston, Illinois, during the 1976 election year. As expected, she found that the respondents who were the most intelligent and the most experienced in political matters were most able to comprehend complex stories and to remember earlier stories from the media. Graber's respondents tuned out much of the flood of available media information. For instance, they ignored two-thirds of the available newspaper stories. Of those stories that caught their attention, 43 percent concerned government or politics. When asked to recall a set of important news stories that were at least a month old, respondents could recall only 23 percent of them with sufficient detail to give four or more statements of fact or opinion about them (Graber 1984, 81–89). Graber interprets these findings optimistically, concluding that people know how to handle information overload. They are perhaps most concerned with their own interests and pleasures, but they also display a moderate willingness to perform their civic duties. People discard much of the "chaff" from news stories while still assimilating the crucial essentials (Graber 1984, 97).

Graber theorizes that respondents notice and evaluate new information by applying their particular "schemas," or prior set of beliefs. For instance, many respondents discounted statements by politicians because they applied a schema that categorized politicians as publicity seekers. Similar to what the Minimal Effects Model suggests, people minimize the impact of the mass media on their political beliefs by applying their schemas to news stories.

The News Source and Comprehension. It is often debated whether newspapers or television informs people more about public affairs. When people are surveyed on the subject, most claim to get more of their news from television than from newspapers, and the trend is

TABLE 8.4 Media Usage in 1992 Presidential Campaign

TV News				Daily Newspaper			
Days watched during week		Attention to campaign news		Days read during week		Attention to campaign news	
None	11%	None, very little	23%	None	23%	None, very little	56%
1–6	42	Some, quite a bit	57%	1–6	36	Some, quite a bit	35%
7 days	48	A good deal	20%	7 days	39	A good deal	9%

Source: NES, 1992 election data.

increasing. Table 8.4 shows one example of this survey evidence. During the 1992 presidential campaign, people generally reported that they watched news on television more regularly than they read the newspapers. People also claimed to pay more attention to the presidential campaign on television than in the newspapers.

On the other hand, recent evidence suggests that tables like Table 8.4 exaggerate people's reliance on television for their news (Robinson and Levy 1986, 231–41). People pay different degrees of attention to the broadcast and the print media. Watching television news or listening to radio news is the most passive form of attention. Indeed, the set may be on, but without concentration from the viewer or listener. One important early research project set up cameras in people's homes to observe the occupants' attention to television sets that were turned on. The researchers discovered that only about half the times that the news was on was anybody watching (Bechtel et al. 1972). (Only commercials got less attention!) Reading a newspaper or a magazine requires more active concentration. Also, the print media provide the greater depth of information and allow citizens to absorb information at their own pace. If the entire transcript of a half-hour network news broadcast were set to print, it would take no more space than the front page of a daily newspaper.

Repeated studies provide evidence that reading newspapers makes one more informed than does watching television news. For instance, when Graber's 21 respondents were able to recall certain stories from the news, they were much more likely to report newspapers to be the source than television (Graber 1984, 85). Similarly, when Robinson and Levy (1986, 96–103) conducted a multivariate statistical analysis of news comprehension, they found that newspaper reading (and newsmagazine reading) had a far greater impact on news comprehension than did viewing television news.

Still, the power of television to engage the viewer should not be underestimated. Newman et al. (1992) conducted an experiment in which they presented (roughly) the same information to volunteers either in a real newspaper story or in a real television news report. Their before-after comparisons of political information suggested that on balance, people retain just as much if not more of the basic facts of an issue (such as apartheid in South Africa or the AIDS epidemic) when the information is obtained watching the network news as they do from reading a newspaper account. While the content of television news may ordinarily lack the depth and context of detailed newspaper accounts, presenting information with pictures by itself does not lessen learning.

Media Messages and Policy Preferences

In an ambitious study, Page et al. (1987) tried to estimate the influence of television reports on the content of public opinion. They collected 80 instances from the late 1960s into the early 1980s where the same survey question about an important question of public policy was administered to national samples over a period of years. Page and his colleagues then attempted to see whether television content between the two surveys could account for the observed change. This exercise involved extensive monitoring and coding for more than a decade's worth of network news programs.

On the average, Page et al. discovered that opinion did not change much in the short run of even a few years. But when change occurred, the direction tended to be consistent with the preponderant direction of the messages on network news. The authors examined the impact of many different sources of information on network news (e.g., presidents, the opposition party, interest groups). The source that best predicted opinion change was television commentary—from anchorpersons, reporters in the field, or special commentators. According to the estimates, each viewpoint presented in a commentary could bring about as much as 4 percentage points of opinion change. But Page et al. are cautious when interpreting why television commentary predicts opinion change. They do not claim that individual newscasters are themselves the major source of opinion change. Rather, their message frequently overlaps or reinforces the dominant elite message that filters through the public via the media. Or news commentators or others with whom they agree may be perceived as simply reflecting an agreed-upon consensus which may strongly influence the formation of citizen opinions (Page et al. 1987, 35).

In other words, when the messages on television network news seem to advocate a particular change of policy, it is a good bet that public opinion will change modestly in the same direction. But instead of television messages causing the opinion change, another possibility could be that both television messages and public opinion are responding to some other source of influence.

Agenda Setting

The potential influence of the mass media on political thinking is not limited to influence on policy preferences. In addition, the mass media can set the agenda, or determine the public's choices regarding which policy questions are important. A small study of the 1968 presidential election conducted by McCombs and Shaw (1972) is the precursor to a growing body of research on "agenda setting." McCombs and Shaw asked their survey respondents to name the "main things ... government should concentrate on doing something about." The issues named turned out to be the same issues stressed in newspaper and television coverage of the campaign. McCombs and Shaw argued that this relationship is more than a sharing of concern by the public and the media decision-makers, since the public, they argued, obtains its information from the media. They suggest that the media set the political agenda for the public. By this argument, the media do not so much influence what people think as what they think about.

Although there has been much follow-up research on the effectiveness of the media in setting the public agenda, the first reports did not lend themselves to easy generalizations (McCombs 1981; O'Keefe and Atwood 1981). Some recent analyses, however, show clear evidence of media agenda setting, either from statistically analyzing actual changes in the public agenda or from observing perceptions when the media agenda is changed experimentally. Let us take a brief look at this evidence.

Changes in the Agenda over Time. For years, the Gallup Poll has asked Americans: "What is the most important problem facing the country today?" Changes in the national response to this question provide a crude but serviceable indicator of changes in national concerns. Historically, responses have centered on foreign policy and economic concerns. Foreign policy has dominated since the first readings in the 1940s, although various economic problems stood in first place for much of the 1950s and 1960s. Only civil rights, peaking in 1964 with 20 percent concerned, and issues of social control, peaking with 25 percent in 1973, have rivaled foreign policy and the economy as the focus of public concern (Smith 1985).

Looking for evidence of agenda setting, Michael MacKuen (1981) conducted an elaborate statistical analysis of national responses to the "most important problem" question over a 15-year period (1962–1977).

MacKuen found that, for most issues, public concern tracked media attention, as measured by the level of reporting of the issue in the newsmagazines. For some issues, MacKuen found the public's level of concern responding more to media concern than to the objective circumstances. For instance, media attention to crime predicted public concern about crime better than did the actual crime rate. Similarly, media attention to the war in Vietnam predicted public concern about the war better than did American troop levels (MacKuen 1981, 84–88).

Experimentally Manipulating the Agenda. Ideally, the best way to ascertain the degree to which the mass media can influence the agenda would be by experimentally manipulating what people read or watch. We could imagine, for example, that we could change the content of network news programs and then observe how people react. Iyengar and Kinder (1987; see also Iyengar et al. 1982) did exactly that in their experiments with the network news. Iyengar and his colleagues paid some ordinary citizens to participate in their studies of television viewing. Subjects were divided into different groups to watch the previous evening's network news together for six consecutive days. Unknown to the subjects, each group saw a different altered version. One such experiment went as follows. For one group, a news story about defense preparedness was edited into each news program. For a second group, a news story about pollution was inserted. For the third group, an inflation story was inserted. Thus, each group got a week-long dose of messages concerning one particular problem.

Reportedly, none of the subjects suspected that they were viewing edited versions of the news. The most interesting results from the study were the responses to the "most important problem" question before and after the experiment. Those given pollution stories and those given defense stories registered significantly abnormal increases in concern about pollution and defense, respectively. The inflation group did not change much, apparently because they already expressed a strong concern about inflation in their initial questionnaires prior to the experiment and could hardly increase the level of their response. Further analysis suggested that the subjects in each group began to evaluate President Carter according to how they saw Carter's handling of their manipulated topic. Iyengar and his colleagues show not only that the content of the media can influence the agenda, but that the choice of issues for the agenda can influence people's evaluation of the president.

Sophistication and Agenda Manipulation. An interesting question is how political sophistication is related to agenda setting. Illustrating that this question has not been fully settled, MacKuen and Iyengar et al. give different answers. Iyengar et al. report that their least sophisticated respondents were the most responsive to experimental manipulation of the agenda. This seems reasonable, since less sophisticated people lack the stored information that helps to discount propaganda in the media. However, the less sophisticated subjects were shown news programs under artificial conditions. Would they have been as attentive and persuaded in a natural setting? MacKuen (1984) finds the least sophisticated respondents to be the most immune to actual changes in the media's agenda. Evidently the most sophisticated are easiest for the media to lead, because only the sophisticated ordinarily pay enough attention.

The evidence that citizens respond to the media's agenda serves to remind that people are dependent on the information they receive. But media influence on what we think to be important implies nothing about the motives of the people who set the media's agenda. Media decision-makers often select stories for our attention because they view these stories to be what the public wants or in the public's interest. To a considerable degree, objective circumstances drive the media agenda. For instance, news media feed us the most stories about inflation when the inflation rate is highest (Behr and Iyengar 1985). But to a considerable extent, the media's choices for the public agenda may simply reflect the voices of those who clamor to be heard. Government officials, and the president in particular, exert a strong influence on the media's political agenda. Particularly at the local level, officials sometimes avoid making decisions the public would favor by keeping them off the agenda (Berkman and Kitch 1986, 175–310; Graber 1980, 193–223).

The Media as Cue-Givers

Certain political contests are sufficiently ambiguous in their interpretation that the news media take upon themselves the role of referee, to tell us who won. Election outcomes are an obvious case. Although we ordinarily do not need media pundits to tell us which candidate garners the most votes, media commentary may help us decide if the election winner achieved a "landslide" or earned a policy mandate. For midterm elections, where the summary outcome is the percentages of Senate and House seats and governorships won by the Republicans and the Democrats, the media help determine which party performed better than expected. Media interpretation is particularly intrusive in presidential primary elections, where the key issue generally is not the number of delegates the candidates win in the particular state, but momentum: which candidates are gaining and which are faltering, and who "really" won by surpassing expectations.

Presidential debates provide a subtle setting for media cue-giving. Although research shows that presidential debates foster considerable learning about the candidates and where they stand on issues, these debates change the minds of surprisingly few voters. The 1988 presidential debate was typical in this regard. In polls after the 1988 debates, few voters claimed to change their presidential preference. Many voters watch presidential debates as rooting partisans, cheering on their favorite candidate. Naturally, they want to know who "won." The mass media transmit the consensus verdict of the debate outcome.

The 1976 and 1984 presidential debates provided vivid illustration of how postdebate media messages can alter perceptions of the outcome. The second 1976 Ford-Carter debate contained President Ford's famous "Poland gaffe." Attempting to make the point that Poland was a sovereign nation, Ford startled knowledgeable observers by stating that Poland was not dominated by the Soviet Union. Research on audiences that were watching confirm, however, that most viewers did not give the remark much attention or attribute to it much importance (Steeper 1978). Polls conducted immediately after the debate suggested no consensus regarding who won. But over the next few days, as the media highlighted the message of Ford's gaffe, polls began to show a clear consensus that Ford had lost.[1]

The 1984 example was similar. In the first 1984 debate, President Reagan gave such a faltering performance that it raised new questions about whether his advanced age had weakened his ability. Yet the verdict was close in the polls on the night of the debate, with Mondale "winning" by only from 1 to 9 percentage points. The media declared Mondale the winner, however, and even began to report openly about whether Reagan was too old. One night after the debate, the ABC News/*Washington Post* poll found the public seeing Mondale was the winner by a lopsided 55 to 19 margin. Still one night later, the *New York Times*/CBS News poll respondents saw Mondale the winner by an even bigger 66 to 17 margin (Sussman 1984). This was a dramatic turnabout in public perceptions, fueled by cues from the mass media plus public discussions. To complete the story, Reagan and Mondale debated again two weeks after the first debate. Reagan cracked a joke about his age and in general improved his performance. Media commentators immediately declared him back on track. Two more weeks later, Reagan was reelected handily.

Newspaper Endorsements and the Vote

Does a newspaper's editorial stance influence the political opinions of its readers? Newspaper endorsements are often thought to be particularly crucial at the local level. Especially when the election is non-partisan or involves an extremely long ballot, the newspaper's decision regarding what to report or whom to endorse can be very important. As one newsperson reportedly once said, "You can't tell the players without a scorecard, and we sell the scorecards" (Banfield and Wilson 1963, 159). Newspapers achieve excellent success in endorsing local candidates who win. But this can be partially attributed to newspapers' endorsements of candidates who look like winners rather than to any influence of the newspaper on the electoral decision. At the local level, the effect of newspaper endorsement has been studied mainly for elections with lengthy ballots where voters are asked to select more candidates than they can possibly know anything about. For this particular type of election, where voter confusion is at its maximum, studies suggest that newspaper support is the key to victory (Mueller 1970b; Hooper 1969).

Some studies have examined national election data in an attempt to relate people's voting decisions to the endorsements of the newspapers they read. Even with statistical controls for party identification and other relevant variables, these studies show a fair-sized relationship between endorsements and votes, at the presidential, gubernatorial, and senatorial levels (Robinson 1974; Coombs 1981). These studies, however, present some difficulty for the making of causal inference. When survey respondents have a choice of newspaper, they may select the newspaper that represents their partisan views. Thus, any relationship between the endorsement decision of the respondent's favorite newspaper and the respondent's own voting decision could be the result of the respondent's newspaper selection rather than the newspaper's influence.

Another reason why it is difficult to research endorsement influence is that, as we saw earlier in this chapter, newspapers almost always endorse Republican candidates. This makes it difficult to match voters who read Republican newspapers with those who read Democratic newspapers. But one exception to the Republican endorsements habits of American newspapers provided a unique opportunity to study endorsement effects. In the 1964 presidential election, more newspapers endorsed President Lyndon Johnson (42 percent) than his Republican opponent, Barry Goldwater (35 percent). With this relatively even division, Erikson (1976b, 207–34) was able to compare the vote in communities where the local newspaper(s) endorsed the Democrat with the vote in communities where the local newspaper(s) endorsed the Republican. Statistical controls were imposed for the community's previous vote, the particular state, and the size of the city. Even with these controls, the 1960–1964 vote shift was about 5 percentage points more

Democratic where the endorsements were Democratic than where they were Republican.

Presidential Manipulation and the Mass Media

Of all public officials, only the president can command the time on television to present his case to the people. One change that television has brought about is the greater ease with which American presidents can communicate directly with the American people. Each modern president has used the television forum to promote public support for his policy initiatives. Their success, however, has been mixed. Recall the study of television impact by Page et al. (1987). They found that television newscasts' presentations of presidential policy preferences are followed by only modest movement of public opinion. However, they also found the public response to be greater at times when the president enjoys high popularity.

On domestic policy, polls show only one clear instance of a presidential initiative gaining popular support. This instance was President Lyndon Johnson's leadership of public opinion in support of the civil rights bill of 1964 that guaranteed equal access for all races to public accommodations such as hotels and restaurants. Between June 1963 (during Kennedy's administration) and January 1964, public support for the proposed law rose from a slim plurality (49 to 42 percent) to a commanding majority of 61 to 31 percent.[2] This is a shift far greater than would normally occur on a controversial issue over a 7-month period.

The more normal result of a presidential attempt to sway public opinion is exemplified by President Reagan and tax reform. Throughout the early years of his presidency, Reagan urged the public to support tax reform. In 1985, Reagan signed a tax reform bill from Congress that was much to his liking. But Congress's achievement of tax reform resulted from internal dynamics that had little to do with public opinion. Throughout the battle for tax reform, the public was essentially indifferent to the prospect of major change in the tax laws and was cynical about the possible impact. People eventually became interested only after the bill became law, when they began to wonder how it would affect them personally.[3]

On foreign policy, however, presidents can be quite persuasive with public opinion. Perhaps the clearest case is the response to President Reagan's justification to the nation for the invasion of the Caribbean island nation of Grenada in 1983. Immediately following the invasion but before the president spoke to the nation, only 53 percent approved of the invasion. Immediately after President Reagan addressed the nation, however, approval shot up to 64 percent.[4] The most lasting impact of Grenada was on the public's evaluation of Reagan's job performance. Before the invasion, Reagan's approval ratings had been in the doldrums, comparable to Jimmy Carter's at his equivalent point in the presidential term. After the invasion, Reagan's ratings began a long climb upward.

When a foreign policy crisis unfolds, the media focus uncritically on the president as the national spokesman. In what has been labeled the "rally around the flag" effect, presidents make short-term gains in public favor whenever they deal with a foreign policy crisis (Mueller 1970a, 29). In terms of the Gallup approval rating, Truman gained 9 points when he decided to resist the 1950 Communist invasion of South Korea; Eisenhower gained 8 points following the 1956 Suez crisis; and Kennedy gained 13 points following the 1962 cuban missile crisis. More recent examples are boosts in popularity for Johnson after the Dominican Republic invasion (1965), for Nixon after the Cambodian invasion (1970), for Ford after the Mayaguez incident (1975), for Carter after the Camp David Summit (1978), and for Reagan after the invasion of Grenada.

Bush's successful handling of the short Gulf War with Iraq in early 1991 provides one of the most impressive examples of a "rally effect." Between January and March of 1991, Bush's approval rating soared from a respectable but middling 55 percent to the unheard-of heights of 87 percent. As with all rallies, however, this one was short-lived. As the national economy skidded during 1991 and 1992, Bush's approval level dropped into the danger zone below 50 percent. In an event totally unanticipated in early 1991, Bush lost his 1992 reelection bid.

Even crises that reflect badly on the President normally produce surges in presidential popularity. Eisenhower gained following the U-2 incident and summit collapse of 1960, as did Kennedy after the disastrous Bay of Pigs Invasion of 1961. Until Bush's Gulf War success, the strongest short-term gain in the history of Gallup's approval ratings was Carter's 19-point gain in November 1979 following Iran's seizure of American hostages.

The reason for the rally around the President in times of crisis is often interpreted as a sort of unthinking frenzy of patriotism where citizens choose to support the leader without considering whether the leader is right or wrong. This imagery may be too simplistic. Richard Brody (1991) argues a different scenario. According to Brody, people support their president in times of crisis because that is the their rational option given the one-sided nature of the information presented to them. In a time of crisis, the President has peoples' attention and controls the available information. Rival political elites potentially could create some news by criticizing the President, but in typical rally circumstances, their political interest is to keep quiet except to be supportive. With little in the news that contradicts the President, the flow of news is one-sided. Lacking an alternative frame of references, citizens support the President.

On the other hand, a crisis that becomes prolonged to the point where rival politicians begin to criticize can bring a president nothing but woe. Jimmy Carter may have benefited in the short run from a hostage crisis, but his failure to solve the crisis contributed to his defeat in 1980. Lyndon Johnson's failure to end the Vietnam War provides another example. Early in Johnson's presidency, public opinion supported both Johnson and the war effort. But the Johnson administration tragically miscalculated the extent to which a reasonably popular president could maintain support for an unwinnable land war in Asia.

Ronald Reagan's Iran-Contra scandal (1986–78) is an example of a foreign policy crisis that for obvious reasons caused the president's popularity to fall rather than rise. As the revelations about Iran-Contra emerged in the news media, Reagan's popularity plummeted 20 points. The uncritical media attention usually offered a president in a crisis was naturally absent as the Iran-Contra story unfolded, with its revelations of arms sales to Iran and proceeds used for illegal military aid to the Nicaragua Contras (Brody and Shapiro, 1989; Hurwitz et al. 1989; Krosnick and Kinder, 1990).

Conclusions

In one sense the Minimal Effects Model of media influence is correct. People rarely make major changes in their political attitudes as a result of messages in the mass media. Researchers instead uncover more modest effects. People attend to the media with considerable selectivity, processing new information into previous mental cubbyholes. Media messages can influence opinions in several ways, but the effects are generally modest.

8-3 Television and Election Campaigns _____

One important political change of the past forty years is the way television has altered the conduct of political campaigns. Television has allowed political candidates to campaign directly to the American people. But not all the effects of televised campaigns may be desirable. Televised campaigns bring about the potential for candidates' electoral success to be determined by their mastery of the more superficial aspects of television campaigning, or even simply their ability to raise money for television advertisements.

Television and Presidential Elections

The 1952 presidential campaign was the first campaign of the television era. The nature of that campaign has nurtured some modern myths—maybe true, maybe not—about television's impact on presidential election politics. Eisenhower's ease in front of the television camera helped him develop the image of a warm-hearted but stern former military commander. Moreover, Eisenhower's campaign relied heavily on television advertising under the direction of Madison Avenue's Rosser Reeves. Pushing the slogan that Americans "like Ike," Reeve's advertising strategy marked the beginning of modern television campaigning, which would only become more sophisticated as the years progressed.[5]

Meanwhile, "Ike's" opponent, Governor Adlai Stevenson of Illinois, also contributed to the mythology of television's dominance in modern campaigning. Like Eisenhower, Stevenson had an enthusiastic core of supporters and generally was viewed favorably by the American public. But he suffered from one important handicap. Stevenson did not like television and resisted his advisors' attempts to exploit its potential. (Stevenson reportedly did not even own a television set at the time.) While Ike smiled before the cameras and made the first effective use of spot television ads, Stevenson conducted an old-fashioned campaign, directing carefully crafted speeches to small audiences. Stevenson's campaign committee did pay to have a few of his speeches televised nationally. But as is now generally recognized, simply letting the live cameras roll at a campaign rally is not an effective use of advertising on television.[6]

Ultimately we cannot know how much television contributed to the 1952 presidential outcome. We do know, however, that the *belief* is widespread that the candidates' ability to exploit television, along with their media advisors' cleverness, determines the success of presidential candidates. Election results continue to feed myths about the power of television. The electoral success of Ronald Reagan provides the best example. And if television explains success, it can also rationalize failure. Walter Mondale, the Democrats' unsuccessful presidential candidate in 1984, explained his failure with the observation that, unlike Reagan, he had "never warmed up to the television." And following Dukakis's defeat in 1988, many Democrats found their candidate's inept television campaign to be a convenient scapegoat.

Whether valid or not, political campaign managers share some common perceptions of how to conduct a successful campaign. Campaign directors set up campaign rallies and appearances as media events. The immediate audience in physical attendance is less important than the millions of television viewers who may see a snippet of the event reported on their sets at home. Therefore, campaign advisors try to find the right hook for the day's events that might capture the attention of television journalists. Too many events or too many different themes endanger the campaign's control of the television agenda. And the candidate should not be too accessible to reporters, for he or she might say something newsworthy that will become the unintentional story on the evening news.

Republican presidential campaigns have more successfully followed the textbook for television campaigning than their more disorganized Democratic opponents. Like Ronald Reagan before him, in 1988 George Bush made a limited number of campaign appearances, in carefully staged settings with specific, if narrow, themes. The television cameras could not help but present the message that Bush's "handlers" wanted to present for that day. The Dukakis campaign was unable to exert the same level of control of its news coverage. Clinton's 1992 television campaign obviously was more successful, but still regarded at the time as less professional than Bush's Republican operation.

But why should the Republicans run more effective presidential campaigns? Because the Republicans have dominated recent presidential elections, each new candidate can call upon an experienced and capable team of campaign organizers. The Democratic presidential candidate will typically rely on trusted advisors with no national campaign experience rather than the "failed" organizers of the previous quest. Some observers also suspect that recent Republican presidential candidates have obtained favorable media treatment because the press tends to favor likely winners. Consider the near-counterexample: When Dukakis appeared to be leading early in 1988, he was getting the more favorable media treatment. Once electoral fortunes reversed, campaign coverage favored the new front-runner, Bush (Patterson, 1987). In 1992, Bush's status reversed, as he developed the scent of a likely loser. By most accounts, the 1992 press coverage favored Clinton (Sabato 1993).

One frequent complaint against television news coverage of campaigns is television's emphasis on the visual aspect of campaigns at the expense of the more cerebral. Television is a poor medium for the flow of ideas in campaigns. Campaign messages can be presented only briefly on the television news. Some fear that as a consequence, complicated ideas lose out to cheap slogans. One might think that by covering campaign events, television news would present significant portions of candidate speeches directly to the viewer. Instead, television presents candidates talking in small "sound bites." Back in the 1968 presidential campaign, the typical network news sound bite was one full minute. By 1988, the average sound bite lasted only nine seconds (Hellin 1992). In 1992, network news executives vowed to reform, but by most accounts, network coverage of the 1992 campaign was a slim improvement over the recent past.

If television news does not present candidate speeches, what does it actually show when it reports on political campaigns? Unfortunately, television reporters rarely intervene to inform their audiences about the policy issues that separate rival candidates. Instead they emphasize campaign hoopla—the "horse race," superficial campaign events, and campaign personalities (Graber 1980; Joslyn 1984; Patterson 1993). According to the count by the Center for Media and Public Affairs, only 40 percent of the general election campaign stories on the networks dealt with policy issues in 1992, an increase of 4 percentage points over 1988 (Stanley and Niemi 1994). The deemphasis of policy issues is not solely the fault of the television medium, however. When newspapers report on a campaign, they show the same tendency.[7] Reporting on the horse race or the personalities may be easier than reporting on the policy issues. It produces less controversy and more audience interest.

Television and Presidential Primaries

Television coverage not only has altered the conduct of general elections but also has contributed to the way that political parties nominate their candidates. Earlier in this century, primary elections were not particularly important. Candidates were often chosen by party conventions or party caucuses, which left most voters out of the decision-making. Even in instances when candidates were chosen in party primaries, party leaders could usually dominate the selection. Now, the vast majority of state and local nominations are determined by primary election. And party leaders no longer dominate, since candidates can appeal directly to the primary electorate, via television.

At the presidential level, primary elections have taken on importance only recently, with television playing a major role. In 1968, the Democratic Convention resolved to "reform" the party's delegate selection process. As a result, states began to employ the presidential primary as their means of selecting national convention delegates pledged to particular candidates. Because state laws often needed to be changed, these reforms affected both the Democratic and Republican parties. With each presidential year since 1968, active campaigning for the presidential nomination began earlier in the campaign season than it had before.

Television plays a major role in this focusing of the outcome toward a single winner within each party. The first part of the primary campaign may be fought largely away from the limelight of network television, at the person-to-person level in states like New Hampshire with its early primary, or Iowa, which has a complicated caucus procedure that causes presidential candidates to woo party activists. Even when networks cover these events, they draw little nationwide attention.

The eventual verdicts of these primaries and caucuses, however, suddenly concentrate national attention upon a few front-runners. Inevitably, the national media spotlight an unexpected winner, or at least a new dark horse, in the early primary field. The 1984 Democratic primaries provide the classic case of a primary candidate surging from nowhere to claim national attention. Senator Gary Hart squeaked into a second-place showing in the Iowa caucus and then charged to a surprise victory in the New Hampshire primary. Almost instantly, Hart went from relatively obscure senator to a household name. Via the magic of television, Americans could take a look at the serious presidential hopeful who, only a week or so before, few could identify.[8]

Throughout the 1984 primary season, Mondale and Hart fought from primary to primary for the nomination. But did the mass media, and television in particular, provide voters with the kind of information that would help them make intelligent choices? What voters knew about these two candidates, apart from what they looked like, was a set of slogans. Hart campaigned as the candidate of "new ideas." Mondale's retort, borrowed from a successful hamburger commercial, was "Where's the beef?" Actually, Hart's campaign spelled out some new ideas, with which voters might agree or disagree. But television commentators rarely discussed the content of Hart's ideas and in fact often ridiculed "new ideas" as an empty slogan. For the media, the important aspect of the campaign was the horse race. Mondale, of course, defeated Hart for the nomination but lost the general election.

Television News and an Informed Electorate

Earlier in this chapter we discussed evidence that television news may be less effective than newspapers as a source of political information. Studies have extended this finding to political campaigns as well. People seem to learn a lot more about the political issues of campaigns from newspapers than from television news.

In an early study of media influence, Patterson and McClure (1976) interviewed a panel of Syracuse, New York, citizens in early September and again in November of the 1972 election year. In their later interviews they asked their respondents about their media habits, particularly how often they had followed the campaign on network news and in the newspapers. In both interviews, they asked their respondents where the presidential candidates (Nixon and McGovern) stood on each of 18 national issues.

Not surprisingly, as the 1972 campaign progressed, Patterson and McClure's respondents increased their knowledge of candidate positions. The surprising aspect was that viewing television network news seemed to make little difference. Patterson and McClure report that people who claimed to be network news viewers increased their knowledge of candidate positions by 28 percent on the average. But people who claimed to *not* watch network news gained almost as much: 25 percent. Meanwhile, self-identified newspaper readers showed a 35 percent gain in information compared with a mere 18 percent gain for nonreaders. Patterson and McClure (1976, 51) bluntly interpret their result: "those individuals who faithfully tuned in network news during the election learned not much more than people who spent that time doing something else."

Using NES data, Joseph Wagner (1983) examined the effect of media reliance on voter information in the 1976 presidential contest. Wagner compared frequent readers of political news in newspapers with those who were not regular newspaper readers but did claim to "frequently" or "sometimes" watch the nightly news. Wagner found that newspaper readers were more perceptive of the policy differences between the two presidential candidates (Ford and Carter) than were those who relied only on television. Wagner found the relationship to persist even with statistical controls for respondent education and other background variables. Seemingly, then, reliance on newspapers makes one more informed about political issues than does reliance on television news.

Of course it may not be startling to find that television informs less than newspapers. But to what extent is television more informative than nothing at all? As part of his study of the 1976 campaign, Wagner compared the television-reliant respondents with the few who claimed

TABLE 8.5 Patterns of Attention to Newspaper and Television News, 1992

		Television Viewing		
		Regular viewer	Occasional viewer	Nonviewer	All cases
Newspaper Reading	Regular reader	11%	4%	1%	16%
	Occasional reader	10%	18%	9%	37%
	Nonreader	10%	27%	9%	47%
	All cases	31%	49%	19%	100%

Cell entries are percents of total sample

Source: NES, 1992 election data.

to be attentive to neither television nor newspapers. The small number of respondents who belonged to this unexposed group made this comparison tentative. Surprisingly, however, Wagner found that the television-reliant respondents were no more informed about the candidate positions than were the inattentive.

Using the 1992 NES election data, we offer some additional demonstrations of how newspapers and television news inform voters during presidential campaigns. We divided 1992 NES respondents into three categories of television news watching. "Regular viewers" claimed both to watch television news at least 6 days a week and to follow television news of the campaign with "quite a bit" or "a good deal" of attention. "Nonviewers" claimed to watch no television news or pay no attention to campaign news. "Occasional viewers" were in between these two extremes. We rated newspaper readership similarly. "Regular readers" claimed both to read newspapers at least six days a week and to follow the campaign in newspapers with "quite a bit" or "or a good deal" of attention. "Nonreaders" claimed to not read newspapers or pay no attention to campaign news. "Occasional readers" were in between.

Rating respondents according to three categories on viewing and three categories on reading gives a combined set of categories with a total of nine cells. Frequencies with which people belonged in each of the nine cells are shown in Table 8.5. This table reflects the growing dominance of television over newspapers as a news source. But the same individuals who attended to one medium generally attended to the other. Regular viewing and regular reading tended to go together. So did nonviewing and nonreading. Our interest is in sorting out the separate effects of reading and watching. For this, we pay special attention to the relatively rare respondents who either follow the campaign a lot on television but not in the newspapers or vice versa.

Table 8.6 shows the basic results. Part (a) of Table 8.6 shows the percentage of respondents who said they were "very interested" in the campaign. As we move from nonviewer to regular viewers or from nonreaders to regular readers, we see that campaign interest increases. This relationship between media attention and campaign interest is clear for both viewing and reading. For each level of television viewing, newspaper readers are more interested than nonreaders. For each level of newspaper reading, television news viewers are more interested than nonviewers. All this fits with common sense. Interest in the campaign should make one want to follow the campaign more closely both in newspapers and on television; perhaps, following the campaign either in newspapers or on television also makes one more interested.

But now note, in part (b) of Table 8.6, what happens when we substitute information about candidate policy positions for campaign interest. High scorers correctly rated Bush to the right of Clinton on all five issues examined. The relationship between newspaper reading and information is clear. At each level of television news viewing, regular newspaper readers are the most informed about candidate policy position. However, the same pattern is not found for the effect of television news viewing. At each level of newspaper reading, television news viewing related only weakly to information.

Taken together, the evidence we have examined is damaging for the proposition that television news coverage of presidential campaigns informs the viewing public. Regularly watching television news during a presidential campaign may encourage people to become more interested in the campaign. But regular watching of television news is not associated with attention to policy issues or perceptiveness regarding a candidate's stand on policy issues.

TABLE 8.6 Responsiveness in the 1992 Presidential Campaign, by Media Attention

(a) % "Very Interested" in the Election

| | | Television News Viewing | | |
		Regular viewer	Occasional viewer	Nonviewer
	Regular reader	83%	61%	44%
Newspaper Reading	Occasional reader	61%	37%	31%
	Nonreader	54%	19%	11%

(b) % with High Information about Candidate Positions

| | | Television News Viewing | | |
		Regular viewer	Occasional viewer	Nonviewer
	Regular reader	38%	41%	48%
Newspaper Reading	Occasional reader	30%	29%	6%
	Nonreader	18%	17%	9%

Source: NES, 1992 election data.

Television Campaign Ads and an Informed Electorate

News programs do not constitute the only television outlet for political candidates. Candidates often conduct a major portion of their campaigns via television advertisements—usually in the form of 30-second "spot ads." Although expensive, ads have the advantage that, unlike with news broadcasts, candidates possess full control of their content. Even when their content is distorted, television ads frame issues for the electorate. George Bush's "Willie Horton" ads in 1988 provide a notorious example. These ads highlighted a Massachusetts prisoner who committed a rape while on a weekend furlough when Bush's opponent, Michael Dukakis, was governor. Without a counter response from Dukakis, these ads left the impression with voters that Dukakis was generally indifferent toward criminal behavior. The "Willie Horton" ad is but one example of the growing trend toward negative advertising, with candidates spending almost as much money attacking their opponents as they do promoting themselves (Jamieson 1992).

Is spending for television more effective than other kinds of campaign spending? While campaign directors almost unanimously see television advertising as effective, only about 20 percent of congressional candidates' campaign expenditures actually go to television advertisements (Goldenberg and Traugott 1984, 86–88, 117). Thus even if spending does win votes, we cannot be certain that television advertising is the key. Research by Gary Jacobson, however, does show that candidates are more visible in the mass media when overall campaign expenditures increase. For instance, when a congressional challenger spends only about $25,000 on the campaign, only about 45 percent of the prospective voters are able to recall something about the candidate from the mass media. But when the challenger spends about $500,000, two-thirds recall the candidate from the mass media (Jacobson 1987, 123).

One of the most interesting analyses of the effectiveness of campaign ads is from Patterson and McClure's Syracuse study. Recall that their study found that people who watched the most television news did not learn much more than the average viewer about candidate campaign positions. Patterson and McClure (1976, 93–139) also ascertained how much television in general their respondents watched during the fall campaign. Their presumption was that people who watched the most TV were the most exposed to campaign ads on TV. They found that heavy television watchers did not change their views of the candidates any more than those who were light watchers. In this sense, Patterson and McClure cast doubt on the effectiveness of the television ads. They also found, however, that heavy television watchers learned considerably more about candidate policy positions over the course of the campaign than did light watchers. This presents an interesting irony.

Although Patterson and McClure may overstate the case, they suggest that people learn more about where the candidates stand on issues from watching them posture in television ads than from watching the coverage on the television news.

The Media and Campaigns: An Assessment

The quality of democracy depends on the degree to which citizens can make informed decisions at the ballot box. How well citizens perform this task depends not only on citizens' interest in and capability of processing political information, but also on the quality of the information that is available to them. Contemporary scholarship tends to view modern media campaigns negatively, with their emphasis on negative advertising and their issueless news coverage (e.g., Jamieson 1992, Sabato 1993, Patterson 1993). But contemporary scholarship also treats the voters generously. The prevailing view of the electorate is that it makes the best use of its judgment *given the limited information that reaches it* (Page and Shapiro, 1991; Brody 1991; Popkin 1991). Studies that trace the evolution of voters during the campaign show that despite the limitations of the mass media, considerable learning takes place. Voters appear more informed about issues as the campaign goes on (Patterson and McClure 1976, Buchanan 1991), and more focused on relevant criteria for making a vote choice (Gelmon and King 1993). The mass media's shaping of campaigns and the potential for improvement present interesting questions that are far from fully answered.

8-4 Conclusion

The mass media pervade our society in a way that would have been unimaginable to the founders of the American Republic. One can still debate whether the condition of American democracy is better or worse as a result. At the time of the United States' origin, the smaller society with no mass media resulted in a different conception of public opinion than is common today. The sociologist C. Wright Mills described the idealized view of public opinion that once prevailed:

> Two centuries ago, before the mass media as we know them today, it was thought that in a democracy the public of public opinion consisted of small groups of people talking among themselves, electing spokesmen for their group, who in turn talked among themselves. (Mills, 1963, 535).

The notion was of a public opinion originating with the informed public and moving "upward" to affect societal institutions. With the modern media, influence moves directly "downward" from the mass media—and the institutions they reflect—to public opinion as a mass audience. With democratic institutions, audience members are supposed to send their signals back upward, influencing government behavior with their votes and other actions. The important function for the mass media in a democracy is to help their audiences perform their duties as democratic citizens responsibly.

In at least one respect, the mass media perform their democratic role reasonably well. As a reflector of societal values, the media reinforce public acceptance of the rules of democracy. In other respects, however, different observers with different political viewpoints may complain about the media's failure to properly enlighten the public. Changing or reforming the media would not be an easy task. Meaningful changes would be difficult to legislate. And it would probably be unrealistic to try to mobilize the mass media to reform themselves.

Human beings are resourceful at avoiding the influence of media messages. Yet, public opinion and mass media messages are at least somewhat related. There is no clear evidence that this relationship is more than minimal, however, or that the direction of influence is entirely from the media to the public.

Notes _____

1. Immediately after the debate, a national poll showed that the public saw Ford the winner, 48 to 28. By the following evening, Carter was perceived the winner 61 to 19. (Steeper 1978, 85).
2. AIPO News Release, February 2, 1964. The exact question was, "How would you feel about a law that would give all persons—Negro as well as white—the right to be served in public places, such as hotels, restaurants, theaters?"
3. In January 1985, the *Washington Post*/ABC News Poll asked people's views of the "Treasury I" tax reform proposal: The response was 32 percent for, 18 percent against, with the remainder claiming either they had no opinion or they had not heard of the plan. In September 1986, just before the passage of a tax reform bill, the *Washington Post*/ABC News poll recorded sentiment in favor. 23 to 15 percent, with the remainder with no opinion. *Source: Washington Post National Weekly Edition* (1986).
4. CBS News/*New York Times* "prespeech" and "postspeech" October 1973 surveys.
5. On the history of campaign advertising, see Jamieson (1992).
6. On Stevenson and television in 1952, see Halberstam (1979).
7. By one count (Hershey 1989), in 1988 newspaper stories of campaign strategy outnumbered stories of campaign policy issues by about 2 to 1.
8. On the media and momentum in presidential primaries, see Brady and Johnston (1987), and Bartels (1987).

CHAPTER 9

Elections as Instruments of Popular Control

In a democracy, the public supposedly controls the behavior of its public officials by exercising its influence at the ballot box in a rational fashion. We call this the Rational Activist Model. Ideally, each voter would select a candidate who best represents his or her views on matters of public policy. At least in a two-candidate election, the collective choice would then be the candidate who is closer to most voters on the issues. The policy result would be the closest correspondence possible, given the choice of candidates, between the collective preferences of the electorate and government policy.

But representation of the public interest via democratic elections is not as simple in practice as it is in theory. It is possible, for instance, to hold elections in which none of the candidates on the ballot offer policy choices that voters find attractive. Or, even when the candidates present a relevant menu of policy choices, the electorate may—through some combination of misguidance, ignorance, and indifference—vote "irrationally" by voting into office a candidate who does not represent their interests. Also, if office-holders perceive that the electorate is not watching, or that it does not care, they may feel free to make policy decisions without consideration of public opinion.

Looking at the matter in a positive rather than negative fashion, we can state the conditions that do allow elections to be an effective instrument for inducing policy decisions that are responsive to public opinion. First, the candidates should offer a meaningful choice of policy options that appeal to voters, and once elected, the winner should try to carry out campaign pledges. Second, the voters should be informed about the issues that separate the candidates and vote for the candidate who best represents their own views. Clearly, the fulfillment of each one of these conditions depends on the other. For example, political leaders pay the greatest attention to public opinion when they believe that the public is alert enough to throw them out of office if they do not. Similarly, voters have the greatest opportunity to vote intelligently on the basis of policy issues when the politicians act from the assumption that the public is going to do so.

In the present chapter, we examine the behavior of the electorate when it carries out its assigned responsibility. Then in the following chapters we examine the responsiveness of political elites to public opinion.

9-1 Political Campaigns and the Voter _____

During each political campaign, voters are bombarded with news and propaganda about the candidates who seek their favor. Judging by the attention that politicians give to the voters at election time, one might conclude that the voter reacts to campaign stimuli in the fluid manner that the voter does as a consumer, reacting to advertising stimuli in the mass media. Just as the person about to purchase a product, such as a detergent, might vacillate in his or her choice of brands until the moment of purchase, so might the voter waver between the candidates until entry into the voting booth forces a final decision. But as we saw in Chapter 8, this image of the voting process underestimates the voter's ability to resist political messages.

As discussed in Chapter 3, most American voters have a more or less permanent attachment to either the Republican or the Democratic Party. It is through this filter of party identification that most voters view the partisan aspects of the political world. The anchor of party identification prevents most voters from wavering in their choice of candidates during a campaign, and they do not change the party they vote for from one election year to the next. We know from National Election Study surveys that, of people who vote in two successive presidential elections, about 80 percent will vote for the same party's presidential candidate both times (Converse 1962). Similarly, most voters decide whom they will support for president as early as convention time and stick to this choice over the course of the campaign. About 80 percent of the voters each November vote for the candidate who had been their August preference (Benham 1965). When partisans do change their candidate choice during the campaign, one usually finds an initial attraction to the opposition's candidate followed by a return to the fold by election day.

Below the presidential level, the percentage of voters who stick with their party's choice is even higher. For lesser offices, the amount of information that reaches voters is often too slight to give them any reason to go against their party. Only in nonpartisan elections and primary contests (where party identification cannot be a criterion of choice) do voters vacillate in an erratic manner. In fact, voter preferences in primary contests are so fluid that pollsters have great difficulty predicting outcomes, even when they monitor opinion as late as a day or two before the election (Bartels and Broh 1989).

Of course, if party identification were the sole determinant of how people vote, election results would simply reflect the balance of Democratic and Republican identifiers. And since the ratio of Democratic to Republican identifiers changes only modestly in the short run, election results would be almost identical from one election to the next. In fact, election results often depart considerably from the voter division that would occur with a strict party-line vote.

When an election is decided essentially on a party-line basis, the result is called the "normal vote." Assuming a 50/50 split by Independents and only a minimum partisan defection rate (equal on both sides), the normal vote in a national election would produce a victory for the Democrats, who would obtain about 54 percent of the two-party vote (Converse 1966; see also Petrocik 1989). This calculation reflects the Democrats' edge in party identification that more than counterbalances the effect of a higher turnout rate among Republicans than Democrats.

The normal vote is approximated by the nationwide returns of midterm elections, in which national issues are seldom important, while Republican and Democratic trends generated by various state and local contests cancel themselves out. When election results depart appreciably from the normal vote expectations, the "short-term partisan forces"[1] of the campaign favor one party more than the other. In presidential elections, strong short-term forces often push the election results away from the normal vote baseline. This difference between presidential and midterm elections is shown in Figure 9-1.

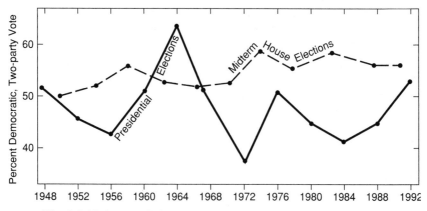

Fig. 9-1 Voting trends in presidential and midterm House election.

The midterm vote for the U.S. House of Representatives since 1950 has consistently stayed within the range of between 50 and 59 percent Democratic, varying slightly around the 54 percent Democratic vote baseline. (The U.S. House vote in presidential years shows the same pattern.) Barring the jolt of a genuine partisan realignment favoring the Republicans, the Democratic Party seems destined to control the U.S. House of Representatives.

In post–World War II presidential elections, the vote has been close to "normal" only five times: in 1948, 1960, 1968, 1976, and 1992. With "normal" elections at the national level being Democratic victories, the Democrats won four of these close-to-normal elections while barely losing one (1968).

In seven of the twelve presidential elections since World War II, the outcome was outside the range of the "normal vote," with one party or the other benefiting from "short-term partisan forces." In six of these seven instances (Eisenhower in 1952 and 1956, Nixon in 1972, Reagan in 1980 and 1984, Bush in 1988), the short-term forces swung strongly in the Republicans' favor. Only in the Democratic landslide election of 1964 did the short-term forces decidedly favor the Democratic presidential candidate. The post–World War II range of variation in the two-party presidential vote is from 61–39 Democratic (1964) to 61–39 Republican (1972). With the wide range of short-term forces at the presidential level, the modest Democratic edge in the normal vote clearly is no handicap to Republican presidential candidates.

The departure of election results from the normal vote does not signify that the usual role of party identification in shaping electoral decisions has broken down. Instead, one finds that the party favored by the short-term forces is the beneficiary of most of the short-term partisan defections and wins most of the Independent votes. Figure 9-2 shows this pattern over the twelve presidential elections from 1948 through 1992.

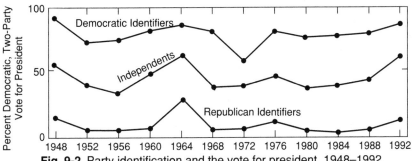

Fig. 9-2 Party identification and the vote for president, 1948–1992. (Source: NES election data.)

When the short-term forces favor the Republicans, Democrats "defect" beyond their usual rate; Republicans are even more loyal to their party than usual, and Independents vote overwhelmingly Republican. With pro-Democratic short-term forces, the pattern is the reverse—with unusually frequent Republican defections and a Democratic trend among Independents.

Short-Term Forces Below the Presidential Level

For state and local elections, the "normal" vote reflects the partisan balance of the particular state or local constituency rather the nation as a whole. Due to the kinds of people who reside in the area, the local normal vote often is very one-sided in favor of the Republicans or Democrats. Election results will reflect the local normal vote plus any short-term forces that carry over from national politics (or from higher-level state or local contests). In addition, the local vote will reflect the short-term forces generated by the local candidates and their campaign. One way of thinking about local short-term forces is as the "personal" vote generated by the candidates themselves (Cain et al. 1987).

Although candidates for local office run less visible races than presidential candidates, their own campaigns help to determine their electoral fate. The importance of local campaigns is indicated by the fact that as many as half the voters in a national election will report that they split their ticket rather than vote for one party's candidate for all offices. Because of this ticket splitting, the same constituency will often vote the Democratic candidate into one office and the Republican candidate into another.

As for president, election outcomes below the presidential level depend in large part on the short-term forces of the specific campaign. By one estimate, short-term forces for the statewide offices of governor and U.S. senator are about as large as for president (Erikson et al. 1994, Ch. 8). The implication is that statewide (and perhaps local) outcomes readily depart by 10 or 15 percentage points from the state (or local) normal vote. Even where one party dominates, the disadvantaged party often can win when it fields the stronger candidate.

Who Are the "Floating Voters"?

Election outcomes are the result of both the normal vote and short-term partisan forces of the campaign. Voters whose choice is determined by the campaign rather than a long-term partisan commitment are called "floating voters." An important question is: How informed are the floating voters? If the floating voters are more politically informed than the average, we would think that election trends are essentially the response of the most politically alert segment of the public. But if the reverse is true—that floaters are more politically ignorant than the average—then we might be compelled toward the more dismal conclusion that election trends are largely the result of campaign propaganda of the sort that appeals to the voters least capable of making an informed evaluation.

Thanks to a classic article by Converse (1962) and a more recent elaboration by Zaller (1992), we have some good but complicated theory regarding floating voters. Consider a candidate's decision whether to pitch the campaign at inattentive and unsophisticated voters or at attentive and sophisticated voters. On the one hand, the more attentive voters are easier to reach with new campaign messages. On the other hand, these attentive voters are more hardened in their views. Their accumulated storage of political information helps to bolster their initial views against intruding information. For example, a Republican who is highly informed about politics is better equipped to discount Democratic propaganda than one who is more politically ignorant. Less attentive voters are more easily swayed, but only if new information reaches them.

Given these complications, the information level of floating voters depends considerably on the intensity of the campaign and the flow of information. When the information flow is low, the least attentive voters are so uninformed that they lack any basis for switching back and forth between candidates. They vote according to their initial partisan predisposition, if they vote at all. Attentive voters, meanwhile, although more resistant to influence from campaign propaganda, sometimes change their candidate choice when new information reaches them. However, when the information flow is high, even the least attentive voters receive some information. Since these least attentive voters are the most influenced by new information they receive, they contribute disproportionately to electoral volatility.

The battle for the presidency attracts great interest and large voter turnout, with almost all voters receiving some campaign exposure. For example, awareness of the candidates' names is nearly universal during a presidential campaign. The universal intake of new information during a presidential campaign loosens a great number of voters from their partisan moorings—particularly among the least attentive voters. The tiny fraction of presidential voters who manage completely to avoid the campaign maintain stable candidate preferences throughout the campaign. But setting these few cases aside, partisan defections and preelection wavering in candidate choice are most frequent among voters with the least exposure to the presidential campaign.

Table 9.1 illustrates the relationship between our information scale, introduced in Chapter 3, and partisan defection in the 1992 presidential election. Among Democrats, it was the least informed who "de-

TABLE 9.1 Vote for President, 1992, by Information Level and Party Identification

	Information		
	Low	Medium	High
Democratic identifiers			
Clinton	78%	80%	89%
Perot	12	12	7
Bush	11	8	5
	100%	100%	100%
Independent identifiers			
Clinton	39%	41%	49%
Perot	31	26	27
Bush	30	33	25
	100%	100%	100%
Republican identifiers			
Clinton	13%	11%	4%
Perot	19	20	16
Bush	68	69	80
	100%	100%	100%

Information scale based on correctness of relative placement of candidates on issues. For details, see the Appendix.

Source: NES, 1992 election data.

fected" to vote for Bush or Perot; similarly, among Republicans, the least-informed voters were more likely to "defect" to Clinton or Perot. Since the pro-Democratic short-term forces brought more Republican than Democratic defections, one can say that among partisans, it was the least informed who helped the most to tilt the election toward Clinton and away from Bush. Relatively uninformed Republicans were only weakly committed and abandoned Bush in large numbers, while a lesser number of weakly committed uninformed Democrats went against the tide by abandoning Clinton. Meanwhile, the more informed partisans held firm for their party.

Table 9.1 also shows the voting behavior of self-proclaimed Independents in the 1992 presidential election. Free of partisan attachments, Independents respond the strongest to campaign short-term forces. In 1992, Independents favored Clinton over Bush decisively and, not surprising given their lack of partisan commitment, were the strongest partisan category for Ross Perot's independent candidacy. Within each information category, over two-thirds of the Independents rejected Bush. Among Independents, the most informed were the most likely to vote for Clinton, while the least informed were the strongest category for Perot.

The net result of this analysis is that Clinton's percentage point lead over Bush was higher among the least informed (+17 percent) than among the highly informed (+10 percent):

	Low information	High information
Bush %	31%	37%
Clinton %	48	47
Perot %	21	16
	100%	100%
Clinton% − Bush%	+17%	+10%

This is the usual pattern of presidential elections: The least-informed voters exaggerate the partisan trend. In 1988, for example, low-information voters were more supportive of winner Bush than were high-information voters. As Converse argues, it sometimes seems that ". . .not only is the electorate as a whole quite uninformed, but it is the least informed members within the electorate who seem to hold the critical 'balance of power' in the sense that alternatives in the governing party depend disproportionately on shifts in their sentiment (Converse 1962, 578).

We might even be tempted to conclude that the most effective presidential campaign would be one aimed directly at the voter who is normally inattentive and uninformed about politics. But recall that the inattentive voter is a less accessible target of campaign messages. Note, too, the tendency of the least informed to dilute their influence by not voting. Based on self-reports, the 1992 vote turnout within the least- and most-informed categories were:

	Low information	High information
Voted	60%	92%
Did not vote	40	8
	100%	100%

The electoral contribution of the least-informed citizens is diluted by their low motivation to vote.

9-2 Policy Issues and Voters _____

Despite our current knowledge about voting behavior, scholars do not fully agree on the precise role that policy issues play in elections. From what we know about the capabilities of average American voters, we are not surprised that many scholars are skeptical about whether candidates' policy proposals and ideological leanings affect many voter decisions. Among the most pessimistic are the authors of *The American Voter,* undoubtedly the single most influential book on voting behavior. They found the electorate to be almost wholly without detailed information on the issues of the day, unable to judge the rationality of government policies, and unable to appraise the appropriateness of the means necessary to arrive at desirable ends (Campbell et al. 1960, 543).

The American Voter, however, was based on the two Eisenhower elections from the quiescent 1950s. Several studies of more recent elections—most notably *The Changing American Voter*—offer a rather different interpretation of the capabilities of the American voter (Nie et al. 1976).[2] Beginning with the Johnson-Goldwater election of 1964, political issues and political ideology have become increasingly important as determinants of the vote in the United States. The reason for this growth of issue voting is that parties and candidates have become more polarized on liberal vs. conservative lines. But just how important issues have become remains controversial.

For voters to be influenced by policy issues when they cast their ballots, two conditions must be met. First, the voters must be aware of the differences between the policy views of the candidates. Second, the voters must be motivated to vote on the basis of the issues that divide the candidates. Evidence of issue voting is strongest when the divergence between the candidate stances is strong and the issue is of considerable importance to the electorate.

Here, we examine the evidence of policy voting in presidential elections. Most of the data analysis that follows is from the National Election Study (NES) survey of the 1992 presidential election. As measured via survey analysis, the degree of issue voting in 1992 was typical of recent presidential elections.

Voter Perceptions of Candidate Differences, 1992

A necessary condition for voting on the basis of candidates' policy positions is that the voters perceive actual policy differences between the candidates. Following the usual procedure of NES surveys, in 1992 the National Election Study researchers asked respondents for their perceptions of the presidential candidates' positions on a series of seven-point scales representing several issues. Table 9.2 arranges these data to show how voters rated Democratic candidate (and winner) Bill Clinton relative to his Republican opponent, incumbent George Bush.

Individuals could rate Clinton to the left of Bush (correct), rate Bush to the left of Clinton (incorrect), or place the two candidates in a tie

TABLE 9.2 Voter Perceptions of Issue Differences Between Presidential Candidates, 1992

Issue	Clinton Left of Bush	Bush Left of Clinton	Same or Incomplete Ratings
Liberal/conservative ideology	71	11	18
Domestic spending	58	8	36
Defense spending	57	8	35
Abortion	67	5	27
Guaranteed jobs, standard of living	58	8	36

Source: NES, 1992 election data. Each percentage is based on voters only.

(presumably incorrect). Additionally, on each issue scale some voters (generally around 25 percent) gave no candidate ratings, either because they did not have a position themselves or because they claimed not to know the position of one or both of the major candidates.

Table 9.2 shows that when voters perceived the candidates to be different on an issue, they almost invariably saw Clinton to the left of Bush. Still, voters often rated the candidates the same or gave incomplete ratings. On all issues, however, a majority of voters ordered the candidates correctly. The sharpest perception was on the liberal-conservative ideology scale, where 71 percent saw Clinton to the left of Bush.

The respondent ratings of candidate ideology shown in Table 9.2 provided the basis for classification on our information index. Of 1992 voters, 29 percent were "high-information" scorers, meaning that they saw Clinton to Bush's left on all five items shown in Table 9.2. "Low-information" scorers comprise 29 percent of the voting total, and they score in the guess range regarding net candidate placement. (See the Appendix.) The remaining 42 percent were in between. Thus, roughly speaking, a third of the voting electorate is clearly tuned in to the candidates' ideological differences, another third is not, and about one third is somewhere in between. As usual, our picture of the electorate is mixed.

Policy Issues, Ideology, and Votes, 1992

In order to vote on the basis of policy issues, it is not enough to become aware of the candidates' policy differences. In addition, voters must find these choices sufficiently important to influence their vote choices. With policy voting, we would observe people voting for the candidate closest to their own views. This would usually mean liberals voting Democratic and conservatives voting Republican.

Table 9.3 presents some simple evidence of policy voting in the 1992 presidential election. This table shows that over a variety of issues, vot-

TABLE 9.3 1992 Presidential Vote by Policy Opinions

Policy	% Clinton	% Perot	% Bush	
Abortion				
Permit	57	21	21	= 100%
Restrict	38	16	46	= 100%
Gays in military				
Permit	59	19	22	= 100%
Disallow	31	19	50	= 100%
Defense spending				
Less	57	21	22	= 100%
More	41	17	42	= 100%
Domestic spending				
More	65	16	19	= 100%
Less	23	23	55	= 100%
Aid to minorities				
Favor	69	14	17	= 100%
Oppose	36	20	44	= 100%
National health care				
Favor	61	19	20	= 100%
Oppose	28	19	54	= 100%
Death penalty				
Oppose	70	12	19	= 100%
Favor	41	21	38	= 100%
Prayer in schools				
Oppose	48	20	32	= 100%
Favor	47	17	36	= 100%
Aid to Russia				
More	47	19	34	= 100%
Same, less	47	19	33	= 100%

Source: NES, 1992 election data.

ers who prefer the liberal position gave the most support to Clinton, while voters preferring the conservative position gave the most support to Bush. Some of the issues shown were actively discussed in the 1992 campaign, with the candidates taking divergent stands: abortion, gays in the military, environmental spending, national health care, and the general issue of relative degree of spending and services by the national government. Taking each of these issues separately, one sees a sharp tendency for liberals to support Clinton and conservatives to support

TABLE 9.4 Presidential Vote by Two Summary Measures of Liberalism-Conservatism, 1992

	Self-Identification on Ideological Scale						
	Extremely Liberal					Extremely Conservative	
	1	2	3	4	5	6	7
% Clinton	82	83	69	47	27	14	24
% Perot	18	10	23	24	25	13	18
% Bush	0	6	8	28	47	73	58
(% of Voters)	(3)	(82)	(13)	(32)	(21)	(17)	(3)

	Ten-Item Composite Issue Index*						
	Most Liberal						Most Conservative
	-10 to -8	-7 to -5	-4 to -2	-1 to +1	+2 to +4	+5 to +7	+8 to +10
% Clinton	92	82	59	49	29	12	2
% Perot	8	12	26	17	22	18	13
% Bush	0	6	15	34	49	70	85
(% of Voters)	(6)	(10)	(21)	(23)	(22)	(11)	(4)

*For construction of the ten-item composite issue index, see Chapter 3.

Source: NES, 1992 election data.

Bush. Three other issues—defense spending, the death penalty, and aid to blacks—involved subtler shadings of disagreement between the candidates but still have been long-standing battlegrounds of partisan disagreement. Here, too, we see liberals and conservatives dividing in their candidate choice. Two other issues, school prayer and aid to Russia, while arguably representing a conservative and liberal side, were not a matter of much partisan controversy in 1992. On these two issues, one can see little if any tendency for liberal and conservative voters to support different candidates.

Since so many issues seem to matter, we should be able to improve our vote predictions by taking into account voter positions on many issues simultaneously, rather than one issue at a time. Table 9.4 shows the relationship between general liberal-conservative ideology and the 1992 vote two ways.

First, the table shows the vote as a function of ideological identification, where ideological identification is measured using the full seven-point scale from "extremely liberal" to "extremely conservative." Ideological identification predicts fairly well, particularly for voters on the liberal side of the spectrum. Of the 3 percent calling themselves "extremely liberal," 82 percent voted for Clinton; the remaining 18 percent supported Perot, with none for Bush. Self-identified "conservatives" were far less loyal to Bush than liberals were to Clinton. Many "conservatives" supported Perot or even Clinton, apparently on nonideological grounds.[3]

The second part of Table 9.4 shows the vote as a function of a ten-item composite liberal-conservative index introduced in Chapter 3. Here the degree of prediction is even better. Six percent of the voting respondents scored in the most liberal range—from minus 8 to minus 10 on the index. Not one of these most liberal respondents (84 in number) voted for Bush: 92 percent chose the most liberal candidate, Clinton, while 8 percent chose Perot. At the conservative end of the scale, 3 percent of the voting respondents scored between +8 to +10. Of these, 85 percent voted for Bush, with the remainder splitting 13 percent for Perot and only 2 percent for Clinton.

From this demonstration, voters with consistently liberal or conservative views are highly predictable in their vote choice. But most voters are not at either ideological extreme. At least one-fourth are near the exact center—in the -1 to +1 range on the ten-point scale—and must be described as decidedly moderate or centrist. Many others appear only vaguely liberal or conservative, and their votes do not always follow from their ideological direction.

TABLE 9.5 1992 Presidential Vote by Ideology with Party Identification Controlled

	Democrats			Independent			Republicans		
Ideological Self-Identification									
	Lib.	Mod.	Con.	Lib.	Mod.	Con.	Lib.	Mod.	Con.
% Clinton	90	79	68	68	41	21	18	14	5
% Perot	10	13	14	22	36	28	44	21	16
% Bush	*	8	18	10	23	51	37	65	79
(% of voters)	(16)	(11)	(8)	(9)	(12)	(13)	(2)	(8)	(21)

	Democrats			Independent			Republicans		
*Ten-Item Issue Index***									
	Lib.	Center	Con.	Lib.	Center	Con.	Lib.	Center	Con.
% Clinton	90	77	72	65	41	22	27	11	5
% Perot	9	13	9	25	31	24	14	24	14
% Bush	1	11	18	10	28	54	59	66	82
(% of voters)	(15)	(16)	(6)	(9)	(17)	(9)	(2)	(13)	(13)

*Less than 1 percent.
**Ideology scale collapsed so -10 to -3 = liberal; -2 to +2 = center; +3 to +10 = conservative.
Source: NES, 1992.

In part, the predictability of votes from ideology as shown in Table 9.4 is due to voters simply responding to their partisan background: Liberals tend to identify with the Democratic Party and conservatives with the Republicans (Chapter 3). Thus, just by voting their party identification, voters tend to support the candidates closest to their views. Issue voting is further enhanced by party defections and issue voting by Independents. Table 9.5 illustrates this by showing the relationships between ideology and the vote within the three categories of party identification.

Conservative Democrats and liberal Republicans, while rare, are the partisan groups most prone to "defect" in their presidential vote. Meanwhile, Independents present the clearest example of issue voting. Neutral in terms of partisanship, they generally vote Democratic if liberal and Republican if conservative.

Information and Ideological Voting

As one would expect, ideological voting is most prevalent among voters who are highly informed about candidate positions. In surveys, the observed relationship between ideology and vote choice becomes most pronounced when we select the most informed voters (Knight 1985; Jacoby 1991; Lyons and Scheb 1992; Pierce 1993). Figure 9-3 illustrates how issue voting rises with information.

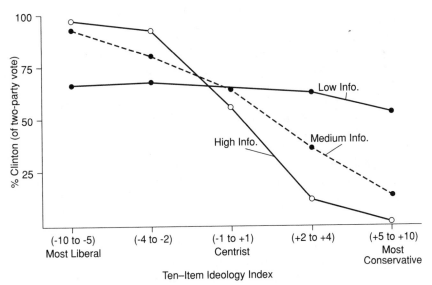

Fig. 9-3 Issue Voting by Level of Information, 1992

The figure divides 1992 respondents into those low, medium, and high on our scale of information about candidate differences on issues. For each group, Figure 9-3 shows the relationship between the ten-item index of respondent liberalism-conservatism and the vote. For this figure, Perot voters are discarded to ease the presentation. Graphed percentages represent the Clinton proportion of the two-party vote.

Note first that low-information voters show almost no issue voting: Their vote is mildly pro-Clinton whether their issue positions are liberal, centrist, or conservative. Among these least-informed voters, it could hardly be otherwise than that liberals and conservatives are nearly indistinguishable in their vote. Voters who are confused or wrong about candidate positions could not vote coherently on the basis of policy issues. While these uninformed voters were largely rejecting the same George Bush whom they had supported in 1988, it was not ideology that caused the transformation.

In contrast, examine the behavior of the highly informed voters (who saw Bush to the right of Clinton on all four issues examined plus ideological direction). Among liberals, virtually all supported Clinton, presumably because they saw Clinton closer to them than Bush was on the issue; among conservatives, virtually all supported Bush, presumably because they saw him closer to their point of view. Meanwhile, those highly informed voters who were in the middle did not divide evenly. Instead, they tilted toward Clinton, influenced by other factors such as the economy. To the extent ideological considerations tipped the 1992 election, the movement by informed Independents in the middle of the ideological spectrum was responsible.

We learn from this exercise that when voters are informed about the ideological differences among candidates, ideology is a strong influence on vote choice. The degree to which voters choose candidates based on ideology depends in large part on the degree of ideological division between the candidates and the degree to which these differences are publicized. When Democratic and Republican candidates are similar ideologically, ideological differences between Democratic and Republican voters are also slight beyond those that derive from voting on the basis of party identification. Studies of different elections (e.g., Nie et al. 1976) show that the stronger the candidates' ideological differences, the more will ideological voting follow.[4]

Easy vs. Hard Issues

For voters, questions of public policy are "hard" issues in the sense that they require a certain amount of attention and sophistication.

Many voters lack the political resources necessary to monitor and evaluate the candidates' policy proposals. Recall from Chapter 3 that no more than a quarter of the electorate (sometimes less) can be classified as sophisticated "ideologues" who evaluate parties and candidates in left-right policy terms. But even if unsophisticated voters do not make judgments about the desirability of specific policies, they can evaluate candidates in terms of relatively "easy" issues. One example of an "easy" issue evaluation is whether a candidate appears to favor or represent the interests of certain groups more than others. This, recall from Chapter 3, is a "group benefit" response to voting. Another "easy" kind of issue evaluation is to decide whether conditions seem to be good or bad under the current incumbent or incumbent party. This, recall from Chapter 4, is "nature-of-the-times" voting. Neither group benefit nor nature-of-the-times voting requires any direct knowledge of either specific policies or what the candidates claim they would do if elected. But each allows one to case a seemingly informed vote with a minimum of information costs.

Group-based voting. Voters can orient themselves to parties and candidates on the basis of which groups they seem to be for or against. In this way, voters need to recognize which groups they like and dislike and learn the party with which each of these groups is aligned. No investment in determining candidate positions or the relative benefits from these is required. Group-based voting is voting on the basis of "ideology-by-proxy" (Campbell et al. 1960, 219–20). For example, a relatively prosperous citizen can learn to vote Republican simply by adopting the belief that Republicans favor the rich. In this way, our prosperous citizen votes the same as if he or she were able to develop a conservative ideology to rationalize economic self-interest.

The most frequent form of group-related voting is based on the perception that the Democrats favor the working class and the disadvantaged, while the Republicans favor the rich and privileged. This can be seen from an inspection of the open-ended evaluations of the candidates Bush and Clinton in the 1992 NES survey. NES voters in 1992 (as in other years) were given the opportunity to articulate their likes and dislikes about the two presidential candidates. Those claiming to like Clinton because he was for the working people ("common people," "little people," "working people," etc.) or dislike Bush because he was for the privileged ("big business," "Wall Street," "upper class," etc.) totaled 14 percent of the sampled voters. Those who admitted that they liked Bush because he favored the rich or disliked Clinton because he favored the poor totaled a mere 1 percent of the voter sample. These group-related attitudes did predict votes:

	Clinton for Poor and/or Bush for Privileged Is:	
Vote	Reason to like Clinton or dislike Bush	Reason to like Bush or dislike Clinton
Bush	9%	70%
Perot	13	18
Clinton	78	12
	100%	100%
Percent of voters	*14%*	*1%*

Because voters who prefer their candidate to represent the poor greatly outnumber those who publicly state a preference for candidates who favor the rich, Democratic candidates would seem to be favored when elections are fought along class lines. (Of course, many voters would privately applaud the Republicans for favoring the privileged but not admit this to an interviewer.) Elaborate statistical analysis shows that on balance, group-related attitudes are one source of electoral advantage for the Democrats (Stokes 1966; Kagay and Caldiera 1980).

In the contemporary United States, race is often thought to be the basis of considerable group-related voting. It is often argued that just as many vote Democratic because they see the Democrats as better for blacks, others vote Republican because they also see the Democrats as more responsive to black interests (Carmines and Stimson 1980). One might expect evidence of voting on the basis of parties' or candidates' racial alignments to be readily identified by responses to NES open-ended likes/dislikes questions, in the same manner as for the rich vs. poor alignment. But voters shy away from volunteering racial concerns to interviewers. Just as very few admit to favoring policies that favor the rich, very few will claim that they are influenced to vote either for or against a candidate who favors blacks' interests.[4]

Race was not as visible a factor in 1992 as in earlier elections. In 1988, Bush's emphasis on (black) prisoner Willie Horton's escape from furlough on his opponent Mike Dukakis's watch as governor of Massachusetts was seen by many as an appeal to white racial fears. One indirect measure of racial (not necessarily racist) sentiment from the NES 1988 survey is respondents' relative ratings of whites and blacks (among other groups) on a "thermometer" scale from "0" (very cold) to "100" (very warm). In 1988, slightly more than half the white voters claimed warmer feelings toward other whites than toward blacks. Following is how reported racial sentiment predicted the 1988 vote (white voters only):

Vote	Rate whites higher	Rate races equal or blacks higher
Bush	66%	54%
Dukakis	36	46
	100%	100%

Preferring whites to blacks increased a white voter's probability of voting for Bush by about 10 percentage points in 1988. Of course, not all whites who happen to rate whites higher than blacks in a casual survey of feelings toward groups are racially prejudiced. But racial attitudes are likely to have something to do with the fact that, as a group, whites who claimed to prefer whites to blacks voted more for George Bush in 1988.

Nature-of-the-times voting. Still another voter shortcut is nature-of-the-times voting—evaluating whether times are good or bad (or will improve or get worse) and rewarding or punishing the incumbent party accordingly. Especially when little other information is available, the incumbent's (or incumbent party's) recent performance may be the best forecast of future prospects under a continuation of the existing regime. Nature-of-the-times voters may not have specific policies in mind, but they can throw the rascals out if the obvious signs indicate that it is time, in Campbell's words (1964, 755), to let "a new bunch of fellows run things for a while."

To measure retrospective voting, the 1992 NES respondents were asked:

"Do you feel that things in this country are going in the right direction or do you think things have pretty seriously gotten off on the wrong track?"

Vote	Right Direction	Wrong Track
Bush	62%	27%
Perot	13	20
Clinton	26	53
	100%	100%
Percent of sample	*17%*	*83%*

The overwhelming sentiment that the nation was on the "wrong track" certainly contributed to Bush's defeat. Much of the judgment about the nation's direction concerns the economy. The National Elections Study regularly asks respondents to evaluate whether over the past year, the nation's economy "has gotten better, stayed the same, or gotten worse."

For 1992, the question predicted the vote as follows:

Vote	Economy has gotten better	Economy has stayed about the same	Economy has gotten worse
Bush	77%	51%	26%
Perot	13	18	19
Clinton	11	31	55
	100%	100%	100%
Percent of voters	*4*	*23*	*72*

Whether one saw the economy as bad or good correlated strongly with 1992 presidential votes. One reason is that survey respondents sometimes respond to economic questions with rationalizations of their vote choice. (Did the 4 percent who somehow saw improvement in the 1992 economy say so because they backed Bush or did they vote Bush because they liked the economy?) But even allowing for this source of contamination, it is likely that economic perceptions caused many vote choices, and the one-sided nature of economic perceptions in 1992 contributed greatly to Bush's electoral downfall.[5]

Candidate Evaluations

Still another important set of voter motivations has nothing to do with issues. We refer to voters' evaluations of the personal characteristics and leadership abilities of the candidates. Simply put, voters tend to support candidates whom they like and trust. Whether a voter likes a candidate may transcend any policy differences or even overcome a strong party identification.

To examine "candidate evaluations" in the 1992 presidential contest, we return to the open-ended evaluations of the candidates in 1992, when NES respondents were asked their likes and dislikes of Bush and Clinton (but not Perot). Here we consider only net likes and dislikes in terms of the two major candidates' personal characteristics, such as leadership and experience (e.g., "Bush is a proven leader," "Bush doesn't care about people like us") and "personalities" (e.g., "Clinton cares," "Clinton is too slick"). If Bush-likes and Clinton-dislikes outnumbered Bush-dislikes and Clinton-likes, the direction of the respondent's candidate evaluations was pro-Bush. The opposite pattern was pro-Clinton. Many other respondents were neutral in their candidate evaluations.[6] Net candidate evaluations predict 1992 votes as follows:

Vote	Like Bush Better	Neutral	Like Clinton Better
Bush	58%	28%	16%
Perot	19	21	7
Clinton	22	50	77
	100%	100%	100%
Percent of voters	40%	30%	30%

In terms of personal attributes, 40 percent saw Bush more favorably and 30 percent saw Clinton more favorably. However, Bush won barely half the votes from those who liked him best and barely one quarter of those who were neutral on personality traits. These figures suggest the following perspective on Bush's defeat: Bush's mild edge in likability kept him from even more serious electoral damage in 1992.

Prediction and Causation

Policy issues, ideological identifications, group attitudes, retrospective evaluations, candidate evaluations, and party identifications all seem to predict the vote. The more variables we take into account, the better the prediction. To see that most votes can be "predicted," let us simultaneously predict 1992 presidential votes from the three best predictors: party identification, the ten-issue ideological scale, plus net candidate evaluations. We simply score each predictor as pro-Democratic, neutral, or pro-Republican, and sum them to make a scale from -3 (liberal Democrats who like Clinton better) to +3 (conservative Republicans who like Bush better). The results are shown in Table 9.6. To simplify the presentation, Perot voters are excluded.

TABLE 9.6 Predicting 1992 Presidential Votes from the Summary of Partisan Attitudes

	Pro-Clinton						
	-3	-2	-1	0	+1	+2	+3
% Clinton	98	98	89	67	29	7	2
% Bush	2	2	11	33	71	93	98
	100	100	100	100	100	100	100
(Percent of voters)	(8)	(17)	(17)	(17)	(14)	(16)	(10)

'Perot voters are not included. Index scores represent sum of partisan directions (+ = Republican, – = Democratic) on party identification, ten-item ideological scale, and net candidate evaluations. Minus 3 voters are liberal Democrats who like Clinton better. Plus 3 voters are Republicans who like Bush better.

Source: NES, 1992 election data.

Table 9.6 scores 17 percent as neutral on the three predictors, and even these otherwise "neutral" voters voted 2 to 1 for Clinton over Bush, perhaps in response to the poor economy. For the remaining 83 percent who revealed a partisan tilt to their relevant attitudes, the vast majority voted in accord with attitudes. Over 85 percent with pro-Bush attitudes voted for Bush. Over 90 percent of those with pro-Clinton attitudes voted for Clinton. If we examine the fraction who seemingly voted contrary to their attitudes, we could probably find plausible reasons to explain their vote. Of the 18 percent of the voting sample who were directionally consistent on party, ideology, and candidate evaluation, 98 percent voted as predicted. Clearly, when voters possess consistent reasons to vote one way or another, their votes are consistent with those reasons.[7]

We must be cautious, however, in attributing causal connections. Voters have a need to maintain cognitive consistency between their partisan attitudes and their vote. Of course, the obvious way to achieve this consistency is to vote according to one's partisan attitudes. The problem is that when people decide whom to vote for, they may also rearrange their political attitudes to fit their vote decision. Once citizens decide to vote Republican, for example, they tend to develop new attitudes even more favorable to the Republican point of view. Thus, when a 1992 Bush supporter asserts that the economy is going well, that Bush is a great leader, or that Bush is right on the issues, we might suspect that some of these attitudes are generated to support the vote choice rather than the reverse. Of special concern is the voters' need to maintain cognitive consistency between their issue stances, their perceptions of the candidates' issue stances, and their choice of candidate.

Consider the voter whose views are initially out of alignment—for example, the voter might have liberal views combined with an initial attraction to the more conservative Republican candidate. How our voter would resolve this dilemma depends on which of the three elements—perceptions of the candidates, policy views, and candidate preference—is the weakest link. If our voter feels strongly about his or her policy views and is certain that the favored candidate opposes them, the voter could resolve the dilemma by reversing the candidate choice. This would be an example of policy voting. If the candidate's stands are only vaguely known, the easiest way out might be to shift one's estimate of the candidate stances. This process, known as "projection," is a frequent way out of the dilemma. Voters who see conservative candidates as liberals or vice versa are often projecting their favored views onto their favored candidates (or projecting views they dislike onto candidates they dislike).[8]

A third resolution of the dilemma would be for the voter to change a relatively weak policy stance to make it consistent with the position of the favored candidate. This process is known as "rationalization." Rationalization makes it impossible to disentangle fully the causal process that produces a correlation between voters' policy views and their candidate choice. Consider, for example, the many voters in 1992 observed to be both conservatives and Bush supporters. Presumably the reason why conservatives supported Bush was that as conservatives, they were attracted to Bush's conservatism. But in theory, part of the reason could have been that liking George Bush (for whatever reason) made his supporters think better of his policy positions.

Does rationalization seriously contaminate survey analyses of the vote? Every report of a relationship between voter attitudes and voter decisions should be read cautiously, with an eye for the possibility that the seeming evidence of policy voting may be contaminated by widespread voter rationalization. Probably, however, electoral analysts err on the side of overcaution. Elaborate statistical analyses suggest that concern about voter rationalizations may be overdrawn (Page and Jones 1979; Markus and Converse 1979; Markus 1982). Still, we cannot be sure.

9-3 Explaining Election Outcomes _____

Explaining election outcomes requires a different level of analysis than explaining voter decisions. At the "microlevel," analysts try to account for why people vote the way they do. At the "macrolevel," analysts try to account for short-term forces and electoral trends, for example why Clinton beat Bush in 1992. The variables that explain individual decisions at the microlevel are often insufficient to account for macrolevel electoral change. For example, we have emphasized the role of voters' liberal-conservative ideologies and party identifications for predicting microlevel voting decisions. But aggregated to the national level, macro ideology and macro party identification ordinarily do not change sufficiently to account for electoral trends.[9] Political journalists may interpret a Democratic victory as the result of a liberal mood on the part of the electorate or a Republican victory as a conservative reaction. But as we saw in Chapter 4, the public shows little cyclicality between liberalism and conservativism. Similarly, short-term changes in party identification are thought to be too sluggish to create much movement in the national vote.[10] For instance, between 1988 and 1992, there was insufficient change in net ideology or net partisanship to account for reversal of party fortunes at the presidential level. To identify causes of electoral change, we must look to variables that change the most from one election to the next: the nature of the times and the candidates themselves.

Changing Economic Evaluations

Political parties and presidential candidates get helped and hurt by the electorate's reaction to the "nature-of-the-times." The public often changes its net evaluation of the relative problem-solving capabilities of the Democratic and Republican parties. Polling agencies have periodically asked public samples which party is more likely to bring about peace or bring about prosperity.

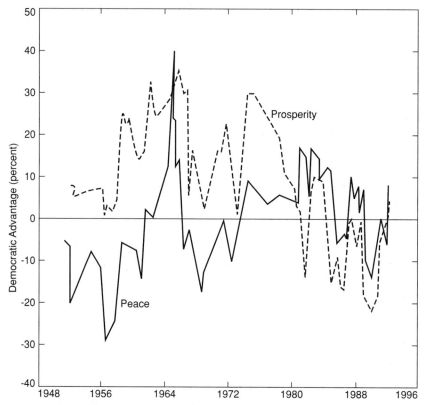

Fig. 9-4 Ratings of parties on peace and prosperity. Prosperity: "Which political party do you think will keep the country prosperous?" Peace: "Which political party do you think would be more likely to keep the United States out of World War III?" For each, the Democratic advantage is the percent responding democratic minus the percent responding Republican. (Sources: Gallup polls reported in Harold W. Stanley, and Richard G. Niemi, *Vital Statistics of American Politics,* 4th ed. [Washington DC: Congressional Quarterly Press, 1993], pp. 167–168.)

These judgments (see Figure 9-4), largely driven by retrospective evaluations of the incumbent party's recent performance, can serve as an electoral barometer. They follow predictable rules. The incumbent party is most likely seen as the party of "peace" when the nation is not at war and as the party of "prosperity" when the economy is in good shape. For instance, during the early part of Bush's term, with the Cold War over and near the end of ten years of uninterrupted economic growth, both the "peace" and the "prosperity" indicators gave good news to the Republicans. With the onset of the recession, however, the "prosperity" advantage shifted decisively back to the Democrats.

The effects of the economy on presidential elections can be observed directly. For twelve post–World War II elections, Figure 9-5 graphs the vote (for the incumbent party) as a function of per capita income growth in the election year.

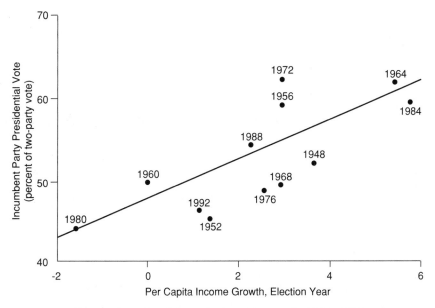

Fig. 9-5 Presidential vote by income growth, 1952–1992

Clearly, the more the election year growth in per capita income, the stronger the national vote for the President's party.[11] It might even seem that all the President must do for his party to win the next election is to time the upward swings of the economic cycle to coincide with election years in the political cycle. Perhaps fortunately, it is not always that simple. Some presidents (e.g., Carter and Bush) have found themselves presiding over election year economic recessions instead of prosperity. And the incumbent party does not win with great regularity anyway. Of the eleven presidential elections from 1952 through 1992, the incumbent party won five but lost six.

Changing Candidate Evaluations

One important source of changing short-term electoral forces is the changing cast of candidates. For election to any level of office, the personal attractiveness of the major-party candidates can be a decisive factor. At the presidential level, the electorate's attraction to the Republican candidate and to the Democratic candidate can vary dramatically from one election to the next. Using multivariate statistical techniques, analysts have generated estimates of the net contributions of presidential candidates' personal attractiveness to presidential election outcomes.[12] The estimates are generated from NES respondents' "candidate evaluations" from the likes and dislikes expressed about candidates' personalities and leadership abilities.

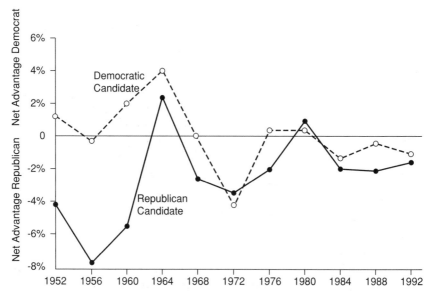

Fig. 9-6 Partisan advantage accruing from candidate evaluations 1952–1992 (Sources: Michael R. Kagay and Greg A. Caldeira, "A Reformed Electorate? Well at Least a Changed Electorate, 1972–1976," in William J. Crotty, ed., *Paths to Political Reform* [Lexington, MA: D. C. Heath, 1979]; updated for 1980 from Herbert B. Asher, *Presidential Elections in American Politics: Voters, Candidates, and Campaigns since 1952,* 3d. e. [Homewood, IL: Dorsey, 1084], p. 164; updated for 1984–92 by the authors.)

Figure 9-6 presents the estimated candidate effects, 1952 to 1992. As the figure shows, the public's evaluations of candidate personalities and capabilities constitute a major determinant of electoral change. The most popular candidate of recent decades was Dwight ("Ike") Eisenhower, elected twice in the 1950s. Eisenhower was a popular general (from World War II), who engaged the voters with his warm smile. Most candidates have been favorably viewed by voters, but not to the extent that the 1950s voters "liked Ike." Two candidates who were viewed particularly negatively were Barry Goldwater (Republican in 1964) and George McGovern (Democrat in 1972). According to the estimates, each cost their party about 4 percentage points just in terms of likability and leadership. Each lost in a major landslide.

A careful reading of Figure 9-6 will show that Clinton was viewed less favorably than Bush in 1992. (Clinton's net evaluations were in fact slightly negative, similar to Dukakis's in 1988). Earlier presidents (Kennedy, Carter, Reagan) had also ascended to the presidency while handicapped by being less popular personally than their opponent. In each instance, other issues overrode personal appeal to decide the election. Reagan was an example of a president who was able to convert an initial skepticism (in 1980) into a personal reelection mandate (in 1984).

Candidate Issue Positions

Changing candidates provide more than a revolving set of personal attributes for the voter to judge. Each new candidate also brings a new set of policy positions. Even though the electorate is relatively fixed in its policy preferences, candidate positions do change. With each change of candidate, the shift in policy position can change the equation regarding which candidate is closest to the electorate's net preferences. Shifting candidate positions allow policy issues to affect election outcomes. Let us examine how.

Part of the popular lore of politics is that in a two-person race, the candidate who stakes out the middle ground of the political spectrum will win by virtue of appealing to the moderate voter. In terms of their own personal views, candidates tend to be more liberal (Democrats) or conservative (Republicans) than their electorates. Yet the belief that moderate voters decide elections pushes candidates toward the center of the spectrum.

This logic is spelled out in a model of the vote developed by Anthony Downs (1958, Ch. 8). Figure 9-7a depicts the basic Downs model. This figure presents voter positions as a bell-shaped distribution on the liberal-conservative spectrum. The Downs model assumes policy voters who prefer the candidate closest to their views on this spectrum. If both candidates are stationed near the center, as in Figure 9-7a, neither will have the policy edge. But if one candidate veers toward one of the ideological extremes (as does the conservative in Figure 9-7b), then policy voters in the middle will support the opponent, giving that more moderate candidate the victory.

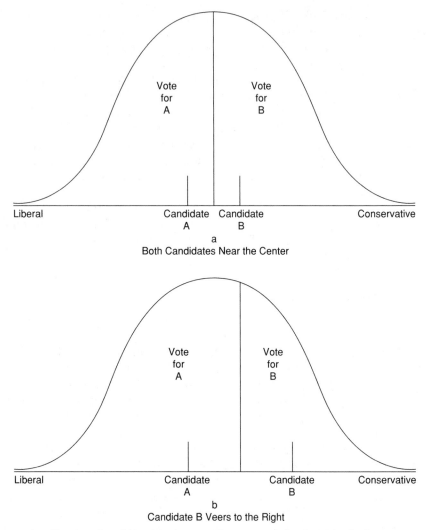

Fig. 9-7 Candidate ideology and voter response (hypothetical).

The Downs model predicts that Democratic candidates get more votes when they take moderate rather than liberal positions, and that Republican candidates get more votes when they take moderate rather than conservative positions. These hypotheses have received considerable support in research on congressional (U.S. House and Senate) elections (Erikson 1971; Wright 1978; Johannes and McAdams 1981; Wright and Berkman 1986; Erikson and Wright 1993).

Table 9.7 presents one illustration from the 1990 midterm election. Six conservative U.S. House Republicans are each matched with a

TABLE 9.7 Moderates are Better Vote-Getters than Conservative Among Republicans in U.S. House Elections, 1990

			Republican Percent of Two-Party Vote			
Republican Member	District	Conservatism Score	Member	Bush 1988	Member's Lead Over Bush	Difference
Hyde	IL 6	92	67	69	-2	+9
Porter	IL 10	69	69	62	+7	
Lightfoot	IA 5	90	68	48	+20	+2
Gandy	IA 6	63	72	50	+22	
Vander Jagt	MI 9	92	55	63	-8	+16
Davis	MI 11	50	61	53	+8	
Solomon	NY 28	81	68	59	+11	+2
Fish	NY 21	43	75	62	+13	
Walsh	NY 27	61	64	53	+11	+8
Horton	NY 29	31	72	53	+19	
Paxon	NY 31	92	57	57	0	+11
Houghton	NY 34	72	71	60	+11	
Averages:						
Conservative		86	63	58	+5	+8
Moderate		56	70	57	+13	

Republican House members were paired as conservatives and liberals if they represented contiguous districts within the same state and were at least 20 points apart on the ideological index. The ideological index is the average of the conservatism rating by the conservative American Constitutional Union and 100 percent minus the liberalism rating by the liberal Americans for Democratic Action.

more moderate House Republican from a politically similar neighboring district. For each pair, the more moderate is the better vote-getter, as measured by the candidates' 1990 showing relative to President Bush's 1988 vote in the district. Although this tendency is not as easily shown for House Democrats, moderate Democrats also tend to be better vote-getters than their liberal brethren.

If the electoral margins of House members are affected by their policy stances, certainly the outcomes of presidential elections must also be affected by the positions of the candidates. One common explanation for Republican success in recent presidential elections is that recent Democratic candidates have been too liberal for the electorate's taste. To shed some light, we can examine NES survey data. Since 1972, NES respondents have been asked not only to place themselves on the seven-point version of the ideological scale, but also to locate both presidential candidates on the scale as well.

Figure 9-8 traces the historical record. In all six elections traced in Figure 9-8, the average voter position has been slightly right of center

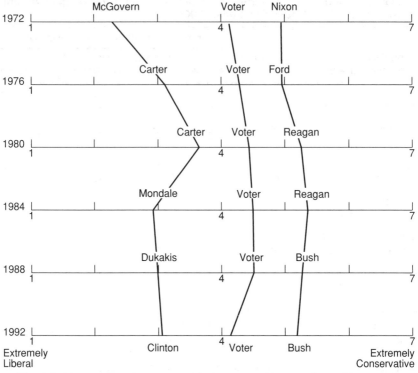

Fig. 9.8 Mean ratings by voters of their own positions and candidate positions, on 7-point liberal-conservative scales, 1972–1992.

on the seven-point scale. The Republican candidate was always perceived farther right than the average voter position and the Democrat farther left. In five of the six elections, more voters saw the Republican as closer to themselves on the right than the Democrat was to themselves on the left. The one exception was 1980, when President Carter positioned himself close to the center while his opponent Reagan was seen as something of a right-winger. Of course Carter still lost, but for nonideological reasons.

For the six elections, relative ideological proximity between candidates and voters accounts most clearly for the 1972 outcome. The Democratic candidate, George McGovern, was perceived as considerably left of center and lost accordingly. In the other elections, nonideological factors contributed considerably. In 1976, the Republican candidate, President Gerald Ford, was handicapped by the legacy of Watergate plus a sluggish economy. In 1980, Carter was handicapped by the continuing saga of the Iran hostage crisis plus a sluggish economy plagued by unwanted inflation. In 1984, President Reagan was helped more by his personal appeal, the economic recovery, and the afterglow of the invasion of Grenada than by his slight ideological edge over Democrat Walter Mondale. In 1988, Bush's victory over Dukakis was helped by an edge in candidate appeal as much as by the slight edge in ideological proximity. We discuss the 1992 outcome separately.

Issues and Clinton's 1992 Victory

Earlier we examined the contribution of various voter motivations to individual voter decisions in the 1992 presidential election. Now let us piece together the available information to account for the 1992 presidential outcome. Why exactly did the public choose Bill Clinton for president and reject George Bush? The 1992 electorate did not suddenly turn more Democratic or more liberal in 1992. Why, then, did the electorate that placed George Bush in the White House in 1988 switch to Clinton in 1992?[13]

One common conjecture about the 1992 election is that Bush lost because he was unable to pin the "liberal" label on Clinton as he had successfully done to his unfortunate 1988 opponent, Michael Dukakis. As a governor of a Southern state and a founder of the centrist Democratic Leadership Council, Clinton attempted to present a moderate image. On certain specific issues like the death penalty, for example, Clinton clearly rejected the unpopular liberal position.

Still, as the 1992 campaign played out, Clinton became viewed as almost as liberal as the electorate saw Dukakis four years before. As Figure 9-8 shows, in terms of ideological placement, the 1992 electorate saw Clinton almost equidistant from the average voter ideologically (with Bush seen closer by a very slight margin). Thus neither candidate had a clear edge in terms of ideological closeness to the electorate in 1992.

Still another possible explanation for Clinton's popularity is that Clinton was a more appealing candidate than previous Democratic nominees, such as Dukakis, Mondale, Carter, or McGovern. As measured by the NES likes/dislikes measure of candidate evaluation, however, Clinton was more disliked than liked during the 1992 campaign. (See Figure 9-6.) In fact, the likes/dislikes measure showed him marginally less appealing in terms of personality and leadership attributes than Dukakis in 1988. Meanwhile, Bush maintained his generally positive appeal on personality and leadership. By the likes/dislikes estimates, Bush may have gained one percentage point and Clinton lost one percentage point due to their personal evaluations. Thus, personal appeal cannot explain Clinton's victory.

Almost certainly, the main cause of Bush's defeat was voter dissatisfaction with the economy. As economic conditions worsened late in his term, Bush's popularity plunged, with his approval rating settling well below 50 percent by early 1992. Statistical analysis of NES survey data supports the interpretation that if 1992 perceptions of economic conditions were as optimistic as economic perceptions had been in 1988, Bush would at least have come close to victory.

9-4 Conclusions

When the Rational Activist Model is fulfilled, elections are decided by voters choosing candidates on the basis of their policy views. By this standard, the record of recent presidential elections is mixed. Tracing back to the 1964 presidential election, Democratic and Republican presidential candidates have polarized on liberal vs. conservative grounds sufficiently to give the voters a clear ideological choice. At the "microlevel," many individual voters are motivated by the ideological menu when they cast their ballots. But they are also motivated by non-policy considerations. At the "macrolevel," the electorate's collective reactions to candidate positions do help to shape their electoral verdict, but in conjunction with other considerations.

Apart from policy issues or ideology, there are additional determinants of the vote. As we have seen, people sometimes vote for or against the incumbent party on the basis of its past performance. One would find difficulty condemning this behavior as irrational. In addition, two very important predictors of peoples' votes are their party identifications and their evaluations of the personal characteristics of the candidates. To the extent that people vote on the basis of a party identification that is based on policy or ideological considerations (such as when a staunch conservative is committed to the Republican Party) and to the extent that the candidates are ideologically typical of their party (see Chapter 11), party voting can be viewed as rational.

But what about voting on the basis of the candidates' personal characteristics? One of the best predictors of a person's vote is simply whether the voter likes the personal qualities of the Democratic candidate more than the Republican. We may be tempted to view voting on such a nonissue (or even apolitical) basis to be voting on the basis of irrelevant considerations. But this view may be mistaken. Morris Fiorina (1977a, 618) puts the question well:

> Considerable misconception surrounds the discussion of the importance of candidate qualities for the voting decision. Various authors have suggested that voting on the basis of candidate qualities is irrational, or at least of lower order of rationality than voting on the issues. . . . Such suggestions apparently stem from the erroneous belief that attitudes toward

the candidates reflect no more than Ike's smile, Nixon's beard, or Kennedy's accent. Actually, the bulk of the citizenry's impressions of the candidates focuses on qualities which are of legitimate relevance to the latter's capacity to govern: experience, leadership ability, and so on. . . . Why should a candidate's intelligence, administrative ability, etc. be any less a legitimate issue than where he stands on Medicare or aid to Israel?

That the voters choose the candidate they find to have the greatest character, competence, or trustworthiness is quite reasonable, even if their candidate is not the one that is closest to the voters on policy issues.[14] Unfortunately, however, voters do not always have the necessary information to make good judgments about a candidate's character until after they have elected him as president.

The collective decisions the voters make at election time contain elements of both stability and change. That most voting decisions are based on long-standing partisan loyalty adds an element of stability. Electoral shifts are normally only temporary, because voters shifting toward the advantaged party or candidate do not change their identification in the process. Consequently they may surge in the opposition partisan direction in a subsequent election, or even do so when voting in another contest held on the same date. Yet it is conceivable that circumstances could be so polarizing as to cause permanent transfers of partisan loyalties rather than temporary partisan defections. The most recent such realignment period, centered in the 1930s, produced a change from a considerable Republican advantage in national voting loyalties to a long-term Democratic edge in party identification that persists today. This change can be interpreted as at least a partial ratification by the American electorate of President Roosevelt's then unprecedented expansion of federal government services that were applied to cope with the equally unprecedented Great Depression. If another realignment is on the near horizon, it could restore the Republican Party to the predominant position, or weaken it further. Or it could change the focus of the issues that separate the two parties without producing a net change in the distribution of party loyalties. If any of these possibilities become true, the public will have arranged its partisan loyalties as a long-term electoral response to the decisive issues of the day.

Notes

1. On the concept of short-term partisan forces in elections, the classic article is Campbell (1964).
2. Several studies report increased issue voting in presidential elections, beginning in the 1960s. See Schulman and Pomper (1975); Declercq et al.

(1975); Kirkpatrick et al. (1975); Miller et al. (1976); Miller (1987); and Romero (1989).

3. Reasonable scholars have disagreed on the role of ideology in voting behavior. Compare Luttbeg and Gant (1985); Tedin (1987); and Knight (1985).

4. Scholars disagree on the importance of racial sentiment in U.S. elections. Compare Carmines and Stimson (1980) and Abramowitz (1993).

5. On voter reaction to the economy, see Kiewiet (1983); Fiorina (1981); Markus (1988); Kinder et al. (1989); and MacKuen et al. (1992).

6. Measuring candidate evaluations from the likes/dislikes responses has a long tradition. See Campbell et al. (1960). Some studies have measured candidate evaluations from "thermometer" ratings of the candidates. Thermometer ratings measure more than candidate likability and perceived leadership ability, and usually predict the vote so well that they can be considered surrogates for the vote decision. The result is the relatively empty prediction that people vote for the candidates they like best.

7. That it is easy to predict a person's vote decision from measured attitudes has been known for some time. See, for example, Campbell et al. (1984) and Kelley (1983).

8. "Projection," for example, can account for many of the instances of misperception shown in Table 9.2. For two recent discussions of projection, see Conover and Feldman (1989) and Lodge et al. (1989).

9. On the linkages between the macro- and the microlevels of analysis as they pertain to aggregated vote decisions, see Wright (1989).

10. The assertion that changes in party identification are not strong enough to affect elections may be less correct than once believed. See MacKuen et al. (1989).

11. On the economy and presidential elections, see Tufte (1978); Hibbs (1987); Fair (1988); and Erikson (1989).

12. Figure 9-5 is based on Donald E. Stokes's (1966) "partisan components analysis," which is designed to estimate the relative effects of different partisan attitudes on election results. Stokes applied the model to elections from 1952 through 1964. His results were subsequently updated by Kagay and Caldiera (1984). Recent results have been updated by the authors of this book. The procedure is based on a statistical analysis of SRC/NES respondents' reported likes and dislikes about parties and candidates. First the content of the likes and dislikes is divided into six components: the Democratic candidate, the Republican candidate, government management, domestic policy, foreign policy, and group benefits. The impact of each component on the election outcome is determined from a statistical analysis of how influential each component is in determining the vote, and how one-sided the evaluations are for the particular component in the particular election.

13. For early reports on the 1992 election, see Pomper (1993) and Frankovic (1993).

14. There is evidence that the most sophisticated voters are the most attentive and responsive to candidates' personal attributes. See Miller et al. (1986).

CHAPTER 10

The Public and Its Elected Representatives

In the previous chapter, the public showed some ability to utilize elections as a policy expression as prescribed by the Rational-Activist Model. While this public competence falls far short of the democratic "ideal," policy-responsive voters can alter the outcome of a close election. In this chapter, we turn to the political leaders' ability to achieve consistency between public opinion and public policy by way of two additional models of political linkage which we discussed in Chapter 1. The Sharing Model considers the agreement between the opinions of leaders and the public that may make policy consistent with public opinion, and the Role-Playing Model focuses on the personal concern of leaders to reflect the preferences of their constituents.

These three models receive the most extensive evaluation here as they posit characteristics of the representatives that condition their response to the public. The Interest Groups and Political Party Models, positing mediating institutions presumed to encourage political linkage, are covered in the next chapter.

10-1 Opinion Sharing Between Policymakers and the Public

The simplest form of linkage between public opinion and the policy decisions of political leaders would be the simple sharing of common opinions by followers and leaders. Consider, for example, the result if we elected representatives by lottery. Just as a randomly selected sample of survey respondents is representative of the generally population within a certain margin of error, so would an assembly of 435 randomly selected people acting as a House of Representatives be representative of the population. If such an assembly could act without being distracted by the demands of powerful interest groups or the actual rules of Congress that impede change, then—for better or worse—its decisions would reflect public opinion. In actuality the Congress (and other legislatures) may even be less representative than a random sample, if for no other reason than that members are supposedly chosen for their superior capabilities rather than their typicality.

How then do members of Congress and other political leaders differ from the general population? To answer this question we must find the traits that motivate some but not others to pursue a political career and the traits that favor success in achieving this goal. When people who are active in politics—whether as a local party official or an elected legislator—are interviewed, they often report that a spur to their political career was a very politically active family. The consensus based on several studies is that about 40 percent of the people who are presently politically active grew up in politically active homes. Thus, assuming only 10 percent of the public (at the most) are very active in politics themselves, almost half of our political leaders come from the 10 percent of the nation's families that are most politically active (Prewitt 1970, 66).

Office-holders also differ from the public in that they are often recruited to run for office. Intense political interest alone cannot push a person into a political, leadership role. To contest an election seriously, the would-be political leader must attract the base of support necessary to win. In some cases, the political leader is a "self-starter" who, because of his or her political interest and ambition, announces candidacy and then is able to accumulate support. In other cases, the future leader is selected by the local business or party elite for the task of getting elected. Sometimes the community or party leaders can choose from among many active aspirants for the role. But often at the local level, previously nonpolitical people end up as officeholders through the urging of friends or business associates. Kenneth Prewitt (1970) finds these "lateral entrants" to politics among members of the nonpartisan city councils he studies. James Barber (1965) finds them among members of the highly partisan Connecticut legislature. Many are what he

TABLE 10.1 Occupations of Congressmembers (1993) Compared with the Public (1990) (in percentages)

Occupation	U.S. Senate	U.S. House	U.S. Labor Force
Farmer	6	4	1
Manager (business)	24	31	9
Teacher	11	15	5
Lawyer	58	42	1
Journalist	8	6	.
All others	4	5	84

˙Less than .5 percent. Senate and House percentages add to greater than 100 percent due to multiple listings. "All other" category does not include prior occupation of government or politics.

Sources: Ornstein et al., 1994; *Statistical Abstract of the United States,* 1992.

calls "reluctants"—serving not because of their raw ambition or political interest, but because of the insistence of others.

Because the most wealthy and best-educated people are most likely to be politically interested and articulate and have the visibility to be tapped for a leadership role, we are not surprised that these are the people who become some of our political leaders. Put simply, there is an upper-status bias to the political-leadership opportunity structure. For example, as Table 10.1 shows, the occupations of the members of Congress are predominantly professional or managerial. In a society where only 18 percent of the work force is engaged in such occupations, lawyers and businesspeople are particularly overrepresented in Congress. Lawyers and businesspeople are somewhat overrepresented in state legislatures as well. Additionally, greater percentages of legislators are white, male, Protestant, and over 30 years old than are found for the general adult population.[1]

In part, the overrepresentation of the affluent and educated in the councils of government stems from the middle-class leadership structure of the two major political parties. Even the Democratic party—supposedly the more representative of the working class—draws its leaders from the middle class. By contrast, in many other democracies, the presence of a Socialist or Labor party draws working-class people into greater political activity. In Norway, for example, political participation is not correlated with affluence as it is in the United States (Rokkan and Campbell 1960). Although Socialist and Labor parties do not draw their leaders exclusively from the working class that they represent, they do at least open the door for the political recruitment of blue-collar workers, a door that is rather closed in this country (Epstein 1967, 167–200).

There is not anything inherently sinister about the status differentiation between political leaders and the general public because the disproportionate concentration of political leadership skills in the hands of the better educated and prosperous may make it all but inevitable. For example, even the delegates to the "reformed" Democratic National Convention of 1972 were still far better educated and more affluent than the general population, although they were representative on the basis of race, sex, and age. Even movements of economic protest draw their leaders from the most affluent strata within the protest group. For example, Lipset (1950, 166) finds this to be the pattern within agricultural protest movements: "The battle for higher prices and a better economic return for their labor has been conducted by the farmers who need it least."

The status "bias" to the leadership structure does not necessarily mean that the political views of political leaders typify their class instead of that of the general public. For example, the 1972 delegates to the Democratic Convention obviously did not express the prevailing views of the economically comfortable. To be sure, there are potential sources of misrepresentation in the group background of political leaders. For example, one might suspect that state legislatures would be more eager to pass "no-fault" insurance laws if they contained fewer lawyers.[2] Or the city council that is overstocked with local businesspeople might well be suspected of reflecting the prevailing norms of the local business community rather than the views of the general population.

A more general consideration is that whatever their individual ideologies, the generally affluent leaders might resist wealth-redistribution legislation that would work against their self-interest. For example, a study of the attitudes of national convention delegates (in 1956) found that one of the few issues on which delegates of both parties were clearly more conservative than the public was that of making the rich pay a greater share of the taxes (McClosky et al. 1960). Of course, one could argue that virtually all political viewpoints found in the general population are also shared by some of the prosperous and better educated—and these might be our leaders. Even among the affluent, few are sufficiently politically motivated to run for public office. Those who do, do not always represent the political views of their economic group. Thus, one can hope that there is sufficient diversity of viewpoint among the candidates for office from which the people make their selections at the polls. And if not, there is still the possibility that electoral pressure can divert the behavior of political leaders away from unrepresentative personal preferences.

We can also try a direct approach to the question of whether political leaders and the general public share the same opinions by comparing the political attitudes of the two groups. Back in Chapter 6 we already

TABLE 10.2 Comparison of Public and Congressional Opinion on Selected Policy Issues, 1978

	Public	U.S. House Members
Defense: Percent that say money for national defense should be decreased	23	26
SALT: Percent in favor of SALT II	67	74
Health insurance: percent in favor of "National Health Insurance fully paid by the government"	47	45
Tax cut: percent opposed to a "large federal income tax cut"	53	51
Abortion: percent favoring "government paying for abortions for the poor"	41	35

Source: Kathleen A. Frankovic and Laurily K. Epstein, "Congress and its Constituency: The New Machine Politics," paper delivered at American Political Science Association Meeting, Washington, D.C., September 1979.

discussed one difference between public and leadership attitudes—leaders' greater support for civil liberties. For routine policy issues, however, only a few sets of data exist from which to assess the correspondence between the policy views of the public and its elected leaders.

One opportunity to assess the correspondence between public and leader opinion derives from CBS/*New York Times* polls that have compared public and congressional responses to current political issues: in 1970 (by CBS) and in 1978 and 1982 (by CBS/*New York Times*). Examples for 1978 are shown in Table 10.2. For both the 1970 and 1982 surveys, the distributions of responses by the public sample and by U.S. House members generally differ by only a few percentage points.[3]

For a final comparison of public and decision-maker opinion, Table 10.3 compares the survey responses of a large public sample with those of a large national sample of state legislators, from a study of state politics by Uslaner and Weber (1983). Collectively, the views of the legislators closely parallel the views of the national public. Over the ten issues, the average difference between public and legislator preferences is only 8 percentage points. On most of these issues, the public appears more liberal than the legislators, but only slightly so.

That the public and its elected leaders have similar opinions on a variety of issues may seem a surprise, given the general differences in income, education, and other background characteristics between the public and its leaders. The biases of leadership selection could have us expect that elected officials would share the opinions of the upper class rather than the opinions of the public as a whole. Does the apparent absence of an upper-class bias to leadership opinions imply that electoral

TABLE 10.3 Policy Preferences of the Public and of State Legislators on State Policies, 1968–1974

	Percentage Favoring "Liberal" Policy Position	
Policy	Public	Legislators
Capital punishment opposition	36	35
Abortion in first three months	51	53
Firearms permits	74	51
Teacher unionization	68	59
Teacher strikes	37	26
Police and fireman unionization	65	60
Police and fireman strikes	31	16
Marijuana legalization	17	17
No-fault auto insurance	76	76
Parochial school aid	57	45

Source: Eric M. Uslaner and Ronald E. Weber, "Policy Congruence and American State Elites: Descriptive Representation versus Electoral Accountability," *Journal of Politics,* 45 (February 1983), p. 188.

politics works to weed out political candidates whose views are incongruent with public opinion? Another question, not easily answered, is to what extent the elected leaders' relatively representative preferences guide their behavior in office so that government policies also become consistent with public opinion. There are forces—such as the inertial drag of legislative rules and norms, the opposition of powerful pressure groups, and the failure of executive leadership—that can prevent even a representative Congress or state legislature from doing what the public seems to want.

10-2 Leadership Responsiveness to Public Opinion ____

We have seen that there is some sharing of political preferences by people and their elected representatives. Thus, if the representatives' preferences guide their behavior in office, there will be at least a modest amount of agreement between public opinion and policy. But this observed tendency for elected leaders to reflect the opinions of their constituencies is a fragile foundation for democratic representation. Given the obvious limits to voter rationality, and the biases in the recruitment of political leaders, it is a wonder that we can find so much similarity of opinions between the public and its elected leaders. Moreover, a general pattern of opinion sharing is of no help in those instances when the public and its representatives do hold different views. However, elected officials sometimes follow public opinion rather than their own private inclinations, playing the role of the

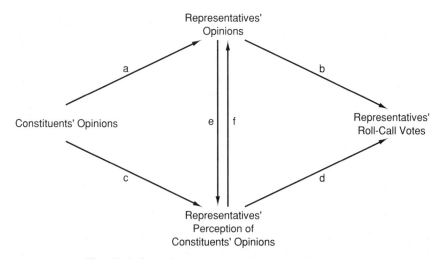

Fig. 10-1 Path diagram of constituency influence.

electorate's instructed delegates—what we have labeled the Role-Playing Model.

Figure 10-1 presents one classic formulation of the dynamics of legislative representation. This diagram is adapted from Warren E. Miller and Donald E. Stokes's (1963) classic study of congressional representation in 1958. First, via elections, constituency opinion helps determine the opinions of the legislators (path a). Second, legislators' opinions obviously influence legislators' actions (path b). Next, we see the Role-Playing Model. Legislators enhance representation when they correctly perceive constituency opinion (path c), but only if their perceptions of constituency opinion influence their behavior (path d). [Paths e and f provide minor complications: Legislators can convince themselves that their views reflect the public's (e) or change their private opinions in response to their perceptions of constituency views (f).]

For this Role-Playing Model to work, two conditions must be met. One requirement is that the representative has an incentive to choose the public's preference over his or her own. This incentive may be the representative's belief that following public opinion is ordinarily the "right" thing to do. Or the incentive may be the representative's fear that electoral defeat would be the consequence of ignoring public opinion. The second requirement is that the representative must know what public opinion is. We discuss this second requirement in a later section.

Seemingly crucial to the people's having much real control over what their leaders do is a strong desire by public officials to take public opinion into account. Ascertaining the strength of this desire is difficult. As V.O. Key lamented in 1961, "We have practically no systematic information about what goes on in the minds of public men as they ruminate about the weight to be given to public opinion in governmental decision" (Key 1961a, 490).

Political scientists uncover some clues to the motivations of elected leaders by studying the attitudes and behavior of politicians. A good starting point is Miller and Stokes's study of Congress in 1958. Miller and Stokes were interested in how frequently elected officials follow their perception of constituency views. As part of their study, they interviewed their sampled congressmen regarding both their own positions and what they perceived their constituencies' positions to be on several issues, representing the policy dimensions of civil rights, social welfare, and foreign policy.

Miller and Stokes found that in each area the representatives' personal preferences and their perceptions of constituency preference were about equally (and positively) correlated with their roll-call behavior. From this evidence, Congress members apparently give about as much weight to their perceptions of constituency views as they do to their own opinions.

Legislators and the Role of Instructed Delegate

For nearly every circumstance in which one human being interacts with another, such as being a parent, asking a question in the class-room, interviewing for a job, or serving as a representative in govern-ment, people hold beliefs about what the proper behavior would be in those circumstances. The sets of beliefs prescribing behavior for each social situation are normally labeled "roles." Roles vary greatly in their richness, with some encompassing very broad ranges of expected be-havior and others giving only minimal direction. Our concern here is with the role of the political representative and, more specifically, with that role as perceived by representatives.

Several researchers have explored the various aspects of how legis-lators see their roles, or their perceptions of how they are expected to behave. Over thirty years ago, John Wahlke, Heinz Eulau, and their as-sociates (1962) identified three types of representative roles. One type are the "trustees," who believe it is their duty to follow the dictates of their conscience regarding what is best for the constituency. At the op-posite extreme are "delegates," who believe they should follow the wishes of their constituents even if those wishes are contrary to their own. Finally, because the researchers found many representatives who claim they act as trustees on some issues and delegates on others, a conditional or mixed role was defined, which they call the "politico." Many researchers have administered elaborate questionnaires to state legislators and members of Congress to classify them according to their representative roles. In most studies, trustees outnumber delegates, with many legislators preferring the in-between delegate designation (Wahlke et al. 1962; Sorauf 1963: Davidson 1969; Soule 1969; Kuklinski and McCrone 1981; Friesema and Hedlund 1981). Thus, based at least on self-perception, the legislator who conscientiously fol-lows public opinion may be in the minority.

The sorting of legislators on the basis of their legislative roles is a significant enterprise only if their role designations help us predict their actual behavior. Theoretically, delegates are more responsive to constituency interest than trustees are. Two studies of California leg-islators suggest this is the case (Kuklinski and Elling 1977; McCrone and Kuklinski 1979). These studies compare delegates, politicos, and trustees in terms of the extent to which their roll-call voting corre-sponded to constituency voting on a series of referenda. True to theory, the first of these studies (by Kuklinski with Elling) found a far higher correlation between constituency liberalism and roll-call liberalism for delegates than for trustees, with politicos in between. The second study (by McCrone and Kuklinski) also reports that among California legislators the delegates are the most responsive to perceived constituency opinion and are the most accurate in estimating actual constituency opinion.

As we have seen, the role most conducive to political linkage—that of delegate—appears to be favored by only a minority in most legislatures. To be sure, many legislators would find it too humiliating to admit to being merely the voice of others. Indeed, most of us applaud the "courage" of the "statesmanlike" legislator who votes with his independent judgment rather than with the views of his constituency—particularly when we agree with that judgment.

Beyond asking legislators about how they perceive their role, it is difficult to ascertain how much political leaders believe they should heed public opinion because they think it is what they ought to do. We cannot test the validity of this aspect of the Role-Playing Model directly, for it is impossible to enter politicians' minds and locate their value structures. However, some observers of politics have argued that the widespread belief that public opinion should be followed is a major source of democratic linkage between the public and its leaders. V.O. Key, for example, saw within the subculture of political leaders that a value of fundamental importance is a "regard for public opinion, a belief that in some way or another, it should prevail" (Key 1961b, 538).

Legislative Responsiveness to Constituency Opinion

Examining what elected representatives do rather than what they say produces considerable evidence that representatives respond to the threat of potential electoral defeat. Legislators show greater attention to public opinion as election day looms than when the last election is just over. Similarly, when their district's lines are redrawn, legislators can be observed to change their voting record to match the new constituency. Here we examine some of this evidence, from state legislatures and the U.S. Congress.

Kuklinski's (1978) study of California legislators offers unusually graphic evidence of the responsiveness of legislators to the periodic threat of losing reelection. Kuklinski assesses representation by means of the correlation between constituency liberalism (as expressed in frequent referendum results) and the legislator's roll-call liberalism. Figure 10-2, from Kuklinski's study, indicates that legislators can give substantial representation to their constituencies. California assemblymen—who face reelection every two years—consistently do so throughout the years examined. For California state senators, however, who face reelection only every four years, the pattern is more cyclical. The half of the California senators who faced reelection in 1970 were substantially more responsive in 1970 than in succeeding years when the electoral threat diminished. Completing the pattern, those facing reelection in 1972 sharply improved their representation in 1972 and just as sharply showed a decline thereafter. These examples suggest that representatives do respond to perceived electoral threats by seeking to better reflect their constituents' views as election time approaches.

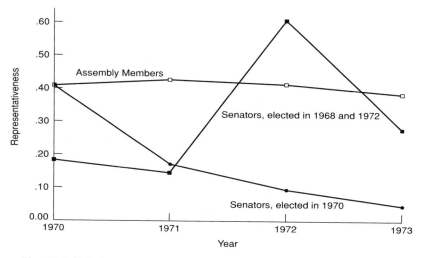

Fig. 10-2 Relationship between the temporal proximity of elections and representatives of California State Legislators. (Source: James H. Kuklinski, "Representatives and Elections: A Policy Analysis," *American Political Science Review,* 72 [March, 1978], p. 174.)

The six-year senatorial term makes the U.S. Senate a particularly useful laboratory for watching elected leaders respond to public opinion. We might presume that senators act more constrained by opinion in their state late in their six-year term, as reelection time approaches, than early in the six-year cycle just after getting elected. Democratic senators, whose personal beliefs are generally more liberal than those of their statewide constituencies, would act less liberal as their term progresses but then return to more liberal positions once reelected. Republican senators, whose personal beliefs generally are more conservative than those of their statewide constituencies, would act less conservative as their term progresses but then return to more conservative positions once reelected. In a study of Senate roll-call voting, Martin Thomas (1985) reports exactly these patterns.

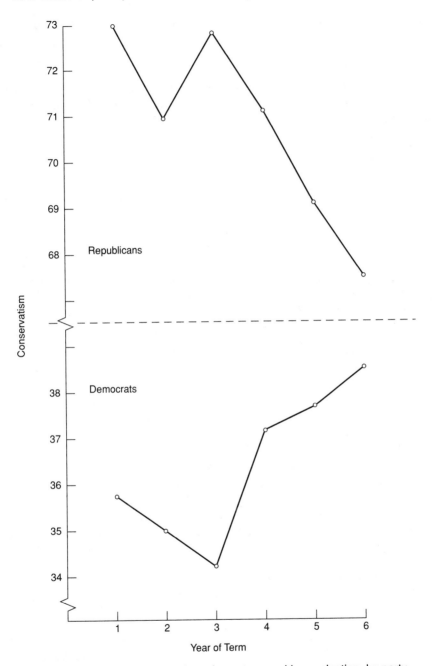

Figure 10-3 Mean conservatism of senators seeking reelection, by party and year of term. (Source: Martin Thomas, "Election Proximity and Senatorial Roll Call Voting," *American Journal of Political Science,* 29 [February 1985] p. 103)

As shown in Figure 10-3, both Democratic senators and Republican senators moderate their roll-call record as reelection time approaches. This figure is based on senators who seek reelection only. Interestingly, Thomas shows that senators who do not run again also moderate their views through the fifth year, but they return to their original positions in the sixth year when the retirement decision has been made.

With their two-year term, U.S. House members must continually try to stay elected. Although we cannot watch their behavior change with the election cycle, an opportunity is sometimes present to watch them change when their constituency changes. U.S. House constituencies change every 10 years following the U.S. Census, as district lines must be redrawn to reflect population changes. Amihai Glazer and Marc Robbins (1985) have statistically demonstrated that U.S. House members respond to these district changes in their roll-call voting. They measure changes in constituency opinion by comparing the past presidential voting of the new and the old district. By this measure, when the House member gets a more liberal district, the member usually becomes more liberal; when the members gets a more conservative district, the member usually becomes more conservative.

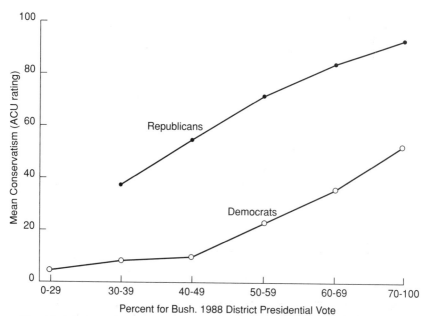

Fig. 10-4 U.S. House members' roll-call conservatism, 1989, by district vote for Bush, 1988.

For congressional districts, the district vote for president is a serviceable indicator of the district's ideological tendencies. Districts that tend to vote Democratic for president tend to be more liberal, and districts that tend to vote Republican for president tend to be more conservative. And a district's presidential voting is a good predictor of its Congress member's voting record. For instance, Figure 10-4 shows that the constituency vote division in the 1968 Bush-Dukakis election is a good predictor of House roll-call voting in 1989. Within each party, the most conservative House members represented the most conservative (i.e., pro-Bush) districts. This apparent responsiveness to constituency opinion helps explain why neither party in Congress acts as a homogeneous unit. When Democratic representatives vote like Republicans or Republican representatives vote like Democrats, chances are that they are responding to the apparent liberalism-conservatism of the district.

Political Ambition

The belief that their reelection chances hinge on how well they represent constituency opinion will not influence officeholders much unless they care about getting reelected. As Joseph Schlesinger (1966, 2) has described the positive functions of political ambition, "no more irresponsible government is imaginable than one of high-minded men unconcerned for their political futures." Politicians at the top of the political ladder usually try to continue in office for as long as possible. For example, presidents normally want to stay in office for their constitutional allotment of two full terms. Even Truman and Johnson, who both opted for retirement in the spring of their reelection years, did so only after the results of the first presidential primaries indicated that even renomination by their party would have been a difficult hurdle.

Most governors (about 75 percent) also seek reelection when not constitutionally prohibited by term limits. Ambition also runs high for Congress members. When up for reelection, about 85 percent of senators and 90 percent of House members try for for another term. Even when Congress members "retire," they rarely leave political life; most House members who "retire" actually do so to seek the higher office of U.S. senator or governor.

A theme that runs through studies of Congress is that the goal of staying elected guides an overwhelming portion of what Congress does. Douglas Arnold (1990) claims that reelection is the dominant congressional motivation. Kingdon (1973) shows that pleasing constituency interests dominates congressional decision-making even on routine legislation. Mayhew (1974a) argues that the structural organization of the House of Representatives is best understood as a collective response to the members' need to stay elected. Fenno (1978) finds that in their frequent trips home, representatives are often compelled to explain their roll-call votes to the satisfaction of important constituents. Of course the desire to stay elected is not the sole congressional motivation. Parker (1992) reminds us that representatives focus on generating safe reelection prospects to free themselves in order to pursue their policy agendas.

Promoters of term limits for office-holders argue that the continuous preoccupation with staying elected *detracts* from the policy-making function. One concern is that elected officials may overrespond to the less enlightened aspects of public opinion. As V. O. Key (1961a, 490) once observed: "Public men often act as if they thought the deciding margin in elections was cast by fools; moreover, by fools informed enough and alert enough to bring retribution to those who dare not demonstrate themselves equally foolish."

Interestingly, the inclination to hold onto office for several terms is a relatively recent phenomenon. In the nineteenth century, House and Senate members quite frequently returned to private life after a term or two (Price 1971). This is the pattern in many state legislatures even today, particularly in states offering low legislative pay (Squire 1988, 1992). With variation from state to state, for state legislatures the retirement rate is about 22 percent (Jewell and Breaux 1988, Table 1). Many "retirements," however, are to pursue alternative electoral opportunities. Incumbents interest in reelection is least in local settings, such as city councils and school boards (Luttbeg 1966a; Prewitt 1970; Karnig and Walter 1977).

The rate at which members of a legislative body retire appears to have very delicate effects. Observers of Congress often moan that the institution is handicapped by the presence of too many aged members who refuse to give up their seats. Students of state legislatures offer the opposite complaint; that frequent retirements (often to seek higher office as well as to go back home) produce a depletion of experienced personnel. Our chief concern is that the retiring legislator may be relatively indifferent to public opinion.

One should not necessarily infer that the nonambitious office-holder's escape from electoral pressure typically frees him or her to pursue worthy goals that are too advanced for public opinion to accept. Surely, many politicians are strongly motivated to advance their conception of the "public interest." But this pursuit of accomplishments only feeds their ambition for further public service, which requires reelection. This reasoning suggests the hypothesis that the political leaders with the strongest policy motivations tend to feel the most electoral pressure to satisfy public opinion—at least on matters that concern them least.

10-3 How Elected Officials Learn Public Opinion _____

Even if political decision-makers want to follow public opinion, they cannot do so effectively unless they know what the people want. According to political lore, good politicians have acute political antennae that detect the prevailing political mood when they wander among the "grass roots." Of course, the policymaker is also sometimes able to "read" public opinion more directly by examining the results of available opinion polls.

Politicians and Opinion Polls

Like the rest of us, politicians have access to commercial opinion polls such as the Gallup Poll. But politicians often seek further intelligence regarding public opinion by commissioning their own polls. The first president to poll the public in earnest was Franklin Roosevelt in the late 1930s. While his next two successors, Truman and Eisenhower, had little use for private polling, presidential polling picked up in earnest with John Kennedy. Starting with Kennedy, virtually every major presidential decision has been made with the benefit of private polls. Presidents seek updates regarding public attitudes toward current policies, public reactions to future policy options, and, especially, information on their own personal standing with the voters. In many instances, the private intelligence gained from polls guided presidential decision-making. For instance, Presidents Kennedy and Johnson both pushed Medicare with a particular insistence because their polls offered the confidence that Medicare was a winning issue with the electorate (Jacobs 1993).

Politicians below the presidential level also do their own polling, as do the major political parties. Senate and House members spend about 3 percent of their sizable campaign war chests on polling their states or districts (Fritz and Morris 1992). (Nonincumbents spend considerably less.) Although the general purpose of this polling is to ascertain the status of their "horse race" with current or future opponents, private constituency polls can also register signals regarding shifts in the constituency concerns.

Like everybody else, the politician must read opinion polls with caution. Even an officeholder with no other goal than staying elected would be unwise to base every decision on what the polls show to be the majority preference. Let us examine the reasons why.

As we saw in Chapter 3, the distribution of opinion on an issue can vary with the exact question wording. Consequently, the side of the issue on which majority opinion lies may shift with the seemingly innocuous change in the question wording. Given such circumstances, following public opinion as registered by a single reading on the issue may make little political sense.

Actually, the policy option that would yield the political leader the most votes (and satisfy the most people) is not always the majority position anyway. For example, according to unsubstantiated political lore, the minority who are gun enthusiasts have managed to defeat several politicians who advocate strict gun control even though polls show a majority favor strict gun registration laws. Presumably, the average person, when asked, favors gun control but will not translate this conviction into action at the ballot box; the gun enthusiast will.

Paradoxically, the way to build a winning majority at the polls may sometimes be to create a coalition of intense minorities. Suppose, for example, opinion on three issues is divided 80 to 20, with the different minorities on each issue feeling several times more intensely about the matter than those on the other side do. Then if one candidate supports the majority side on all three issues, and the other appeals to the minority side, the candidate of the minorities could win 60 percent of the vote (20 times 3), assuming all vote on the basis of the issues. There would be nothing inherently undemocratic about the majority side losing out on each question, as a majority of voters would have more to gain from their representation on the one question they feel strongly about than they would from representation on the other two issues.

Politicians may sometimes feel free to ignore the polls because they recognize that the public generally expects its political leaders to use their own judgment, acting as trustees rather than delegates. In one Iowa poll, most respondents said state legislators should act according to their conscience rather than according to constituency preferences when there was a conflict between the two (Hedlund 1975). The public seems to react with displeasure at being asked to do what it thinks it elects officials to do, namely, make decisions. For example, many defeats of fluoridation referenda seem based on public displeasure at the failure of elected officials to take a stand on the issue by passing the buck to the voters (Crain et al. 1969, 138).

Acting as a trustee rather than as an instructed delegate may have still another payoff. At election time, voters make retrospective judgments of the apparent success or failure of past policies, perhaps even more than on the policy issues under current debate. If the politician expects to be rewarded or punished for the "nature of the times," polls of current public sentiment about what ought to be done offer little help. For example, a president exercises good political judgment when he makes economic policy on the basis of expert opinion rather than on the basis of a poll taken to see what people think would work best.

The war in Vietnam provides an important example of a discrepancy between the public's policy preference at the moment and the public's eventual reaction to the consequences of that policy. According to the polls, the public supported the war at the time the crucial steps of escalated involvement were taken. If the high officials in the Kennedy-Johnson administrations had foreknowledge of the extent of the public's eventual opposition to a prolonged war, perhaps they would have made different decisions. Here, politicians had to make crucial guesses about public reactions to their possible options—for which polls could not give answers.

Other Ways of Learning Constituency Opinion

When asked how they learn constituency opinion, politicians claim not to rely much on polls. But more informal methods of estimating public opinion also contain pitfalls. Crowd reactions, obviously, can be misleading indicators, given the disproportionately politicized and partisan nature of political audiences. How accurate are other sources of opinion cues—constituency questionnaires, election returns, constituency group composition, the mail, and the people back home to whom the representative talks?

Constituency Questionnaires. Unlike the president, lower-level elected officials (such as state legislators) rarely have the resources to conduct their own polls. But one group of officeholders who do make frequent use of polls (albeit of a nonscientific sort) are members of the U.S. House of Representatives. Thanks to their franking (free mailing) privilege, House members can send questionnaires to each household in their district for only the printing costs. Most House members utilize this privilege to poll constituents. Since the "polls" are administered by mailed questionnaires, they have a low return rate, perhaps as low as 15 percent on the average. This can permit the views of a small minority (typically the better educated and more wealthy) to be mistaken for "public opinion." But one might argue that since the minority who take the trouble to respond to congressional polls presumably feel most intensely about the issues, any bias in the poll results would be weighted in favor of the more attentive constituents who will vote according to their beliefs.

Election Returns. After elections, a popular fad is to analyze the results to determine the new "mood" of the voters. We saw earlier that changes in the voters' partisan preferences are not the result of ideological mood swings. Republican gains do not necessarily mean the public has swung farther to the right, for example. The winning politician who mistakenly interprets his landslide victory to be a mandate for his favorite programs may experience a sudden erosion of his popular support. The urge to decipher meaning from particular issue-oriented election contests can also lead to errors, if the judgment is made without consideration of the general partisan trend.

For example, in retrospect, an overinterpretation of election results by concerned political observers may have been the reason why official Washington overestimated the popular support for demagogic Senator Joe McCarthy in the early 1950s. Although, at first, other senators disassociated themselves from McCarthy's unsubstantiated claims that some indefinite number of known Communists were running loose in the State Department and elsewhere in government, the defeat of several of McCarthy's senatorial critics in the 1950 and 1952 elections silenced the remainder. In retrospect, we see that most of the defeated McCarthy opponents would have lost anyway in the anti-Democratic tide (Polsby 1960). Almost unnoticed, McCarthy trailed his party's ticket when he won reelection from Wisconsin voters in 1952. Actually, McCarthy was never supported by a clear majority of the public; most of his supporters came from predictable sources such as small-town Republicans. If otherwise alert politicians had paid closer attention to the polls than to isolated and misleading election returns, the "climate of opinion" that assumed McCarthy was invincible may never have been created. As it was, McCarthy's downfall—forced by his attack on the U.S. Army—was as sudden as the initial rise of what became known as "McCarthyism."

Although politicians may overinterpret partisan electoral trends or electoral fate of certain candidates who are linked to particular causes, they may learn something meaningful about the general political preferences of their constituencies from how their constituencies vote in comparison with others. Earlier (Figure 10-4) we saw that roll-call voting by U.S. House members correlates with presidential voting. Although we do not know whether this relationship results because House members consciously try to adjust their behavior in direct response to election returns, we can reasonably infer that district presidential voting normally will be a good gauge of whether the district is a relatively conservative or a relatively liberal district. Although the extent to which constituency opinion is related to partisan voting has not been fully explored, one Florida study finds that the 1968 presidential election returns were a good predictor of referendum voting on certain issues in state legislative districts. Moreover, legislators appeared to respond to the cue of past district voting when they were asked to predict the referendum verdicts in their districts (Erikson et al. 1975).

Group Characteristics. Politicians sometimes take their cues regarding public opinion from their knowledge of the group composition of their constituency. For instance, politicians sometimes appear sensitive to the concerns of African-Americans in direct proportion to the proportion of their constituents who are black. Politicians use constituency wealth as an indicator of constituency receptivity to new taxing or spending policies, or the constituency's education level as a signal of constituency receptivity to liberal social policies. Politicians with older than average constituencies show particularly sensitivity to the needs of the elderly. And more than one otherwise conservative politician have supported gay rights when representing a sizable gay minority. Beyond the most obvious indicators, however, constituency social composition is an incomplete guide to public opinion. District demography may be of little help if the district is socially diverse or the issue is obscure.

The Mail. Political officeholders place only slight stock in the mail they receive as a source of constituency opinion. Skepticism is highest when a barrage of letters clearly originates from a pressure-group campaign. But, setting such cases aside, is there any bias to the mail that political leaders receive? Writing a letter to an elected official is not a regular activity for the average person. Only about 15 percent of the public admit to ever having written a public official, and about two-thirds of all letters written to officials originate from 3 percent of the public (Converse et al. 1965). For some reason, people who write letters to public officials tend to occupy the right side of the political spectrum. Politicians who measure public opinion solely from the content of their mail would judge public opinion to be more conservative than it is (Verba and Brody 1970).

The Vocal Minority. To the casual observer, public opinion might appear to be obvious without having to resort to the numbers in scientific polls. Why not simply tune into a radio talk show and listen to the voice of the people? Or, for the visually inclined, why not consult the tone of the political letters to the editor in the local newspaper? The problem of course would be that the views of talk show callers and newspaper letter writers present a distortion of general opinion. They do represent the views of a "vocal minority."

If one were to ascertain public opinion by monitoring the vocal minority, one would be fooled into seeing a public that is more conservative and Republican (and irate) than it actually is. Like people who write letters to politicians, people who write letters to their local newspaper are more conservative than the general public (Converse et al. 1965; Verba and Brody 1970). Perhaps even to a greater extent, talk show callers too are decidedly more conservative than the general public (Kahout et al. 1993). One reason for the vocal minority's conservatism is their social status and leisure time. The typical member of the vocal minority is wealthier, more educated, and older than the average citizen, and such people tend to be more politically conservative. Second, newspapers and talk shows sometimes screen letters and calls for ideological content.

Most politicians are sufficiently sophisticated to discount the views of the vocal minority as representative of general opinion. But quite possibly the exaggerated conservatism of those who speak out causes politicians to see public opinion as more conservative than it actually is.

Attentive Constituents. One important aspect of the life of elected officials is their "home style" (Fenno 1978) when they interact directly with local constituents. Elected officials strive to maintain personal contact with many constituents, including partisan allies, members of various local groups, plus other people who are simply friends. Politicians often use these conversations with attentive constituents to try to sense changes in the public mood. Constituents from whom elected officials seek advice are more knowledgeable than the average, and also higher in socioeconomic status than the average voter (Boynton et al. 1969). Attentive opinion can be a leading indicator of what ordinary citizens will soon be thinking, but their views may be atypical because of their higher status.

How Accurately Do Officials See Public Opinion?

Given the multiple devices that officeholders employ to sense public opinion, how accurate are their perceptions of public opinion? One approach to answering this question is to sample opinion and then see how closely the public's representatives can predict what it is. In their study of congressional representation, Miller and Stokes sampled opinions in congressional districts and then asked the districts' representatives what they thought the opinion of their home constituency would be.

On civil rights issues, Miller and Stokes found the correlation between constituency opinion and the representative's perception of it to be a fairly robust +.74—a not surprising indication that representatives of pro-civil rights black constituencies and anti-civil rights Deep South districts are aware of their constituencies' views. Correlations were also positive on social welfare issues (+.17) and foreign policy issues (+.25). Although the latter correlations are relatively weak, one reason is the sampling error in the estimates of constituency opinion. There is reason to believe that if constituency opinion were estimated from larger samples, the correlations between constituency opinion and congressional perceptions of it would be considerably higher (Erikson 1978).

Perhaps the most difficult test for the representatives' political antennae to pass is correct estimation of constituency opinion on issues that do not attract much public attention. Accordingly, Ronald Hedlund and H. Paul Friesema (1972) quizzed Iowa state legislators about their constituencies' majority preference on four statewide referendum questions that were about to be put before the voters. On four questions, the accuracy of the legislators' predictions varied from 59 to 92 percent. (Simply by guessing randomly, the legislators would have been correct half the time.) The predictions on home rule for cities (92 percent) and reapportionment (82 percent) were reasonably accurate. But the rates of successful prediction on holding annual legislative sessions (59 percent) and giving the governor the item veto (64 percent) were only slightly beyond the guess range. Hedlund and Friesema argue that the home rule and reapportionment referenda attracted greater public interest than annual legislative sessions and item vetoes. This suggests greater accuracy in representatives' predictions of public opinion in those areas where the public expresses the most interest.

Following up on the Iowa study, Erikson et al. (1975) asked Florida legislators to predict the percentage-point breakdown in their district and in the state on three "straw ballot" referendum issues in 1973. One of these straw ballot issues dealt with the volatile question of "forced" school busing to achieve racial balance. Here the legislators' estimates were not far off the mark; for example, the 56 responding House members erred by an average of only 7 percentage points in predicting their district's anti-busing vote. But estimates were less accurate on the less publicized, remaining straw ballot issues. On the question of allowing prayers in schools, the average error in prediction was 11 percentage points; on the question of rejecting the dual (or segregated) school system, the average was 12 percentage points. Once again, the legislators' awareness of public opinion is weaker when the public focus on the issue is weak.

Recall from Table 10.3 the ten issues on which Uslaner and Weber ascertained public opinion and legislator opinion in the states. As part of their study, Uslaner and Weber (1979) also obtained indirect ("simulated") measures of constituency opinion, plus legislators' perceptions of constituency opinion. They estimated that across the ten issues, state legislators averaged about a 20-percentage-point error in predicting constituency opinion. Their most ironic result is that on nine of the ten issues, legislators' estimates of constituency opinion tended to be farther from constituency opinion than the legislators' own opinions were. In other words, the legislators would have done a better job of representing constituency opinion by acting on their own beliefs than on their rather erroneous estimates of what their constituents wanted. The Miller-Stokes data show a similar pattern. Across two of the three sets of issues, constituency opinion correlates slightly more strongly with the elected representative's opinion than with the representative's perception of constituency opinion.

Both the Uslaner-Weber and the Miller-Stokes estimates of constituency opinion have their own errors of measurement, thus requiring
cautious interpretation. But these studies suggest that legislators do at
least as good a job of representing constituency opinion by following their
own views as they do by trying to follow their perception of constituency
opinion. This tentative conclusion carries negative implications about
legislators' ability to infer constituency opinion. But the positive side is
the extent to which the representation process results in congruence between the views of constituencies and their representatives.

10-4 Do Elected Officials Need to Follow Public Opinion?

We have seen that although politicians sometimes have difficulty
reading public opinion, they apparently do at least try to consider public opinion when making decisions—partly from fear of electoral retribution if they do not. Actually, one might suspect that public officials do
not need to weigh public opinion very heavily in order to get reelected.
Incumbent officeholders do not lose reelection bids at a rate that should
stimulate electoral anxiety. Furthermore, most people do not monitor
their leaders' policy with sufficient attention to produce massive voter
reactions. Could it be that elected officials have more freedom from
public opinion than they realize?

Incumbency

Judging from their reelection rates, it may seem that elected politicians have little reason to fear the wrath of the voters. In most election
years, over 90 percent of U.S. House incumbents who seek reelection get
returned to office. For U.S. senators, the reelection rate is only slightly
lower. State legislators are also secure. Their reelection rate is about 92
percent, but with important variations among states (Jewell and
Breaux 1988, Table 2). Governors are somewhat more vulnerable, winning reelection about 80 percent of the time they seek another term.
Governors are electorally insecure because, like presidents, they are
held accountable for the nature of the times during their administration. Legislators face less electoral difficulty than executives because
voters find difficulty in tracing the consequences of legislators' actions
or in holding them individually responsible for government outputs,
such as the state of the economy.

There are four separate reasons why incumbents almost always win
reelection.[4] First, many elections are partisan contests, decided along
partisan lines. Consequently, elections tend to favor the locally domi-

nant party. Where one party dominates the other, even an office-holder with a low personal standing can win repeated victories.

A second reason why incumbents generally win is because the status of incumbency gives them an advantage over their opponents. In U.S. House elections, incumbents gain 5 percent or more of the vote or more between the time of their first victory and their first reelection attempt. (Alford and Brody 1993). The process that accounts for this "incumbency advantage" is not fully understood, but it seems that House members are able to exploit their powers of office (or "perks"), such as their free mailing privileges, for electoral advantage. Another factor may be a cautious tendency of voters to support whoever is already in office. U.S. senators and state governors do not seem to enjoy as great an incumbency advantage as U.S. House members. At the state legislative level, the possible role of an incumbency advantage has not been subjected to much research (but see Breaux and Jewell 1992).

Still a third reason why incumbents generally win is that incumbents tend to obtain a strong, positive, "personal" vote due to their attractive candidate qualities. Candidates with strong personal appeals tend to win elections. Winners, therefore, tend to be strong candidates. And when winners seek reelection as incumbents, they generally continue to be strong candidates.

The electoral success of incumbents may signal both something wrong and something right about the status of representation. When elected officials are repeatedly returned to office because people vote for the dominant party or because people vote for the security of the familiar incumbent, incumbents can act unbound by constituency opinion. Under these circumstances, representation suffers. But there is also a positive side. Part of the reason for incumbent success is that candidates who do things to please voters are allowed to stay in office the longest. Incumbents who represent their constituencies on policy issues are allowed to stay in office the longest.[5]

Voters' Attention to Policy Positions

To what extent do voters react to the content of their leaders' policy decisions and policy proposals for the future? In the previous chapter we saw some evidence of policy voting, particularly at the presidential level. But especially in subpresidential contests, the public's information is usually too low to allow the expectation of much policy voting. The best data in this regard concern people's awareness of the U.S. House of Representatives and their particular representative.

Congress is not a very salient institution to most people. When asked which party has more representatives, more give the correct answer than the incorrect one. But with an adjustment for correct guessing, the best estimate is that typically less than half the congressional-election voters cast their ballot with firm knowledge of which party is in control (Stokes and Miller 1962, 537). Once, following the 1966 election, a plurality in an SRC poll incorrectly responded that the Republicans controlled Congress—apparently confusing the big Republican gains that were reported in the news media with a Republican majority.[6] When people are asked how good a job Congress is doing, one might suspect that their response would depend on their party identification and the party in power—Democrats would like Congress best when the Democrats control it, for example. But it does not work out this way. People more frequently rate the performance of Congress to be good when their party controls the White House but not Congress, than when their party controls Congress but not the White House (Davidson et al. 1968, 60–63).

When we turn to voters' knowledge of their individual congressmen and congressional candidates, no improvement is found. First of all, the local news media rarely give much coverage to the roll-call stands of members of Congress or to the substantive issues to congressional campaigns. Consequently, even if more people had the urge to follow the congressional politics of their district, they would have great difficulty in doing so. Only slightly more than half the public can even name their congressional representative. Similarly, at election time only about half will claim to have read or heard anything about their representative in Washington or the opposing candidate. When interviewers probe to find out what the voter has read or heard about the incumbent congressional candidate, the answer is typically a vague reference such as "he (or she) is a good person," or "he (or she) knows the problems." In National Election Surveys, only about 15 percent express reactions to their U.S. House member in terms of positions taken on specific legislation (Jacobson 1987).

On even hotly debated congressional issues, few people know where their Congress member stands. Table 10.4 shows the results of two surveys asking people their Congress member's position on a particular matter. One issue is funding for development of a supersonic transport plane (SST) shortly after Congress rejected it in 1971. Most people polled were unable to state how their representative voted on the SST. Those who tried to answer the question were wrong almost as often as they were right—suggesting that even those who tried to answer were mostly guessing. Thus, the voters were almost totally unaware of how their congressional representative voted on an issue that had commanded a substantial share of newspaper headlines for a period of months. Evidently, members of Congress were able to vote on the SST without attracting much public attention back home.

The second issue presented in Table 10.4 is women's rights, from a study by Patricia Hurley and Kim Hill (1981). The specific congres-

TABLE 10.4 Voter Awareness of Representative's Position: Two Examples

Voter's Perception of Representative's Position	Representative's Actual Vote on SST, 1971	
	For SST	*Against SST*
For SST	12%	3.5%
Against SST	14	27.5
Not sure	74	69
	100%	100%
	Representative's Actual Vote on ERA Extension, 1978	
	For Extension	*Against Extension*
Pro-equal role for women	63%	48%
Women's place is in the home	10	19
In between	27	33
	100%	100%

Source: On Supersonic Transport, John Kraft, Inc., "A Review of Voter Attitudes in Ten Key Congressional Districts," August 1971, a Report to the American Businessmen's Committee for National Priorities. Percentages are district means. On ERA extension, recomputed from Patricia A. Hurley and Kim Quaille

sional action is the 1978 vote on extending the deadline for ratification of the equal rights amendment. The perceptions obtained from the public samples are estimates of where the respondent's U.S. representative stood on the general issue of women's rights. Respondents were only slightly more willing to rate their representative as being for equal rights if the representative actually favored an extension of the ERA deadline than if the representative did not.

From these survey findings, one might well wonder whether the representatives need to pay any attention to the views of their constituency when they weigh the alternatives of each legislative decision. As Warren Miller and Donald Stokes (1963, 54) put it: "Congressmen feel that their individual legislative actions may have considerable impact on the electorate, yet some simple facts about the Representative's salience to his constituents imply that this could hardly be true."

Indeed, we may have a major political linkage between mass opinion and leader response that is generally overlooked—although the public is not watching, leaders sometimes do what they think the public wants because they mistakenly believe the public is paying attention! If this is true, then leaders' responsiveness to public opinion would quickly evaporate once somebody points out to them that surveys show the public to be rather indifferent to what they do. On the other hand, maybe the politicians do not exaggerate the importance of their record to their electoral fate as much as the polls seem to suggest. Let us explore the reasons why officeholders do have to tread carefully when they consider violating something called public opinion.

First, the high reelection rate of incumbent officeholders does not actually provide much security because the officeholder may want to win not only the next election, but also several thereafter. Consider the case of U.S. House members, who have a success rate of over 90 percent per reelection attempt. Most will survive their next election, but in the long run about one-third eventually leave office via an electoral defeat (Erikson 1976c, 613–32). Such odds on long-term electoral survival can give House members reason to pay special attention to constituency desires.

Second, the easiest way for voters to become aware of their elected leader's record is for it to be exploited by an opponent as a stand against public opinion. Therefore, although name recognition generally wins votes, lack of public knowledge of a political leader's policy stands may sometimes actually be a sign of successful representation. Put another way, if members of Congress became more casual in their consideration of constituency views—for example, if representatives of liberal districts started acting like conservatives and vice versa—the polls might show much more evidence of constituency awareness, and on election day, more incumbents would be defeated. David Mayhew (1974a, 37) puts it this way:

> When we say "congressman Smith is unbeatable," we do not mean there is nothing he could do that would lose him his seat. Rather we mean, "Congressman Smith is unbeatable as long as he continues to do the things he is doing." If he stopped answering his mail, or stopped visiting his district, or began voting randomly on roll calls, or shifted his vote record eighty points on the ADA scale, he would bring on primary or November election troubles in a hurry.

Third, one should note that there does exist a sprinkling of informed voters who shift their political weight according to the policy views of the candidates. Even if these alert voters compose a tiny fraction of the total, their opinion leadership allows them to influence election outcomes to an extent beyond what their numbers would indicate. As information about the representative diffuses downward from relatively informed opinion leaders to the mass public, many voters may "get simple positive or negative cues about the Congressman which were provoked by his legislative actions but no longer have a recognizable policy content," as Miller and Stokes (1963, 55) suggest. By responding to such cues, a significant number of voters may act as if they are relatively informed about their representative's record. As a result, the collective electoral decisions in congressional contests may be more responsive to roll-call records than our knowledge about individual voters would indicate.

In the previous chapter, we saw that the result of this process is visible in election returns. Members of Congress lose votes when they take ideologically extreme public positions. Normally, such vote loss due to policy stands is not sufficient for defeat, since the representative is often protected by a modest incumbency advantage and a one-party district. But the few who do lose can often blame their own policy stands for their misfortune.

10-5 Conclusion

This chapter has examined two mechanisms by which elected leaders follow public opinion. By the Sharing Model, elected leaders tend to do what their constituents want for the simple reason that elected leaders are drawn from the constituencies that elect them. When we consider the relationship between the legislator's views and the mean (or median) views of the legislator's specific geographic constituency, the Sharing Model provides little guarantee of representation. Just because a person is selected as the representative does not guarantee that this representative represents the average views of the constituency. The Sharing Model works best in the aggregate, in the sense that a large legislative body should normally represent the views of the larger population from whom it is collectively elected.

To obtain correspondence between (average) constituency views and the positions of elected leaders, we must rely on the electoral process. Via the Rational-Activist Model (see Chapter 9), voters elect those candidates who represent their own views, so that winners hopefully reflect constituency opinion better than do losers. Because they believe that their constituents are watching, elected leaders try to anticipate the reactions of their electorate in advance. This is the Role-Playing Model at work. Because of the fear of electoral sanctions (or simply because they believe it to be what they ought to do), elected leaders play the role of "delegate," trying to please their constituents. By doing so, they provide their constituents with policy representation.

The general public shows some ambivalence regarding the desired role of their representatives. Should our elected leaders follow our instructions (as delegates following the Role-Playing Model) or should they follow their own beliefs regarding our best interests, regardless of the electoral consequences (as our trustees)? As we have seen, elected leaders try hard to stay elected, and they generally succeed. In other words, they are good at their job—that of professional politician. In recent years, many voters have been attracted to the idea of term limits for elected officials, as a way of ridding politics of career politicians. Opponents of term limits counter that if we do not like our elected leaders we should remove them at the ballot box, not by constitutional provision. This controversy is far from settled.

Notes _____

1. On the social and economic characteristics of American legislators, see Jewell and Patterson (1981), Thompson and Moncrief (1992), Bullock (1992), and Freeman and Lyons (1992).
2. Within state legislatures, lawyers more frequently vote against no-fault insurance than do non-lawyers (Dyer 1976).
3. Comparing opinions of the mass public with those of elites is difficult, since the results of the comparison can depend on the issues that are chosen. In 1982, the CBS/*New York Times* survey included questions about school prayer and a constitutional amendment to balance the budget. Elites appear more liberal on these issues because they are more aware of the complexities than the mass public, who treat questions about prayers and balanced budgets as referenda on God and the virtue of thrift, respectively. On the practical issues of what Congress should spend its money on, the 1982 mass and congressional samples were remarkably similar.

   In 1970, U.S. senators were also interviewed. Senators displayed slightly more liberal views than either the public or the House members. For an analysis of the 1970 findings, see Backstrom (1977). For an analysis of the 1978 data, see Bishop and Frankovic (1981).
4. Another subtle reason for the high rate of incumbent reelection is a pattern of strategic retirements. Although incumbents rarely retire, those who are likely to lose present an exception. Thus, one reason why we do not see more incumbents kicked out of office by the voters is that electorally vulnerable incumbents often prefer not to risk giving their voters the pleasure. One wave of incumbent retirements in advance of the voters' wrath occurred in 1992. About one-third of the U.S. House members burdened by excessive overdrafts in the House "banking" scandal declined to run for another term (Banducci and Karps 1994).
5. This discussion is drawn from Erikson and Wright (1993).
6. Following the 1966 election, 44 percent said the Republicans have "elected the most Congressmen"; 21 percent said the Democrats did; the remainder said they did not know. *Source:* Survey Research Center, *1966 Election Study Codebook*.

CHAPTER 11

Parties and Interest Groups: Mediating Institutions and Representation

This chapter discusses the two remaining political linkage models: the Political Parties Model and the Interest Groups Model. Democratic theorists concerned with the political linkage between public opinion and the behavior of elected leaders often posit an important role for the mediating institutions of political parties and interest groups. In its own way, each of these institutions can provide a means for a less than fully attentive public to attain its desired policy goals.

When political parties take distinctive stands on issues, party labels provide a mechanism for voters' own views. Rather than having to select among individual candidates for each of the many offices, the voters need only to select among the different parties based on their policy programs. For this model to work, parties should not only offer different programs, but also be able to enact their programs when placed in office. Interest groups have advantages that are not normally available to the mass public. Unlike ordinary citizens, organized interest groups can pay full-time attention to policymaking actions of government: They have personnel holders on hand in Washington D.C. or the state capital to persuade officeholders toward the policy views of their group. During election campaigns, interest groups can contribute money to candidates and urge their members to vote for candidates who represent their views. Obviously these activities can alter public policy away from public opinion as well as toward it. When interest groups reflect public opinion, their influence on the actions of elected officials helps promote accountability. When group opinion differs from public opinion, group influence works against democratic representation. Therefore a key question is how frequently elected leaders follow the public will when they in fact are responding to the pressures of organized groups.

11-1 Political Parties and Representation _____

According to the Political Parties Model, party labels clarify the political choices available to the voters. For this model to work, two conditions are necessary. First each political party would outline the program it would enact if its candidates were elected; thus the candidates' party labels signify what the candidates will do if elected. Second, each voter would make his or her selection at the polls on the basis of the party that best represents his or her views. This model simplifies the task of the policy-oriented voter. Instead of monitoring each candidate's campaign statements and hoping that they reflect what the candidates would do if elected, the voter would need only to learn the differences between the parties' programs and use party labels as a cue to rational voting. Ideally the party programs would be determined by an internal consensus that would govern the behavior of the party's elected officials.

As we have seen, voters do not always behave according to the prescription of the Political Parties Model. Although most voters identify with a political party and party identifiers generally vote for their party's candidates, Republican and Democratic identifiers are not greatly polarized on policy differences between the two major parties. Thus, party voting by the mass public only to a limited degree can be considered policy voting.

Whether voters are given the opportunity to rationally select candidates on the basis of party labels depends on the existence of differences between the programs of the two parties. Here we examine the extent to which Republican and Democratic leaders actually differ in their policy presences, in the programs they offer to the voters, and in their behavior in office. Observers often say that to win elections, political parties must appeal to the moderate voter. In addition, parties must also appeal to their loyal activists who are often located at their party's ideological directions—toward the center by the party's desire to win elections, and away from the center, toward the ideological preferences of the party leaders and activists.[1]

To keep parties near where the voters are, the electorate must do its part. A policy-motivated electorate will stimulate election-hungry parties toward the electorate's point of view. But suppose that the electorate is too disinterested or uninformed to keep the parties honest? Then elections would be decided solely on nonpolicy grounds and policies would depend solely on the whims of the partisan victors.

Ideology and Party Leaders

Although ideology is only a modest source of partisan division between ordinary Republican and Democratic voters, ideology is often a strong motivation for party activists. The ordinary voter of somewhat conservative persuasion who is raised a Democrat might be content to remain a Democrat. Similarly, the mildly liberal voter who grew up a Republican might stay with the Republican party. For most voters, politics is not that important to compel a matching ideology and party identification. But political activists are different. When a strong ideology motivation spurs an individual to political activism, the individual will usually develop an affinity for the ideologically appropriate party.[2]

The earliest comparison of the personal beliefs of Republican and Democratic leaders is a study by Herbert McClosky, Paul Hoffman, and Rosemary O'Hara (1960). In 1957 and 1958, they gathered identical kinds of data from a public sample of supporters of the political parties and from delegates to the 1956 political party conventions. For each of 24 policy issues, the researchers reported the percentages of both leaders and followers preferring an increased government commitment. They found that issue differences were greater between Republican and Democratic leaders than between Republican and Democratic followers (party identifiers). Republican delegates were to the right of Republican identifiers and Democratic delegates were to the left of Democratic identifiers. Of the two sets of 1956 delegates, the Democrats were more representative of the general electorate. In fact, the difference was not close: even Republican identifiers as a group were ideologically closer to the Democratic delegates than to the Republican delegates.

Studies of delegates to national conventions since 1956 have continued to show each party's delegates to be more "extreme" than the party rank and file. Whether one party is more extreme than the other will vary. In 1972 it was the Democrat's turn to be the least representative. Reversing the 1956 pattern, delegates were so far to the left that rank-and-file Democrats were closer to the Republican delegates on the issues (Soule and McGrath 1975; Kirkpatrick 1975). Since 1972, the parties have been relatively balanced in their extremity (Miller and Jennings 1987, Ch. 9). In terms of ideological identification, Democratic

TABLE 11.1 Ideological Identification of National Convention Delegates, 1976–1992

	1976		1980		1984		1988		1992	
Ideology	Dem.	Rep.	Dem.	Rep.	Dem.	Rep.	Dem.	Rep.	Dem.	Rep.
% Liberal	40	3	46	2	48	1	43	0	47	1
% Moderate	47	45	42	36	42	35	43	35	44	32
% Conservative	8	48	6	58	4	60	5	58	5	63

Source: Harold W. Stanley and Richard G. Niemi, *Vital Statistics of American Politics*, 4th ed. (Washington: CQ Press, 1994), p. 149.

delegates tend to be liberal or moderate but rarely conservative; Republican delegates tend to be conservative or moderate but rarely liberal. Table 11.1 displays these patterns for delegates over five sets of national conventions.

Political parties obtain their political energy from their activists. But while the classic role of party leader is to balance the ideological preferences of the activists with the pragmaticism necessary for winning elections, party activists may be more concerned with ideological correctness than with electoral victory. Increasingly, with the decline of the traditional party organizations and the growing openness of party conventions brought by recent reforms of party rules, ideologues are moving into party leadership positions and determining the nominations of party candidates. There is an irony here. As the leadership structure of the political parties is becoming more internally democratic, the potential for greater policy choice between the parties is created. This increases the conflict between the parties' policies and the preferences of their less-active rank-and-file supporters.

Voter Perceptions of Party Locations

Regardless of the preferences of party leaders, how far apart are the parties (from their supporters and from each other) in terms of public perceptions? To try to answer this question, we examine how 1992 voters view Democratic and Republican ideological positions relative to their own positions. Averaging over four issues (including ideological identification), we measure NES respondents' net positions and perceptions of party positions on the seven-point scales. We set aside non-

TABLE 11.2 Voter Perceptions of Their Policy Positions Relative to the Two Major Parties

	Respondent Party Identification					
Perceived Respondent Party Difference	**Strong Dem.**	**Weak Dem.**	**Indep.**	**Weak Rep.**	**Strong Rep.**	**All Cases**
Respondent left of both parties	43%	28%	19%	5%	4%	20%
Respondent in between two parties˙	55	67	62	62	47	59
Respondent right of both parties	2	5	19	33	50	21
	100%	100%	100%	100%	100%	100%

˙Includes respondents who see self at same location as one party but not another (11%).

Source: NES, 1992 election data. Based on respondent (voters only) perceptions on eight issues. Includes only voters who (on average) saw Democrats to the left of Republicans.

voters and voters who (averaged over for issues) saw no party differences or saw the Republicans (mistakenly) on the left. For each voter who correctly saw the Republicans to the right of the Democrats, we ascertained the voter's perception of his or her *own* position relative to the two parties.' [Those who, according to our measure, perceive their position as perfectly represented by one party—e.g., seeing the Republicans as just right but the Democrats as too liberal—are scored with those in between the two parties.]

Table 11.2 displays the relevant data. Overall, slightly more than half the voters who correctly order the parties ideologically see themselves as in between the Democrats on their left and the Republicans on their right. The remainder are about evenly split between voters who see themselves to the right of even the Republicans (and therefore the Democrats as well) and voters who see themselves as well to the left of even the Democrats (and therefore the Republicans).

Table 11.2 also shows perceptions of party positions broken down by party identification. The most interesting groups are the "strong Democrats" and "strong Republicans." A full 43 percent of the strong Democrats see themselves to the left of both parties. Similarly, 50 percent of the strong Republicans see themselves to the right of both parties. The two parties need to satisfy these polarized partisans. But they also need to woo the portion of the electorate—mainly weak partisans and Independents—in the middle.

Each party's "strong" identifiers are typical of the party's primary electorate. Activists tend to dominate low-turnout party primaries, with an important segment urging the party in a more extreme ideological direction. But to the extent primary electorate chose "extreme" candidates over moderates, the party will risk alienating voters in the center. Each party's more moderate candidates may have the greatest chance to become general election winners, but they face the problem first in securing the nomination from a hostile primary electorate.[3]

And what of that half of the relevant electorate who appear to be ideologically located in between the two parties? These centrist voters seemingly face a distasteful choice of giving power either to a party that is too conservative or a party that is too liberal. However, these voters also have the opportunity to split their ticket, voting for a balance of some Democrats and some Republicans. The desire of moderate voters for an ideological balance of party power may help to explain the frequent pattern of divided party control. Arguably, moderate voters should prefer the ideological balance of one party controlling the presidency and the other controlling Congress to unified control by either party. Such thinking might account for the instances, such as during the 1980s, when the U.S. electorate balanced a Republican president with a Democratic Congress (Fiorina 1992).

This balancing of party control is particularly evident in midterm elections in which the presidential party almost always loses seats in Congress. Not only do midterm voters elect fewer Congress members of the President's party than two years before; they also generally elect fewer members of the President's party than they do when the President's party is out of power. In other words, each party historically has been more favorably treated by midterm voters when it is *out* of power at the presidential level (Erikson 1988).

The Relevance of Party Platforms

At national conventions every fourth year, each party devotes considerable time to spelling out the details of its platform in order to detail the party's "official" position on the issues of the day. Party platforms are often dismissed as mere ritualistic documentation since they are rarely read, quickly forgotten, and not officially binding on a party's candidates. Nevertheless, as research by Gerald Pomper (1980, Chs. 7 and 8) shows, careful reading of party platforms provides some clues as to what the parties would do if they came to power.

Pomper examined the content of the Democratic and Republican platforms from 1944 to 1976. He (with Susan Lederer) found about half the platform statements to be relatively meaningless rhetoric ("The American Free Enterprise System is one of the greatest achievements of humankind") or statements about the issues that are too vague or broad to be meaningful ("The Anti-Trust Laws must be vigorously enforced"). About another quarter of the platform statements qualify as policy approval ("In the Nuclear Test Ban Treaty, we have written our commitment to limitations on the arms race"). Finally, about one-quarter are detailed policy statements like "The Security of the American Trade Unions must be strengthened by repealing 14B of the Taft-Hartley Act." Although voters almost never read party platforms directly, platform statements reach voters indirectly, "through interest groups, mass media, candidates' speeches, and incomplete popular perceptions" (Pomper 1980, 152).

Of particular relevance is whether parties keep their policy promises once in office. Pomper finds that about two-thirds of the winning presidential party's pledges become at least partially fulfilled during the next four years. Somewhat over half the pledges of the nonpresidential party do as well. When both parties offer the same pledge in their platforms, the pledge is fulfilled in some fashion about 80 percent of the time. Pomper (1980, 176) concludes, "We should take platforms seriously, because politicians take them seriously." A recent statistical analysis by Ian Budge and Richard Hofferbert (1990) reinforces Pomper's conclusion. They were able to trace changing federal expenditure patterns to changing priorities found in party platforms, particularly the platform of the presidential party.

Party Voting in Legislatures

Ideally from the standpoint of the Political Parties Model, the electorally dominant party not only would have articulated a program that achieves voter approval, but would be in a position to enact that program once in a power. The dominant congressional party, for example, would be able to enact its preferred legislation, particularly if the president is of the same party and gives encouragement. As is well known, however, events do not always work out this way in the American system. The president often has difficulty pushing his proposals through Congress even when his party is in the majority. Since 1932, the Republicans have controlled both the presidency and Congress only for

TABLE 11.3 Party Voting in the U.S. House on Eight Selected Roll Calls in 1991, 1992, 1993

		Republicans	Democrats	All
Bar employers from hiring replacement workers for striking workers (1991)	For:	16	230	247
	Against:	149	33	182
Require 7-day waiting period for purchase of handgun (1991)	For:	60	179	239
	Against:	102	83	186
Provide abortion services for overseas military personnel and their families (1991)	For:	35	184	220
	Against:	129	79	208
Decrease taxes on middle class, raise taxes on wealthy (1992)	For:	1	219	221
	Against:	163	46	209
Cut $3.5 billion for U.S. troops stationed in Europe (1992)	For:	39	180	220
	Against:	117	68	185
Limit funds for SDI (Stars Wars) (1992)	For:	26	174	201
	Against:	135	82	217
Require major employers to provide unpaid leave to tend to newborn or family illness (1993)	For:	40	224	265
	Against:	134	29	163
Pass Clinton Administration $16 billion stimulus package (1993)	For:	3	231	235
	Against:	168	22	190

Source: "Key Votes," Michael Barone and Grant Unifusa, *The Almanac of American Politics 1994* (Washington: The National Journal, 1993), pp. xvii, xviii.

two early Eisenhower years (1953–54). More frequent has been Democratic control of both branches. Often, Democratic presidents have had their policies blocked in Congress by the so-called "conservative coalition" of Republicans and conservative Southern Democrats. The conservative coalition has occasionally (notably in the early Reagan years) been the decisive factor in the victory of a Republican president's legislative agenda.

This discussion may seem to suggest that party labels are not very relevant in Congress. However, that is far from the truth. In fact, party affiliation is the single best predictor of roll-call voting in Congress. Table 11.3 shows the party breakdown on selected U.S. House roll calls in 1991–1993, during the late Bush and early Clinton presidencies. Although this table illustrates that neither party in Congress acts as an all-cohesive unit, it also shows that party affiliation is a strong predictor of roll-call voting. Each of the eight issues shown in Table 11.3 is a "party vote" (defined as a vote in which a majority of Republicans oppose a majority of Democrats). In recent Congresses, some 40 to 60 percent of roll-call votes have been party votes. On party votes, Congress members vote about 80 percent with their party on the average, and about 20 percent with their opposition (Rohde 1992; Hurley 1989; Patterson and Caldiera 1988).

In Congress, party voting is most prevalent on issues with a discernible liberal vs. conservative content, especially those dealing with the government's role in the economy and social welfare legislation. Especially on civil rights, the ideological distinctiveness between the

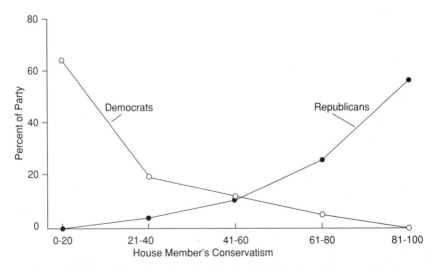

Fig. 11-1 Party differences in roll call votes (ACU index of conservatism), 1989.

congressional parties is growing rather than weakening. Figure 11-1 summarizes these party differences in terms of overall voting records, for House members in 1989. As summed over many issues, most Republicans are more conservative than most Democrats.

In state legislatures, the average rate of party voting is slightly higher than in Congress, but there is considerable variation (LeBlanc 1969; Patterson 1976). While systematic party differences on issues are virtually nonexistent in some state legislatures, some state legislative parties behave as disciplined units. The source of this occasional discipline is sometimes a powerful presiding officer who can penalize members of his party for not supporting party positions, and sometimes it is the party caucus. When a legislative party operates according to the "strong caucus" system, members of the party democratically decide a party position on certain issues, which is sometimes binding on its members. There has been little exploration of the sources of these differences among the state legislatures, or the impact such differences might have on public policy.

Party discipline is seldom evident in Congress, because it is not in the members' best interest: If all Republicans in Congress were forced to vote with their party's conservative majority and all Democrats were forced to vote with their liberal majority, many would be kicked out of office by their local constituencies.[4] Interestingly, however, congressional parties once acted as cohesive units. In the latter party of the nineteenth century, party discipline was maintained in the U.S. House because the Speaker of the House held broad powers over the members. When the Speaker's powers were diluted in the "revolution of 1910–1911," power reverted for a short time to the parties' caucuses. Especially during Woodrow Wilson's administration (1913–1920), each party's caucus regularly voted on issues, and members were often bound (with the rarely exercised excuse of matter of conscience) to vote for the party's majority position. The strong caucus system, however, was short-lived. Given the diversity of viewpoints within the congressional parties and a heightened sensitivity to constituency interests (due in part to increased congressional ambitions to stay elected), to hope that the strong-caucus system would return in Congress would be unrealistic.

Party Labels as a Basis for Policy Choice

Elected leaders from the Democratic and Republican parties differ on ideology in large part because Democrats and Republicans represent different geographic constituencies. But what about the choice that the two parties offer within the same constituency? In this section we examine the ideological choice provided by the Republican and Democratic parties at the constituency level. We first consider candidates in individual House contests. Then, we briefly look at the ideological choice provided by competing parties within the American states.

Party Choice in Congressional Elections. In U.S. House races, the electorate's choice is not between the *typical* congressional Democrat and the *typical* congressional Republican, for the reason that congressional candidates often adjust their issue stances according to the prevailing constituency views. A liberal district will generally be given a choice between a relatively liberal Democrat and a relatively liberal Republican. Similarly, a conservative district will be given a choice between Democrat and Republican candidates who are both relatively conservative for their party. We are interested in the extent to which candidates at the district level diverge from each other and give the constituency votes a meaningful choice.

Almost always, when a district's congressional candidates differ on important issues, the Democrat is the more liberal and the Republican is the more conservative. Table 11.4 shows this for the 1982 congressional candidates. Column I shows, for each of 10 issues, the percentage of the contested districts in which the Republican took the liberal position and the Democrat the conservative position. As the table makes clear, this pattern is rare. Columns II and III show instance of

TABLE 11.4 Candidates' Positions on 10 Issues, 1982 Contested House Elections

	Candidates' Positions			
	I	II	III	IV
Republican:	Lib.	Con.	Lib.	Con.
Democrat:	Con.	Con.	Lib.	Lib.
Constitutional Amendments				
States prohibit abortion	6%	16%	33%	45%
Prayer in public schools	5	13	28	54
For balanced budget	1	22	10	67
Equal rights amendment	2	8	41	50
Issues				
Nuclear freeze with Soviets	3	13	22	62
Domestic content, foreign cars sold in U.S.	6	18	28	48
Cancel July 1983 tax cut	2	19	7	72
Cut military spending increase	3	8	55	34
Reduce domestic social programs	2	15	20	62
Increase regulation of air pollution	6	57	5	33

Source: Robert S. Erikson and Gerald G. Wright, "Voters, Issues, and Candidates in Congressional Elections," in Lawrence C. Dodd and Bruce I. Oppenheimer (eds.), *Congress Reconsidered,* 3rd ed. (Washington, D.C.: Congressional Quarterly Press, 1985), p. 94.

agreement, either liberal or conservative. Column IV shows the dominant pattern of liberal Democrats vs. conservative Republicans.

Generally, a congressional voter has an easy decision rule for casting a partisan ballot: To help elect the most conservative candidate, vote Republican; To help elect the most liberal candidate, vote Democratic. Suppose, for instance, we score each of the 1982 candidates from Table 11.4 from 0 to 10 based on his or her number of conservative positions on the 10 issues (extreme liberals score 0: extreme conservatives score 10). By this measure, the Republican was the more conservative candidate in 93 percent of the contests, the Democrat was the more conservative in 3 percent, and ties occurred in the remaining 4 percent. This result is not unique for the 1982 election. A similar pattern has been found in studies of the 1966, 1974, and 1978 House elections (Sullivan and O'Conner 1972; Wright 1986).

Clearly, the parties present a meaningful choice to the public. For example, when the public desires a more conservative Congress, it can simply elect more Republicans. On the other hand, attributing changes in the partisan makeup of Congresses to policy motives on the part of the electorate can be hazardous. Ideology can rarely be a cause of partisan change in Congress, for the reason that the American electorate rarely moves ideologically. (See discussions in Chapters 3, 9.) Although the numbers of Republicans and Democrats in Congress will vary from one election to the next, these changes generally can be traced to such factors as economic conditions, presidential coattails, and Watergates— not to changes in policy preferences by the public. Yet the mechanism of choice is available for the public to create a policy shift in Congress— and in state legislatures and other political arenas as well.

We can see the policy result of a large net shift in congressional party strength for the example of 1964. In that election, an unusually high number of Democrats were elected to Congress on the coattails of President Johnson's landslide victory. The combination of a large Democratic majority (in fact a northern Democratic majority) and an activist president resulted in the passage of a lot of liberal legislation (Medicare, federal aid to education, the Voting Rights Act) that had been delayed for years.

More recently, in 1980 an abnormal number of Republicans were swept into Congress on Ronald Reagan's coattails. The result was the Reagan tax cut and other legislation that was part of the conservative Reagan agenda. Both the 1964 and 1980 elections had important policy consequences. But in each instance it is very debatable whether the electorate intended a clear mandate for a change in the ideological direction on national policy (Wright 1986).

The shock of a major shift in the party composition of Congress may be a necessary requirement for major changes in national policy.

Realigning elections provide the special case of electoral change producing policy changes that perhaps can be traced directly to public demands. Realigning elections—1896 and 1932 are the best examples—produce not only changes in the party strengths in Congress, but also

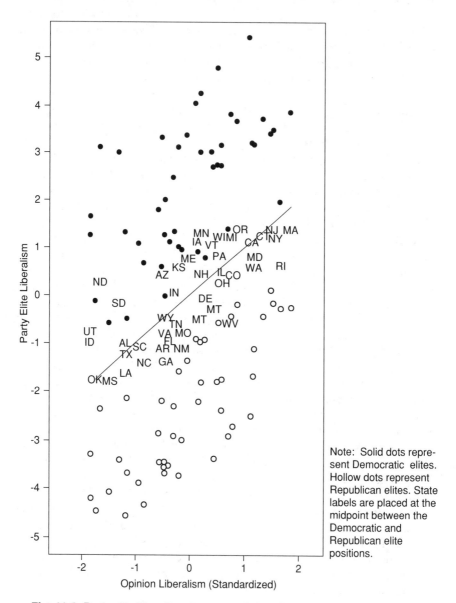

Note: Solid dots represent Democratic elites. Hollow dots represent Republican elites. State labels are placed at the midpoint between the Democratic and Republican elite positions.

Fig. 11-2 Party elite liberalism by state opinion. Source: Erikson, Wright, and McIver 1993.

increased cohesiveness within the dominant party (Brady 1988; Sinclair 1977).

Party Choice in State Elections. The assertion that parties provide a choice need not be restricted to the congressional arena. Party differences can be seen at the state level too. Figure 11-2 illustrates. For each of the 48 states, this figure presents ideological estimates for the Republican and Democratic state party elites plus the state electorate. For the two sets of party elites, each estimate is a composite based on the ideological responses of the state parties' national convention delegates, state legislators, county chairmen, and congressional candidates. The state electorate estimates are based on cumulative CBS/*New York Times* polls.

Figure 11-2 shows both how Democratic and Republican state parties are ideologically distinct from one another. The figure also shows the flexibility of the two parties in responding to state opinion. In each state, the Democratic party is to the left of the Republicans, with the electorate in the middle. But the two party positions are not the same in each state. The more liberal the state electorate, the more liberal are both parties.

The result of this process is that at the state level, party success is determined less by the ideological taste of the state electorate than by the relative ideological closeness of the two parties to the state electorate. In many conservative Southern states, for example, the more liberal Democratic party is electorally dominant. In some liberal states (e.g., New York, Vermont, Wisconsin), the more conservative Republican party does very well. These seeming anomalies occur as a result of the state electorate rewarding the party that stands closest to the state electorate's views (Erikson et al. 1992).

The Importance of Party Competition

The importance of parties is evident during circumstances when parties cease to play a major role—when elections are held on a truly nonpartisan basis, as in many American cities and sometimes for state offices. Reformers once saw nonpartisan elections as ideal because they weaken the role of corrupt political parties. But we now know that nonpartisan elections make it more difficult for voters to get their preferred policies enacted and to hold leaders accountable for their actions (Cassel 1986).

When both major parties compete effectively for the electorate's favor, we would expect close elections. Sometimes, however, party competition breaks down and one party enjoys a monopoly. This has not happened at the national level since the "Era of Good Feelings" around

1820. Often at the state and local levels, however, one party becomes so dominant as to win almost every election.

In theory, the effect of strong party competition should be to enhance representation. With election outcomes uncertain, each party gets an added incentive to woo the marginal voter who otherwise would be ignored. The opposite result would occur under one-party dominance. The dominant party would not need to make policy appeals to a public whose loyalty (or apathy) they have already won.

V.O. Key (1949) argued that the lack of party competition in the American South allowed the once dominant Democratic party in Southern states to ignore public opinion, with the result that the "haves" enacted public policy at the expense of the "have-nots." There has been, largely as a result of Key's position, a conviction among political scientists that parties would be more respohsive to public opinion were competition among state political parties to increase. The states have been moving more toward two-party systems, both in the South and nationwide. As the parties become more evenly matched in the contests for control of governorships and state legislatures, this can only be a positive step in terms of the Political Parties Model. On the negative side, party competition for individual legislative seats has been decreasing (Tucker and Weber 1992). The results of this trend, if any, remain unclear.

Does Party Control Matter?

Readily following from our discussion, which party controls the levers of power can have important policy consequences. We have already seen that elected politicians often do turn party platform pledges into law. We can also examine different policies under different types of party control. The major policy consequences that flow from party control concern redistribution, with Democratic policies tending to favor the Democrats' constituency of lower-income voters and Republican policies tending to favor the Republicans' upper-income voters. Innovations in social welfare legislation, for example, are most frequent when Democrats are strong in Congress and, especially, when the Democrats hold the White House (Browning 1986, Ch. 8; see also Kiewiet and McCubbins 1985). Statistically speaking, unemployment (a major concern of the less affluent) is more likely to decline under Democratic presidents. And inflation (a major concern of the more affluent) is more likely to decline under Republican presidents (Hibbs 1987, Ch. 7). There is also statistical evidence that the income gap between the rich and the poor goes up under Republican presidents and down under Democratic presidents (Hibbs and Dennis 1988).

Of course there are important limits to the policy consequences of party control. From a radical perspective, the choices between the policies of the Democrats and Republicans can be viewed as merely slight variations on the status quo. If one's taste in policy runs toward policies like government ownership of industry legalization of drugs, or abandonment of the public school system, one will not be well represented by either major party. Moreover, the U.S. system of separation of powers and checks and balances slows down the connection between policy proposals and policy enactment. Finally, keep in mind that elected officials are electorally motivated. Once elected, politicians will often moderate their policy positions in order to stay elected rather than satisfy the claims of their active partisan constituencies.

Conclusion

Many elements of the Political Party Model are confirmed. Although neither the Republican nor the Democratic party is a disciplined organization, the leaders and activists within the two major parties are ideologically distinct form one another. Although candidates of the two parties generally avoid their party's ideological extreme in order to get elected, their own strong views and those of their active supporters help push their public positions away from the political center. In this way, Republican and Democratic policy differences carry over into the policy choices that the parties offer the voters. In Congress and other political forums, Republicans and Democrats behave in ideologically opposite ways. Admittedly, the exact ideological choice provided by U.S. political parties will not satisfy everybody. But any failure of the Political Parties Model appears to come more from the public's failure to respond to the choices offered by the political parties than from the parties' failure to satisfy the conditions of the model.

11-2 Interest Groups and Representation _____

Like the Political Parties Model, the Interest Groups Model allows for an intermediate agent (in this case, organized groups) between individuals and their government leaders. Group members need not engage in extensive activity themselves, but can instead rely on their group's leaders and lobbyists to represent their interest. Members may be called upon, however, to contribute to the group's strength by giving money, writing letters to officials, demonstrating, or voting for the group's endorsed candidates. Elected leaders, according to the model, satisfy public opinion when they respond to (and anticipate) group pressures. To the extent the Interest Groups Model is working, the influence of different interest groups will reflect their membership and the intensity with which their views are held. When conflicting demands of different interest groups collide, the policy result would be a compromise, with each side getting its way in proportion to the strength of its membership support.

To evaluate the Interest Groups Model, we need to know whether its suppositions are correct. First, in what ways can interest groups get officeholders to respond to their demands? Unless combinations of individuals can influence policy by engaging in interest-group activity, the model cannot work. Second, do the leaders of interest groups know and support the preferences of their members? If there is no linkage between an organization's mass membership choices and the behavior of its leaders, interest groups cannot furnish any linkage between public opinion and public policy. Third, and most important, to what extent does group opinion represent public opinion? The model cannot hold if many individuals possess strong political views that are unexpressed by organized groups, or if opinions brought to bear by organized groups ignore the full range of relevant opinion.

Interest Group Influence

No scholar has attempted to give any kind of quantitative assessment of the net impact of interest-group activity on public policy, and offering one here would be beyond our capabilities. Although to assert that public policy is always (or most always) the result of group influence would be an overstatement, most observers agree that group influence in the policy process is considerable. While interest groups are noted for their influence at the administrative level (the general public pays the least attention at the policy-implementation phase) their influence at the legislative level is of central concern here.

Organized groups try to get elected leaders to see their point of view. A group will be more successful in this regard if its lobbyists share the same value as the legislators with whom they interact, if its lobbyists have relevant information to offer the legislature, or perhaps if its lobbyists are simply more visible than others. Everything being equal, legislators try to please interested parties, or at least those who do not alienate them.

Always important to an interest group's success will be the group's potential influence on the electoral process. Legislators will respond more to a group's interests if the group has contributed or will contribute money to their political campaigns. Also, the legislator will be more responsive if the group can give a creditable claim that it represents a sizable and attentive voting block. In rare cases, a group may achieve influence by the anticipated threat that it can go over the legislature's head to influence the views and votes of the general public.

Lobbying. How important is lobbying activity in determining legislative outcomes? Despite obvious drawbacks, one way to try to answer the question is to ask legislators or lobbyists. When members of Congress are asked to make such an assessment, they rank lobbying activity among the least important of possible influences on congressional decisions. For example, it is more influential than party leadership positions, but less important than constituency opinion (Kingdon 1973, Chs. 1, 5). Washington lobbyists also assess their influence as modest (Milbrath 1963). State legislators generally downplay the influence of lobbyists when queried by political scientists. But state-level lobbyists see themselves as more influential than do the legislators (Zeigler and Baer 1969).

Some states have strict lobbyist registration laws requiring lobbyists to signify which bills interest them and what their positions are. These strict laws provided Wiggins, Hamm, and Bell an unusual opportunity to assess interest-group success in Iowa, California, and Texas. For a random selection of bills form 1977 to 1983, they found interest groups to be less active and influential than one might expect (Wiggins et al. 1984; see also Wiggins 1983). Between 19 and 26 percent of the bills had no interest groups involved, and between 20 and 25 had only a single group involved. Overall, about half the bills had no evident input from organized groups, even though interest groups in the examined states are reputed to be influential. Most importantly, the eventual legislative outcome corresponded to the predominant interest-group position only slightly more than half the time. Governors had a much higher success rate than did groups. The overall impression of this research is one of interest groups limiting their involvement and only marginally shaping legislative outcomes in the states.

Lobbying is most effective, however, on issues outside the public spotlight. Generally, a group will be most successful if its goal would greatly benefit the group and cost little to others. Examples of such benefits include tax breaks, agricultural subsidies, oil import quotas, veteran's benefits, land tariffs on various commodities. Unfortunately, from the standpoint of the Interest Groups Model, the beneficiaries of such policies are "special interests" that cannot claim to represent public opinion. Narrow but specialized interests have an advantage not only because they have a unity of purpose but also because the public is often not aware of their activities. Meanwhile, groups that depend on a large mass membership for support are often handicapped when their members become satisfied by public relations gestures and symbolic rewards (see Edelman 1965).

Money, PACs, and the Electoral Process. Interest groups influence the political process via their monetary contributions to election campaigns. Politicians obtain campaign contributions from three sources: their political party, individual contributors, and "political action committees." Political action committees (PACs) often are the financial conduits for organized interest groups. Consider PAC contributions to federal candidates in the 1992 campaign (reported in Stanley and Niemi 1994, 178, 210): Through their subsidiary PACs, labor unions contributed 94 million dollars while, via their PACs, corporations and trade associations contributed an even greater 185 million dollars. Issue-oriented and ideological PACs contributed lesser amounts. Overall, PACs were responsible for 37 percent of House campaign contributions and 24 percent of Senate campaign contributions. PAC contributions to congressional campaigns have been increasing, fourfold between 1978 and 1992. While PACs are limited by law to $5,000 per candidate (individual contributors face a $1,000 limit), this limit results in candidates seeking smaller amounts from more groups.

Except for those who are independently wealthy, political candidates need contributions to spend the amount they believe necessary to run an effective campaign. In 1988, U.S. House members spent almost 400 thousand dollars per campaign, even though this amount was rarely necessary. Challengers typically spend much less, but only challengers who outspend their incumbent opponent have much chance of victory. The greatest spending is for open seats, where the Republican and Democratic candidates now on average spend half a million dollars each for the right to replace the retiring incumbent. U.S. Senate campaigns, which are statewide, now routinely cost well over a million dollars. Democratic and Republican candidates benefit about equally from PAC money. The major discrimination is against potential "long-shot" candidates upon whom PACs will not waste their money and against possibly worthy candidates who hold views too independent to attract PAC interest.

The role of PACs in campaign finance is widely regarded as giving too much power to well-financed groups at the expense for ordinary voters. More is involved than simply the effect of money on election outcomes. The argument goes as follows. Contributors give to campaigns not as philanthropic generosity to the deserving class of righteous politicians but as policy investments. Otherwise, why would groups contribute so much to unopposed candidates or concentrate their contributions upon electorally safe members of congressional committees that must pass upon legislation relevant to the group? Although contributions are often given in gratitude for legislative support of the group's positions in the past rather than for explicit future favors, legislators can enhance their expectation of future group support if they support the group position in advance. And once they receive a PAC's support, individual legislators become even more receptive to the group's position. A legislator who votes against a PAC's interest can find the PAC's future contributions withdrawn or even given to an electoral opponent. Even when a PAC mistakenly backs the losing horse in an election, the PAC will often recover influence by funding the winner. In fact, PACs often spread their investment by contributing to both candidates in an election.

With reelection rates of over 90 percent, and with evidence showing that the money they spend in a campaign is rarely crucial to their reelection, we might ask why members of Congress could not boldly act independent of PAC influence. One argument is that politicians do not like to take electoral chances that they can avoid. Certainly many politicians take PAC money without being influenced by it. And many others avoid all PAC money on principle. But there can be little doubt that legislators generally pay extra attention to the views of those who give them money. Political scientists tend to be somewhat cautious in their conclusion, because testing for statistical evidence of PAC influence is not easy. Scholars who have reviewed the evidence, however, do see a tentative statistical pattern whereby Congress members give more weight to contributor opinion than their overall voting record, constituency preferences, and party affiliation would suggest.[5]

Interest groups and their PACs are also major players in presidential primary elections, where each party's presidential nominees are determined. However, since 1976, presidential primary campaigns have been funded partially with private (PAC or individual) money and partially by matching federal funds. Also beginning with the 1976 presidential election, *general* election campaigns for the presidency have been fully funded by the public (with a spending cap), thereby reducing group influence at the presidential level. A possible additional reform step will be public financing of congressional campaigns. Some states have already moved to public financing of some state campaigns. Although incumbent members of Congress are the major beneficiaries of PAC money, they have two incentives to switch to public financing for themselves. First, they would be freed from the distasteful task of chasing PAC money to focus on their primary function of legislation. Second, if incumbents and challengers were funded equally from the federal treasury, the conventional thinking is that challengers would be even more handicapped than now, because nonincumbents need more money to overcome their invisibility to the voters (Jacobson 1989, 133-34). Quite possibly, if the role of money in electoral politics could be neutralized, the change in the performance of Congress and other political arenas could be breathtaking.

Many informed observers doubt that significant reform of campaign financing would greatly diminish the overall role of interest groups in the policy process because organized groups would still possess the advantages of information, expertise, and direct monitoring of government officials which the general public does not possess. The hoped-for change would be that a group's bankroll would play a lesser amount in determining its degree of influence. When elected leaders respond to potential votes rather than potential cash, the different organized groups compete on a more level playing field.

Interest Groups and Public Relations. In addition to giving campaign contributions, groups sometimes attempt to influence public opinion directly, via propaganda campaigns. The interest groups with a large mass-membership base, such as labor unions, place the greatest emphasis on public relations as a technique for influencing legislative and administrative action. The public-relations efforts of labor unions are largely aimed at influencing the opinions and voting behavior of their members. The success of these efforts is limited, but visible. V.O. Key once showed, for example, that the AFL-CIO was somewhat successful at convincing union members of the central AFL-CIO plank to repeal key features of the allegedly anti-union "Taft-Hartley Act" in the early 1950s (Key 1961b, 509). Union leaders also have some influence on the voting behavior of their members. Union members are about 20 percent more likely to vote Democratic than nonunion counterparts in similar life situations (Campbell et al. 1960, 306; Erikson, Lancaster, and Romero 1989). Also unions devote considerable effort to stimulating voter turnout among members.

Since most interest groups do not have a large mass membership, their efforts to indoctrinate their members cannot affect the mass opinion distribution very much even if their indoctrination efforts are entirely successful. However, ordinary interest groups often spend vast amounts of money to influence the opinion of the general public. Such efforts hold the greater promise of immediate rewards to the group when the public affects policy directly via referendum. Since public opinion on an issue is largely uninformed at the time it is put to a referendum, the propaganda effort of interested interest groups can sometimes greatly influence the outcome. For example, fluoridation referenda often go down to defeat, even though most people favor fluoridated water at times when it is not a "hot" issue in their community. Largely responsible for fluoridation defeats is the fear-exploiting propaganda of the antifluoridation forces, which overcome the more "establishment-oriented" propaganda from the other side. Facing a referendum decision on fluoridation, the previously uninvolved voter may ask a friend for the pros and cons and be told that one side says fluoridation minimizes tooth decay, while the other side says it causes unanticipated medical hazards and, besides, may be the first step toward the poisoning of our water supply by the communists. Not being able to sort out the credibility of the arguments, our voter will assign them equal weight and go for the one that promises the least risk (Abelson 1968, 20-27).

The frequent and important referenda on environmental protection are also subject to effective fear-invoking propaganda, emanating from business groups that don't want stricter controls. When the issue is environmental protection, the propaganda antidote that can sometimes reverse public opinion is the exploitation of fear of losing jobs and, perhaps, fear of higher prices. A common technique of groups opposed to policies up for public referenda is to alarm the public of the uncertainty involved with the change as well as to cast suspicion on the motives of those advocating change (Magelby 1989). For the public, an important antidote to group propaganda can be simply learning which groups take which side on an issue. For instance, in a confusing California referendum on automobile insurance regulation, the insurance industry's position went down to defeat in large part because many people learned which side the insurance industry supported and treated it as a negative cue (Lupia 1992).

Organized propaganda efforts are not limited to referenda alone, since an interest group may try to rally mass opinion to influence the outcome of a legislative issue. Nationally, the past activity of the American Medical Association to reverse public support for Medicare proposals is the most visible example. Provoked by President Truman's proposal for a national health care program, the AMA launched a campaign to label it "socialized medicine." The AMA propaganda machine went to work once again in an attempt to overturn public support for President Kennedy's Medicare program, suggesting that the benefits from a private plan would be better. AMA propaganda may have been responsible for temporary but crucial stalling of public support for Medicare during the Kennedy administration. Not until 1965, following the Democratic landslide of 1964, did Medicare gain congressional passage—over the objection of the AMA once again (Jacobs 1993).

Scholarly observers generally agree that except when the public is alerted to its responsibility to vote in a referendum, interest group activity is of little consequence in the shaping of mass opinion. As V.O. Key observed:

> The broad conception of pressure groups as activators of general public opinion which in turn softens up government seldom conforms with the reality. . . . The scale of operation necessary to have substantial impact on public opinion is beyond the resources of most groups. They may reach se-

lected groups of political activists through one channel or another with considerable effect, but by and large their lone efforts to mold mass opinion must be of small consequences. (Key 1961b, 515)

The impact of interest groups on policy, which is often considerable, does not rest with successs of propaganda efforts except for the possibility of an indirect effect when policymakers mistakenly measure the success of interest-group propaganda by its volume.

Representation within Interest Groups

We have studied some of the ways in which interest groups try to influence public policy. Shortly we will evaluate the extent to which opinion within organized groups reflects public opinion. First, however, we shall examine a further aspect of the Interest Group Model. For the model to work, the positions advocated by group lobbyists must be shared by the members. This may not be an easy condition to fulfill, since the internal decision-making structures of organized groups seldom function in the manner of ideal democracies.

If the group's reason for organization is the sharing of a common ideology or common point of view on a single issue, the group's leaders should have no difficulty discerning the members' positions on those issues that were the source of the group's mobilization. One study of two women's groups with opposite positions on the Equal Rights Amendment (National Organization for Women and Women Who Want to be Women) found that the two membership groups not only held opposite views on the ERA (no surprise) but, interestingly, were also sharply divided on other issues as well. Members of the pro-ERA group were generally ideologues of the left who supported liberal causes generally, while members of the anti-ERA group tended to be ideologically committed to right-wing issue positions (Tedin et al. 1977). In general, groups that organize because they share a common political viewpoint draw heavily from ideological and issue-oriented citizens. In this way, the intensity aspect of public opinion gets represented in the political process via the group process.

Not all organized groups, however, stimulate and maintain membership because the members share commitments to common political views. Such politically active organizations as trade unions and professional associations form for nonpolitical reasons and only incidentally make forays into the political arena. Leaders of these groups have a politically diverse membership that is difficult to represent. For example, union leaders are more liberal and activist than union rank-and-file members, especially on issues peripheral to the trade union cause. An example is civil rights, on which union leaders show a strong liberal commitment that is not shared by their rank-and-file white membership. On the other hand, leaders of conservative business groups and professional groups (such as the American Medical Association) are often more *conservative* than their members.

Does Group Opinion Equal Public Opinion?

Interest group activity only satisfies the Interest Group Model if the opinion of groups corresponds to the opinion of the public. We have little direct information about the congruence of group opinion and public opinion. Perhaps the only direct evidence is from a study by Luttbeg and Wiggins (1983) from Iowa, one of the states where lobbyists must record their interests on prospective legislation. For 14 bills before the Iowa legislation, Luttbeg and Wiggins compared interest-group positions with public opinion, as surveyed by *Des Moines Register* and *Tribune* polls. In only two instances did public opinion disagree with the majority of the groups that registered a position. These data carry obvious limitations, but they do suggest that the Interest Group Models may provide some political linkage.

Admittedly, the correspondence between group opinion and public opinion from this Iowa study could be a happy accident, not generalizable beyond the particular Iowa setting. To rely fully on group opinion as a reflection of public opinion would require confidence that all points of view have equal access to the interest-group arena. This, of course, is a tall order.

If group opinion were to reflect public opinion, organized group membership should be spread evenly throughout society. In one typical poll, 62 percent of the respondents reported that they belong to at least one voluntary association such as a club, union, or business organization. But only 31 percent reported membership in an organization where political discussions take place (Verba and Nie 1972, 1976). As with other forms of political participation, people are more likely to belong to groups if they are among the most wealthy or most educated. For example, whereas most Americans in the lowest third in socioeconomic status belong to no groups, most in the upper third are active members of one or more organizations (Verba and Nie 1972, 203–04).

The Incentive to Organize

We have seen that certain people are more likely than others to join organized groups, with the most frequent joiners being among the wealthy and better educated. We can also observe that most lobbyists represent business, labor, professional, or agricultural groups— groups to which most people do not belong.[6] Many opinions clearly do not receive articulation by organized groups, while others are amply represented by group spokespersons. Is there any way then to save the Interest Groups Model as a means by which interest groups advance the preferences of *public* opinion? One might argue that people with the most intense views are at least representative of people who care the most. By this argument, if a set of unorganized individuals were to perceive a strong common interest, they would form an organized interest group. If potential groups that are not organized remain so, they are reasonably content with the way things are (Truman 1951).

The flaw in this argument is that spontaneous organization for political actions is too costly to expect the effective mobilization of a group simply because its potential members share an intense concern. To form an organization, some individuals must undertake the cost of recruiting members. More importantly, the incentive to join a dues-paying political group is limited because potential members can obtain the same benefits of the group's potential activity whether they join or not. Mancur Olson (1968) calls this the "free rider" problem. As Olson has shown, most politically powerful interest groups did not originally organize over a common political cause. Instead, key interest groups, such as labor unions, professional groups, business groups, and farm groups, developed their memberships because of common incentives to share nonpolitical benefits from organization. Only after the groups grew from offering nonpolitical services to their members did they become effective in the political arena. This argument should not be taken too far, however, as groups sometimes do organize around a momentary issue only to disappear afterward. Olson's insightful analysis suggests a further problem with the Interest Groups Model. Because politically oriented groups are difficult to organize, existing organizations tend to be defenders of the status quo.

Some observers see the problem as a difference in resources between the organized special interest group and a disorganized public. In recent years, so-called "public interest groups" (Common Cause and Ralph Nader's organizations, for example) have entered the political arena in order to restore a balance (Berry 1989). Although these groups have not mobilized the general public into a cohesive political force, they have not been without their political influence as they lobby for their versions of "the public interest." Also in recent years, there has been a proliferation of organized groups representing such causes as the advancement of women, consumers, taxpayers, and the environment. Although these groups receive financial support from only a fraction of the people they claim to represent, they are recognized as an important new force in the political arena. A model is provided by the activities of the NAACP and other civil rights groups which for years have articulated the grievances of American blacks. Although civil rights groups had been underfinanced and often ignored, their persistent activities were in large part responsible for the political advances blacks have made over the past three decades.

Conclusion

Because the positions voiced by influential organized groups do not necessarily correspond to even the most strongly held view within the general public, the actual group process seldom follows the prescription of the Interest Groups Model. If group activity were the sole input into governmental decision, it seems unlikely that decisions would follow public opinion. The problem is that the group process results in some opinions carrying more weight than others.

Although some people obtain more representation from group activity than others, observers do not all agree that interest groups operate against the public interest. A fact of political life is that some people—particularly the wealthy, educated, articulate, and already politically powerful—are in the best position to advance their political preferences. This fact is only made clearer when we examine the role of interest groups in politics. Although the Interest Groups Model may not describe reality, perhaps we should ask whether we would prefer if all interest group access to government officials could somehow be eliminated. While the "special interest" would lose access, so would the spokespersons for the general public. Rather than wish interest-group influence could be reduced, perhaps we should concentrate on ways to make the process more equitable.

Notes _____

1. Recall from the Downs model (Chapter 9) that candidates motivated solely by electoral concerns should move toward the center of the political spectrum. The same logic applies to political parties as actors. Of course neither candidates or parties will be found exactly at the center. Considerable research has focused on why candidates and parties do not converge, with much of the attention given to the preferences of the candidates and their activist supporters. Relevant literature includes Aldrich (1983), Poole and Rosenthal (1984), and Erikson, Wright, and McIver (1993).
2. On the partisan background of party activists, see Kweit (1986) and Nesbit (1988).
3. Although the image of primary elections as driven by the preferences of ideologues of the left (for Democrats) and right (Republicans) is a common one, support from survey analysis is elusive. See Norrander (1989).

4. For a good discussion of this point, see Mayhew (1974a). Congressional party leaders play an important role in converting the assortment of political demands into coherent policy. See Kiewiet and McCubbins (1991); Sinclair (1993).

5. For example, Jacobson (1989, 141) concludes: "Still, at least some [Congress] members, on some issues (those drawing little public or district attention) seem to vote in a way that reflects prior PAC contributions independent of ideology, partisanship, or local interests." Similarly, Schlozman and Tierney (1986, 255-56) conclude: "Most [studies] have uncovered statistically significant relationships of varying strength . . . between PAC receipts and rollcall votes, controlling for other relevant factors such as party, constituency characteristics, and ideology." As both Jacobson and Schlozman and Tierney also note, the available statistical evidence is divided and uneven. In his review of the evidence, Sorauf (1988, 312) states it this way: "The results have been disappointingly mixed and ambiguous. Some studies find modest relationships and an independent effect of contributions but others do not—an outcome probably the result of the different methodologies and the different groups and votes in the various projects.

6. For example, in 1981, 71 percent of all organizations represented by lobbyists in Washington were business organizations, 4 percent were labor organizations, 2 percent were agricultural organizations, and 17 percent were professional organizations (Schlozman and Tierney (1986, 62-81).

CHAPTER 12

Public Opinion and the Performance of Democracy

According to democratic theory, the health of a democracy depends on the existence of a politically informed and active citizenry. By carefully monitoring government affairs, citizens could develop informed opinions about policies that would represent their interests. By working for and voting for candidates who represent their views, and by making their views known to elected leaders, citizens could collectively translate their various policy preferences into government action. The resulting set of policies that governments would enact would represent a reasonable compromise between competing claims of equally powerful and informed citizens. This description represents the democratic ideal. In this concluding chapter we assess the degree to which American democracy approaches this democratic ideal and speculate about possible ways to achieve improvement.

12-1 Assessing the Impact of Public Opinion on Policy

We have discussed five models that have the potential to provide public policy consistent with what the public would prefer. By voting for leaders who share its views, the public can fulfill the basic needs of the Rational-Activist Model. If reliable voting cues are furnished by political parties, policy-oriented voters can fulfill the Political Parties Model by choosing the party platform most compatible with their views. Aside from voting, people can influence policymakers by bringing the preferences of the groups to which they belong to bear on officials, thus fulfilling the Interest Groups Model. In addition, linkage between opinions and policy can be furnished by two models that do not demand public coercion of leaders. If policymakers try to follow public opinion and perceive that opinion accurately, the Role-Playing Model would be fulfilled. Finally, because leaders and followers share many of the same political beliefs, even the Sharing Model provides political linkage.

By itself, each of these sources of political linkage may provide only a small increase in the degree to which officials are responsive to the public. Their total effect may, in fact, be slight, since to show that public opinion can influence policy is not a demonstration that public opinion is followed all or even most of the time. Perhaps the evidence we need is some sort of counting of the frequency with which government policies are in accord with public opinion. A truly definitive study following this design would need information at the national, state, and local levels across a broad range of policies as to whether the process of political linkage results in public policy that is consistent with public opinion. We would want to be able to say which of the linkage models proves most viable and on what issues. We would want to assess the consequences of linkage failure for the public's opinions about its government, for its participation in political affairs, and ultimately for political stability. Unfortunately such a study does not exist.

Since presently available evidence of the frequency of political linkage is limited, conclusions based on it must be very tentative—perhaps limited to only the specific issues studied, the level of government considered, and the time period involved. Moreover, congruence between majority opinion and government policy may not always be the best indicator of political linkage, since government decisions can be responses to the intense opinions of a minority rather than to the preferences of the majority. Also, as we have seen, "majority" opinion on an issue fluctuates with the exact wording of a survey question. Keeping these cautions in mind, let us see what the evidence shows about the congruence between public opinion and government policy.[1]

Evidence at the National Level

If acts of Congress were determined by the demands of public opinion, then Congress would act whenever public opinion built to majority support or higher behind a proposed program. Because polls do not regularly monitor opinions on specific proposals before Congress, we seldom know how much support the public gives to a policy before its enactment. However, polls can offer clues regarding how well Congress serves the broad policy guidelines preferred by the public.

One issue on which we can assess this consistency between opinion and policy is Medicare—which became law in 1965. As early as 1935, a presidential commission had proposed a plan for national health insurance that would have provided universal coverage. In 1945, President Truman endorsed such a plan. Twenty years later Congress passed a comprehensive health insurance plan, but only for the elderly. Why was there such a delay? One reason was that although most people favored government assistance, they were not insistent. For example, consider the results of an SRC poll in 1956 (when the health care issue was dormant) that asked people whether the government should "help people get doctors and health care at low cost" and also asked for an appraisal of government performance to date (too much, less than it should, about right, or "haven't heard yet what the government is doing"). Although opinion was more than 2 to 1 in favor of government participation, only 30 percent said government was doing less than it should. The crystallized opposition—who both opposed government participation and said the government either was doing about right or was going too far—made up only 15 percent of the sample (recomputed from Key 1961a, 269). Most people apparently did not have a coherent opinion one way or the other. Even when Medicare became a central issue in the 1960s, few were attentive. In a 1962 quiz of the public, only 57 percent of the respondents said they had heard of Medicare and had any understanding of it. In fact, only 7 percent knew the basic facts—that it would be financed by Social Security and limited to people receiving old-age insurance (Nadel 1972, 540). Only after Medicare became law in 1965 did most people become aware of its general provisions.

Perhaps if people had become politically mobilized by their views on medical care, Medicare or something even more extensive would have been enacted much sooner. As things stood, the powerful American Medical Association was able to forestall satisfaction of a feeble-voiced public. In fact, neither Medicare nor its predecessors even emerged from the House Ways and Means Committee in more than very diluted form until the 1964 Democratic landslide tipped the committee's balance in favor of such legislation (Marmor 1970; see also Jacobs 1993).

While the importance of public opinion in the enactment of Medicare remains ambiguous, we need to analyze more than a single issue. To develop a strong statistical argument that policy corresponds (or seems to follow) public opinion, we need to find a consistent pattern of congruence over many issues. One form of congruence would be a pattern of policy changes usually following the direction of majority opinion. Even stronger evidence would be both opinion and policy changing in the same direction, so that opinion change would predict a corresponding policy change.

Alan Monroe (1979) has examined opinion-policy congruence over the period from 1960 to 1974. Each usable poll question ascertained whether or not the public preferred a specific change in national policy. For each of the issues, Monroe then determined whether the specific policy change eventually took place. His basic findings are shown in Table 12.1. On the 74 issues for which the public favored the status quo, the desired outcome of no change occurred 76 percent of the time. On the 48 issues on which the public preferred change, the desired outcome of designated change occurred 59 percent of the time. Evidently, the

TABLE 12.1 Congruence between Policy Preference among the Mass Public and Policy Outcomes at the National Level

	Preference	
Outcome	Status Quo	Change
Status Quo	76%	41%
Change	24	59
	100%	100%
	(*N* = 74)	(*N* = 148)
Consistent = 64%		

Source: Alan D. Monroe, "Consistency between Public Preferences and National Policy Decisions," *American Politics Quarterly,* 7 (January 1979), p. 9. Copyright © 1979 by Sage Publications. Reprinted by permission of Sage Publications, Inc.

public is less likely to get its way when it prefers change than when it prefers the status quo. Of course, that the American political system tends to be status-quo-oriented has often been observed. That is, an intense minority (for example, opponents of gun control) can often block change. But in either case, the public's preference becomes policy more often than not. Over all cases—preferences for change and preferences for the status quo—Monroe finds policy corresponding to public opinion almost two-thirds of the time.

In a related study, Page and Shapiro (1983) examine over 300 instances of opinion *change* recorded by polls between 1935 and 1979. They find a healthy correspondence between the direction of the change in public preferences and the direction of the change in public policy. In the 231 instances where opinion and policy both changed, they changed in the same direction instead of opposite directions 66 percent of the time. Page and Shapiro do not entirely rule out the possibility of some spurious relationship: Political elites could "educate" the public to like the policies they enact for their own interest. Support for the inference that opinion causes policy is strengthened, however, by the fact that their observed policy changes almost always followed the change in opinion rather than the other way around.

Recently, scholars have been exploring long-term-over-time relationships between opinion and national policy in search of statistical evidence of opinion influencing policy. Several positive results have been reported. The clearest evidence is for defense spending, with changes in defense spending seemingly following from shifts in public perceptions of need (Bartels 1991; Hartley and Russett 1992). Spending levels for domestic purposes also appear responsive to public preferences (Wlezien 1993). Recent statistical evidence even suggests that Supreme Court decisions respond to shifts in public opinion (Mishler and Sheehan 1993).

Time-series evidence of an opinion-policy linkage at the national level can also be presented in terms of the electorate's ideological mood on the one hand and a composite of national policies on the other. As our measure of public opinion we use Stimson's "mood" indicator of public liberalism. Recall (Chapter 4) that mood represents a composite of trends over several survey questions regarding national policy. As a measure of national policy, we combine three separate measures of Senate roll-call liberalism, three similar measures of House roll-call liberalism, two roll-call-based measures of presidential liberalism and an index based on positions taken by the President's solicitor-general before the Supreme Court (Stimson et al. 1994).

Figure 12-1 overlays the scores on these two indexes from 1956 to 1990, showing a seeming connection between mood and policy. When public opinion turns more liberal or conservative (and these movements of mood are small in magnitude), the index of national policy appears to follow. Although correlation does not prove causation, it would seem that the ideological tone of national policy draws its momentum from slight shifts in ideological taste on the part of the U.S. public.

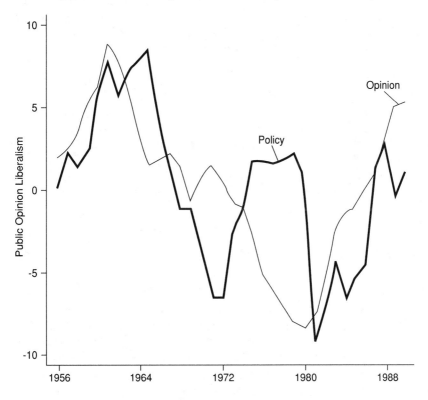

Fig. 12-1 Public Opinion and Policy Liberalism, 1956–90

Evidence at the State Level

At the state level, the opinion-policy linkage can be analyzed by seeing whether states where the public is most in favor of a given policy tend to be the states that enact that policy. Unfortunately, this kind of analysis is limited by the fact that polls rarely report reliable state-by-state breakdowns of opinion for comparison. Surprisingly, the best state-level opinion data are from polls conducted in the 1930s when national polls were based on much larger samples than today. One study examined three state-level issues for which there were available opinion data in 1936 (Erikson 1976a). On each of these issues—capital punishment, child labor regulation, and woman jurors—a strong correlation between state opinion and state policy was found. While these examples suggest an opinion-policy linkage, further analysis of this sort is hampered by the lack of available state opinion data.

For a recent analysis of state policy, Erikson, Wright and McIver (1993) pooled several CBS/*News York Times* surveys from the 1976–1988 period. Pooling of several surveys together provided over 100,000 national respondents and large samples within individual states. Their measure of state opinion is based on the ideological self-identification (liberal, moderate, conservative) of the state samples. Their measure of state policy is a composite of eight state policies with a liberal versus conservative content. They find a large correlation (+.81) between the opinion measure and the policy measure. This relationship is shown here in Figure 12-2.

Figure 12-2 shows that the ideological tendency of state public opinion and the ideological tendency of state policy almost always go together. The most liberal states enact the most liberal policies, and the most conservative states enact the most conservative policies. Although we cannot be totally secure about the causal direction, these data strongly suggest that public opinion matters when states make important policy decisions.

Evidence at the Local Level

At the local level of government we know very little about the relationship between public opinion and policy decisions. There appear to be no studies that systematically attempt to determine whether existing differences among local policy choices are related to local political opinions. One study, however, examined the relationship between political participation levels and "policy congruence" for citizens and leaders in 55 American cities. Policy congruence is a measure of the extent to which citizens and elected officials agree on what are the most important local problems. A study by Sidney Verba and Norman Nie (1972) and a further analysis of the same data by Susan Hansen (1975) reveal that the higher

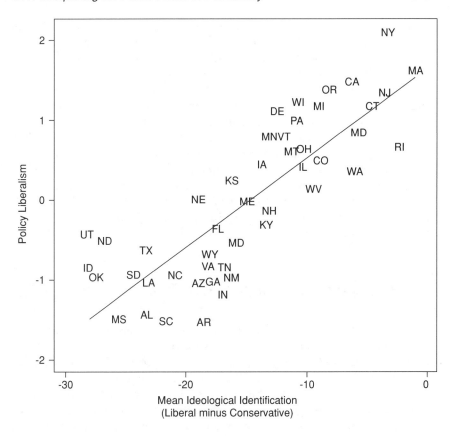

**Fig. 12-2. State Policy Liberalism and Public Opinion
Source: Erikson et al., 1993.)**

the community's level of public participation—particularly its level of voting participation—the greater the congruence between mass and elite perceptions of community problems. Of further consequence are competitive elections. Hansen finds the combination of high voting turnout and close local elections produces the greatest citizen-leader congruence scores. Contrary evidence exists, however. Luttbeg (1986b) finds in a study of 37 Texas cities that leaders were the most anxious about satisfying public opinion in cities with the *least* competitive elections.

Summary

Although the evidence is certainly incomplete, the few relevant studies that test for an opinion-policy linkage suggest that public opinion is far from inconsequential. At the national level we find that opinion and national policy are in agreement more often than not. At the state level we find that state opinion can be a good predictor of state policy. At the local level we find that high citizen participation is associated with citizen-leader agreement on important problems, although we have no data concerning solutions to those problems.

Such findings should not be surprising, because as we have seen, there are several linkages at work translating even feebly voiced public opinion into policy. This information, however, should not be cause for complacency about the current state of American democracy. Other forces besides public opinion shape government decisions. In addition, the opinions that sometimes influence policy may not be informed or, from our point of view, enlightened opinions. On the positive side, the evidence that a rather inattentive public can sometimes influence policy suggests that a more attentive public would have even greater control over policy decisions.

12-2 Interpreting the Public's Role in Democracy _____

As this book describes, the public generally does not live up to its prescribed activist role. Moreover, while public opinion can often influence government policy, in reality public opinion is not the sole determinant of policy outcomes. Why not? Public control of government decisions depends on both the extent to which people actually participate in policies and the equality of people's resources for effective participation. The first point is obvious: It seems logical that the more people participate in politics, the more they can influence government decisions. But some people can participate more effectively than others because they command a greater share of the necessary resources such as money, information, articulateness, and access to decision makers. How inequitable one views the distribution of these political resources can determine one's view of how democratic the political system actually is. Some observers see effective political power concentrated in the hands of a "power elite" who control policy outcomes for their own interests. Others more optimistically see the inequality in the distribution of power limited basically to the different political skills that individuals have and their interest in using them.[2] Because this debate over the equality of the distribution of political power is not easily decided by scientific inquiry, we shall not enter it directly here. But, taking into account that the tools of effective political participation are not equally distributed, how can we assess the less than active political role of the public? We shall discuss four different plausible conclusions.

Public Apathy as Mass Political Incompetence

Perhaps the easiest view of the public's limited role in government affairs is that people are simply incapable of doing any better. The frequency with which people fail to hold political opinions, the rarity of the liberal or conservative "ideologue," and the difficulty in locating rational policy-oriented voters may all indicate that people generally lack the skills necessary to make sophisticated judgments about their political leaders and policies. Worse yet, the political views that people do hold may be intolerant, naive, or simply wrong. Viewed from this perspective, an increase in public participation would only make the situation worse because "bad" public opinion would drive "good" policymakers toward undesirable acts.

If the mass public is viewed as being inherently incapable of playing a useful role, then the remedy of trying to "uplift" public opinion becomes ineffective. Instead, one might have to rely on the proper training or careful recruitment of political leaders as a means of producing desired outcomes. If such desired outcomes include the preservation of the substance of democracy, then one must prescribe both a limited public role and the instillation of a heavy dose of democratic values among political elites. Thomas Dye and Harmon Ziegler (1987), who arrive at this position, call it the "irony of democracy."

Public Apathy as Rational Disengagement

Possibly the reason that most people do not allow politics to intrude far into their lives is that to do so would be irrational. From a strict cost-vs.-benefit standpoint, one should not follow public affairs closely, since the investment would get one nowhere. One's vote is useless because it is fantasy to assume that one vote can decide an election's outcome except in the most extraordinary circumstances. Even when one's economic interest are directly at stake in the political arena (which may be rare), organizing like-minded people for collective political pressure is irrational because the costs of organization outweigh the possible benefits one could expect.[3] The cynic might also suggest that increased public knowledge of governmental affairs would only produce greater political withdrawal, as people who learn about their leaders' corruption and unresponsiveness will feel even more helpless at the prospect of changing things.

If this logic is correct, then people who do participate in politics usually are motivated by something other than tangible personal gains. Perhaps they "irrationally" participate in order to gratify a felt obligation or civic duty. If the major determinant of an individual's sense of obligation to participate is preadult political socialization, then a reformer might hope to increase public participation by improving the "training" of the next generation of citizens. Alternatively, one might hope to eliminate rational withdrawal from politics by somehow increasing the rewards of political participation.

Public Apathy as Elite Manipulation

One can also interpret the public's low participation in politics as the result of manipulation by leaders and their allies. When one observes political docility on the part of people who seemingly should have strong reasons for political protest, one can easily draw the conclusion that the individuals are being misled by propaganda. Whether or not one can support such an interpretation depends on one's convictions that the individuals in question are actually oppressed. A convinced Marxist, for example, can readily view the lack of class consciousness on the part of American workers as a sign of deception by the existing power structure. Similarly, a member of the John Birch Society might attribute the public's lack of concern about what he sees as a pervasive Communist conspiracy to be a sign of the effectiveness of the conspiracy.

One does not have to believe in a complex conspiracy in order to view political quiescence as the result of elite manipulation. Because most political events are remote from people's everyday lives, people willingly view these events through the interpretation of their leaders. Also, since people want to believe that their political system is benign rather than corrupt or evil, they readily find reassurance from optimistic interpretations of the existing order and resist the voices that tell them otherwise.[4]

If one sees people as unwilling to accept "truth" because they do not want to disturb their cherished beliefs, the obvious remedy would appear to be heavy doses of correct information. But how to make this remedy effective remains unclear.

Public Apathy as Public Contentment

Rather than viewing public apathy as a sign that the classical democratic model does not hold, one can interpret apathy as an indicator of public contentment. If people do not concern themselves with political matters, then they must not have any additional demands to make on their government. Conversely, when many people do participate in politics, it is a distressing signal either that government has ignored public needs or that conflicts between societal groups are no longer being successfully resolved by political leaders.[5]

Actually, the view that public apathy means public satisfaction rests on the assumption that the public is rather politically sophisticated. It assumes that people are capable of articulating any grievances they might have, that people feel that their expression of grievances would be effective, and that people are not easily led to ignore their interests. Only if these assumptions are made can one conclude that the lack of political participation indicates that people's needs are met by the proper working of a democratic system.

Although they contradict one another, each of these four possible explanations of the public's lack of political participation contains a grain of truth. For example, the public may not be capable of participation in all government decisions, particularly when the decision depends on proper evaluation of advanced technical knowledge. Equally obvious is that people can take only limited time from their personal affairs to participate in politics. Moreover, people may decide not to participate because they feel (perhaps mistakenly) that they can trust their political leaders. Finally, people may sometimes retire from the political arena because they have no particular grievances.

Simply holding them up to the light of scientific evidence cannot determine which of the explanations of low participation in politics is most valid, since individual observers will view the evidence through the filter of their own preconceptions and values. How observers view such matters as human nature, people's basic interest, and the benevolence of government can shape how strongly they conclude that political inactivity signifies incapability, rational withdrawal, manipulation, or contentment. Similarly, the extent to which observers see their own opinion in harmony with majority opinion might influence their views of whether public control of government should increase or decrease.

12-3 The Expansion of Political Participation _____

Whether increased public political participation is desirable also depends on the type of political participation. Few would applaud the increased mass participation that would result in civil war or mass mobilization in support of an antidemocratic movement. But few would fear an increase in informed, democratic participation—particularly if we ignore possible disagreement over what "informed democratic participation" means. When there is little mass participation, the burden of responsibility falls on the political elites—both to insure the continuation of the democratic rules and also to make policy decisions that are fair and equitable. But if one agrees that the purpose of democracy is to insure that political leaders are held accountable to the people, one can hardly applaud when people do not actively seek to protect their own interests. Are there any ways to increase the number of active participants while at the same time insuring that this participation will be rational and democratic?

Seemingly part of the answer would involve some way of creating a more politically informed public. Since the public can hardly be blamed for its political ignorance when it is given little information on which to make its political judgments, we can favor more thorough political reporting by the news media and the efforts of various "public interest" groups (such as Ralph Nader's organizations and Common Cause) to increase public awareness. Hopes should not be set too high, however, because information campaigns do not always reach the people who are most in need of them. Also, we must recognize the possibility of side effects produced by increased public knowledge, such as greater public cynicism or an intensification of conflict between politically aroused mass groups.

Possibly, an increase in mass political participation could be brought about by the difficult task of creating a culture or climate of opinion that encourages more participation. The place to start would be with children, whose political values and expectations are not yet formed. Since to politicize American families that are not already politically active would be difficult, the public schools would be a more plausible agent than the family for the encouragement of greater participation—perhaps, as some suggest, by instituting greater student participation in classroom decision making. But even if this would work in principle, it may be politically impossible to implement, since people generally see the proper role of schools as instilling loyalty and respect for authorities rather than permitting premature sharing of classroom authority by pupils. Of course, even more than early schooling, the college experience prepares young people for activist political roles. Thus the trend toward increasing attendance in institutions of higher education may provide some increase in public activism, although it has thus far failed to do so.

Simply changing the laws in certain ways may be the most realistic means of bringing about at least modest increases in political participation. For example, the voting rate might increase considerably if obstacles to voter registration are eliminated so that voters could register automatically rather than having to take the time and effort to do this on their own. Political influence would become more evenly distributed if laws to limit and regulate campaign contributions can effectively weaken the influence of wealthy special interest groups.

Perhaps the existing methods for translating public opinion into government policy are inaccurate relics from a technically primitive time when ballot casting, face-to-face communication, and geographic representation were the only feasible conduits for public expression. New methods might be tried to encourage greater citizen participation. Participation could be encouraged by giving people greater opportunity to participate directly in local decisions, including perhaps more participatory democracy in nongovernmental organizations such as the factory, school, or church. Also people could play a more direct role by deciding policy questions in referenda instead of letting their elected leaders decide them. Finally, it may now be technologically feasible to allow people to vote in referenda via telephonic communication from the comfort of their home.

There is no question that greater citizen participation is a desired democratic value. But it is debatable whether additional opportunities to participate would lead to wiser government decisions than elected leaders presently make. While proposals for expanding participation deserve serious consideration, their practicability and desirability remain uncertain.

Notes _____

1. Three good reviews of the relationship between public opinion and public policy are Burstein (1981), Shapiro and Jacobs (1989), and Jacobs and Shapiro (1994).
2. The most widely cited representatives of these opposing viewpoints are Mills (1956) and Dahl (1961).
3. For the development of this particular point, see Olson (1968).
4. For a provocative discussion of opinion manipulation, see Edelman (1965).
5. For an articulation of this view, see Wilson (1962).

The National Election Study and the General Social Survey Questions

Two major national surveys, designed specifically for academic analysis, are conducted on a regular basis. These are the National Election Study (NES) done by the Center for Political Studies at the University of Michigan (conducted in even number years), and the General Social Survey (GSS), done by the National Opinion Research Center at the University of Chicago (usually conducted yearly). For academic purposes, these surveys are much more valuable than surveys done by commercial polling organizations. One reason is that the interviews are done in person rather than over the phone. Another is that the questionnaires are quite lengthy, usually including hundreds of items administered over a period of more than one hour. Also, many items are repeated over time allowing for the analysis of changes.

Throughout this book, responses to opinion questions asked in either the NES or GSS opinion surveys are examined. As their content usually appears in abbreviated form, the complete wordings for the most frequently used questions in the book are presented below. Where appropriate, responses are labeled as [L] for liberal and [C] for conservative, according to how these terms are applied to the response alternative within the text.

Questions from the 1992 NES Survey _____

1. PARTY IDENTIFICATION

Two questions are used to measure party identification. First, respondents are asked:

> Generally speaking, do you usually think of yourself as a Republican, a Democrat, an Independent, or what?

This basic question provides the division between the three kinds of partisans. For the second question, partisans are probed regarding the strength of their partisanship, and Independents are probed to see whether they lean toward one of the major parties.

Republicans and Democrats are asked:

Would you call yourself a strong Republican [Democrat] or not so strong Republican [Democrat]?

Independents are asked:

Do you think of yourself as closer to the Republican Party or to the Democratic Party?

Independents who choose a party are called *Independent Leaners*. Many Independents respond that they lean toward neither party. They are often called *Pure Independents*.

The net result is a 7-point scale of partisanship.

1. Strong Democrat
2. Not so strong (or "weak") Democrat
3. Independent, leaning Democrat
4. Pure Independent
5. Independent, leaning Republican
6. Not so strong (or "weak") Republican
7. Strong Republican

Unless otherwise noted, we use the simpler three-way division: Democrats (1 and 2), Independents (3, 4, and 5), and Republicans (6 and 7).

2. LIBERAL/CONSERVATIVE IDEOLOGY

People are asked to choose an ideological position on a 7-point scale. Respondents are first asked:

We hear a lot of talk these days about liberals and conservatives. Here is a 7-point scale on which the political views that most people might hold are arranged from extremely liberal to extremely conservative.

Then they are asked:

Where would you place yourself on this scale, or haven't you thought much about it?

1. Extremely liberal
2. Liberal
3. Slightly liberal
4. Moderate, middle-of-the-road
5. Slightly conservative
6. Conservative
7. Extremely conservative
8. Don't know
9. Haven't thought much about it

Where we show the basic division between self-identified liberals and conservatives, we combine responses 1, 2, and 3 as *liberal* and 5, 6, and 7 as *conservative*.

In recent years, the NES has used the following variation of the 7-point scale for most of its issue questions. Respondents are first presented with two extreme positions on the issue. Then they are asked to place themselves with regard to the issue on a scale ranging from one to seven. Shown the scale, respondents are asked: "Where would you place yourself on this scale or haven't you thought much about it?" The scale position 1 generally represents the extreme liberal viewpoint and scale position 7 generally represents the extreme conservative viewpoint. For convenience, we often compress the scale, combining the responses 1, 2, and 3 as *liberal* responses and 5, 6, and 7 as *conservative* responses, with neutral "4" respondents and those who admit they "haven't thought much about it" combined as "non-opinion holders."

Following are the seven 7-point issue scales used by NES in 1992.

3. GOVERNMENT SERVICES/SPENDING SCALE

Some people think the government should provide fewer services, even in areas such as health and education, in order to reduce spending. . . .Other people feel it is important for the government to provide many more services even if it means an increase in spending. . . .Where would you place yourself on this scale?. . .

[C] Government should provide many fewer services; reduce spending a lot.

[L] Government should provide many more services, increase government spending a lot.

(On this one item, NES scores 1 to 7 as conservative to liberal. We reverse the polarity so that 1 represents the liberal and 7 the conservative end of the scale, consistent with other items.)

4. GOVERNMENT JOB AND STANDARD OF LIVING SCALE

Some people feel the government in Washington should see to it that every person has a job and a good standard of living. Others think the government should let each person get ahead on his own. Where would you place yourself on this scale? . . .

[L] Government see to a job and a good standard of living
[C] Government let each person get ahead on own

5. NATIONAL HEALTH INSURANCE

There is much concern about the rapid rise in medical and hospital costs. Some people feel there should be a government insurance plan that would cover all medical and hospital expenses for everyone. Others feel that all medical expenses should be paid by individuals and through private insurance plans like Blue Cross or other company paid plans. Where would you place yourself on this scale? . . .

[L] Government insurance plan
[C] Private insurance plan

6. MINORITY AID SCALE

Some people feel that the government in Washington should make every effort to improve the social and economic positions of blacks and other minority groups. Others feel that the government should not make any special effort to help minorities because they should help themselves. Where would you place yourself on this scale? . . .

[L] Government should help minority groups
[C] Minority groups should help themselves

7. DEFENSE SPENDING SCALE

Some people believe that we should spend much less for defense. Others feel that spending should be greatly increased. Where would you place yourself on this scale? . . .

[L] Greatly decrease defense spending
[C] Greatly increase defense spending

8. WOMEN'S ROLE SCALE

Recently there has been a lot of talk about women's rights. Some people feel that women should have an equal role with men in running business, industry, and government. Others feel that women's place is in the home. Where would you place yourself on this scale? . . .

[L] Women and men should have equal roles
[C] Women's place is in the home

The seven-point issue scales were used as part of the 10-item composite index of liberal-conservative policy positions, used in Chapters 3 and 9. For this composite scale, each component item is added as -1 (liberal), +1 (conservative), or 0 (other). The remaining four issues for this scale are:

9. CAPITAL PUNISHMENT

Do you favor or oppose the death penalty for persons convicted of murder?

Responses favoring the death penalty are classified as conservative; responses opposing the death penalty are classified as liberal.

[L] Oppose
[C] Favor

10. RUSSIA SCALE

Should federal spending on aid to countries of the former Soviet Union be increased, decreased, or kept the same?

[L] Increase
[C] Decrease

11. GAYS IN THE MILITARY

Do you think homosexuals should be allowed to serve in the United States Armed Forces or don't you think so?

[L] Yes, think so
[C] Don't think so

12. ABORTION

There has been some discussion about abortion during recent years. Which of the opinions on this page best agree with your view?

1. By law, abortion should never be permitted.
2. The law should permit abortion only in case of rape, incest, or when the woman's life is in danger.
3. The law should permit abortion for reasons other than rape, incest or danger to the woman's life, but only after the need for abortion has been clearly established.
4. By law, a woman should always be able to obtain an abortion as a matter of personal choice.

For purposes of ideological classification, responses 1–3 are coded as conservative, and response 4 is coded as liberal.

For five of the NES issue questions in 1992, respondents were also asked to locate the position of the major-party presidential candidates, Bush and Clinton. These questions were 2, 3, 4, 7, and 12. Respondents' relative placements of Bush and Clinton were used to create an index of political information and knowledge, used in Chapters 3, 8, and 9. To construct this scale, every correct answer (Bush to the right of Clinton) was scored as +1. Every incorrect answer (Bush to the left of Clinton) was scored as -1. Every tied response was scored as zero. These scores were summed to create a composite knowledge score ranging from -5 (all incorrect) to +5 (all correct).

The -5 to +5 composite scores were grouped into three categories of high, medium, and low. "High" scores were perfect +5s. "Low" scores were +1 or less. For the lower scorers, the mean on the original -5 to +5 was zero, or in the guess range on candidate placement. All not scored at high or low were scored as "medium" on political knowledge.

Questions from the General Social Survey _____

13. ABORTION

Please tell me whether or not you think it should be possible for a pregnant woman to obtain a legal abortion . . .

A. If there is a strong chance of a serious defect in the baby?

B. If she is married and does not want any more children?
C. If the woman's own health is seriously endangered by the pregnancy?
D. If the family has very low income and cannot afford any more children?
E. If she became pregnant as a result of a rape?
F. If she is not married and does not want to marry the man?
G. If the woman wants it for any reason?

14. POLITICAL TOLERANCE

The GSS asks tolerance questions with a variety of groups as the target. The general form of the question, using atheists as the target group, is:

There are always some people whose ideas are considered bad or dangerous by other people. For instance, somebody who is against all churches and religion. . . .

A. If such a person wanted to make a speech in your (city/town/community) against churches and religion, should he be allowed to speak or not?
B. Should such a person be allowed to teach in a college or university, or not?
C. If some people in your community suggested that a book he wrote against churches and religion should be taken out of your public library, would you favor removing this book, or not?

References

Abelson, Robert. 1968. "Computers, Polls, and Public Opinion: Some Puzzles and Paradoxes." *Trans-Action* 5 (Sept.): 20-27.

Abramowitz, Alan I. 1994. "Issue Evolution Reconsidered: Racial Attitudes and Partisanship in the U.S. Electorate." *American Journal of Political Science* 38 (Feb.): 1-25.

Abramson, Paul R. 1983. *Political Attitudes in America.* San Francisco: Freeman.

Abramson, Paul R., and Ada W. Finifter. 1981. "On the Meaning of Political Trust: New Evidence from Items Introduced in 1978." *American Journal of Political Science* 25 (May): 297-306.

Abravnel, Martin B., and Ronald J. Busch. 1975. "Political Competence, Political Trust, and the Action Orientation of University Students." *Journal of Politics* 37 (Feb.): 69-81.

Achen, Christopher. 1975. "Mass Political Attitudes and the Survey Response." *American Political Science Review* 69 (Dec.): 1218-31.

Acock, Alan, Harold D. Clarke, and Marianne C. Stewart. 1985. "A New Model for Old Measures: A Covariance Structure Analysis of Political Efficacy." *Journal of Politics* 47 (Nov.): 1062-84.

Adelson, Joseph, and Robert P. O'Neil. 1966. "Growth of Political Ideas in Adolescence: The Sense of Community." *Journal of Personality and Social Psychology* 4 (July): 295-306.

Adorno, Theodore W., et al. 1950. *The Authoritarian Personality.* New York: Harper.

Aldrich, John H. 1983. "A Downsian Spatial Model with Party Activism." *American Political Science Review* 77 (Dec.): 974-90.

Alford, John R., and David W. Brady. 1993. "Personal and Partisan Advantage in U.S. Congressional Elections." *Congress Reconsidered.* 5th ed. Ed. Lawrence C. Dodd and Bruce I. Oppenheimer. Washington, DC: Congressional Quarterly.

Alford, Robert R. 1963. *Party and Society.* Chicago: Rand.

Almond, Gabriel A. 1950. *The American People and Foreign Policy.* New York: Harcourt.

Almond, Gabriel A., and Sidney Verba. 1965. *The Civic Culture.* Boston: Little.

Altmeyer, Bob. 1981. *Right Wing Authoritarianism.* Winnipeg: U of Winnipeg P.

———. 1988. *Enemies of Freedom: Understanding Right Wing Authoritarianism.* San Francisco: Jossey-Bass.

Alwin, Duane F., Ronald L. Cohen, and Theodore M. Newcomb. 1991. *Political Attitudes Over the Life Span.* Madison, WI: U of Wisconsin P.

Andersen, Kristi. 1979. *The Creation of a Democratic Majority, 1928-1936.* Chicago: U of Chicago P.

Anderson, Lee, et al. 1990. *The Civics Report Card.* Princeton, NJ: National Assessment of Educational Progress, Educational Testing Service.

Arnold, Douglas. 1990. *The Logic of Congressional Action.* New Haven: Yale UP.

Arterton, F. Christopher. 1974. "The Impact of Watergate on Children's Attitudes Toward Authority." *Political Science Quarterly* 89 (June): 269-88.

Astin, Alexander. 1991. *The American Freshman: National Norms for Fall 1991.* Los Angeles: American Council on Education.

Backstrom, Charles H. 1977. "Congress and the Public: How Representative Is One of the Other?" *American Politics Quarterly* 5 (Oct.): 411-36.

Bagdikian, Ben H. 1972. "The Politics of American Newspapers." *Columbia Journalism Review* 10 (Mar./Apr.): 9-10.

Baloyra, Enrique A. 1979. "Criticism, Cynicism and Political Evaluation: A Venezuelan Example." *American Political Science Review* 73 (Dec.): 981-94.

Banducci, Susan A., and Jeffrey A. Karp. 1994. "Electoral Consequences of Scandal and Reapportionment in the 1992 House Elections." *American Politics Quarterly* 22 (Jan.): 3–26.

Banfield, Edward C., and James Q. Wilson. 1963. *City Politics.* New York: Vintage.

Barber, James David. 1965. *The Lawmakers.* New Haven: Yale UP.

Bartels, Larry. 1987. "Candidate Choice and the Dynamics of the Presidential Nominating Process." *American Journal of Political Science* 31 (Feb.): 1-30.

———. 1988. *Presidential Primaries and the Dynamics of Public Choice.* Princeton, NJ: Princeton UP.

———. 1991. "Constituency Opinion and Congressional Policy Making: The Reagan Buildup." *American Political Science Review* 85 (June): 457-74.

———. 1993. "Messages Received: The Political Impact of Media Exposure." *American Political Science Review* 87 (Mar.): 267-86.

Bartels, Larry, and C. Anthony Broh. 1989. "The Polls—A Review: The 1988 Presidential Primaries." *Public Opinion Quarterly* 53 (Winter): 563–8

Bechtel, Robert D. R., Clark Achelpohl, and Rogers Akers. 1972. "Correlates Between Observed and Questionnaire Responses to Television Viewing." *Television in Day-to-Day Life: Patterns of Use.* Ed. Eli A. Rubinstein, George A. Comstock, and John P. Murray. Washington, DC: GPO (HEW Publication HSM 72-9059).

Beck, Paul Allen. 1974. "A Socialization Theory of Partisan Realignment." *The Politics of Future Citizens.* Ed. Richard G. Niemi. San Francisco: Jossey-Bass.

―――. 1977. "The Role of Agents in Political Socialization." *Handbook of Political Socialization.* Ed. Stanley A. Renshon. New York: Free.

Beck, Paul Allen, and M. Kent Jennings. 1991. "Family Traditions, Political Periods, and the Development of Partisan Orientations." *Journal of Politics* 53 (Aug.): 742-63.

Behr, Roy, and Shanto Iyengar. 1985. "Television News, Real-World Cues, and Changes in the Public Agenda." *Public Opinion Quarterly* 49 (Spring): 38-57.

Benham, Thomas W. 1965. "Polling for a Presidential Candidate: Some Observations in the 1964 Campaign." *Public Opinion Quarterly* 29 (Summer): 177-78.

Bennett, W. Lance. 1980. *Public Opinion in American Politics.* New York: Harcourt.

Benson, John M. 1981. "The Polls: A Rebirth of Religion?" *Public Opinion Quarterly* 40 (Fall): 337–48.

Bereday, George Z. F., and Bonnie B. Stretch. 1963. "Political Education in the USA and USSR." *Comparative Education Review* 7 (June): 9-16.

Berelson, Bernard, Paul Lazarsfeld, and William McPhee. 1954. *Voting.* Chicago: U of Chicago P.

Berkman, Ronald L., and Laura W. Kitch. 1986. *Politics in the Media Age.* New York: McGraw.

Bernstein, Alan. 1992. "Bush's Popularity Falls in Own Houston District." *Houston Chronicle,* 25 July, Section A.

Berry, Jeffrey M. 1989. *The Interest Group Society.* 2nd. ed. Glenview, IL: Scott.

Bigman, Stanley K. 1948. "Rivals in Conformity: A Study of Two Competing Dailies." *Journalism Quarterly* 25 (Autumn): 125–31.

Bishop, George F., and Kathleen A. Frankovic. 1981. "Ideological Consensus and Constraint Among Party Leaders and Followers in the 1978 Election." *Micro-Politics* 3: 87-111.

Bishop, George F., Alfred J. Tuchfarber, and Robert W. Oldendick. 1978. "Change in the Structure of American Political Attitudes: The Nagging Question of Question Wording." *American Journal of Political Science* 22 (May): 250-69.

Bishop, George F., et al. 1980. "Pseudo-Opinions on Public Affairs." *Public Opinion Quarterly* 44 (Summer): 198-209.

Blumer, Herbert. 1948. "Public Opinion and Public Opinion Polling." *American Sociological Review* 13 (Oct.): 542-54.

Bogart, Leo. 1972. *Polls and the Awareness of Public Opinion.* 2nd ed. New Brunswick, NJ: Transaction.

Bolce, Louis, Gerald De Maio, and Douglas Muzzio. 1992. "Blacks and the Republican Party: The 20 Percent Solution." *Political Science Quarterly* 107: 63-79.

Boyer, Ernest, and Mary Jean Whitelaw. 1989. *The Condition of the Professoriate: Attitudes and Trends, 1989.* New York: Harper.

Boynton, G. R., Samuel C. Patterson, and Ronald D. Hedlund. 1969. "The Missing Links in Legislative Politics: Attentive Constituents." *Journal of Politics* 31 (Aug.): 700-21.

Bradburn, Norman, and Seymour Sudman. 1988. *Polls and Surveys.* San Francisco: Jossey-Bass.

Brady, David W. 1988. *Critical Elections and Congressional Policy Making.* Stanford, CA: Stanford UP.

Brady, Henry E., and Richard E. Johnston. 1987. "What's the Primary Message: Horserace or Issue Journalism?" *Media and Momentum: The New Hampshire Primary and Nomination Politics.* Ed. Gary R. Orren and Nelson W. Polsby. Chatham, NJ: Chatham House.

Brady, Henry E., and Gary R. Orren. 1992. "Sources of Error in Public Opinion Surveys." *Media Polls in American Politics.* Ed. Thomas E. Mann and Gary R. Orren. Washington, DC: Brookings.

Brady, Henry E., and Paul M. Sniderman. 1985. "Attitude Attribution: A Group Basis for Political Reasoning." *American Political Science Review* 79 (Dec.): 1061-78.

Brandes, Lisa. 1992. "The Gender Gap and Attitudes Toward War." Paper presented at the annual meeting of the Midwest Political Science Association, April 9-12.

Breaux, David, and Malcolm Jewell. 1992. "Winning Big: The Incumbency Advantage in State Legislative Races." *Changing Patterns in State Legislative Careers.* Ed. Gary F. Moncrief and Joel A. Thompson. Ann Arbor, MI: U of Michigan P.

Brehm, John. 1993. *The Phantom Respondents.* Ann Arbor, MI: U of Michigan P.

Brody, Richard A. 1991. *Assessing the President.* Stanford, CA: Stanford UP.

Brody, Richard A., and Catherine R. Shapiro. 1989. "Policy Failure and Public Support: The Iran-Contra Affair and Public Assessment of President Reagan." *Political Behavior* 11 (Dec.): 353-70.

Brody, Richard A., and Lee Sigelman. 1983. "Presidential Popularity and Presidential Elections: An Update and Extension." *Public Opinion Quarterly* 47 (Fall): 325-28.

Broh, C. Anthony. 1983. "Presidential Preference Polls and Network News." *Television Coverage of the 1980 Presidential Campaign.* Ed. William C. Adams. Norwood, NJ: Ablex.

Brown, Peter A. 1991. "Ms. Quota." *The New Republic* 204 (April 15): 18-19.

Browning, Robert X. 1986. *Politics and Social Welfare Policy in the United States.* Knoxville, TN: U of Tennessee P.

Bryce, James. 1900. *The American Commonwealth.* New York: Macmillan.

Buchanan, Bruce. 1991. *Electing a President.* Austin, TX: U of Texas P.

Budge, Ian, and Richard I. Hofferbert. 1990. "Mandates and Policy Outputs: U.S. Party Platforms and Federal Expenditures, 1950-1985." *American Political Science Review* 84 (Mar.): 248-61.

Bullock, Charles. 1992. "Minorities in State Legislatures." *Changing Patterns of State Legislative Careers.* Ed. Gary F. Moncrief and Joel A. Thompson. Ann Arbor, MI: U of Michigan P.

Burnham, Walter Dean. 1970. *Critical Elections and the Mainsprings of American Politics.* New York: Norton.

Burstein, Paul. 1981. "The Sociology of Democratic Politics and Government." *Annual Review of Sociology.* vol 7. Ed. Ralph H. Turner and James F. Short, Jr. Palo Alto, CA: Annual Reviews.

Caddell, Patrick. 1979. "Trapped in a Downward Spiral." *Public Opinion* (Oct./Nov.), 2-8.

Cain, Bruce, John Ferejohn, and Morris Fiorina. 1987. *The Personal Vote*. Cambridge, MA: Harvard UP.

Caldicott, Helen. 1986. *Missile Envy: The Arms Race and Nuclear War*. New York: Bantam.

Campbell, Angus. 1964. "Issues and Voters: Past and Present." *Journal of Politics* 26 (Nov.): 745-57.

Campbell, Angus, Philip E. Converse, Warren E. Miller, and Donald E. Stokes. 1960. *The American Voter*. New York: Wiley.

Campbell, Angus, Gerald Gurin, and Warren E. Miller. 1954. *The Voter Decides*. Evanston, IL: Row.

Campbell, James E. 1985. "Sources of the New Deal Realignment: The Contribution of Conversion and Mobilization to Partisan Change." *Western Political Quarterly* 38 (June): 357-76.

Cantril, Albert H. 1991. *The Opinion Connection*. Washington, DC: Brookings.

————. 1992. "A Setback for All Public Polls." *The Public Perspective* 3 (Jan./Feb.): 23-24.

Cantril, Hadley. 1951. *Public Opinion 1935-1946*. Princeton, NJ: Princeton UP.

Carmines, Edward G., John P. McIver, and James A. Stimson. 1987. "Unrealized Partisanship: A Theory of Dealignment." *Journal of Politics* 49 (June): 377-99.

Carmines, Edward G., and James A. Stimson. 1980. "The Two Faces of Issue Voting." *American Political Science Review* 74 (Jan.): 78-91.

————. 1989. *Issue Evolution: Race and the Transformation of American Politics*. Princeton, NJ: Princeton UP.

Cassel, Carol A. 1986. "The Non-Partisan Ballot in the United States." *Electoral Laws and their Consequences*. Ed. Bernard Grofman and Rend Lipjart. New York: Agathon. ————. 1993. "A Test of Converse's Theory of Party Support." *Journal of Politics* 55 (Aug.): 664-81.

Chandler, Robert. 1972. *Public Opinion*. New York: Bowker.

Childs, Harwood. 1965. *Public Opinion: Nature, Formation and Role*. Princeton, NJ: Van Nostrand.

Chong, Dennis. 1993. "How People Think, Reason and Feel about Civil Liberties." *American Journal of Political Science* 37 (Aug.): 867-99.

Cirino, Robert. 1972. *Don't Blame the People*. New York: Random/Vintage.

Citrin, Jack. 1974. "The Political Relevance of Trust in Government." *American Political Science Review* 68 (Sept.): 973–1001.

Clymer, Adam. 1993. "Opposition to Baird Grows As Senators Hear the People." *New York Times*, 22 January, Section A:3.

Combs, Michael and Susan Welch. 1982. "Blacks, Whites and Attitudes Toward Abortion." *Public Opinion Quarterly* 46 (Winter): 510-20.

Connell, Robert W. 1987. "Why the 'Political Socialization' Paradigm Failed and What Should Replace It." *International Political Science Review* 8 (July): 215-23.

Conover, Pamela, and Stanley Feldman. 1981. "The Origins and Meaning of Liberal and Conservative Self-Identifications." *American Journal of Political Science* 25 (Nov.): 617-45.

————. 1989. "Candidate Perceptions in an Ambiguous World: Campaigns, Cues, and Inference Processes." *American Journal of Political Science* 33 (Nov.): 912-41.

Converse, Jean. 1987. *Survey Research in the United States.* Berkeley, CA: U of California P.

Converse, Philip E. 1962. "Information Flow and the Stability of Partisan Attitudes." *Public Opinion Quarterly* 26 (Winter): 578-99.

———. 1964. "The Nature of Belief Systems in Mass Publics." *Ideology and Discontent.* Ed. David Apter. New York: Free.

———. 1966. "The Concept of the Normal Vote." *Elections and the Political Order.* Ed. Angus Campbell et al. New York: Wiley.

———. 1976. *The Dynamics of Party Support.* Beverly Hills, CA: Sage.

———. 1987. "Changing Conceptions of Public Opinion in the Political Process." *Public Opinion Quarterly* 51 (Spring): 12-24.

Converse, Philip E., Aage R. Clausen, and Warren E. Miller. 1965. "Electoral Myth and Reality: the 1964 Election." *American Political Science Review* 59 (June): 332-35.

Converse, Philip E., and Gregory B. Markus. 1979. "Plus ca change . . .: The New CPS Election Study Panel." *American Political Science Review* 73 (Mar.): 32-49.

Cook, Elizabeth Adell, Ted. G. Jelen, and Clyde Wilcox. 1992. *Between Two Absolutes.* Boulder, CO: Westview.

Cook, Fay Lomax, and Edith J. Barnett. 1992. *Support for the American Welfare State.* New York: Columbia UP.

Cooley, Charles H. 1922. *Human Nature and the Social Order.* New York: Scribner's.

Coombs, Steven Lane. 1981. "Editorial Endorsements and Electoral Outcomes." *More Than News: Media Power in Public Affairs.* Ed. Michael Bruce MacKuen and Steven Lane Coombs. Beverly Hills, CA: Sage.

Craig, Stephen G. 1993. *The Malevolent Leaders.* Boulder, CO: Westview.

Crain, Robert L., Elihu Katz, and Donald B. Rosenthal. 1969. *The Politics of Community Conflict: The Fluoridation Decision.* Indianapolis: Bobs.

Crespi, Irving. 1988. *Pre-Election Polling: Sources of Accuracy and Error.* New York: Russell Sage.

Dahl, Robert A. 1961. *Who Governs?* New Haven: Yale UP.

———, ed. 1966. *Political Opposition in Western Democracies.* New Haven: Yale UP: 40-41.

———. 1971. *Polyarchy.* New Haven: Yale UP.

———. 1982. *Democracy in the United States.* Chicago: Rand.

———. 1989. *Democracy and Its Critics.* New Haven: Yale UP.

Dalton, Russell. 1980. "Reassessing Parental Socialization: Indicator Unreliability versus Generational Transfer." *American Political Science Review* 74 (June): 421-38.

Davidson, Roger H. 1969. *The Role of the Congressman.* New York: Pegasus.

Davidson, Robert H., David M. Kovenock, and Michael K. O'Leary. 1968. *Congress in Crisis: Politics and Congressional Reform.* Belmont, CA: Wadsworth.

Davis, James A. 1992. "Changeable Weather in a Cooling Climate Atop the Liberal Plateau." *Public Opinion Quarterly* 56 (Fall): 261-95.

Dawson, Richard, Kenneth Prewitt, and Karen Dawson. 1977. *Political Socialization.* 2nd ed. Boston: Little.

Day, Christine L. 1990. *What Older Americans Think: Interest Groups and Aging Policy.* Princeton, NJ: Princeton UP.

Declercq, Eugene, Thomas L. Hurley, and Norman R. Luttbeg. 1975. "Voting in American Presidential Elections, 1956-1972." *American Political Quarterly* 3 (July): 222-46.

Delli Carpini, Michael X. 1986. *Stability and Change in American Politics: The Coming of Age of the Generation of the 1960s.* New York: New York UP.

Delli Carpini, Michael X., and Scott Keeter. 1992. "The Public's Knowledge of Politics." *Public Opinion, the Press, and Public Policy.* Ed. J. David Kennamer. Westport, CT: Praeger.

Delli Carpini, Michael X., and Lee Sigelman. 1986. "Do Yuppies Matter? Competing Explanations of their Political Distinctiveness." *Public Opinion Quarterly* 50 (Winter): 502-18.

Dennis, Jack, and Carol Webster. 1975. "Children's Images of the President and Government in 1962 and 1974." *American Politics Quarterly* (Oct.): 211-38.

Deutscher, Irwin. 1973. *What We Say / What We Do.* Glenview. IL.: Scott.

Dillman, Don A. 1978. *Mail and Telephone Surveys.* New York: Wiley.

Downs, Anthony. 1958. *An Economic Theory of Democracy.* New York: Harper.

Dreyer, Edward. 1971-72. "Media Use and Electoral Choices: Some Political Consequences of Information Exposure." *Public Opinion Quarterly* 35 (Winter): 544-53.

Duckitt, John. 1989. "Authoritarianism and Group Identification: A New View of an Old Construct." *Political Psychology* 10 (Feb.): 63-84.

Durr, Robert. 1993. "What Moves Policy Sentiment?" *American Political Science Review* 87 (Mar.): 158-72.

Dye, Thomas R., and Harmon Zeigler. 1987. *The Irony of Democracy.* 7th ed. Belmont, CA: Wadsworth.

Dyer, James A. 1976. "Do Lawyers Vote Differently? A Study of Voting on No-Fault Insurance." *Journal of Politics* 38 (May): 452-56.

Easton, David. 1965. *A Systems Analysis of Political Life.* New York: Wiley.

Easton, David, and Jack Dennis. 1969. *Children and the Political System.* New York: McGraw.

Eber, Ralph, and Richard Lau. 1990. "Political Cynicism Revisited: An Information Processing Reconciliation of Policy-Based and Incumbency-Based Interpretations of Changes in Trust in Government." *American Journal of Political Science* 34 (Feb.): 236-53.

Edelman, Murray. 1965. *The Symbolic Uses of Politics.* Urbana, IL: U of Illinois P.

Efron, Edith. 1971. *The News Twisters.* Los Angeles: Nash.

Elms, Alan. 1972. *Social Psychology and Social Relevance.* Boston: Little.

Engelberg, Stephan. 1993. "A New Breed of Hired Hands Cultivates Grass-Roots Anger." *New York Times,* 17 March, Section A:1, 11.

Epstein, Edward Jay. 1974. *News From Nowhere.* New York: Random.

Epstein, Leon D. 1967. *Political Parties in Western Democracies.* New York: Praeger.

Erikson, Robert. S. 1971. "The Electoral Impact of Congressional Roll Call Voting." *American Political Science Review* 65 (Dec.): 1018–32.

———. 1976a. "Is There Such a Thing as a Safe Seat?" *Polity* 8 (Summer): 613-32.

———. 1976b. "The Relationship Between Public Opinion and State Policy: A New Look at Some Forgotten Data." *American Journal of Political Science* 20 (Feb.): 25-36.

———. 1976c. "The Influence of Newspaper Endorsements in Presidential Elections: The Case of 1964." *American Journal of Political Science* 20 (May): 207-34.

———. 1978. "Constituency Opinion and Congressional Behavior: A Reexamination of the Miller-Stokes Representation Data." *American Journal of Political Science* 22: 511-35.

———. 1979. "The SRC Panel Data and Mass Attitudes." *British Journal of Political Science* 9 (Jan.): 89-114.

———. 1988. "The Puzzle of Midterm Loss." *Journal of Politics* 50 (Nov.): 1011-29.

———. 1989. "Economic Conditions and the Presidential Vote." *American Political Science Review* 83 (June): 567-73.

———. 1993. "Counting Likely Voters in Gallup's Tracking Poll." *The Public Perspective* 4 (March/April): 22-23.

Erikson, Robert S., Thomas D. Lancaster, and David W. Romero. 1989. "Group Components of the Presidential Vote, 1952-1984." *Journal of Politics* 51 (May): 337-46.

Erikson, Robert S., Norman R. Luttbeg, and William B. Holloway. 1975. "Knowing One's District: How Legislators Predict Referendum Voting." *American Journal of Political Science* 19 (May): 231-46.

Erikson, Robert S., and Kent L. Tedin. 1981. "The 1928-1936 Partisan Realignment: The Case for the Conversion Hypothesis." *American Political Science Review* 75 (Dec.): 951-62.

———. 1986. "Voter Conversion and the New Deal Realignment." *Western Political Quarterly* 39: 729-32.

Erikson, Robert S., and Gerald C. Wright. 1993. "Voters, Candidates, and Issues in Congressional Elections." *Congress Reconsidered.* 5th ed. Ed. Lawrence C. Dodd and Bruce I. Oppenheimer. Washington, DC: Congressional Quarterly, 91-114.

Erikson, Robert S., Gerald C. Wright, and John P. McIver. 1994. *Statehouse Democracy: Public Opinion and Policy in the American States.* New York: Cambridge UP.

Erskine, Hazel. 1962a. "The Polls: Race Relations." *Public Opinion Quarterly* 26 (Winter): 137-48.

———. 1962b. "The Polls: Attitudes." *Public Opinion Quarterly* 26 (Winter): 293.

———. 1962c. "The Polls: The Informed Public." *Public Opinion Quarterly* 26 (Winter): 669-77.

———. 1967. "The Polls: Negro Employment." *Public Opinion Quarterly* 31 (Fall): 132-53.

———. 1972. "The Polls: Pollution and Its Costs." *Public Opinion Quarterly* 36 (Spring): 120-35.

———. 1975. "The Polls: Health Insurance." *Public Opinion Quarterly* 39 (Spring): 128-43.

Fair, Ray C. 1988. "The Effect of Economic Events on Votes for President: A 1984 Update." *Political Behavior* 10 (Summer): 168-79.

Farrand, Max. 1961. *The Records of the Federal Convention of 1787*. Vol. 1. New Haven: Yale UP.

Feldman, Kenneth, and Theodore M. Newcomb. 1969. *The Impact of College on Students*. Vol. 2. San Francisco: Jossey-Bass.

Feldman, Stanley. 1989. "Reliability and Stability of Policy Positions: Evidence from a Five-Wave Panel." *Political Analysis* 1: 25-60.

Feldman, Stanley, and John Zaller. 1992. "The Political Culture of Ambivalence: Ideological Response to the Welfare State." *American Journal of Political Science* 36 (Feb.): 268-91.

Fenno, Richard F., Jr. 1978. *Home Style: House Members in Their Districts*. Boston: Little.

Ferree, G. Donald. 1993. "Counting Likely Voters: A Reply to Erikson." *The Public Perspective* 4 (March/April): 22-23.

Field, John O., and Ronald E. Anderson. 1969. "Ideology in the Public's Conceptualization of the 1964 Election." *Public Opinion Quarterly* 33 (Fall): 380-88.

Finkle, Steven E. 1985. "Reciprocal Effects of Participation and Political Efficacy: A Panel Analysis." *American Journal of Political Science* 29 (Nov.): 891-911.

———. 1993. "Re-examining the 'Minimal Effects' Model in Recent Presidential Campaigns." *Journal of Politics* 55 (Feb.): 1-21.

Finkle, Steven E., and James B. Rule. 1975. "Relative Deprivation and Related Psychological Theories of Civil Violence: A Critical Review." *Research in Social Movements, Conflicts and Change*. vol 9. Ed. Kurt and Gladys Lang. Greenwich, CT: JAI.

Finkle, Steven E., Edward N. Muller, and Karl-Dieter Opp. 1989. "Personal Influence, Collective Rationality, and Mass Political Action." *American Political Science Review* 83 (Sept.): 885-903.

Fiorina, Morris P. 1977. "An Outline for a Model of Party Choice." *American Journal of Political Science* 21 (Aug.): 601-25.

———. 1981. *Retrospective Voting in American National Elections*. New Haven: Yale UP.

———. 1992. *Divided Government*. New York: Macmillan.

Fischer, Claude S. 1975. "Toward a Subcultural Theory of Urbanism." *Social Forces* 53 (Mar.): 420-32.

Foote, Joe S., and Michael E. Steele. 1986. "Degrees of Conformity in Lead Stories in Early Evening Network Newscasts." *Journalism Quarterly* 63 (Spring): 19-23.

Franklin, Charles H., and John E. Jackson. 1983. "The Dynamics of Party Identification." *American Political Science Review*. 77 (Dec.): 957-73.

Franklin, Charles H., and Liane C. Kosaki. 1989. "The Republican Schoolmaster: The Supreme Court, Public Opinion and Abortion." *American Political Science Review* 83 (Sept.): 751-71.

Frankovic, Kathleen A. 1992. "The CBS News Call-In: 'Slipups in the Broadcast.'" *The Public Perspective* 3 (March/April): 19-21.

———. 1993. "Public Opinion in the 1992 Campaign." *The Election of 1992*. Ed. Gerald M. Pomper. Chatham, NJ: Chatham House.

Free, Lloyd A., and Hadley Cantril. 1968. *The Political Beliefs of Americans.* New York: Simon.

Freeman, Patricia, and William Lyons. 1992. "Female Legislators: Is There a New Type of Woman in Office?" *Changing Patterns in State Legislative Careers.* Ed. Gary F. Moncrief and Joel A. Thompson. Ann Arbor, MI: U of Michigan P.

Friesema, H. Paul, and Ronald D. Hedlund. 1981. "The Reality of Representational Roles." *Public Opinion and Public Policy.* Ed. Norman R. Luttbeg. Itasca, IL: Peacock.

Fritz, Sara, and Dwight Morris. 1992. *Handbook of Campaign Spending.* Washington, DC: Congressional Quarterly.

Gaertner, Samuel L., and John F. Dovidio. 1986. "The Aversive Form of Racism." *Prejudice, Discrimination, and Racism.* Ed. John F. Dovidio and Samuel L. Gaertner. New York: Academic.

Gallup, George, and Saul Rae. 1940. *The Pulse of Democracy.* New York: Simon.

Gamson, William. 1968. *Power and Discontent.* Homewood, IL: Dorsey.

Gans, Herbert J. 1980. *Deciding What's News.* New York: Random.

Garcia, F. Chris. 1973. *Political Socialization of Chicano Children.* New York: Praeger.

Gelman, Andrew, and Gary King. 1993. "Why Are American Presidential Polls So Variable When Votes Are So Predictable?" *British Journal of Political Science* 23 (Oct.): 409-51.

Gibson, James L. 1986. "Pluralistic Intolerance in America." *American Politics Quarterly* 14 (Oct.): 267-93.

———. 1987. "Freedom and Tolerance in the United States." (NORC: Unpublished Codebook).

———. 1988. "Political Intolerance and Political Repression During the McCarthy Red Scare." *American Political Science Review* 82 (June): 512-29.

———. 1992. "The Political Consequences of Intolerance: Cultural Conformity and Political Freedom." *American Political Science Review* 86 (June): 338–56.

Gibson, James L., and Richard D. Bingham. 1985. *Civil Liberties and the Nazis: The Skokie Free-Speech Controversy.* New York: Praeger.

Gibson, James L., and Kent L. Tedin. 1988. "The Etiology of Intolerance for Homosexual Politics." *Social Science Quarterly* 69 (Sept.): 587-604.

Ginsberg, Benjamin. 1982. *The Consequences of Consent: Elections, Citizen Control and Popular Acquiescence.* Reading, MA: Addison.

———. 1986. *The Captive Public.* New York: Basic.

Glazer, Amihai, and March Robbins. 1985. "Congressional Responsiveness to Constituency Change." *American Journal of Political Science* 29 (May): 259-73.

Goldenberg, Edie N., and Michael W. Traugott. 1984. *Campaigning for Congress.* Washington, DC: Congressional Quarterly.

Goldstein, Robert. 1978. *Political Repression in Modern America: From 1870 to the Present.* Cambridge, MA: Schenkman.

Graber, Doris A. 1980. *Mass Media and American Politics.* Washington, DC: Congressional Quarterly.

———. 1988. *Processing the News.* New York: Longman.

Greeley, Andrew. 1992. "Religion Around the World: A Preliminary Report." (Chicago: NORC).

Green, Donald Philip, and Bradley Palmquist. 1990. "Of Artifacts and Partisan Stability." *American Journal of Political Science* 34 (Aug.): 872-902.

Greenberg, Edward. 1970. "Black Children and the Political System." *Public Opinion Quarterly* 34: 335-48.

Greenstein, Fred I. 1965. *Children and Politics.* New Haven: Yale UP.

———. 1969. *Personality and Politics.* Chicago: Markham.

———. 1992. "Can Personality and Politics Be Studied Systematically?" *Political Psychology* 13 (Mar.): 105-28.

Groves, Robert, and Robert Kahn. 1979. *Surveys by Telephone.* New York: Academic.

Hahn, Harlan. 1968. "Northern Referenda on Fair Housing." *Western Political Quarterly* 21 (Sept.): 483-95.

Halberstam, David. 1979. *The Powers That Be.* New York: Knopf.

Hallin, Daniel. 1992. "Sound Bite News: Television Coverage of Elections." *Journal of Communication* 45 (Spring): 5-24.

Hamilton, Richard. 1975. *Restraining Myths: Critical Studies of U.S. Social Structure and Politics.* New York: Halsted.

Hansen, Susan Blackwell. 1975. "Participation, Political Structure, and Concurrence." *American Political Science Review* 69 (Dec.): 1181-91.

Haratwig, Frederick, and Charles Tidmarch. 1974. "Children and Political Reality: Changing Images of the President." Paper presented at the 1974 annual meeting of the Southern Political Science Association.

Hartley, Thomas, and Bruce Russett. 1992. "Public Opinion and the Common Defense: Who Governs Military Spending in the United States?" *American Political Science Review* 86 (Dec.): 905-15.

Harvey, G. Ted. 1972. "Computer Simulation of Peer Group Influence on Adolescent Political Behavior." *American Journal of Political Science* 16 (Nov.): 588-621.

Harvey, O. J., and G. Beverly. 1961. "Some Personality Correlates of Concept Change Through Role Playing." *Journal of Abnormal and Social Psychology* 27 (Mar.): 125-30.

Hawkins, Robert P., Suzanne Pingree, and Donald Roberts. 1975. "Watergate and Political Socialization." *American Politics Quarterly* 4 (Oct.): 406-36.

Hedlund, Ronald D. 1975. "Perceptions of Decisional Referents in Legislative Decision-Making." *American Journal of Political Science* 19 (Aug.): 527-42.

Hedlund, Ronald D., and H. Paul Friesema. 1972. "Representatives' Perceptions of Constituency Opinion." *Journal of Politics* 34 (Aug.): 167-76.

Herbst, Susan. 1993. *Numbered Voices: How Public Opinion Has Shaped American Politics.* Chicago: U of Chicago P.

Hero, Alfred O. n.d. "Public Reactions to Federal Policy: Some Comparative Trends." Unpublished paper.

Herrera, Richard. 1992. "The Understanding of Ideological Labels by Political Elites: A Research Note." *Western Political Quarterly* 45 (Dec.): 1021-35.

Hershey, Marjorie Randon. 1989. "The Campaign and the Media." *The Election of 1988: Reports and Interpretations.* Ed. Gerald M. Pomper. Chatham, NJ: Chatham House.

Hershey, Marjorie Randon, and David B. Hill. 1975. "Watergate and Preadults' Attitudes Toward the President." *American Journal of Political Science* 19 (Nov.): 703-26.

Herson, Lawrence J.R., and C. Richard Hofstetter. 1975. "Tolerance, Consensus and the Democratic Creed." *Journal of Politics* 37 (Dec.): 1007-32.

Hertsgaard, Mark. 1988. *On Bended Knee: The Press and the Reagan Presidency.* New York: Farrar.

Herzon, Fred. 1972. "A Review of Acquiescence Response Set in the California F-Scale." *Social Science Quarterly* 53 (June): 62-78.

Hess, Robert D., and Judith V. Torney. 1967. *The Development of Political Attitudes in Children.* Chicago: Aldine.

Hibbs, Douglas A., Jr. 1987. *The American Political Economy: Macroeconomics and Electoral Politics in the United States.* Cambridge, MA: Harvard UP.

Hibbs, Douglas A., Jr., and Christopher Dennis. 1988. "Income Distribution in the United States." *American Political Science Review* 82 (June): 467-90.

Hitchens, William A. 1992. "Voting in the Passive Voice." *Harper's* 284 (April): 45-52.

Hofstetter, Richard. 1976. *Bias in the News.* Columbus, OH: Ohio State UP.

Hooper, Michael. 1969. "Party and Endorsement as Predictors of Voter Choice." *Journalism Quarterly* 43 (Summer): 302-05.

Hugick, Larry, and Guy Molyneux. 1993. "The Performance of the Gallup Tracking Poll: The Myth and the Reality." *The Public Perspective* 4 (Jan./Feb.): 12-14.

Hurley, Patricia A. 1989. "Parties and Coalitions in Congress." *Congressional Politics.* Ed. Christopher Deering. Chicago: Dorsey.

Hurley, Patricia A., and Kim Quaille Hill. 1981. "The Prospects for Issue Voting in Contemporary Congressional Elections: An Assessment of Citizen Awareness and Representation." *Public Opinion and Public Policy.* 3rd ed. Ed. Norman R. Luttbeg. Itasca, IL: Peacock.

Hurwitz, Jon, and Mark Peffley. 1987. "How Are Foreign Policy Attitudes Structured? A Hierarchical Model." *American Political Science Review* 81 (Dec.): 1099-1120.

Hurwitz, Jon, Mark Peffley, and Paul Raymond. 1989. "Presidential Support During the Iran-Contra Affair." *American Public Opinion* 17 (Oct.): 359-85.

Hyman, Herbert. 1959. *Political Socialization.* Glencoe, IL: Free.

Inkeles, Alex. 1961. "National Character and the Modern Political System." *Psychological Anthropology: Approaches to Culture and Personality.* Ed. Francis L. K. Hsu. Homewood, IL: Dorsey.

Iyengar, Shanto. 1993. *Is Anyone Responsible? How Television Frames Political News.* Chicago: U of Chicago P.

Iyengar, Shanto, and Donald R. Kinder. 1987. *News That Matters.* Chicago: U of Chicago P.

Iyengar, Shanto, Mark. D. Peters and Donald R. Kinder. 1982. "Experimental Demonstrations of 'Not-So-Minimal' Consequences of Television News Programs." *American Political Science Review* 76 (Dec.): 848-58.

Jackman, Mary. 1978. "General and Applied Tolerance: Does Education Increase Commitment to Racial Integration?" *American Journal of Political Science* 22 (May): 302-24.

Jackman, Mary R., and Robert W. Jackman. 1983. *Class Awareness in the United States.* Berkeley: U of California P.

Jackman, Mary, and Michael J. Mulha. 1984. "Education and Intergroup Attitudes: Moral Enlightenment, Superficial Democratic Commitment or Ideological Refinement." *American Sociological Review* 49 (Aug): 751-69.

Jackman, Robert W. 1972. "Political Elites, Mass Publics, and Support for Democratic Principles." *Journal of Politics* 54 (Aug.): 753-73.

Jacob, Philip E. 1956. *Changing Values in College.* New Haven: Hazen Foundation.

Jacobs, Lawrence R. 1993. *The Health of Nations: Public Opinions in the Making of American and British Health Policy.* Ithaca, NY: Cornell UP.

Jacobs, Lawrence R., and Robert Y. Shapiro. 1993. "Polling and Opinion on Health Care Reform." *The Public Perspective* 4 (May/June): 22-27.

———. 1994. "Studying Substantive Democracy." *PS: Political Science and Politics* 27 (Mar.): 9-17.

Jacobson, Gary C. 1987. *The Politics of Congressional Elections.* 2nd ed. Boston: Little.

Jacobson, Gary C. 1989. "Parties and PACs in Congressional Elections." *Congress Reconsidered.* 4th ed. Ed. Lawrence C. Dodd and Bruce I. Oppenheimer. Washington, DC: Congressional Quarterly.

Jacoby, William G. 1988a. "The Impact of Party Identification on Issue Attitudes." *American Journal of Political Science* 32: 643-61.

———. 1988b. "The Sources of Liberal-Conservative Thinking: Education and Conceptualization." *Political Behavior* 10 (Winter): 316-32.

———. 1991. "Ideological Identifications and Issue Attitudes." *American Journal of Political Science* 35 (Feb.): 178-205.

Jamieson, Kathleen Hall. 1992. *Dirty Politics.* New York: Oxford UP.

Jaros, Dean, Herbert Hirsch, and Frederick Fleron. 1968. "The Malevolent Leader: Political Socialization in an American Sub-Culture." *American Political Science Review* 62 (June): 564-75.

Jelen, Ted G. 1992. "Political Christianity: A Contextual Analysis." *American Journal of Political Science* 36 (Aug.): 662-92.

Jelen, Ted G. 1993. "The Political Consequences of Religious Group Attitudes." *Journal of Politics* 55 (Feb.): 167-77.

Jennings, M. Kent. 1987. "Residuals of a Movement: The Aging of the American Protest Generation." *American Political Science Review* 81 (June): 365-81.

Jennings, M. Kent. 1992. "Ideological Thinking Among Mass Publics and Political Elites." *Public Opinion Quarterly* 56 (Winter): 419-41.

Jennings, M. Kent, Lee H. Ehrman, and Richard G. Niemi. 1974. "Social Studies Teachers and Their Students." *The Political Character of Adolescence.* Ed. M. Kent Jennings and Richard G. Niemi. Princeton, NJ: Princeton UP.

Jennings, M. Kent, and Gregory B. Markus. 1984. "Partisan Orientations Over the Long Haul: Results from the Three-Wave Political Socialization Panel Study." *American Political Science Review* 78 (Dec.): 1000-18.

Jennings, M. Kent, and Richard G. Niemi. 1974. *The Political Character of Adolescence.* Princeton, NJ: Princeton UP.

———. 1982. *Generations and Politics*. Princeton, NJ: Princeton UP.

Jensen, Richard. 1968. "American Election Analysis: A Case of History and Methodological Innovation and Diffusion." *Politics and Social Science*. Ed. Seymour Martin Lipset. New York: Oxford UP.

Jewell, Malcolm E., and David Breaux. 1988. "The Effect of Incumbency on State Legislative Elections." *Legislative Studies Quarterly* 13 (Nov.): 495-514.

Jewell, Malcolm E., and Samuel Patterson. 1981. *The Legislative Process in the United States*. 7th ed. New York: Random.

Johannes, John R., and John P. McAdams. 1981. "The Congressional Incumbency Effect: Is It Casework, Policy Compatibility, or Something Else? An Examination of the 1978 Election." *American Journal of Political Science* 25 (Aug.): 512-52.

Johnstone, John, Edward Slawski, and William Bowman. 1976. *The Newspeople*. Urbana, IL: U of Illinois P.

Joslyn, Richard. 1984. *Mass Media and Elections*. Reading, MA: Addison.

Jowell, Roger, Barry Hedges, Peter Lynn, Graham Farrant, and Anthony Heath. 1993. "The 1992 British Election: The Failure of the Polls." *Public Opinion Quarterly* 57 (Summer): 238-63.

Kagay, Michael R., and Greg A. Caldiera. 1980. "A Reformed Electorate? Well, At Least a Changed Electorate." *Paths to Political Reform*. Ed. William J. Crotty. New York: Heath.

Karnig, Albert K., and B. Oliver Walter. 1977. "Municipal Elections Registration, Incumbent Success and Voter Participation." *The Municipal Yearbook 1977*. Washington, DC: International City Management Association: 65-72.

Katosh, John, and Michael Traugott. 1981. "The Consequences of Validated and Self-Reported Voting Measures." *Public Opinion Quarterly* 45 (Winter): 519-35.

Keene, Karlyn H. 1991. "Feminism Vs. Women's Rights." *The Public Perspective* 3 (Nov./Dec.): 3-4.

Kelley, Stanley J., Jr. 1983. *Interpreting Elections*. Princeton, NJ: Princeton UP.

Kelly, Michael. 1993. "A Left Turn by Clinton? Centrists Feel Left Out." *New York Times,* 23 May, Section A.

Kenski, Henry. 1988. "The Gender Factor in a Changing Electorate." *The Politics of the Gender Gap*. Ed. Carol M. Mueller. Beverly Hills, CA: Sage.

Kerlinger, Fred N. 1984. *Liberalism and Conservatism*. Hillsdale, MI: Earlbaum.

Kernell, Samuel. 1978. "Explaining Presidential Popularity." *American Political Science Review* 72 (June): 506-23.

Kesler, Charles. 1979. "The Movement of Student Opinion." *National Review* 23 (Nov.): 1448.

Key, V.O., Jr. 1949. *Southern Politics in State and Nation*. New York: Knopf.

———. 1961a. "Public Opinion and the Decay of Democracy." *Virginia Quarterly Review* 37(Autumn): 488-512.

———. 1961b. *Public Opinion and American Democracy*. New York: Knopf.

Kiecolt, K. Jill, and Laura E. Nathan. 1985. *Secondary Analysis of Survey Data*. Beverly Hills, CA: Sage.

Kiewiet, D. Roderick. 1983. *Macroeconomics and Micropolitics.* Chicago: U of Chicago P.

Kiewiet, D. Roderick, and Matthew D. McCubbins. 1985. "Congressional Appropriations and the Electoral Connection." *Journal of Politics* 47 (Spring): 59-82.

———. 1991. *Congressional Parties and the Appropriations Process.* Chicago: U of Chicago P.

Kinder, Donald. 1986. "The Continuing American Dilemma: White Resistance to Racial Change 40 Years After Myrdahl." *Journal of Social Issues* 42 (Mar.): 151-72.

Kinder, Donald R., Gordon S. Adams, and Paul W. Gronke. 1989. "Economics and Politics in the 1984 American Presidential Elections." *American Journal of Political Science* 33 (May): 491-515.

Kinder, Donald R., and Don Herzog. 1993. "Democratic Discussion." *Reconsidering the Democratic Public.* Ed. George E. Marcus and Russell L. Hanson. University Park, PA: Pennsylvania State UP.

Kinder, Donald R., and D. Roderick Kiewiet. 1979. "Economic Grievances and Political Behavior: The Role of Personal Discontents and Collective Judgments in Congressional Voting." *American Journal of Political Science* 23 (Aug.): 495-527.

———. 1981. "Sociotropic Politics." *British Journal of Political Science* 11 (Apr.): 129-61.

Kingdon, John W. 1973. *Congressmen's Voting Decisions.* New York: Harper.

Kirkpatrick, Jean. 1975. "Representative in the American National Conventions: The Case of 1972." *British Journal of Political Science* 5 (July): 262-322.

Kirkpatrick, Samuel A., William Lyons, and Michael R. Fitzgerald. 1975. "Candidates, Parties, and Issues in the American Electorate: Two Decades of Change." *American Politics Quarterly* 3 (July): 247-83.

Kirscht, John P., and Ronald C. Dillehay. 1967. *Dimensions of Authoritarianism: A Review of Research and Theory.* Lexington, KY: U of Kentucky P.

Knight, Kathleen. n.d. "Liberalism and Conservatism." *Measures of Political Attitudes.* Ed. John P. Robinson, Philip Shaver, and Lawrence Wrightsman. New York: Academic. Forthcoming.

———. 1985. "Ideology in the 1980 Election: Political Sophistication Matters." *Journal of Politics* 47 (Aug.): 828-53.

Knight, Kathleen, and Carolyn Lewis. 1992. "Ideology and the American Electorate." *Perspectives on American and Texas Politics.* Ed. Kent L. Tedin, Donald S. Lutz, and Edward P. Fuchs. Dubuque, IA: Kendall-Hunt.

Knoke, David, and Michael Hout. 1974. "Social and Demographic Factors in American Political Party Affiliations, 1952-1972." *American Sociological Review* 39 (Aug.): 700-13.

Kolbert, Elizabeth. 1993. "Did the Voting Experts Go Wrong?" *New York Times,* 4 November, Section A.

Kolson, Kenneth L., and Justin J. Green. 1970. "Response Set Bias and Political Socialization Research." *Social Science Quarterly* 51: 527-538.

Kornhauser, William. 1970. *The Politics of Mass Society.* Chicago: Markham.

Krosnick, Jon A., and Matthew K. Kerent. 1993. "Comparisons of Party Identification and Policy Preferences: The Impact of Survey Question Format." *American Journal of Political Science* 37 (Aug.): 941-64.

Krosnick, Jon A., and Donald Kinder. 1990. "Altering the Foundations of Support for the President through Priming." *American Political Science Review* 84 (June): 497-512.

Kuklinski, James H. 1978. "Representatives and Elections: A Policy Analysis." *American Political Science Review* 72 (Mar.): 165-77.

Kuklinski, James H., and Richard C. Elling. 1977. "Representational Role, Constituency Opinion, and Legislative Roll Call Behavior." *American Journal of Political Science* 21 (Feb.): 135-44.

Kuklinski, James H., and Donald J. McCrone. 1981. "Electoral Accountability as a Source of Policy Representation." *Public Opinion and Public Policy*. Ed. Norman R. Luttbeg. Itasca, IL: Peacock.

Kuklinski, James H., Ellen Riggle, Victor Ottati, Norbert Schwartz, and Robert S. Wyer. 1991. "The Cognitive and Affective Basis of Political Tolerance Judgments." *American Journal of Political Science* 35 (Feb.): 1-27.

Kweit, Mary Grisez. 1986. "Ideological Congruence of Party Switchers and Nonswitchers: The Case of Party Activists." *American Journal of Political Science* 30 (Feb.): 184-96.

Ladd, Everett Carll. 1970. *American Political Parties: Social Change and Political Response*. New York: Norton.

———. 1981. "205 and Going Strong." *Public Opinion* (June/July): 7-12.

———. 1989. *The American Polity*. 3rd ed. New York: Norton.

———. 1992. "The Trials of Election Polling." *The Public Perspective* 3 (May/June): 3–11.

———. 1993. *The American Polity*. 5th ed. New York: Norton.

Ladd, Everett Carll, and John Benson. 1992. "The Growth of News Polls in American Politics." *Media Polls in American Politics*. Ed. Thomas E. Mann and Gary R. Orren. Washington, DC: Brookings.

Ladd, Everett Carll, and G. Donald Ferree. 1981. "Were the Pollsters Really Wrong?" *Public Opinion* (Dec./Jan.): 13.

Lane, Robert. 1962. *Political Ideology*. New York: Free.

Langton, Kenneth P., and M. Kent Jennings. 1968. "Political Socialization and the High School Civics Curriculum in the United States." *American Political Science Review* 62 (Sept.): 852-77.

Lasswell, Harold D. 1951. "Democratic Character." *The Political Writings of Harold D. Lasswell*. Glencoe, IL: Free.

Lau, Richard. 1985. "Two Explanations for Negative Effects in Political Behavior." *American Journal of Political Science* 29 (Feb.): 119-38.

Lavrakas, Paul J. 1987. *Telephone Survey Methods*. Beverly Hills, CA: Sage.

LeBlanc, Hugh L. 1969. "Voting in State Senates: Party and Constituency Influences." *Midwest Journal of Political Science* 13 (Feb.): 33-57.

Leege, David C., and Michael R. Welch. 1989. "Religious Roots of Political Orientations: Variations Among Catholic Parishioners." *Journal of Politics* 51 (Feb.): 137-64.

———. 1991. "Dual Reference Groups and Political Orientations: An

Examination of Evangelically Oriented Catholics." *American Journal of Political Science* 35 (Feb.): 28-56.

Levit, Katherine R., et al. 1990. "National Health Care Spending Trends: 1988." *Health Affairs* (Spring): 166-75.

Lewis, I. A. 1990. "Poll Wars and Poll Debacle in Nicaragua." *The Public Perspective* 1: 6.

Lewis-Beck, Michael, and Tom Rice. 1982. "Presidential Popularity and the Presidential Vote." *Public Opinion Quarterly* 47 (Winter): 534-37.

Lichter, S. Robert, and Stanley Rothman. 1979 "Media and Business Elites." *Public Opinion* 4 (Oct./Nov.): 42-46, 59-60.

Light, Paul C. 1988. *Baby Boomers.* New York: Norton.

Light, Paul C., and Celinda Lake. 1985. "The Election: Candidates Strategies, and Decision." *The Elections of 1984.* Ed. Michael Nelson. Washington, DC: Congressional Quarterly.

Lippmann, Walter. 1922. *Public Opinion.* New York: Harcourt.

———. 1925. *The Phantom Public.* New York: Harcourt.

Lipset, Seymour Martin. 1950. *Agrarian Socialism.* Berkeley, CA: U of California P.

———. 1959. "Some Social Requisites of Modern Democracy: Economic Development and Political Legitimacy." *American Political Science Review* 53 (Mar.): 69-105.

———. 1960. *Political Man.* Garden City, NY: Doubleday.

———. 1992. "Polls Don't Lie. People Do." *New York Times*, 10 September, Section A.

Lodge, Milton, Kathleen McGraw, and Patrick Stroh. 1989. "An Impression-Driven Model of Candidate Evaluation." *American Political Science Review* 83 (June): 399-419.

Lodge, Milton, and Patrick Stroh. 1993. "Inside the Mental Voting Booth: An Impression-Driven Process." *Explorations in Political Psychology.* Ed. Shanto Iyengar and William J. McGuire. Durham, NC: Duke UP.

Luker, Kristin. 1984. *Abortion and the Politics of Motherhood.* Berkeley, CA: U of California P.

Lupia, Arthur. 1992. "Busy Voters, Agenda Control, and the Power of Information." *American Political Science Review* 86 (June): 390-403.

Luskin, Robert C. 1987. "Measuring Political Sophistication." *American Journal of Political Science* 31 (Nov.): 856-99.

Luskin, Robert C., John P. McIver, and Edward G. Carmines. 1989. "Issues and the Transmission of Partisanships." *American Journal of Political Science* 33 (May): 440-58.

Luttbeg, Norman R. 1968. "Political Linkage in a Large Society." *Public Opinion and Public Policy.* Ed. Norman Luttbeg. Homewood, IL: Dorsey.

———. 1983. "News Consensus: Do U.S. Newspapers Mirror Society's Happenings?" *Journalism Quarterly* 60 (Autumn): 484-88.

———. 1986. "The Attitudinal Impact of Community and Personal Electoral Competition." Paper presented at the annual meeting of the Southern Political Science Association.

Luttbeg, Norman R., and Michael Gant. 1985. "The Failure of Liberal-

Conservative Ideology as a Cognitive Structure." *Public Opinion Quarterly* 49 (Spring): 80-93.

Luttbeg, Norman R., and Charles W. Wiggins. 1983. "Public Opinion Versus Interest Group Opinion: The Case of Iowa." *Public Opinion and Public Policy.* 3rd ed. Ed. Norman R. Luttbeg. Itasca, IL: Peacock.

Luttbeg, Norman R., and Harmon Zeigler. 1966. "Attitude Consensus and Conflict Within an Interest Group: An Assessment of Cohesion." *American Political Science Review* 60 (Sept.): 655-65.

Lyons, William, and John M. Scheb. 1992. "Ideology and Candidate Evaluation in the 1984 and 1988 Presidential Elections." *Journal of Politics* 54 (May): 573-86.

MacDougall, Curtis D. 1966. *Understanding Public Opinion.* Boston: Little.

MacKuen, Michael Bruce. 1981. "Social Communication and the Mass Policy Agenda." *More Than News: Media Power in Public Affairs.* Ed. Michael Bruce MacKuen and Steven Coombs. Beverly Hills, CA: Sage.

———. 1984. "Exposure to Information, Belief Integration, and Individual Responsiveness to Agenda Change." *American Political Science Review* 78 (June): 372-91.

MacKuen, Michael B., Robert S. Erikson, and James A. Stimson. 1989. "Macropartisanship." *American Political Science Review* 83 (Dec.): 1125-1142.

———. 1992. "Peasants or Bankers: The American Electorate and the U.S. Economy." *American Political Science Review* 86 (Sept.): 597-611.

Magleby, David B. 1989. "Opinion Formation and Partisan Change in Ballot Proposition Campaigns." *Manipulating Public Opinion.* Ed. Michael Margolis and Gary A. Mauser. Pacific Grove, CA: Brooks/Cole.

Margolis, Michael. 1977. "From Confusion to Confusion: Issues and the American Voter (1956-1972)." *American Political Science Review* 71 (Mar.): 31-43.

Markus, Gregory B. 1979. "The Political Environment and the Dynamics of Public Attitudes." *American Journal of Political Science* 23 (May): 338-59.

———. 1982. "Political Attitudes in an Election Year: A Report on the 1980 NES Panel Study." *American Political Science Review* 76 (Sept.): 538-60.

———. 1988. "The Impact of Personal and National Economic Conditions on the Presidential Vote: A Pooled Cross-Sectional Analysis." *American Journal of Political Science* 32 (Feb.): 137-54.

Markus, Gregory B., and Philip E. Converse. 1979. "A Dynamic Simultaneous Equation Model of Public Choice." *American Political Science Review* 73 (Dec.): 1055-70.

Massialas, Byron. 1969. *Education and the Political System.* Reading, MA: Addison.

Mayer, William G. 1992. *The Changing American Mind.* Ann Arbor, MI: U of Michigan P.

Mayhew, David R. 1974. *Congress: The Electoral Connection.* New Haven: Yale UP.

McAneny, Leslie, and Lydia Saad. 1992. "Post Convention 'Bounce': Clinton's Highest in Gallup Records." The Gallup Report 323 (August): 25.

McClosky, Herbert, and Alida Brill. 1983. *Dimensions of Political Tolerance.* New York: Russell Sage.

McClosky, Herbert, Paul J. Hoffman, and Rosemary O'Hara. 1960. "Issue Conflict and Consensus Among Party Leaders and Followers." *American Political Science Review* 59 (June): 406-27.

McCombs, Maxwell E. 1981. "The Agenda-Setting Approach." *Handbook of Political Communication*. Ed. Dan D. Nimmo and Keith R. Sanders. Beverly Hills, CA: Sage.

McCombs, Maxwell E., and Donald L. Shaw. 1972. "The Agenda-Setting Function of the Mass Media." *Public Opinion Quarterly* 35 (Summer): 176-87.

McFarland, Sam G., Vladimir S. Ageyev, and Marina A. Abalakina. 1992. "Authoritarianism in the Former Soviet Union." *Journal of Personality and Social Psychology* 63 (Dec.): 1003-10.

Meloen, J.D., L. Hagendorn, Q. Raaijmakers, and L. Visser. 1988. "Authoritarianism and the Revival of Political Racism: Reassessments in the Netherlands of the Reliability and Validity of the Concept of Authoritarianism by Adorno et al." *Political Psychology* 9 (Sept.): 412–44.

Merelman, Richard. 1971. *Political Socialization and Educational Climates*. New York: Holt.

———. 1972. "The Adolescence of Political Socialization." *Sociology of Education* 45 (Spring): 128-42.

———. 1980. "Democratic Politics and the Culture of American Education." *American Political Science Review* 74 (June): 319-33.

———. 1986. "Revitalizing Political Socialization." *Political Psychology*. Ed. Margaret G. Hermann. San Francisco: Jossey-Bass.

Milbrath, Lester W. 1963. *The Washington Lobbyists*. Chicago: Rand.

Milbrath, Lester W., and M. L. Goel. 1977. *Political Participation*. 2nd ed. Chicago: Rand.

Miedaian, Myriam. 1991. *Boys Will Be Boys: Breaking the Link Between Masculinity and Violence*. New York: Doubleday.

Milgram, Stanley. 1969. *Obedience to Authority*. New York: Harper.

Miller, Arthur H. 1974. "Political Issues and Trust in Government: 1960-1970." *American Political Science Review* 68 (Sept.): 944-61.

———. 1983. "Is Confidence Rebounding?" *Public Opinion* (June/July): 16-21.

———. 1988. "Gender and the Vote: 1984." *The Politics of the Gender Gap: The Social Construction of Political Influence*. Ed. Carol M. Mueller. Beverly Hills, CA: Sage.

Miller, Arthur H., and Stephen A. Borrelli. 1991. "Confidence in Government in the 1980s." *American Politics Quarterly* 19 (Apr.): 147-75.

Miller, Arthur H., Warren E. Miller, Alden S. Raine, and Thad A. Browne. 1976. "A Majority Party in Disarray: Policy Polarization in the 1972 Election." *American Political Science Review* 70 (Sept.): 753-78.

Miller, Arthur H., and Martin P. Wattenberg. 1984. "Politics from the Pulpit: Religiosity and the 1980 Election." *Public Opinion Quarterly* 48 (Spring): 301-11.

Miller, Arthur H., Martin P. Wattenberg, and Oksana Malanchuk. 1986. "Schematic Assessment of Presidential Candidates." *American Political Science Review* 80 (June): 522-40.

Miller, Arthur H., Christopher Wlezien, and Ann Hildreth. 1991. "A Reference Group Theory of Party Coalitions." *Journal of Politics* 53 (Nov.): 1134-49.

Miller, Warren E., and M. Kent Jennings. 1987. *Parties in Transition: A Longitudinal Study of Party Elites and Party Supporters.* New York: Russell Sage.

Miller, Warren E., and Donald W. Stokes. 1963. "Constituency Influence in Congress." *American Political Science Review* 57 (Mar.): 45-46.

Mills, C. Wright. 1956. *The Power Elite.* New York: Oxford UP.

Mishler, William, and Reginald S. Sheehan. 1993. "The Supreme Court as a Countermajoritarian Institution? The Impact of Public Opinion on Supreme Court Decisions." *American Political Science Review* 87 (Mar.): 87-101.

Monroe, Alan D. 1979. "Consistency Between Public Preferences and National Policy Decisions." *American Politics Quarterly* 7 (Jan.): 3-21.

Montaigne, Michel de. 1967. *The Complete Works of Montaigne.* Stanford, CA: Stanford UP.

Moore, David W. 1992a. "The Sure Thing That Got Away." *New York Times*, 25 October, Section A.

———. 1992b. *The SuperPollsters.* New York: Four Walls, Eight Windows.

Moore, Stanley W., James Lare, and Kenneth A. Wagner. 1985. *The Child's Political World.* New York: Praeger.

Morin, Richard. 1991. "The Outcome Is There in Black and White." *Washington Post,* weekly ed., 25 February-3 March: 37.

———. 1992. "Surviving the Ups and Downs of Election '92." *Washington Post,* weekly ed., 9-15 November: 37.

Mueller, John E. 1970. "President Popularity from Truman to Johnson." *American Political Science Review* 64 (Jan.): 22-41.

———. 1973. *War, Presidents and Public Opinion.* New York: Wiley.

Nadel, Mark V. 1972. "Public Policy and Public Opinion." *American Democracy: Theory and Reality.* Ed. Robert Weissberg and Mark V. Nadel. New York: Wiley.

Nesbit, Dorothy Davidson. 1988. "Partisan Changes Among Southern Activists." *Journal of Politics* 50 (May): 322-34.

Neubauer, Dean E. 1967. "Some Conditions of Democracy." *American Political Science Review* 61 (Dec.): 1002-09.

Neuman, W. Russell, R. Just, and Ann N. Crigler. 1991. *Common Knowledge: News and the Construction of Political Meaning.* Chicago: U of Chicago P.

Nice, David C. 1992. "The States and the Death Penalty." *Western Political Quarterly* 45 (Nov.): 1037-48.

Nie, Norman, and Kristi Anderson. 1974. "Mass Belief Systems Revisited: Political Change and Attitude Structure." *Journal of Politics* 36 (Aug.): 540-91.

Nie, Norman H., Sidney Verba, and John R. Petrocik. 1976. *The Changing American Voter.* Cambridge, MA: Harvard UP.

Niemi, Richard G., Stephen C. Craig, and Franco Mattei. 1991. "Measuring Internal Political Efficacy in the 1988 National Election Study." *American Political Science Review* 85 (Dec.): 1407-13.

Niemi, Richard G., John Mueller and Tom W. Smith. 1989. *Trends in Public Opinion.* New York: Greenwood.

Norrander, Barbara. 1989. "Ideological Representatives of Presidential Primary Voters." *American Journal of Political Science* 33 (Aug): 570-87.

Norris, Pippa. 1988. "The Gender Gap: A Cross-National Trend?" *The Politics of the Gender Gap.* Ed. Carol M. Mueller. Beverly Hills, CA: Sage.

Nunn, Clyde Z., Harry J. Crockett, Jr., and J. Allen Williams, Jr. 1978. *Tolerance for Nonconformity.* San Francisco: Jossey-Bass.

O'Keefe, Garrett J., and L. Erwin Atwood. 1981. "Communication and Election Campaigns." *Handbook of Political Communication.* Ed. Dan D. Nimmo and Keith R. Sander. Beverly Hills, CA: Sage.

Olson, Mancur, Jr. 1968. *The Logic of Collective Action.* New York: Schocken.

Oreskes, Michael. 1990. "In Year of Volatile Vote, Polls Can Be Dynamite." *New York Times* 2 November, Section A.

Ornstein, Norman J., Thomas E. Mann and Michael J. Malbin, eds. 1994. *Vital Statistics on Congress 1993-1994.* Washington, DC: Congressional Quarterly.

Orton, Barry. 1982. "Phoney Calls: The Pollster's Nemesis." *Public Opinion* (June/July): 56-57.

Page, Benjamin I., and Calvin Jones. 1979. "Reciprocal Effects of Policy Preferences, Party Loyalties, and the Vote." *American Political Science Review* 73 (Dec.): 1071-89.

Page, Benjamin I., and Robert Y. Shapiro. 1983. "Effects of Public Opinion on Public Policy." *American Political Science Review* 77 (Mar.): 175-90.

———. 1989. "Foreign Policy and the Rational Public." *Journal of Conflict Resolution* 32 (June): 211-47.

———. 1992. *The Rational Public.* Chicago: U of Chicago P.

Page, Benjamin I., Robert Y. Shapiro, and Glenn R. Dempsey. 1987. "What Moves Public Opinion?" *American Political Science Review* 81 (Mar.): 23-43.

Palmer, Paul A. 1936. "The Concept of Public Opinion in Political Theory." *Essays in History and Political Thought.* Ed. Carl F. Wittke. London: Oxford UP.

Parker, Glen R. 1992. *Institutional Change, Discretion, and the Making of the Modern Congress.* Ann Arbor, MI: U of Michigan P.

Parry, Geraint. 1969. *Political Elites.* New York: Praeger.

Pateman, Carole. 1970. *Participation and Democratic Theory.* Cambridge, England: Cambridge UP.

Patterson, Samuel C., Jr. 1976. "American State Legislatures and Public Policy." *Politics in the American States: A Comparative Analysis.* 3rd ed. Ed. Herbert Jacob and Kenneth N. Vines. Boston: Little.

Patterson, Samuel C., and Gregory A. Caldiera. 1988. *British Journal of Political Science* 18 (Jan.): 111-21.

Patterson, Thomas E. 1989. "The Press and Its Missed Assignment." *The Election of 1988.* Ed. Michael Nelson. Washington, DC: Congressional Quarterly.

Patterson, Thomas E., and Robert D. McClure. 1976. *The Unseeing Eye.* New York: Putnam.

Petrocik, John R. 1987. "Realignment: New Party Coalitions and the Nationalization of the South." *Journal of Politics* 49 (May): 347-75.

———. 1989. "An Expected Party Vote: New Data for an Old Concept." *American Journal of Political Science* 33 (Feb.): 44-66.

Phillips, Kevin. 1991. *The Politics of Rich and Poor.* New York: Harper.

————. 1993. *Boiling Point*. New York: Random.

Pierce, John C. 1970. "Party Identification and the Changing Role of Ideology in American Politics." *Midwest Journal of Political Science* 14 (Feb.): 25-42.

Pierce, Patrick A. 1993. "Political Sophistication and the Use of Candidate Traits in Candidate Evaluation." *Political Psychology* 14 (Mar.): 21-35.

Polsby, Nelson W. 1960. "Toward an Explanation of McCarthyism." *Political Studies* 18 (Oct.): 250-71.

Polsby, Nelson W., and Aaron Wildavsky. 1984. *Presidential Elections*. 6th ed. New York: Scribner's.

Pomper, Gerald M. 1972. "From Confusion to Clarity: Issues and American Voters, 1956-1968." *American Political Science Review* 66 (June): 415-28.

————. 1993. "The Presidential Election." *The Election of 1992*. Ed. Gerald M. Pomper. Chatham, NJ: Chatham House.

Pomper, Gerald, M., with Susan S. Lederman. 1980. *Elections in America: Control and Influence in Democratic Politics*. 2nd ed. New York: Longman.

Poole, Keith T., and Howard Rosenthal. 1984. "The Polarization of American Politics." *Journal of Politics* 46 (Nov.): 1061-79.

Popkin, Samuel L. 1991. *The Reasoning Voter*. Chicago: U of Chicago P. Press, Charles, and Kenneth Verburn. 1988. *American Politicians and Journalists*. Boston: Scott.

Prewitt, Kenneth. 1970. *The Recruitment of Political Leaders: A Study of Citizen Politicians*. New York: Bobbs.

Price, H. Douglas. 1971. "The Congressional Career—Then and Now." *Congressional Behavior*. Ed. Nelson W. Polsby. New York: Random.

Price, Vincent. 1992. *Public Opinion*. Newbury Park, CA: Sage.

Ranney, Austin. 1976. *Channels of Power: The Impact of Television on American Politics*. New York: Basic.

Ravitch, Diane, and Chester E. Finn, Jr. 1987. *What Do Our 17-Year-Olds Know*. New York: Harper.

Ray, John J. 1988. "Why the F-Scale Predicts Racism: A Critical Review." *Political Psychology* 9 (Dec.): 669-81.

Reichley, A. James. 1985. *Religion in American Public Life*. Washington, DC: Brookings.

Remmers, H. H., and Richard D. Franklin. 1963. "Sweet Land of Liberty." *Anti-Democratic Attitudes in American Schools*. Ed. H. H. Remmers. Evanston, IL: Northwestern UP.

Robinson, Claude. 1932. *Straw Votes: A Study of Political Predicting*. New York: Columbia UP.

Robinson, John P., and Mark R. Levy. 1986. *The Main Source: Learning from Television News*. Beverly Hills, CA: Sage.

Robinson, Michael Jay, and Maura Clancey. 1984. "Teflon Politics." *Public Opinion* (Apr./May): 14-18.

Rodgers, Harrell R., and Edward B. Lewis. 1975. "Student Attitudes Toward Richard Nixon." *American Politics Quarterly* 4 (Oct.): 432-36.

Rogers, Lindsay. 1949. *The Pollsters*. New York: Knopf.

Rohde, David W. 1992. "Electoral Forces, Political Agendas, and Partisanship in the House and Senate." *The Postreform Congress*. Ed. Roger W. Davidson. New York: St. Martins.

Rokeach, Milton. 1960. *The Open and Closed Mind*. New York: Basic.

Rokkan, Stein, and Angus Campbell. 1960. "Citizen Participation in Political Life: Norway and the United States of America." *International Social Science Journal* 12: 69-99.

Romero, David W. 1989. "The Changing American Voter Revisited: Candidate Evaluations in Presidential Elections, 1952 to 1984." *American Politics Quarterly* 17 (Oct.): 409-21.

Roper, Burns. 1980. "Reading the Signals in Today's Political Polls." *Public Opinion* (Feb./Mar.): 48.

———. 1982. "The Polls Malfunction in 1982." *Public Opinion* (Dec./Jan.): 41-45.

———. 1985. Roper Report 84-1, 3-10, Dec.

Rose, A. M. 1964. "Alienation and Participation." *American Sociological Review* 27 (Dec.): 151-73.

Rosenberg, Milton J., et al. 1970. *Vietnam and the Silent Majority.* New York: Harper.

Roseneau, James N. 1961. *Public Opinion and Foreign Policy.* New York: Random.

Rosenthal, Andrew. 1989. "Broad Disparities in Polls and Votes Raising Questions." *New York Times* 9 November: 1, 13.

Rossi, Eugene J. 1965. "Mass and Attentive Public Opinion on Nuclear Weapons Tests and Fall-out." *Public Opinion Quarterly* 29 (May): 280-97.

Rothenberg, Randall. 1990. "Surveys Proliferate, But Answers Dwindle." *New York Times,* 26 October, Section A.

Rotunda, Ronald D. 1986. *The Politics of Language: Liberalism as Word and Symbol.* Iowa City, IA: U of Iowa P.

Russett, Bruce, and Thomas W. Graham. 1989. "Public Opinion and National Security Policy: Relationships and Impacts." *Handbook of War Studies.* Ed. Manus J. Midlarsky. Boston: Unwin Hyman.

Sabato, Larry. 1993. *Feeding Frenzy: How Attack Journalism Has Transformed American Politics.* 2nd ed. New York: Free.

Sabine, George. 1952. "The Two Democratic Traditions." *Philosophic Review* 61 (Aug): 214-22.

St. Dizier, Byron. 1986. "Republican Endorsements, Democratic Positions: An Editorial Page Contradiction." *Journalism Quarterly* 63 (Autumn): 581-86.

Schlesinger, Joseph. 1966. *Ambition and Politics.* Chicago: Rand.

Schlozman, Kay Lehman, and John T. Tierney. 1986. *Organized Interests and American Democracy.* New York: Harper.

Schneider, William. 1989. "Trouble for the GOP." *Public Opinion* 12 (May/June): 5-6.

Schneider, William, and I.A. Lewis. 1985. "Views on the News." *Public Opinion* 8 (Aug./Sep.): 6-11, 58-59.

Schreiber, E. M. 1978. "Education and Change in American Opinions on a Woman for President." *Public Opinion Quarterly* 42 (Summer): 171-82.

Schulman, Mark A., and Gerald M. Pomper. 1975. "Variability in Electoral Behavior: Longitudinal Perspectives form Causal Modeling." *American Journal of Political Science* 21 (Feb.): 1-18.

Schuman, Howard, and Stanley Presser. 1981. *Questions and Answers in Attitude Surveys: Experiments in Question Form, Wording, and Content.* New York: Academic.

Schuman, Howard, Charlotte Steeh, and Lawrence Bobo. 1985. *Racial*

Attitudes in America: Trends and Interpretations. Cambridge, MA: Harvard UP.

Schwartz, David. 1973. *Political Alienation and Political Behavior.* Chicago: Aldine.

Schwartz, Sandra K. 1975. "Preschoolers and Politics." *New Directions in Political Socialization.* Ed. David C. Schwartz and Sandra K. Schwartz. New York: Free.

Sears, David O. 1986. "Symbolic Racism." *Towards the Elimination of Racism: Profiles in Controversy.* Ed. Phyllis A. Katz and Dalmas Taylor. New York: Plenum.

———. 1991. "Whither Political Socialization Research? The Question of Persistence." *Political Socialization, Citizenship and Democracy.* Ed. Orit Ichilov. New York: Teachers College P.

Sears, David O., and Carolyn L. Funk. 1990. "Self-Interest in Americans' Political Opinions." *Beyond Self-Interest.* Ed. Jane J. Mansbridge. Chicago: U of Chicago P.

Sears, David O., Carl P. Hensler, and Leslie K. Speer. 1979. "Whites' Opposition to Busing: Self-Interest or Symbolic Politics?" *American Political Science Review* 73 (June): 369-84.

Sears, David O., and Donald R. Kinder. 1971. "Racial Tensions and Voting in Los Angeles." *Los Angeles: Viability and Prospects for Metropolitan Leadership.* Ed. W. Z. Hirsch. New York: Praeger.

Sears, David O., and Richard R. Lau. 1983. "Inducing Apparently Self-Interested Political Preferences." *American Journal of Political Science* 27 (May): 223-52.

Sebert, Suzanne K., M. Kent Jennings, and Richard G. Niemi. 1974. "The Political Texture of Peer Groups." *The Political Character of Adolescence.* Ed. M. Kent Jennings and Richard G. Niemi. Princeton, NJ: Princeton UP.

Shantz, Ellen. 1972. "Sideline Citizens." *Political Youth, Traditional Schools.* Ed. Byron Massialas. Englewood Cliffs, NJ: Prentice.

Shapiro, Robert Y., and Lawrence R. Jacobs. 1989. "The Relationship Between Public Opinion and Public Policy: A Review." *Political Behavior Annual.* Vol. 2. Ed. Samuel Long. Boulder, CO: Westview.

Shapiro, Robert Y., and Harpreet Mahajan. 1986. "Gender Differences in Policy Preferences: A Summary of Trends from the 1960s to the 1980s." *Public Opinion Quarterly* 50 (Spring): 47-55.

Sheatsley, Paul B. 1966. "White Attitudes Toward the Negro." *Daedalus* 95 (Winter): 217-38.

Shingles, Richard D. 1981. "Black Consciousness and Political Participation: The Missing Link." *American Political Science Review* 75 (Mar.): 76-91.

———. 1989. "Class, Status, and Support of Government Aid to Disadvantaged Groups." *Journal of Politics* 51 (Nov.): 933-62.

Showalter, Stuart W. 1974. "Evening Network News Selection: A Confirmation of News Judgment." *Journalism Quarterly* 51 (Winter): 712-15.

Sigel, Roberta S., and Marilyn Brookes. 1974. "Becoming Critical About Politics." *The Politics of Future Citizens.* Ed. Richard G. Niemi. San Francisco: Jossey-Bass.

Sigel, Roberta S., and Mariyn B. Hoskin. 1981. *The Political Involvement of Adolescents.* New Brunswick, NJ: Rutgers UP.

Sigelman, Lee. 1981. "Question-Order Effects on Presidential Popularity." *Public Opinion Quarterly* 45 (Summer): 199-207.

Sigelman, Lee and Susan Welch. 1991. *Black Americans' View of Rachial Inequality—The Dream Deferred.* Cambridge, UK: Cambridge U.P.

Silbiger, Sara S. 1977. "Peers and Political Socialization." *Youth and Society* 5 (Mar.): 169-78.

Simon, Rita J., and Jean M. Landis. 1989. "The Polls: Women's and Men's Attitudes About a Woman's Place and Role." *Public Opinion Quarterly* 53 (Summer): 271-76.

Sinclair, Barbara. 1993. "House Majority Party Leadership in an Era of Legislative Restraint." *The Postreform Congress.* Ed. Roger W. Davidson. New York: St. Martins.

Sinclair, Barbara Deckard. 1977. "Party Realignment and the Transformation of the American Agenda: The House of Representatives, 1925-1938." *American Political Science Review* 71 (Sept.): 940-53.

Smith, Eric R.A.N. 1990. *The Unchanging American Voter.* Berkeley, CA: U of California P.

Smith, Eric R.A.N., and Peverill Squire. 1990. "The Effects of Prestige Names in Question Wording." *Public Opinion Quarterly* 54 (Spring): 97-116.

Smith, M. B., J. S. Bruner, and R. W. White. 1956. *Opinions and Personality.* New York: Wiley.

Smith, Tom W. 1984. "Nonattitudes: A Review and Evaluation." *Surveying Subjective Phenomena.* Vol. 2. Ed. Charles F. Turner and Elizabeth Martin. New York: Russell Sage.

————. 1985. "The Polls: America's Most Important Problem." *Public Opinion Quarterly* 54 (Winter): 479–507..

————. 1990a. "The First Straw? A Study of the Origins of Election Polls." *Public Opinion Quarterly* 54 (Spring): 21-36.

————. 1990b. "Liberal and Conservative Trends in the United States." *Public Opinion Quarterly* 54 (Winter): 609-26.

————. 1992. "Changing Racial Labels." *Public Opinion Quarterly* 56 (Winter): 496-514.

Smith, Tom W., and Paul Sheatsley. 1984. "American Attitudes Toward Race Relations." *Public Opinion* (Oct/Nov): 14-15.

Smith, Tom W. and Frederick D. Weil. 1990. "Finding Public Opinion Data." *Public Opinion Quarterly* 54 (Winter): 609-26.

Sniderman, Paul M. 1975. *Personality and Democratic Politics.* Berkeley, CA: U of California P.

Sniderman, Paul M., Richard A. Brody, and Philip E. Tetlock. 1991. *Reasoning and Choice: Explorations in Political Psychology.* New York: Cambridge UP.

Sniderman, Paul M., and Thomas Piazza. 1993. *The Scar of Race.* Cambridge, MA: Harvard UP.

Sniderman, Paul M., Thomas Piazza, Philip E. Tetlock, and Ann Kendrick. 1991. "The New Racism." *American Journal of Political Science* 35 (May): 423-47.

Sniderman, Paul M., Philip E. Tetlock, James N. Glaser, Donald Philip Green, and Michael Hout. 1989. "Principled Tolerance and the American Mass Public." *British Journal of Political Science* 19 (Feb.): 25-45.

Sobel, Richard. 1989. "The Polls—A Report: Public Opinion About United States Intervention in El Salvador and Nicaragua." *Public Opinion Quarterly* 53 (Spring): 114-28.

Sorauf, Frank J. 1963. *Party and Representation.* New York: Atherton.

———. 1988. *Money in American Elections.* Boston: Scott.

Soule, John W. 1969. "Future Political Ambitions and the Behavior of Incumbent State Legislators." *Midwest Journal of Political Science* 13 (Aug.): 439-54.

Soule, John W., and Wilma E. McGrath. 1975. "A Comparative Study of Presidential Nomination Conventions: The Democrats 1968 and 1972." *American Journal of Political Science* 21 (Aug.): 501-18.

Spitz, Elaine. 1984. *Majority Rule.* Chatham, NJ: Chatham House.

Squire, Peverill. 1988. "Why the 1937 *Literary Digest* Poll Failed." *Public Opinion Quarterly* 52 (Spring): 123-33.

———. 1992. "Changing State Legislative Careers." *Changing Patterns in State Legislative Careers.* Ed. Gary F. Moncrief and Joel A. Thompson. Ann Arbor, MI: U of Michigan P.

Stanley, Harold W., and Richard G. Niemi. 1992. *Vital Statistics of American Politics.* 3rd ed. Washington, DC: Congressional Quarterly.

———. 1994. *Vital Statistics of American Politics.* 4th ed. Washington, DC: Congressional Quarterly.

Steeper, Frederick T. 1978. "Public Response to Gerald Ford's Statements on Eastern Europe in the Second Debate." *The Presidential Debates: Media, Electoral and Policy Perspectives.* Ed. George F. Bishop, Robert G. Meadow, and Marilyn Jackson-Beeck. New York: Praeger.

Stembler, Charles H. 1961. *Education and Attitude Change: The Effect of Schooling on Prejudice Against Minority Groups.* New York: Institute of Human Relations.

Stephens, William N., and C. Stephen Long. 1970. "Education and Political Behavior." *Political Science Annual: An International Review.* Vol. 2. Ed. James A. Robinson. Indianapolis: Bobbs.

Stimson, James A. 1975. "Belief Systems: Constraint, Complexity, and the 1972 Election." *American Journal of Political Science* 19 (Aug.): 393-417.

———. 1991. *Public Opinion in America: Moods, Cycles, and Swings.* Boulder, CO: Westview.

Stimson, James A., Michael B. MacKuen, and Robert S. Erikson. 1994. "Opinion and Policy: A Global View." *PS: Political Science and Politics.* 27 (Mar.): 29-35.

Stokes, Donald E. 1966. "Some Dynamic Elements of Contests for the Presidency." *American Political Science Review* 60 (Mar.): 19-28.

Stokes, Donald E., and Warren E. Miller. 1962. "Party Government and the Saliency of Congress." *Public Opinion Quarterly* 26 (Winter): 531-46.

Stouffer, Samuel A. 1949. *The American Soldier.* Princeton, NJ: Princeton UP.

———. 1955. *Communism, Conformity and Civil Liberties.* New York: Doubleday.

Sudman, Seymour. 1976. *Applied Sampling.* New York: Academic.

Sullivan, John L., and Robert E. O'Connor. 1972. "Electoral Choice and Popular Control of Public Policy: The Case of the 1966 House Elections." *American Political Science Review* 66 (Dec.): 1256-68.

Sullivan, John L., James E. Piereson, and George E. Marcus. 1978. "Ideological Constraint in the Mass Public: A Methodological Critique and Some New Findings." *American Journal of Political Science* 22 (May): 233–49.

———. 1982. *Political Tolerance and American Democracy.* Chicago: U of Chicago P.

Sundquist, James L. 1973. *Dynamics of the Party System.* Washington, DC: Brookings.

Sussman, Barry. 1984. "How TV's Power Has Again Transformed Public Opinion." *Washington Post,* national weekly ed., 22 October.

———. 1985. "Pollsters Cheer Up About Public's Opinion of Polls." *Washington Post,* national weekly ed., 25 November.

———. 1986. "In Pollsters We Trust." *Washington Post,* national weekly ed., 25 August.

Taylor, Humphrey. 1993. "Polling and Opinion on Health Care Reform." *The Public Perspective* 4 (May/June): 19-22.

Tedin, Kent L. 1974. "The Influence of Parents on the Political Attitudes of Adolescents." *American Political Science Review* 68 (Dec.): 1579-92.

———. 1976. "On the Reliability of Reported Political Attitudes." *American Journal of Political Science* 20 (Feb.): 117-24.

———. 1977-1978. "Age vs. Social Composition Factors as Explanations for Cleavages on Socio-Political Issues." *Aging and Human Development* 9: 116-31.

———. 1980. "Measuring Parent and Peer Influence on Adolescent Political Attitudes." *American Journal of Political Science* 24 (Feb.): 136-54.

———. 1986. "Change and Stability in Presidential Popularity at the Individual Level." *Public Opinion Quarterly* 50 (Summer): 121-32.

———. 1987. "Political Ideology and the Vote." *Research in Micro-Politics.* Vol. 2. Ed. Samuel Long. Greenwich, CT: JAI.

———. 1994a. "Mass Support for Competitive Elections in the Soviet Union." *Comparative Politics* 27 (Apr.): 241-71.

———. 1994b. "Self-Interest, Symbolic Values and the Financial Equalization of the Public Schools." *Journal of Politics* 56: (Aug) 628–649..

Tedin, Kent L., Richard Matland, and Richard Murray. 1991. "The Acid Test of Gender Voting: The 1990 Election for Governor of Texas." Paper presented at the annual meeting of the Southern Political Science Association.

Tedin, Kent L., and Richard W. Murray. 1981. "Dynamics of Candidate Choice in a State-Level Election." *Journal of Politics* 43 (May): 435-55.

Tedin, Kent L., and Oi-Kuan Fiona Yap. 1993. "The Gender Factor in Soviet Mass Politics: Survey Evidence from Greater Moscow." *Political Research Quarterly* 46 (Mar.): 179-211.

Tedin, Kent L., et al. 1977. "Social Background and Political Differences Between Pro- and Anti-ERA Activists." *American Politics Quarterly* 5 (July): 395-408.

Thomas, Martin. 1985. "Electoral Proximity and Senatorial Roll Call Voting." *American Journal of Political Science* 29 (Feb.): 96-111.

Thompson, Joel A., and Gary F. Moncrief. 1992. "Nativity, Mobility, and State Legislators." *Changing Patterns in State Legislative Careers.* Ed. Gary F. Moncrief and Joel A. Thompson. Ann Arbor, MI: U of Michigan P.

Tierney, John. 1992. "Journalists Reneging on Election Promises." *New York Times,* 31 January, Section A.

Tocqueville, Alexis de. 1966. *Democracy in America.* 1st ed. Ed. J. P. Mayer and Max Lerner. New York: Harper.

Tolchin, Martin. 1986. "The Pollsters Look Back." *New York Times,* 8 November, Section A.

Torres, Aida, and Jacqueline Forrest. 1988. "Why Do Women Have Abortions." *Family Planning Perspectives* 20: 169-76.

Traugott, Michael. 1992a. "A Generally Good Showing, But Much Work Needs to be Done." *The Public Perspective* 4 (November/December): 31-32.

Traugott, Michael W. 1992b. "The Impact of Media Polls on the Public." *Media Polls in American Politics.* Ed. Thomas E. Mann and Gary R. Orren. Washington, DC: Brookings.

Truman, David. 1951. *The Governmental Process.* New York: Knopf.

Tucker, Harvey J., and Ronald E. Weber. 1992. "Electoral Change in U.S. States: System vs. Constituency Competition." *Changing Patterns in State Legislative Careers.* Ed. Gary F. Moncrief and Joel A. Thompson. Ann Arbor, MI: U of Michigan P.

Tufte, Edward R. 1978. *Political Control of the Economy.* Princeton, NJ: Princeton UP.

Turner, Charles, and Elizabeth Martin. 1984. *Surveying Subjective Phenomena.* New York: Russell Sage.

Tussman, Joseph. 1960. *Obligation and the Body Politic.* New York: Oxford UP.

Uslaner, Eric M., and Ronald E. Weber. 1979. "U.S. State Legislators' Opinions and Perceptions of Constituency Attitudes." *Legislative Studies Quarterly* 4 (Nov.): 563-86.

Uslaner, Eric M., and Ronald E. Weber. 1983. "Policy Congruence and American State Elites: Descriptive Representation Versus Electoral Accountability." *Journal of Politics* 45 (Feb.): 183-96.

Vaillancourt, Pauline Marie. 1973. "Stability of Children's Survey Responses." *Public Opinion Quarterly* 37 (Summer): 373-87.

Verba, Sidney, and Richard Brody. 1970. "Participation, Policy Preferences and the War in Viet Nam." *Public Opinion Quarterly* 34 (Fall): 325-32.

Verba, Sidney, and Norman H. Nie. 1972. *Participation in America.* New York: Harper.

Wahlke, John C., et al. 1962. *The Legislative System.* New York: Wiley.

Wald, Kenneth D. 1992. *Religion and Politics in the United States.* 2nd Ed. Washington, DC: Congressional Quarterly.

Wald, Kenneth D., Dennis E. Owen, and Samuel S. Hill. 1989. "Churches as Political Communities." *American Political Science Review* 82 (June): 532-48.

Wattenberg, Martin P. 1986. *The Decline of American Political Parties, 1952-1984.* Cambridge, MA: Harvard UP.

———. 1991. "The Building of a Republican Regional Base in the South." *Public Opinion Quarterly* 55 (Fall): 424-31.

Weatherford, Stephen. 1984. "Economic Stagflation and Public Support for the Political System." *British Journal of Political Science* 14 (Jan): 187–205.

———. 1987. "How Does Government Performance Influence Political Support?" *Political Behavior* 9 (vol. 1): 5-27.

———. 1992. "Measuring Political Legitimacy." *American Political Science Review* 86 (Mar.): 149-68.

Weiner, Terry S. 1978. Homogeneity of Political Party Preference Between Spouses." *Journal of Politics* 40 (Feb.): 208-11.

Weisberg, Herbert. 1987. "The Demographics of New Voting Gap: Marital Differences in American Voting." *Public Opinion Quarterly* 51 (Fall): 335-43.

Weissberg, Robert. 1974. *Political Learning, Political Choice and Democratic Citizenship.* Englewood Cliffs, NJ: Prentice.

Wetstein, Matthew E. 1993. "A LISREL Model of Public Opinion on Abortion." *Understanding the New Politics of Abortion.* Ed. Malcolm Goggin. Newbury Park, CA: Sage.

Wiggins, Charles W. 1983. "Interest Group Involvement and Success Within a State Legislative System." *Public Opinion and Public Policy.* 3rd ed. Ed. Norman R. Luttbeg. Itasca, IL: Peacock.

Wiggins, Charles W., Keith E. Hamm, and Charles G. Bell. 1984. "Interest Group and Party Influence Agents in the Legislative Process: A Comparative State Analysis." Revised version of a paper presented at the annual meeting of the American Political Science Association, September.

Williams, Christine B., and Daniel Richard Minns. 1986. "Agent Credibility and Receptivity Influences in Children's Political Learning." *Political Behavior* 8 (2): 175-200.

Williams, J. Allen, Jr., Clyde Z. Nunn, and Louis St. Peter. 1976. "Origins of Tolerance: Findings from a Replication of Stouffer's *Communism, Conformity and Civil Liberties.*" *Social Forces* 44 (Dec.): 394-408.

Wilson, Francis Graham. 1962. *A Theory of Public Opinion.* Chicago: Greenwood.

Wilson, Thomas C. 1985. "Urbanism and Tolerance: A Test of Some Hypotheses Drawn from Wirth and Stouffer." *American Sociological Review* 50: 117-23.

Wlezien, Christopher. 1993. "From Outputs to Inputs: The Feedback of Budgetary Policy on Public Preferences for Spending." Paper presented at the annual meeting of the American Political Science Association.

Wolf, Alan. 1993. "The New Orthodoxy in the New York Schools." *The New Republic* (March 18): 7-9.

Wolfinger, Raymond, and Michael G. Hagen. 1985. "Republican Prospects: Southern Comfort." *Public Opinion* (Oct./Nov.): 9.

Wright, Gerald C., Jr. 1978. "Candidates' Policy Positions and Voting in U.S. House Elections." *Legislative Studies Quarterly* 3 (Aug.): 445-64.

———. 1986. "Elections and the Potential for Policy Change in Congress." *Congress and Policy Change.* Ed. Gerald C. Wright, Jr., and Leroy Reiselbach. New York: Agathon.

———. 1989. "Level-of-Analysis Effects on Explanations of Voting: The Case of U.S. Senate Elections." *British Journal of Political Science* 18 (July): 381-98.

Wright, Gerald C., Jr., and Michael Berkman. 1986. "Candidates and Policy in

United States Senate Elections." *American Political Science Review* 80 (June): 567-88.

Wyer, Robert S., Jr. and Victor C. Ottati. 1993. "Political Information Processing." *Explorations in Political Psychology.* Ed. Shanto Iyengar and William J. McGuire. Durham, NC: Duke UP.

Yang, Soon Joon, and Richard D. Alba. 1992. "Urbanism and Nontraditional Opinion: A Test of Fischer's Subcultural Theory." *Social Science Quarterly* 73 (Sept.): 596-609.

Zaller, John. 1992. *The Nature and Origins of Mass Opinion.* Cambridge, England: Cambridge UP.

Zaller, John, and Stanley Feldman. 1992. "A Simple Theory of the Survey Response: Answering Questions and Revealing Preferences." *American Journal of Political Science* 36: 579-616.

Zeigler, Harmon, and Michael Baer. 1969. *Lobbying: Interaction and Influence in American State Legislatures.* Belmont, CA: Wadsworth.

Zukin, Cliff. 1992. "Yes, But . . . Public Opinion Is a Top-Down Process." *Public Opinion Quarterly* 56 (Fall): 311-14.

Index